DEBT REPAYMENT CAPACITY

Cash Flow Forecasting for Borrowers and Lenders

Albert R. McMeen, III

American Management Association

New York • Atlanta • Boston • Chicago • Kansas City • San Francisco • Washington, D.C.
Brussels • Toronto • Mexico City

Library of Congress Cataloging-in-Publication Data

McMeen, Albert R., 1942–
    Debt repayment capacity : cash flow forecasting for borrowers and lenders / Albert R. McMeen, III.
      p. cm.
    Includes bibliographical references and index.
    ISBN 0-8144-5956-0
    1. Assets (Accounting).   2. Financial statements.   3. Credit.
4. Cash flow.   I. Title.
HF5681.A8M38   1992
657'.72—dc20
                                        92-6496
                                          CIP

Printing number

10 9 8 7 6 5 4 3 2 1

Contents

Preface

This book offers a unique approach to the task of interpreting financial statements, since its specific goal is determining quantitatively the capacity of a firm to repay debt. **Debt** is defined as the giving up of specific control over funds in exchange for a contractual obligation to repay interest (rent for the funds) and the principal in accordance with a strict time schedule. It is this payment schedule that distinguishes debt from equity investment in which the investor has more control, at least theoretically, over the investment but is entitled to no specific promise of repayment and thus is subject to greater risk, albeit with potentially a higher return. Therefore, lending is a form of investment that provides the lender with more limited, but hopefully more reliable, returns than equity investors.

Since conservative investors wish lower risks and are willing to take lower returns in exchange, business managers have the option of obtaining these low-cost funds, investing them in their projects, and earning a surplus return for their equity investors. This is called leveraging a firm's stockholder equity and is a prime method of allowing expansion of economic activity by marshaling the entire spectrum of investors into business enterprises. In their recent article in the *New England Economic Review*, Richard W. Kopcke and Eric S. Rosengren ["Debt and Equity" Mar./Apr. 1990, Federal Reserve Bank of Boston] talk about the breakdown of these traditional boundaries between debt and equity. They say that novel instruments have changed the old relationships between debt and equity. These include higher risk of repayment junk bonds and yield enhancements to conventional bonds like warrants for stock purchases.

Kopcke and Rosengren further discuss the dramatic restructuring of corporate capital bases during the 1980s to replace equity with debt. Authorities have repeatedly estimated that corporations are repurchasing their own stock at the rate of $100 billion each year and replacing it with debt. Many observers are puzzled by the replacement of stock equity with debt instruments. The reasons are clear, even if their veracity is uncertain.

For management these include:

1. Increased control by management, with the remaining stock in friendly hands and more highly priced.
2. Making the firm already saddled with substantial debt burdens less likely to be challenged by takeovers.

3. Better tax treatment, with interest payments deductible but not dividends.
4. Greater variety of lenders than equity sources, with lenders more willing to solicit relationships and provide more tailoring to specific management needs.
5. Management maximizing assets under control, not shareholder wealth.

For lenders these include:

1. Investors have seniority over equity, reducing their potential loss in the event of a bankruptcy.
2. Pension funds are being encouraged to match asset maturities to expected times of beneficiary payouts, encouraging debt-type repayment schedules.
3. Government guarantees encourage deposits to intermediaries and restrict the latter's investments to debt securities.

Kopcke and Rosengren conclude with questions about potential costs of this recapitalization, including financial distress and the corporate takeovers, and they wonder (1) if corporations should be required to maintain minimum capital (and under whose auspices) and (2) how the effect of reduced tax collection is to be addressed.

These elements are behind the focus of this book, because in less risky times the consequences of poor debt, or solvency, analysis were less severe. There was proportionally so much equity investment that lenders were protected, and easy recapitalization permitted most firms to survive troubled times. Today analysis must address the chance of variability of debt repayment in an exhaustive way. Thus, this book (1) examines the basic language and concepts of financial statement analysis—essentially accounting—and (2) presents techniques and tools to assist borrower (treasury) or lender (credit) analysts in their efforts to evaluate loan and investment proposals.

The beginning analyst may find it most expeditious to follow "The Basics" chapters, leaving "The Hard Stuff" chapters for later. The analytical techniques presented in each segment start out simple and become more detailed, allowing analysts to tailor the complexity of their analysis to the complexity of the financial statements and loan request under evaluation.

For the more senior lender, the book provides a reference for rigorous analytical techniques in asset evaluation and cash flow analysis. The material presented goes beyond the traditional approach to credit analysis that only provides a vague subjective base upon which to exercise judgment. Instead, this book achieves the following goals:

1. **GAAP inconsistencies**—It points out inconsistencies in the accounting treatment of certain balance sheet and income statement entries. Accepting the information on a firm's financial statements at face value without considering these inconsistencies can cause an analyst to be overly optimistic about a company's creditworthiness. Just as important, however, it can cause an analyst

to be overly cautious and thus to lose a profitable customer or investment opportunity to a more astute competitor. In the words of Lyn M. Fraiser [*Understanding Financial Statements*, 2nd ed., Prentice-Hall, 1988, Englewood Cliffs, N.J.], there are many obstacles to understanding financial statements, specifically:

1. The large volume of information.
2. The complexity of accounting for business transactions requires estimates.
3. The predisposition of management to manipulate income and reduce the quality of earnings.
4. The difficulty in exactly matching income and expenses.
5. Discretionary expenses that can be deferred, thus smoothing earnings variability.
6. Vague controls on non-recurring and non-operating items.
7. The impact of using a yardstick (money) subject to stretching or shrinking (inflation and deflation).
8. Importance of qualitative information to judge the financial statement's meaning.

2. **Breakup value**—It reevaluates the balance sheet to provide a real guide for liquidation analysis—the back door out of any lending or investment situation. Many current analytical ratios, especially the current ratio and the debt to worth ratio, are based, sometimes without the full realization of the analyst using them, on liquidation concepts. By revaluing the balance sheet to market values, these ratios are again made pertinent to the analysis at hand.

3. **Determining cash flow**—It closely examines the composition of the cash flow derivatives, validating the cash available to repay debt, the front door out of any investment. By examining the soundness of aspects of income, irrespective of the accounting conventions used, confidence in these estimates increases so that they become a firm base upon which to build a forecast of future performance, the eventual aim of financial analysis. The culmination here is a chapter on forecasting.

4. **Industry risk**—Finally, the book quantifies the risk aspects of the industry associated with the projected cash flow to achieve the original purpose of the book: the determination of debt repayment capacity with certain ranges of possible outcome given adequate statistical confidence limits, based on the firm's position within the industry.

Structure

The material is presented in several segments: spreadsheet analysis, ratio analysis, forecasting, and application of industry risk variables. The spreadsheet is the basic document used in financial statement analysis. Just as the printed financial statements present management's opinion of a company's financial position, the derived spreadsheet should present the analyst's opinion of the company's financial condition. The spreadsheet provides a format for analyzing financial statements, it aids the analyst in making historical trend and intra-industry comparisons, and it facilitates basic ratio calculations. The primary task for the analyst preparing the spreadsheet is to adjust the financial statement entries to include information provided both in the financial statement footnotes and from other sources.

Subsequent to respreading the financial statement, the lenders can refocus on the traditional concepts of credit analysis such as working capital management, asset management, liability management, operating performance, and cash flow, confident that they are using valid financial numbers, not just the results of management's efforts at looking good to shareholders and creditors. Now, calculating the ratios and analyzing the trends will accomplish meaningful insights—and not just digest management illusions.

While LOTUS 1-2-3 templates are used throughout the book to ease simple numerical manipulation and comparisons, the real value of this tool comes into play with forecasting. First, constructing forecasts is based on two foundation stones of (1) underlying assumptions and (2) tinkering with these assumptions until the outcome reflects one's best guess about the future. A computerized spreadsheet is perfectly suited for this "what-if" study. Unfortunately, these assumptions are at best independent guesses and will undoubtedly not be actualized. Therefore, the real outcome will not be the same as the forecast.

This problem has troubled many in the financial statement analysis area. Those with analytical skills, sufficient time to contemplate generic problems, and the predisposition to do so have worked to devise alternate solutions. Researchers conducted empirical testing of various ratios against firms that have failed; they created the entire school of bankruptcy prediction, now centered around New York University Professor Edward Altman's Z-factor and similar efforts. While these endeavors have had their successes and are sufficiently valid to deserve careful consideration, they still engage the process of boiling down the issue to a single variable, a yes or no, a black or white, result. Observation of business activities brings realization that the "on or off" characteristics of digital computer memories are inadequate. The need is for analyzing the range of possible outcomes.

With a full understanding of a company's financial condition, the analyst can better evaluate (1) the performance of the company's management—issues such as strategic planning, market share, product leadership, labor relations, supply flexibility, business philosophy, management succession, and shareholder diversity—and (2) industry trends and risk characteristics. The last segment of the book considers the variability of specific industry cash flows over the course of a business cycle and combines these with the cash flow forecasts previously calculated. The result is a range of cash flows based on a confidence interval determined partially by the analysts' faith in management to perform and in some degree on the investors' needs for certainty of return. In conclusion, it is this quantitative combining of, technically, industry risk and an individual firm's cash flow forecast, based on a revaluation of the firm's income statement, that is a new tool for the modern analyst in determining debt repayment capacity.

Information Sources

The basic documents to be employed in the book include the traditional audited financial statements. Without these, the analyst is at a real disadvantage in using numbers to assess the firm. Alternatives remain such as interviewing the management or taking valuable collateral. There are public sources of information for firms from whom the analyst cannot obtain statements for examination or for comparison with firms under study. These include:

1. Dun & Bradstreet, Inc., *Industry Norms and Key Business Ratios*, Business Economics Division, Murray Hill, N.J.
2. Robert Morris Associates, *Annual Statement Studies*, Philadelphia, Pa.
3. Standard & Poor's Corporation, *Analyst's Handbook and Industry Surveys* and *Corporation Records and Earnings Forecaster*, New York, N.Y.
4. Leo Troy, *Almanac of Business and Industrial Financial Ratios*, Prentice-Hall, Englewood Cliffs, N.J.
5. Moody's Investors Service, Inc., *Moody's Manuals*, New York, N.Y.
6. Value Line, Inc., *The Value Line Investment Survey*, New York, N.Y.

Sample Questions

This book covers a broad range of material. After completing it, the investor should feel comfortable in confronting all of the following questions about financial statement analysis:

- How does financial leverage benefit borrowers?
- How does inflation affect the balance sheet and income statement if inflation-adjusted accounting is substituted for GAAP-adjusted historical cost accounting?
- When should minority interest be considered part of net worth?
- How can accounts receivable be analyzed to determine whether collection efforts are aggressive enough?
- Why are return on equity and earnings per share ratios not very helpful to creditors?
- What gives rise to deferred taxes and are they debt or equity?
- Why does spreading the current portion of long-term debt as a current liability make the analysis of the operating cycle more difficult?
- How can you tell whether a firm has been replacing fixed assets as they wear out or become obsolete?
- Why does GAAP make it difficult to compare firms within the same industry with fixed assets of the same age?
- How does inflation affect a firm with sizable liabilities?
- What are the alternatives to income recognition for firms with long-term contracts?
- Why have funds flow and cash flow replaced net income for forecasting purposes?

- How do high fixed costs affect a firm during a business downturn?
- How is "income smoothing" accomplished without extraordinary items?
- Why have the current and interest coverage ratios been made obsolete by the fixed charges coverage ratio?
- Why is bankruptcy no longer related to GAAP net worth or working capital concepts?
- How can the current ratio be "window dressed" before a financial report is issued?

In today's competitive lending environment, the traditional approach to credit analysis is inadequate. This book was written for credit analysts and loan officers who are interested in digging beneath the surface to determine a firm's ability to repay a loan.

Chapter 1

Introduction to Financial Statement Analysis

Overview

Financial statement analysis is a key part of the process of determining debt repayment capacity, and it is the major focus of this book. Analysts sometimes refer to the subject of determining debt repayment capacity as credit analysis. The sense that it involved more than financial statement analysis is found in the construct referred to as the *Five C's* of Credit. Other important aspects of determining debt repayment capacity are understanding the purpose of the investment and investigating the borrowing reputation of the prospective borrower.

The Five C's of Credit

The Five C's of Credit are (1) capital, (2) capacity, (3) character, (4) collateral, and (5) conditions. Let us review them individually.

    1. **Capital**—Traditionally, bankers review the balance sheet to examine the borrower's equity and working capital position. Since companies' assets generally lose about 50% of their balance sheet value during bankruptcy, bankers often require that the borrower have at least as much equity in the business as the outstanding indebtedness. That is, lenders often prefer that the ratio of debt to net worth be less than 1:1.

    2. **Capacity**—Capacity represents the debt repayment capacity of the prospective borrower. Since net income shows how much business has improved since the last accounting period, it is often considered a good indicator of debt repayment capacity. Since the 1970s, however, the complexities of income accounting have dramatically increased. As a result, cash flow analysis (going back to the cash journal and ignoring accrual accounting) has replaced income as the prime indicator of debt repayment capacity.

    3. **Character**—In the past, bank officers had longstanding relationships with clients. Lenders, who saw their borrowers through good and bad times, observed firsthand management's reaction to stressful conditions and were able

to gauge their responses accordingly. Today, loan officer turnover is a common problem among banks. It is thus more difficult for a loan officer to anticipate the actions of management of a borrowing firm as well as lenders were able to in the past. Nonetheless, the integrity of management is as important as ever to the credit decision. Investigating managers' reputations and spending considerable time getting to know them is an integral part of any credit assessment. The debt repayment capacity is useless without the will of management to repay debt.

To identify management's capacity to guide the firm in a changing world, consider the following:

- Get managers to tell stories of past problems to help assess how they deal with stress. In addition, stories of success give an impression of reactions to expansive times, when the pressure is on to expand quickly though moderation might be preferable.
- Do not be misled into thinking that a relatively long time on the job is the equivalent to in-depth experience; this comes only after weathering problem times, however long it takes to savor them.
- Have them investigated by private investigation agencies such as Proudfoots or Bishops.
- Seeking reference information by calling former employers may not help that much (unless you personally know them). They are too afraid of lawsuits to say anything derogatory.
- Construct a management organization chart to assess management depth.

Finally, Louis Harris & Associates, Inc. surveyed portfolio managers on which aspects of character they regarded as most important ["Fourth Survey," *Major Institutional Investor*, New York, November 1975, p. 87]. The winning characteristics were:

- Extensive experience and knowledge of the specific business in which the company is involved
- A management that was willing to admit its mistakes
- Identifiable successors
- Incentive compensation program

4. **Collateral**—Collateral refers to the quality and quantity of assets that can be assigned to a specific lender in the event of financial difficulties. Collateral is required more frequently today than in the past because companies generally have greater debt burdens. When considering taking collateral on an investment, *the lender should fully understand the purpose of the investment, because the way the funds are spent may offer a back door out of the transaction.* The lender can and should ask important questions of the borrower concerning the investment's purpose. Examining how well the borrower has thought through the answers to these questions is part of the lender's responsibility as a financial consultant.

The lender should assess the value of the collateral. Since collateral is the "second way out" of the investment, the lender needs to regularly check on its value. The typical technique for determining asset values is to have them appraised by auction appraisers. Appraisers should have experience auctioning assets similar to those being held as collateral. They should be instructed to assume that the liquidation is disorderly (but not disastrous) when estimating values to be used for determining debt repayment capacity.

After determining the value of the collateral, *the lender should investigate whether other creditors are ahead of the bank in debt priority.* Usually, secured lenders, such as finance or leasing companies, have liens on the company's assets. Frequently, these entities prefer the involvement of the local bank (especially if trouble ensues) and are willing to enter into a collateral sharing arrangement with the bank.

In addition to the above, *the lender should periodically conduct title searches of Uniform Commercial Code filings* at the office of the borrower's county clerk (in some states, the secretaries of state hold the records). There are services that conduct these searches for a fee and supply to the inquiring institution a copy of all liens placed against the borrower's equipment and other assets. Conducting regular title searches is important. If it files within ten days of delivery of equipment, an equipment lender can, for example, obtain a superior position to any **spreading lien** ("any equipment now owned or hereafter acquired") that the bank may have previously taken to protect its interests.

5. **Conditions** — Conditions refer to the economic, regulatory, environmental, supply, and competitive circumstances facing the company. To understand what conditions a firm is operating under, analysts must read the available periodicals and research information specific to the firm under study. Issues that the analyst might consider when assessing a firm's conditions include (1) *production* issues, (2) *marketing* issues, and (3) *government and social* issues, which are expanded upon in Chapter 12.

Investment Purpose

Few financial statement analyses require every tool in this book. Understanding the purpose of the investment will help narrow the scope of the analyst's chore. For example, a long-term investment for expansion of a plant indicates that it may be necessary to analyze data as sophisticated as the firm's capital budget. A seasonal investment for inventory financing requires reviewing the firm's cash budget. The short-term investment is dependent on the asset conversion cycle, and ratio analysis is helpful for successfully forecasting repayment.

The purpose of the investment should contain the basis for its repayment. Thus, investments for the purchase of capital equipment should amortize during the life of the equipment and working capital investments should be repaid at the end of the operating cycle.

Documentation

A financial statement analysis should be thorough and examine all aspects of the situation. It should also be well documented. If a borrower gets into trouble, a well-documented analysis file may be the best defense lenders have to protect themselves from being accused of having made a poor lending decision. Today's court decisions *require this documentation* in matters of lenders' liability suits— where the borrowers sue the lenders for improper judgment—and for evidencing exercise of **due diligence**—legal term meaning careful research—to obtain a valid creditor's position in a bankruptcy action.

Definitions

Assets

The balance sheet presents the financial position of a firm on a specific date. During the following explanations, you may want to refer to Exhibit 1-1, which shows the annual report for United Enterprises, Inc. for 12/31/90.

Assets are often viewed as valuable belongings of the firm, that is, the resources that it uses to produce products or services. The balance sheet first shows the asset account of **cash and time deposits**, which unmistakably have value. Usually, they refer to demand deposits or holdings of money market securities that are very short-term in maturity, are without risk of nonrepayment, and are easily marketable.

The next asset on the balance sheet is **accounts receivable**, which result from a firm's selling products or services to customers on credit. It should be clear that the value of the accounts receivable depends on the ability of customers to make payments as they are due.

The next account is **inventory.** As Note A (3) to Exhibit 1-1 shows, inventory is comprised of three components: raw materials, work-in-process, and finished goods. The breakdown of inventory into its components is usually found only in the footnotes. *Raw materials* are acquired by the firm to create products or services. Generally, the firm will acquire them at the best possible price and not stock more than is needed in the foreseeable future. Therefore, the value of raw materials is nearly equal to their acquisition costs. *Finished goods* are on the balance sheet at the cost of production, but these costs may actually be less than the finished goods' market value. *Work-in-process* is little more than a holding category, where raw material and labor expenditures accumulate in anticipation of satisfactory completion and sale. The value of work-in-process is questionable and depends on the success of the firm's operations.

Fixed assets, the next balance sheet entry, primarily represent those assets related to plant and equipment. They are presented net of depreciation. *Depreciation* is merely the accountant's way of spreading out the expenditure of funds to acquire these fixed assets over the *estimated useful economic life* of the equipment. Let's look at an example.

Home Equity Loan

You are applying for a home equity loan. When the bank loan officer asks you to fill out the section of your balance sheet that indicates your home value, you would list the actual expected selling price of your home, taking out an allowance for a real estate commission. This would probably not surprise the banker.

In United Enterprises' financial statement, however, the accountants have not determined the value of the fixed assets in this fashion. They have focused

(Text continued on page 17.)

Exhibit 1-1.

United Enterprises, Inc. is a diversified manufacturer organized into three operating sectors: industrial products, building products and consumer products. Its industrial products are used in the energy, automotive electronic office equipment and agribusiness industries. Its building products serve commercial, industrial and residential markets with products including doors, windows, moldings and light-source fixtures. Its consumer products included apparel, furniture, artificial flowers and other household items. UEI's corporate strategy is based on programs in four key areas: building on strengths, entering new markets, selective acquisition and securing and protecting special market niches.

TO OUR STOCKHOLDERS:

During 1990, United Enterprises, Inc. continued to make good progress in implementing the longer-term strategies announced in mid-1989. Cost reduction programs and tight asset management resulted in excellent cash generation from our operations.

We strengthened our top management organization through internal promotion and recruiting new, experienced executives. Two acquisitions were completed in 1990 and two more were completed in January of this year. More information about these events appears below in this letter and elsewhere in this annual report to stockholders.

Earnings Results

In 1990, the economic slowdown affected our housing, automotive, agribusiness and energy-related businesses. Sales in 1990 were $971 million, down from $1.04 billion in 1989.

Income from continuing operations was $31 million, compared with $43 million in the prior year. Comparable earnings per share were $1.20 in 1990, and $1.67 in 1989. Although sales and earnings were less than in 1989, most of our operations maintained or strengthened their market positions.

Financial Condition

Our financial condition continued strong throughout the year. Tight asset management programs were aggressively pursued and expenditures were watched closely in 1990; nevertheless, we continued to invest where needed to achieve or maintain strong, competitive positions. We invested $30 million in property, plant and equipment. In addition, we bought 3.4 million of our outstanding common shares for $39 million.

During 1990 we maintained the regular 19-cent per share quarterly dividend

payments. We closed the year with a current ratio in excess of 2:1 and a conservative debt level equal to 34 percent of tangible stockholders' equity.

Strategic Repositioning

In mid-1989, we announced and instituted an aggressive, strategic asset redeployment plan. This long-term plan more narrowly focuses UEI as a manufacturing-based company with primary emphasis on industrial and building products while participating in selective consumer markets where we are major competitors or hold special market positions.

The long-term strategies include a major divestment program, redeployment of financial and management resources, and strategic programs in four key areas for continuing growth and improved quality of earnings. At this time, 10 of the 14 announced divestments have been completed and four acquisitions have been made. Descriptions and examples of actions in the four key areas described below and elsewhere in this report are:

* *Building on strengths* in growing markets where we occupy strong competitive positions is taking place through expanded product offerings such as clad windows and a new series of aluminum windows, as well as expansion beyond traditional geographic markets for wood building products and artificial flowers. Also, a major new plant for oil-field pump equipment came on stream last spring.

* *Entering new markets* to reduce dependence on certain cyclical industries is progressing well. We have lessened dependence on molded-plastic parts for automobiles through increased participation in electronic office equipment housings and components. In addition, utilizing our oil and gas production technology, we have developed a fail-safe safety valve for hydrocarbon processing plant applications.

(continued)

Exhibit 1-1. *Continued.*

* Four *selective acquisitions* that complement existing operations have been made. Matrix Lighting of Pinebrook, New Jersey and Master Lighting of Bristol, Pennsylvania strongly reinforce our outdoor high-intensity discharge and fluorescent light-source products. Supreme Manufacturing and Foodstuffs Equipment add marketing, engineering, manufacturing and broadened product offerings to our agribusiness operations. Matrix and Supreme were acquired in 1990, Master and Foodstuffs were acquired in January of this year.

* Securing and protecting *special market niches* continues mainly through product innovation that is responsive to customer preferences. Examples are office chair designs utilizing ergonomic techniques, introduction of a new high-quality children's clothing line and use of a new improved yarn for men's sportshirts.

Outlook for 1991

Decreasing interest rates, increasing housing starts, and improving economic indicators are gratifying. We believe that a steady recovery should occur in 1991. Our top management team is in place, and our financial condition is strong. We will continue to exercise prudent management controls and to invest our human and financial resources for the longer-term benefit of our stockholders.

The management is grateful for the support given by the Board of Directors, by our thousands of men and women co-workers, and by UEI's stockholders. We will continue to make every effort to justify that support.

Gordon A. Pilgrim
Chairman, Chief Executive
Officer and President
February 25, 1991

MANAGEMENT'S DISCUSSION AND ANALYSIS

Financial Review

UEI entered 1990 with a strong and liquid balance sheet in anticipation of improved business conditions. As the year progressed, that improvement did not materialize; as a result, inventory and receivable levels were lowered during the year. While the stockholders' equity base was reduced by the repurchase of common stock, liquidity and debt ratios were maintained at conservative levels. The balance sheet continues to provide the potential to finance future internal growth and acquisitions.

Major Flow of Funds. During 1990 the bulk of operating cash was provided by continuing operations of $97 million and a net increase in long-term debt of $17 million. This total of $114 million, adding other lesser sources, was used largely for capital expenditures of $30 million, common stock repurchases totaling $39 million, and dividends of $21 million.

In 1989 funds provided from continuing operations of $62 million, when combined with time deposit reductions of $29 million, provided $91 million of available cash. This was used mainly for capital expenditures of $38 million, dividends of $22 million, and a business acquisition of $22 million.

Liquidity. Working capital at year-end 1990, as compared to year-end 1989, increased from $183 million to $189 million and the ratio of current assets to current liabilities increased from 2.0:1 to 2.2:1. At year-end 1988 working capital was $207 million with a ratio of 2.5:1. Working capital turnover, the ratio of sales to working capital, slowed from 5.7 times at year-end 1989 to 5.2 times at year-end 1990. The ratio in 1988 was 4.4 times. Current working capital levels are adequate to meet the normal operating needs of UEI.

Inventories decreased by $20 million during 1990 after increasing $19 million in 1989. The inventory to sales ratio of 17 percent in 1990 approximated the 1989 ratio.

Trade accounts receivable were reduced by $10 million during 1990 after an increase of $10 million in 1989. As a percentage of sales, receivable levels declined slightly to 11.4 percent at year-end 1990.

Debt. At year-end 1990 the Corporation's short-term notes payable of $18 million represented offshore indebtedness incurred by our international agribusiness operation to finance working capital requirements. Total consolidated debt outstanding rose by $17 million to $121 million during 1990. Total debt at year-end 1989 showed a slight decline of $2 million from the preceding year-end.

Interest expense decreased by $2.3 million to $11.9 million during 1990 versus $14.2 million in 1989 and $11.2 million in 1988. The reduced interest expense during 1990 was a result of both lower average rates as well as lower average outstanding balances. The 1989 increase reflects opposite trends in the same two factors.

UEI continued to take advantage of favorable interest rates available under tax-free Industrial Revenue Bond financing during 1990 and placed three issues with banks totaling $11.2 million for up to three years.

Consolidated debt as a percentage of tangible stockholders' equity rose from 27 percent at year-end 1989 to 34 percent at the end of 1990. The increase during 1990 is attributable to the reduction of stockholders' equity as a result of UEI's repurchasing 3.4 million common shares and to increased borrowings. During 1989, this percentage increased from 23 percent to 27 percent.

UEI maintains commercial paper ratings of A-2 from Standard & Poor's Corporation and F-2 from Fitch Investors Service. No commercial paper borrowing was outstanding at year-end 1990.

On June 8, 1990 UEI negotiated a Credit Agreement with seven banks which provides $125 million of borrowing availability on a declining basis over a seven-year period. This facility, plus $25 million in bank lines of credit, provides UEI with significant borrowing capacity.

Share Repurchase. On September 2, 1990 UEI announced that it had purchased 3,137,900 of its common shares from First Metropolis Financial Corp. Ltd. of Vancouver, British Columbia and its affiliate First Metropolis Trust Company. The purchase was for approximately $36 million in cash. In total during 1990 the Company purchased 3.4 million of its common shares for approximately $39 million in cash.

Capital Expenditures. Capital expenditures of $30 million were 114 percent of depreciation expense in 1990. This compares with $38 million in 1989 representing 164 percent of depreciation and $36 million in 1988 representing 183 percent of depreciation. The decline in 1990 expenditures reflects management's careful reinvestment approach during the downturn. The 1990 reduction from the originally projected $50 million level is mostly attributable to the postponement of capacity expansion projects. Capital expenditures during 1991 are estimated to be approximately $36 million which the Company currently expects to fund from operating cash flow.

Acquisitions and Divestitures. During 1990 the Company acquired Supreme Manufacturing Company and Matrix Lighting Company for a total consideration of $10 million consisting of cash and debt. In January 1991 UEI acquired Master Lighting Company and Foodstuffs Equipment Co. for a net cost of $42 million. See Note K of Notes to Financial Statements for further information on these acquisitions.

UEI completed the divestiture of three units during 1990, all of which had been earmarked for sale in the June 1989 divestiture plan. In addition, one other unit was sold in January 1991 for a value of over $4 million. It had been expected that all 14 units originally scheduled for divestiture in the June 1989 plan would be disposed of by December 1990. At this time four units, identified on the balance sheet as net assets held for sale, remain to be sold or liquidated. It is anticipated that this will be accomplished during 1991, generating significant funds for redeployment.

Supplementary Data on Inflation and Changing Prices

Due to persistent inflation in recent years, the Financial Accounting Standards Board (FASB) in their statements #33 and #89 encourages an experimental presentation of certain supplementary financial information under a method referred to as "Current Cost."

Current Cost. The objective is to reflect the effect of changes in specific prices that affect UEI's historical financial information. This method adjusts the historical cost of assets and related expenses to their estimated current cost at the respective balance sheet date or date of sale or use, as appropriate. Current costs are principally estimated by the use of specific government or private price indexes and by appraisals or current price quotations.

(continued)

Exhibit 1-1. *Continued.*

United Enterprises, Inc. and Consolidated Subsidiaries
Consolidated Statement of Income Adjusted for Changing Prices (Unaudited)

Year Ended December 31, 1990 Dollars in millions	As Reported in the Primary Financial Statements (Historical Cost)	Adjusted For changes in Specific Prices (Current Cost)
Revenues	$994.1	$994.1
Deductions:		
Cost of products sold	733.8	746.6
Selling expense	106.7	107.9
General and administrative expense	79.0	79.7
Interest and other deductions	15.1	15.1
	934.6	949.3
Income before income taxes	59.5	44.8
Provision for income taxes (A)	28.3	28.3
Net income (B)	$31.2	$16.5
Effective income tax rate (A)	47.6%	63.2%
Earnings per common share	$1.20	$.57
Purchasing power gain from holding net monetary liabilities during the year (C)		$3.7
Net income plus purchasing power gain		$20.2
Depreciation included above	$26.4	$37.2

The current cost estimates are intended to portray the cost of remanufacturing or rebuilding the same asset in its present condition rather than by replacing it with a technologically improved or new asset.

Although accounting policies employed in preparing the historical financial statements are not changed, the inflation-adjusted figures inherently involve the use of assumptions and estimates. The tables and commentary presented on the next two pages should be viewed in that context and not considered as precise indicators of the effects of inflation on UEI's operating results and financial position.

While it is important that financial statement users develop a better understanding of how inflation affects financial reporting, we believe that the primary focus should continue to be on financial statements based upon transaction-historic prices.

(A) The FASB does not permit a reduction of the inflation adjustments for related income tax benefits ($7.0 million or $.30 per share) because this is not allowable under present tax laws.

(B) UEI's management believes that the current cost results are more indicative of the effects of inflation on its productive facilities and product costs than some other adjustment to general level of inflation because of its more specific revaluation approach. Though the CPI may be a better indicator of general inflationary trends and declines in the dollar's purchasing power, its makeup includes price changes on many consumer items such as food and other household costs which have little or no relationship to UEI's capital expenditures and product costs.

The inflation adjusted results are not indicative of what they would have been if existing productive facilities were actually replaced. New assets would be expected to generate operating efficiencies which would offset to some degree the increased depreciation expense.

(C) This purchasing power gain partially offsets the adverse impact of inflation on inventories and plant facilities. It recognizes the economic concept that although the purchasing power of monetary assets (such as cash and receivables) declines during inflationary periods, it is more than offset by larger monetary liabilities (such as payables, accrued expenses and debt) that will be repaid with inflated dollars. The gain is a product of multiplying the average net monetary liability position by the change in the CPI.

(D) At the end of 1990, the current cost of inventory was $168.0 million and property plant and equipment (net) was $296.4 million.

United Enterprises, Inc. and Consolidated Subsidiaries
CONSOLIDATED STATEMENTS OF INCOME

Years Ended December 31, In thousands	1990	1989	1988
Revenues:			
Net sales	$971,367	$1,041,305	$918,595
Income before income taxes of unconsolidated subsidiaries	7,851	7,030	5,701
Other income--Note F	14,854	9,099	8,929
	994,072	1,057,434	933,225
Deductions:			
Cost of products sold	733,839	783,382	703,095
Selling expense	106,677	102,532	88,896
General and administrative expense	79,024	73,654	67,863
Interest expense	11,939	14,209	11,190
Other deductions--Note F	3,088	3,805	10,055
	934,567	977,582	881,099
Income from continuing operations before income taxes	59,505	79,852	52,126
Provision for income taxes--Notes A (5) and E	28,341	36,504	24,435
Income from continuing operations	31,164	43,348	27,691
Discontinued operations--Notes B and E			
Operating loss, net of income tax benefits (1989--$6,442; 1988--$4,312)	--	(10,619)	(6,565)
Estimated loss on disposal, net of income tax benefit of $26,900	--	(95,400)	--
Loss from discontinued operations	--	(106,019)	(6,565)
Net income (loss)	**$31,164**	**$(62,671)**	**$21,126**
Earnings (loss) **per share**			
Continuing operations	$1.20	$1.67	$1.01
Discontinued operations	--	(4.43)	(.27)
Net income (loss)	$1.20	$(2.76)	$.74

See notes to financial statements.

(continued)

Exhibit 1-1. *Continued.*

United Enterprises, Inc.	Annual Report	Page 6

United Enterprises, Inc. and Consolidated Subsidiaries
CONSOLIDATED BALANCE SHEETS

As of December 31, In thousands	1990	1989
Assets		
Current assets		
Cash	$4,860	$9,837
Time deposits--Note K	31,030	4,952
Trade receivables, less allowances (1990--$2,994; 1989--$2,820)	111,023	120,873
Inventories--Note A (3)	167,669	187,848
Prepaid expenses and sundry receivables	34,465	38,688
Total current assets	349,047	362,198
Investments and other assets		
Net assets held for sale--Note B	55,770	62,755
Excess of cost over net assets of purchased businesses--Note A (1)	47,324	44,333
Investments in and accounts with unconsolidated subsidiaries--Note A (1)	25,017	21,042
Other assets	13,382	14,234
	141,493	142,364
Property, plant and equipment (net)--Notes A (4) and C	186,023	184,275
	$676,563	$688,837
Liabilities		
Current liabilities		
Notes payable to banks	$18,250	$15,951
Accounts payable	45,487	55,719
Accrued expenses and other current liabilities	69,822	72,741
Income taxes--Note E	13,697	17,887
Portion of long-term debt due within one year	13,241	16,830
Total current liabilities	160,497	179,128
Long-term debt--Note D	89,721	71,414
Deferred income taxes	26,100	12,108
Stockholders' equity--Notes E and F		
Special preference stock (1990 involuntary liquidation value--$26,157)	1,503	1,512
Common stock, $1 par value; shares authorized 50,000,000; issued:		
1990--24,506,614; 1989--23,956,928	24,507	23,957
Additional paid-in capital	139,153	131,057
Retained earnings--Notes A (5) and D	284,644	276,376
Equity reductions:		
Common stock in treasury, at cost	(38,532)	(1,570)
Other equity reductions	(11,030)	(5,145)
Total stockholders' equity	400,245	426,187
Contingencies--Note I		
	$676,563	$688,837

See notes to financial statements.

United Enterprises, Inc. Annual Report Page 7

United Enterprises, Inc. and Consolidated Subsidiaries
CONSOLIDATED STATEMENT OF CASH FLOWS

for the years ended December 31, Increase (Decrease) in Cash and Cash Equivalents in thousands	1990	1989	1988
Cash flows from operating activities:			
Operating income	$31,164	$43,348	$27,691
Adjustments to reconcile net income to net cash provided by operating activities			
Depreciation and amortization of properties	26,399	23,321	19,873
Deferred income taxes	11,869	6,652	2,253
Undistributed earnings of affiliates (net)	(3,978)	(2,656)	(3,365)
Change in assets and liabilities (net of effects from businesses acquired)			
Decrease (increase) in trade receivables	12,976	(5,148)	8,495
Decrease (increase) in inventories	25,136	(14,404)	(874)
Increase (decrease) in prepaid expenses and sundries	4,447	(11,483)	6,712
Net increase (decrease) in accounts payable, accrued expenses and other liabilities	(16,976)	18,326	(7,312)
Reclassification of deferred income taxes	8,716	485	
Other (net)	(2,544)	4,519	10,873
Net cash provided by continuing operations	97,209	62,960	64,346
Loss from discontinued operations	--	(106,019)	(6,565)
Items not affecting funds (1989: principally writedown of net investments, less noncurrent deferred tax benefit of $16,812)	--	103,335	5,109
Net cash provided by operations	97,209	60,276	62,890
Cash flows from investing activities:			
Net assets of businesses sold	7,014	16,900	6,459
Net assets of businesses acquired	(9,581)	(22,089)	
Other changes in net assets held for sale	(29)	(21,756)	(9,002)
Additions to property, plant and equipment	(30,202)	(38,245)	(36,329)
Net cash after investing activities	64,411	(4,914)	24,018
Cash flows from financing activities:			
Net change in long-term debt	16,657	(1,634)	(2,339)
Cash dividends declared	(21,209)	(21,517)	(21,578)
Acquisition of capital stock	(38,758)	(1,278)	(8,874)
Net cash after financing activities	21,101	(29,343)	(8,773)
Increase (decrease) in cash and time deposits	$21,101	$(29,343)	$(8,773)
Net assets of businesses acquired are summarized as follows:			
Working capital	$4,856	$8,592	
Excess of cost over net assets of purchased businesses	3,394	845	
Property, plant and equipment	1,691	12,652	
Other	(360)		
	$9,581	$22,089	

(continued)

Exhibit 1-1. *Continued.*

NOTES TO FINANCIAL STATEMENTS

Note A--Summary of Significant Accounting Policies

(1) Principles of Consolidation The financial statements include the accounts of the Corporation and all subsidiaries, except those engaged in insurance businesses. Dividends received from unconsolidated insurance businesses were $2.7 million in 1990, $3.2 million in 1989 and $152 thousand in 1988.

The Corporation carries its investments in subsidiaries at cost plus its interest in their undistributed net earnings. The excess of consideration over fair value of assets acquired for purchased businesses is included in "Excess of cost over net assets of purchased businesses." At December 31,1990, $9.3 million is being amortized generally over a forty-year period. Additional amortization is taken to the extent that, in the opinion of management, there has been a decline in the value of this asset.

(2) Foreign Currency Translation Balance sheet accounts denominated in foreign currencies are translated into U. S. dollars at the current rates of exchange as of the balance sheet dates while revenues and costs are translated at average rates of exchange in effect during the respective periods presented. The net effect of this translation process is reflected as an adjustment to stockholders' equity.

(3) Inventories Inventories are valued at the lower of cost, principally first-in, first-out method, or market. Market values for raw materials are based on current replacement cost and market values for work in process, finished products and merchandise are based on net realizable value. In valuing inventories, allowance is made for obsolescence and slow moving inventory. A summary of inventory components at December 31 is as follows:

In thousands	1990	1989
Finished products and merchandise	$74,801	$77,676
Work in process	40,419	50,939
Raw materials	52,449	59,233
	$167,669	$187,848

(4) Depreciation and Amortization Policy Depreciation and amortization are provided by the straight-line method at annual rates calculated to amortize the cost of assets over their estimated useful lives. Lease amortization on capitalized leases is provided generally over the terms of such leases and included in depreciation expense. Gains or losses on retirements or disposals of properties are credited or charged to income. Repair and mainte- nance expenditures are charged to income as incurred.

(5) Income Taxes The Corporation does not provide for taxes on the undistributed earnings of subsidiaries not consolidated for U. S. federal income tax purposes since it intends to retain these earnings in the businesses. Consolidated retained earnings at December 31, 1990 includes approximately $55.8 million of such undistributed earnings. The additional taxes payable if these earnings were distributed would principally represent the difference between applicable U. S. income tax rates and credits allowed for taxes previously paid by such subsidiaries.

(6) Pension Plans Pension costs charged to expense include normal cost and amortization of prior service costs over periods principally ranging from thirty to forty years. The Corporation's policy is to fund pension cost accrued.

(7) Audit Committee of the Board of Directors The Board of Directors has an Audit Committee, consisting of the outside directors, which meets with the Corporation's senior financial management, the vice president internal auditing and the independent auditors to review internal accounting controls, the scope of the annual audit and the results of their examination.

Note B--Discontinued Operations

In June 1989 the Corporation adopted a plan for the orderly disposition of fourteen operations which have been accounted for as discontinued effective June 30, 1989. Accordingly, their operating results (net of related taxes) prior to that date have been reclassified and reported under the caption "Discontinued operations" in the Consolidated Statements of Income. Aggregate sales volume associated with these operations amounted to $119.7 million for the first half of 1989, and $226.1 million for the year ended December 31, 1988.

The Corporation recorded an estimated pretax loss on disposal of these businesses in 1989 of $122.3 million ($95.4 million after-tax or $3.99 per share) including

United Enterprises, Inc.   Annual Report   Page 9

$86.1 million as provisions for cost valuations and associated disposition costs. This has been reduced to $46.8 million at December 31, 1990, reflecting the disposition of nine units and $11.4 million of operating losses incurred subsequent to June 30, 1989. Cash and notes receivable aggregating $23.9 million have been received in connection with the disposition of the nine units.

The net assets of the units remaining to be sold as of December 31,1990, summarized in the accompanying balance sheets as "Net assets held for sale," consist of the following:

In thousands	1990
Current assets	$28,172
Current liabilities	(4,010)
Net current assets	24,162
Property, plant and equipment	(7,405)
Other noncurrent assets (net)	64,616
Net assets	96,183
Allowance for asset writedowns	(40,413)
Net assets held for sale	$55,770

The caption "Other noncurrent assets (net)" in the preceding table includes $48.1 million of net assets related to the consumer and commercial financing operations of UEI Credit Corp. The following summarized financial statements include the aforementioned operations of UEI Credit Corp. as well as those of an insurance subsidiary.

Balance Sheets	In thousands	
December 31,	1990	1989
Cash and marketable securities	$25,604	$24,813
Finance receivables	209,896	236,750
Other assets	21,033	16,570
Total assets	$256,533	$278,133
Notes payable	$112,347	$130,330
Long-term debt	62,310	66,757
Other liabilities	21,247	23,296
Stockholder's equity	60,629	57,750
Total liabilities and stockholder's equity	$256,533	$178,133

Statements of Income	In thousands	
Years Ended December 31,	1990	1989
Finance revenue	$59,030	$56,609
Income maintenance payments from UEI*	2,448	11,005
	61,478	67,614
Interest expense	(24,877)	(27,354)
Operating and other expenses	(30,570)	(33,110)
Income taxes	(2,399)	(2,769)
Net income	$3,632	$4,381

*The Corporation is a party to income maintenance agreement with certain creditors of UEI Credit Corp. requiring payments to be made to UEI Credit Corp. if its income falls below specified levels.

The assets of UEI Credit Corp. not associated with discontinued operations relate to the insurance subsidiary which, for 1990, had total assets of $25.4 million, revenues of $6.3 million and net income of $2.4 mmllion.

Note C--Property, Plant and Equipment

Property, plant and equipment at December 31, stated at cost, are summarized as follows:

In thousands	1990	1989
Land	$11,494	11,2749
Buildings	93,541	1,930
Equipment	238,083	218,119
	343,118	321,323
Less allowances for depreciation and amortization	157,095	137,048
	$186,023	$184,275

Note D -- Debt

A summary of long-term debt outstanding at December 31 is as follows:

In thousands	1990	1989
8.0% Sinking Fund Debentures due June 1, 2005	$31,300	$31,300
Notes payable to banks due principally by May 31, 1995 at prime rate (10.0% at December 31, 1990)	18,000	--
Industrial Revenue Bonds, payable through 2010 (approximate average interest rate of 7.4%)	31,005	20,165
Other debt, payable through 2007 (approximate average interest rate of 7.9%)	8,560	21,866
Capitalized leases	14,097	14,913
	102,962	88,244
Due within one year	13,241	16,830
	89,721	71,414

The maturities of long-term debt during the next five years are as follows: 1991 - $13.2 million; 1992 - $16.0 million; 1993 - $14.4 million; 1994 - $3.8 million; 1995 - $3.5 million.

The 8.25% Sinking Fund Debentures require annual sinking fund payments of $2.5 million which for 1990 was satisfied with prior year's debenture repurchases.

(continued)

Exhibit 1-1. *Continued.*

At December 31,1990, the Corporation's credit lines amounted to $150 million. Use of these credit lines is permissible under the borrowing latitudes of existing loan agreements and may be used from time to time, as necessary, to support outstanding commercial paper. These lines include $125 million under a declining balance Credit Agreement through May 31, 1996, with interest up to 1/2 percent above prime rate for domestic borrowings and up to 1 percent above the London Inter-bank Borrowing Rate (LIBOR) for Eurodollar borrowings. At December 31, 1990, borrowings of $18 million were outstanding under this agreement.

All series of outstanding Special Preference Stock are presently redeemable at the Corporation's option or convertible into Common Stock at the option of the holder. The Corporation has reserved 1,914,959 shares of Common Stock for conversion of the Special Preference Stock.

Note E -- Income Taxes

The provision for income taxes on continuing operations is summarized as follows:

In thousands	1990	1989
Federal:		
Current	$12,918	$25,232
Deferred	11,869	6,652
Foreign	2,254	1,245
State	1,300	3,375
Continuing operations	$28,341	$36,504

Income from continuing operations before income taxes includes income (loss) related to foreign operations as follows: 1990 - $(5.5) million; 1989 - $2.2 million; 1988 - $4.8 million. A Netherlands subsidiary has a foreign net operating loss carry-forward of approximately $13 million ($4 million at December 31, 1989) which is available for use principally over the next 8 years in offsetting any future taxable income of that operation.

Deferred income taxes (credits) for continuing operations are attributable to the following items:

In thousands	1990	1989
Oil and gas drilling tax shelter	$9,823	$4,491
Depreciation -- net of recapture on disposition of assets	1,928	2,604
Other items	118	(443)
	$11,869	$6,652

Deferred income tax benefits for discontinued operations were as follows: 1990 - none; 1989 - $18.6 million; 1988 - $1.7 million. The 1989 benefit is principally attributable to tax benefits on unrealized losses for operations to be sold in the future.

The effective income tax rate for continuing operations differs from the statutory U. S. income tax rate for the following reasons:

	1990	1989
Statutory rate	34.0%	34.0%
Foreign operations	8.0	6.7%
State and local taxes net of federal benefit	5.6	5.0
Effective rate	47.6%	45.7%

The effective income tax rate for the loss on disposal of discontinued operations in 1989 differs from the statutory U.S. income tax rate due principally to the write-off of goodwill without tax basis, carry-forward capital losses for which no benefit has been taken and the rate attributable to capital losses realized.

The Internal Revenue Service has examined the Corporation's federal income tax returns for 1985 and 1986 and has proposed assessments which are being protested by the Corporation. Additionally, the years 1987 through 1989 are currently under examination. Management believes that adequate provision has been made in the accompanying financial statements for any additional taxes likely to be finally assessed.

Note F -- Other Income and Deductions

Other income in 1990 includes a net gain of $7.3 million ($4 million after-tax, or $.17 per share) associated with litigation settlements.

Other deductions include $5.7 million in 1988 ($3.5 million after-tax, or $.14 per share) for incurred or anticipated losses from the sale or liquidation of the net assets of certain businesses.

Note G--Long-Term Contracts

Amounts related to long-term contracts and programs included in receivables are as follows: retainages, 1990 - $3.0 million, 1989 - $3.7 million; recoverable costs, 1990 - $15.0 million, 1989 - $8.9 million. Collections on the December 31, 1990 amounts are estimated at $15.2 million in

1991 and $2.8 million in 1992.

Note H -- Employee Benefit Plans

The Corporation's expense under its various pension, profit sharing and retirement plans amounted to $8.6 million in 1990, $8.0 million in 1989 and $7.4 million in 1988 for its continuing operations. A comparison of accumulated plan benefits and plan net assets related to continuing operations follows:

Calculated as of January 1, In thousands	1990	1989
Actuarial present value of accumulated plan benefits:		
Vested	$38,563	$33,634
Non-vested	3,568	2,993
	$42,131	$36,627
Market value of plan net assets	$46,118	$40,414

The discount rate used to recognize the time value of money in determining the actuarial present value of accumulated plan benefits was principally at 7 1/2 percent for 1990 and 1989.

The Corporation's share of multiemployer plan accumulated benefit and asset amounts is not presently determinable.

Note I -- Contingencies

The Corporation and certain subsidiaries are defendants or plaintiffs in lawsuits that have arisen in the normal course of business. While certain of the lawsuits involve substantial amounts, it is the opinion of management, based on the advice of counsel, that the ultimate resolution of such litigation will not have a material adverse effect on the Corporation's financial position.

The Corporation is contingently liable for up to $26.7 million in respect to notes receivable and conditional sales contracts discounted. See Note B for the income maintenance agreement with certain creditors of UEI Credit Corp.

Note J -- Industry Segment Data

The Corporation's operations are conducted within three industry segments. Inter-segment sales are usually recorded at prices comparable to normal, unaffiliated customer prices, less certain outside selling expenses not incurred.
The Corporation's foreign operations comprise less than 10 percent of consolidated revenues and assets. Export sales are not significant and no single customer accounts for 10 percent or more of the Corporation's revenue.
Information on the Corporation's industry segments is as follows:

In millions	1990	1989(A)
Revenues		
Industrial	$378.5	426.3
Building	245.6	228.6
Consumer	348.8	389.4
Other including dispositions (B)	(15.0)	(3.0)
Consolidated total	$971.4	$1,041.3
Operating profits		
Industrial	$20.6	$31.0
Building (C)	21.7	19.6
Consumer	34.9	51.1
Unconsolidated subsidiaries	7.9	7.0
General corporate items including interest expense and dispositions(B)	(25.6)	(28.8)
Consolidated total	$59.5	$79.9
Identifiable assets		
Industrial	$222.6	$235.3
Building	121.8	119.6
Consumer	168.4	190.9
Discontinued operations	55.8	62.8
Unconsolidated subsidiaries	25.0	21.0
General corporate items including dispositions(B)	83.0	59.2
Consolidated total	$676.6	$688.8
Capital expenditures		
Industrial	$17.2	$18.8
Building	4.7	8.0
Consumer	6.5	8.8
General corporate items including dispositions (B)	1.8	2.6
Consolidated total	$30.2	$38.2
Depreciation		
Industrial	11.1	9.7
Building	8.4	6.8
Consumer	6.4	6.2
General corporate items including dispositions (B)	.5	.6
Consolidated total	$26.4	$23.3

(A) Reclassified to conform with 1990 presentation.
(B)Includes businesses sold prior to 1989 and not included in discontinued operations.
(C) Includes amounts for the lighting fixtures division acquired in 1989 as follows revenues - $32.2 million; operating profits - $6.8 million

(continued)

Exhibit 1-1. *Continued.*

Note K -- Subsequent Event

In January 1991, the Corporation completed the acquisition of Master Lighting (fluorescent lighting) and Foodstuffs Equipment Co. (automated poultry processing systems) for a total cash consideration of $41.7 million and contingency payments of up to an additional $3 million, dependent upon future earnings levels. The acquisitions will be recorded as of January 1, 1991 under the purchase method of accounting.

If the acquisitions were recorded as though they had occurred at the beginning of 1990, the proforma combined results for 1990 would have been as follows: Sales--$1.036 billion; Net income--$32.8 million; Earnings per share--$1.26. These proforma estimates should not be considered indicative of what would have occurred or of expected future results.

REPORT OF INDEPENDENT AUDITORS

To the Stockholders and Board of Directors of UNITED ENTERPRISES, Inc.

We have examined the consolidated balance sheets of U. S. Industries, Inc. and consolidated subsidiaries as of December 31, 1990 and 1989, and the related consolidated statements of income, additional capital and changes in financial position for each of the three years in the period ended December 31, 1990. Our examinations were made in accordance with generally accepted auditing standards and, accordingly, included such tests of the accounting records and such other auditing procedures as we considered necessary in the circumstances.

In our opinion, the financial statements referred to above present fairly the consolidated financial position of U. S. Industries, Inc. and consolidated subsidiaries at December 31, 1990 and 1989, and the consolidated results of their operations and changes in financial position for each of the three years in the period ended December 31, 1990, in conformity with generally accepted accounting principles applied on a consistent basis.

New York, N.Y.
February 23, 1991
Urnst & Hinney

completely on the historical costs. These are the cash amounts that the firm expended and that eventually will wend their way as expenses to the income statement.

The next asset on the balance sheet is **investments.** Investments may represent not only stocks and bonds issued by other companies but also interests in joint ventures and companies that a firm fully owns, but for various reasons has not consolidated into its financial statements. These assets are expected to produce income or increase in value over time. If they fail to generate income or lose value, then the firm's income will drop.

The final asset category is **intangibles.** Intangible assets are not represented by any physical objects. The firm may have paid a lot for intangible assets and they can have great value.

Radio Station

In the case of a radio station the physical assets just reviewed are of relatively minor consequence in determining the value of the company. Instead, its value is dependent on such intangibles as market share, number of listeners, and income level of the listener audience. An acquirer of a radio station, if it already has a good rating, will have to pay more than the market value of these physical assets: The difference is called **goodwill.**

When buyers create a new balance sheet, they create a goodwill account, perhaps like United Enterprises's, called *excess of cost over net assets of purchased businesses*. While being allowed to carry these expenditures of cash as an asset, generating revenues from the use of these assets depends not only on the rating before being acquired but also on the new buyer's performance in operating the station.

If the new owner fouls up, there may be nothing to resell. This contrasts with buying a piece of land to develop and then finding out the necessary permits are unobtainable. In that case, the land would still have value for someone. If a radio station's goodwill value is ruined, no one may be interested in acquiring it.

This brief rundown of the asset side of the balance sheet moved from assets of clearly defined value, such as cash, to assets that have a much less certain value, such as goodwill. Excluding cash and accounts receivable, assets represent cash paid to others, from which the firm has yet to benefit. Surprisingly, most assets could be considered *expenses waiting to happen*, since inventories and all fixed assets will eventually become expenses on the income statement. The notion of assets as having great value thus needs to be qualified. A fundamental concept of financial analysis is that value in an asset is the *ability to generate a stream of cash payments in the future*.

Liabilities

Let's take a look at the liability side of the balance sheet. The first liability is **notes payable** to banks. These notes support the firm's short-term cash needs to pay **accounts payable** and other liabilities incurred from suppliers before it has collected sufficient accounts receivable. **Accrued expenses** are those that the firm has incurred but has not yet been billed for. Notes payable, accounts payable, and accrued expenses are current liabilities of the firm.

The next liability is **long-term debt.** Long-term debt may include term loans from banks, insurance companies, or suppliers of capital equipment. For a larger organization, long-term debt may include bond issues. For a term loan, a borrower must sign an extensive agreement that may include some financial restraints as well as other restraints. For example, long-term debts may be secured by the assets they finance. In addition, there may be covenants that require the firm to maintain certain financial ratios.

These items on the liability side of the balance sheet may not be all bad. They represent funds provided by suppliers and lenders that prize the firm's existence. Accounts payable suppliers generally receive no interest return during the period from which they must wait for payment for delivered goods. With proper care, these suppliers of funds can be depended on to continue extending financing in the future. In general, debt can be of great value to the firm since lenders usually expect a lower return than equity investors.

Equity

Finally, the equity section of the balance sheet shows the funds shareholders have invested to operate the business. This section is little more than a bookkeeping item. Although there may be several types of equity (including par value, paid-in capital, and retained earnings), the sum is nothing more than *total assets minus total liabilities.* The equity section keeps the balance sheet in balance. Thus, if assets are not worth what they cost, the equity section will bear the brunt of any reduction in their value. On the other hand, if the firm does well, earnings entering in larger measure than expenses outflow cause equity to grow.

Contrasting Current and Long-Term Accounts

Economic analysis focuses on firm operations. The subtotals in the middle of the balance sheet—current assets and total current liabilities—separate the firm's operating section from its long-term investment in assets and sources of capital. Short-term assets should be financed with short-term debts; long-term investments should be financed with long-term debts.

Definition of Capital

One of the most famous economic philosophers, Karl Marx, contrasted long-term funds with short-term operating funds. He saw that a company's operating cycle involved acquiring raw materials, producing products from them, and, finally, reselling products.

As far as Marx was concerned, all increases in value during the operating cycle were a result of labor input—an idea actually first espoused by none other than Adam Smith. Marx further reasoned that because of differences in ownership power, owners did not pay laborers for their true contribution but gave them only a subsistence wage to keep them alive. The surplus funds were used by the owners to unjustly enrich themselves. This latter group he called **capitalists.** In fact, he referred to all the long-term funds supplied on the financial statement as **capital,** and we continue to use this same designation today. Therefore, all *funds contributed for the long-term debt as well as equity are called capital.*

Income Statement

In contrast to the way the balance sheet shows the company's status at a moment in time, *the income statement records the activity of the firm between two dates.* The income statement matches the revenues obtained from the sale of goods or services with the expenses undertaken to produce them. Exhibit 1-1 also shows the income statement for United Enterprises, Inc. In preparing the income statement, accountants attempt to break down expenses and distinguish between those directly related to production and those incidental to it, such as interest expense. They further attempt to distinguish between recurring events and those that are extraordinary in nature, as follows:

1. **Sales**—the cash funds or obligations to pay funds in exchange for goods and services supplied by the firm.

2. **Cost of goods sold**—costs directly associated with the production of goods or the provision of services. Most raw materials' costs flow through this expense category. (Some service firms do not show cost of goods sold, making understanding their operations more difficult.)

3. **Selling, general and administrative expense (SG&A)**—the costs *indirectly* associated with supplying goods or services. They include the administrative costs like the president's salary and selling costs such as the rental cars used by salespeople. Financing costs, however, are not included in SG&A.

4. **Operating earnings before interest and taxes**—the sales less all of the direct and indirect costs associated with producing products or services. It is the most useful number on the income statement for the analyst since it excludes non-recurring items, taxes, and interest expenses, none of which are truly useful in determining a company's capacity to pay debt.

5. **Other income and expense**—separate from direct and indirect costs. Included in this category are interest expense and income, dividends from affiliates, and rent from subletting extra real estate.

6. **Net income**—the so-called "bottom line." From an accounting point of view, it indicates how much wealth the company's operation has generated since its last reporting period—a very philosophical concept.

Another consideration in interpreting the income statement is that its annual or periodic calculation may not coincide with the firm's operating cycle. Since the firm is in the middle of certain operations at the time of the preparation of the financial statements, estimates are required; these estimates, like any opinion, may make the income statement better or worse as a criterion of firm performance, and they need to be carefully examined by the analyst. In the case of a retail business such as R. H. Macy, an annual report makes sense, since the firm has actually completed its operating cycle in the course of the year, and the end-of-year date is during a slow season in the summer. In contrast, the performance of a firm such as Chivas Regal, which makes 12-year-old Scotch, is difficult to portray given the substantial inventory storing required as opposed to the one-year cutoff required by the traditional income statement. If the income statement is not closely tied to the firm's operating cycle, revenues, expenses, and, thus, net income can be but *estimates*.

Finally, the income statement tracks only the operating part of the firm's cash flows. For example, any expenditures for plant and equipment or any generation of funds with long-term debt do not appear on the income statement. The income statement is focused on the production cycle rather than any behind-the-scenes or long-term activity. Therefore, there is a need for the additional component of the cash flow statement.

History of Accounting

Using the financial statements is the same thing as using the accounting principles that are their foundation. These accounting principles have grown over many years in an organic way from primitive record keeping to a complex set of guides appropriate for modern business performance and financial position presentation.

Balance Sheet Supremacy

The balance sheet was the first financial statement invented; at the time, it was all that was required. The concept of the corporation did not exist apart from political organizations, and most business activity took place within the lifetimes of the people who undertook work.

A Trading Caravan

Consider a trading caravan going off into the desert loaded up with goods. Upon arriving at the destination, the traders sell the goods and, having no use for the local currency, spend the proceeds immediately on local products. They then take these goods, return home, and sell them. At that point, the results of the trip are divided and the business activity is wound up. In essence, all the accounting needs would be satisfied with a balance sheet at the beginning of the transaction and one at the end in order to determine the amount of wealth created. An income statement at any other point would be useless.

With analysts focused on the balance sheet, management was tempted to dress up the numbers therein as part of their goal for the financial statements: looking good.

Chivas Regal

Let's consider an example. In accordance with industry practice, Chivas Regal carries its 12-year-old Scotch as current inventory, even though it has no intention of selling the Scotch within the next year. This makes the financial statements look more liquid—assets easily converted to cash at close to their market value—than if most of the inventory were carried long-term.

Macy's

Another way management can dress up financial statements is through the selection of fiscal year-end. While the income statement is not much affected by the year's closing date, the balance sheet is dramatically affected. Think about suggesting to Macy's executives that they close the financial statements on November 30. At that time most of the retailer's assets are invested in inventory, since it is about to enter its busiest season, with 35% of total sales occurring in 30 days. Therefore, short-term borrowings are bound to be very high as the firm strains to provide the supply and variety demanded by its customers.

Before charge accounts were common, department stores frequently had their year-end on January 31 (after an inventory reduction sale); however, if stores still chose that alternative, receivables would be unacceptably high, given the pervasive use of charge accounts. Therefore, January 31 is also a poor choice.

Today the more common department store year-end statement is either June 30 or July 31. These dates allow the stores to collect most of their accounts receivable from their Christmas selling season and also to have (in their slowest quarter) low inventories. The absence of accounts receivable and inventory permits the stores to use their working capital to pay down liabilities and present a financial statement that looks better than one jammed with assets and liabilities relative to equity.

Income Statement Supremacy

Historians report that lending and investment analysis centered around the balance sheet through the 1920s. The growth of sophistication concerning financial statements has been slow and largely propelled by several crises in this century. Foremost among these was the Great Depression in the 1930s, which brought on intense interest in the income statement.

Another way of looking at the analytical shift from the balance sheet to the income statement is to consider that analysts are now less interested in static quality of the balance sheet and more interested in the dynamic aspect of fund flows. A balance sheet does not depict the extent to which funds move through the company. As the income statement got more attention from analysts, the various estimates of revenues and expenses that took place—because business transactions are not completed at the time the income statement and balance sheet are prepared—became more complex.

Cash Flow's Ascent

It took many years for the accounting profession to recognize that the income statement only covered the cash flows involved in the inventory, accounts receivable, and accounts payable portions of the balance sheet. The post-World War II creation of the derived **statement of sources and uses,** which measured changes in various balance sheet accounts in an effort to get at net long-term changes, was an initial attempt (the first generation) to capture cash flows involved with acquiring fixed assets and raising long-term funds.

The second major crisis started in 1969, with the bankruptcy of the Penn Central railroad, which greatly shocked the financial markets. It was the first of many failures in giant corporations, previously thought immune to collapse. Theretofore, the balance sheet predisposed analysts to believe that gigantic size inhibited, if not prevented, insolvency. Since then, the failure of major corporate enterprises has become common.

For the second generation of cash flow, concerned accountants created the **statement of changes in financial position** in APB Opinion #19 in 1971. This has come under criticism for showing only cash flows derived from the income statement instead of actual flows through the cash account.

The third generation created the **statement of cash flow,** now required by the Financial Accounting Standards Board (FASB) through the Statement of Financial Accounting Standards (SFAS) #95. The intention now is to disclose gross cash flow—the checking account transactions.

The organization of these statements and the controversy surrounding them will be discussed later. However, the recent focus on cash flow is a boon for lenders since net income expresses the concept of wealth production, whereas it is only cash flow that repays debt and makes interest payments. The production of wealth as demonstrated in the income statement does not indicate the capacity to pay bills as they come due, which is known as **solvency.** Thus, today's focus comprises repaying debt as well as producing wealth. This level of sophistication entreats for a look at the total cash flowing through the corporation within the year, a look at the cash journal. SFAS #95 seems to be a harbinger of this new sophistication.

Users of Financial Statements

There are potential conflicts between different users of financial statements and these conflicts can shape the way the financial statements look.

Owners and Managers

The prime example of this conflict occurs between entrepreneurial owners and present-day non-owning managers. Entrepreneurial owners' central interests in preparation of the financial statements are (1) to confirm their own understanding of firm's performance for the year and (2) to prepare them according to certain rules for the Internal Revenue Service. Outside of the tax rules, the results are essentially for their own purposes. Even if the financial statements do not show much income, liquidity, or even the current market value of fixed assets, the entrepreneurs' shrewd understanding of their business and that of their competitors allows them to discern how well they are doing and what their chances are for continued success.

As corporations grow larger, different areas of the company are often broken into departments or divisions whose performance is separately measured. This is the birth of the professional manager, one who does not have his personal wealth at stake in the corporation, as does the entrepreneurial owner. Now, this manager operates a production center, and cost accounting measures the relative efficiency of different weeks or months of production. The manager attempts to achieve specific targets laid out by senior management or shareholders of a small corporation. Via these targets entrepreneurial owners or shareholders attempt to align the efforts of managers with the interests of the owners. Generally, bonus programs are offered to managers to obtain this alignment; the programs are based on established benchmarks of successful performance, which are customarily accounting concepts such as net income. This method assumes that net income is the appropriate number to indicate increases in wealth. While the manager may have a different set of goals in mind, such as job security, the bonus program focuses attention on the financial statements.

Wrong Incentives

One example of divergence of incentives of managers and stockholders is the desire for large increases in sales even at the loss of some profit. The reason that the sales increase may be deemed more important is that managers are frequently paid based on total volume of sales. Study after study has shown that managers of larger organizations make more money than those of smaller organizations. In addition, the higher sales generally permit the managers to expand their power base, hiring more junior managers. This flies in the face of the theoretically better basis for higher pay: profitability.

The conflict is further evidenced in such management benefiting arrangements as golden parachutes, which protect management against financial harm resulting from a takeover by dissident shareholders and/or corporate raiders.

Particularly appropriate to this analysis is the issue that managers may take liberties about reporting expenses and revenues, the two primary factors in determining net income. As George Foster states in *Financial Statement Analysis* [2nd ed., 1986, pp. 158–159]:*

No matter how detailed the set of rules issued by accounting policy bodies, creative managers or their advisers will find means of structuring transactions that do not give rise to reported expenses or reported liabilities even though, in spirit, expenses or liabilities exist. This is but one of several reasons why the disclosures in annual reports need not represent either a complete or an unbiased representation of the underlying transactions and events affecting the firm.

*Most references to secondary sources are abbreviated in the text. Complete information is in the Bibliography.

Throughout a financial statement analysis you must remember that **the statements are those of management** and that accountants review them to see that they conform to broad statements, and nothing else. There is much leeway in the manner by which management can make themselves look good.

Customers and Employees

Increasingly emphasized by business school courses, customers and employees are regularly called *stakeholders*. Customers of the firm depend on it as a supplier. They want to have continuous service and to avoid the administrative hassle of having a supplier fail.

Osborne Computer

Supplier failure can be a critical problem. Osborne Computer was an early manufacturer of personal computers. It became dependent on a single Australian supplier for a disk drive controller chip. However, on delivery, the chip did not work as originally specified, and Osborne had to take a much more expensive alternative to fulfill its promises to clients. Although Osborne absorbed the additional expense, the ensuing delays disillusioned dealers, a circumstance that may have contributed to the company's eventual bankruptcy.

IBM

On the other hand, when IBM started selling its personal computer, it used several disk drive suppliers, thus avoiding quality and price problems. Be assured, by the end of the second year of production, IBM had six disk drive suppliers. Where IBM was dependent on a chip supplier, Intel, for its 8088 chip, it purchased 40% of Intel, thus achieving greater control over delivery, production quality, and so on.

Labor unions are attached to the hope of higher wages and future growth so that more employees will be hired by the company. They look at the financial statement to see if it is possible to get higher wages. Extremely high profits will inevitably raise the issue of being financially able to accede to labor's demands at the bargaining table.

Creditors

Creditors of the organization include banks, bondholders, and suppliers. Suppliers are focused on continuing sales to that user. Their markup over manufacturing cost is considerably higher than the return a bank might make on its investment. Thus, they may be willing to take a risk greater than a financial institution. There are even suppliers who require down payments sufficient to cover their cost-of-goods sold, and therefore are much less likely to be concerned with a delay in agreed-upon payments.

In contrast to the suppliers, the lenders receive a restricted return with very little premium for risk. They, therefore, tend to be concerned with safety and are captivated with the plans of their borrowers for maintaining earnings stability.

Shareholders

Management traditionally believes that a steadily upward movement in dividends and earnings is the best assurance of an increasing stock price. Their reasoning is that stockholders value steady growth.

H. J. Heinz

One journalist discussed this issue in a reported deception with the H. J. Heinz audit during the 1970s. Because management was encouraged through its bonus plan to do so, they altered revenue and expense records through various techniques over many years and produced a constant 10% growth in sales and earnings. These techniques included delaying shipments at the end of high-growth years and shipping merchandise on delayed billing, but not showing it as such on audited records, in low-growth years. When all the changes had been sorted out, it was plain that Heinz had been growing anywhere from 4% to nearly 16% per annum, although 10% was the average growth. Each year there were significant swings in earnings and sales related to the business cycle, new product introduction, and competitive pressures, not the steady growth *certified* by the accountants.

Principles of Accounting

You have had a brief introduction to the thought that management may be under the gun to look good by any means necessary, even lying. Therefore, for users of financial statements, the temptation is to rely on the auditors to restrict managers' temptations to tell other than the "fair" financial condition of the firm. Knowing some of these fundamental principles of accounting by which the auditors make their judgment calls is prudent. Furthermore, users need to grapple with the idea that the accountant's job includes converting business transactions to a series of numbers: **monetizing.** Some writers say that the analyst's job is to reverse this number crunching process to get a meticulous picture of the actual business transactions occurring in the firm.

Monetary Unit

The accountant must convert full and partially completed business transactions (work in process) into monetary terms. Looking at a balance sheet, as in Exhibit 1-1, you realize that the cash and accounts receivable are the only assets originally available in monetary terms. Cash includes deposits in the bank, and the accounts receivable measure how much customers owe the firm—in dollars—for the product or services supplied. The remaining assets, in particular inventory and plant and equipment, are estimates rather than actual dollar values. This estimation of non-monetary assets is one of the most difficult problems to be faced in analysis.

Besides trying to figure out how to convert these other assets into dollar terms, the accountant has the additional problem that the monetary measure is not a stable one because of the fluctuating inflation rate. The elastic monetary yardstick will have a negative effect on the "fairness" of the financial statement's description of the firm because accounting principles pretend that it is constant.

Objectivity

The next standard is **objectivity.** This concept particularly illuminates how non-monetary assets are measured using *the market value test.* This is especially problematical with regard to long-term fixed assets since they are purchased and then held for a long time. Therefore, financial analysts are stuck with a standard based on the original market value of an asset. This *historic cost* is adjusted only by depreciation based on management's initial estimates of the equipment's useful economic life.

The balance sheet entry is not adjusted by current estimates of the equipment's value except in cases where accountants believe that obsolescence or decay may affect the value. Then, they will use another principle—**conservatism**—to reduce the value stated on the balance sheet to its least favorable value. (Such value must be verifiable by independent third parties.) The essence of the objectivity problem is that conversion from physical (or intangible) items to monetary units requires estimates whereas the concept of objectivity frowns upon using estimates.

Therefore, accountants rely on the price paid for something in the marketplace. While this basically is a good, objective standard, problems still hinder using market value as the sole test. Notably, the cash (or mixed bag of cash and securities) used in the purchase may or may not correspond to an *independently determined value* of a particular item. Examples of problems include (1) the validity of transactions conducted at "arm's length" with supposedly little subjective influence and (2) pricing pressure due to fads (which can temporarily cause the price of a commodity, a piece of equipment, or a whole business to surge or plunge unrealistically). Let's look at some examples:

The Double Knit Machine

In the late 1960s, most fashion experts decided that the future of men's suits belonged to double knit. Machines that produced double knit thus became extremely valuable. For a 9–18 month period, double knit machines, which cost roughly $20,000 to produce, were selling in the marketplace for $100,000. It appeared that there was no upward limit to the value. Then suddenly, the fad died, and fortunes were lost because these machines were no longer in excessive demand.

CIT Sale

Another example of how the *willing seller* part of the market value definition may be affected by unusual pressure was RCA announcing in the late 1970s that it wished to sell CIT, a finance company. The stated reason was that CIT no longer fit within the RCA family of products. Another conjecture was that RCA's management was having a difficult time managing its diverse operations: It had previously dropped out of the computer industry, soon dropped out of the video disk industry, and eventually was acquired by General Electric.

At the time of the CIT sale, the focus was on RCA's debt level as too high, partially because of the debt incurred for the CIT acquisition. RCA's credit rating suffered and its stock dropped in value because of worries about management's ability to operate a financial firm such as CIT Financial.

Manufacturers Hanover acquired CIT in the early 1980s. The questions about how objective was the *market value* price Manufacturers Hanover paid include: Did the fact that there were few buyers who could acquire a multibillion-dollar financial institution like CIT affect the market price paid?

Market value, theoretically at least, implies the existence of a market: many buyers. The amount paid for something *at market* may not be unblemished. It may be better than most other alternatives but it may not be independent or conclusive. With inflation and obsolescence, not to mention management's overestimation of useful life, there are many instances in which a new reputable estimate is better than an old acquisition price (market value). Nevertheless, the principle of objectivity prevents accountants from showing alternatives.

Independent Verification

The principle of **independent verification** restricts the accountant who audits the financial statements of a firm from having any ownership or financial interest in that firm. It also requires that the records, procedures, and controls of the company be evaluated and verified on a statistical basis. Not every source document composing the books and records will be examined and verified. Statistical verification sounds good, but is it good enough? Let's look at an example.

Pittsburgh Coal

A coal company headquartered in Pittsburgh was unable to supply a potential lender's credit department with *audited* financial statements for a substantial transaction. In view of the amount of money involved, the credit department decided to commit an analyst's time and efforts to perform an audit.

He obtained copies of all the invoices that Pittsburgh Coal had sent the previous year and verified that (1) they totaled up to the sales listed on the income statement and (2) the customers confirmed purchasing that much. The analyst also obtained copies of all invoices that had been submitted to the company and verified that they equaled the cost-of-goods sold. He checked each one of these documents; the analyst called all suppliers and verified the invoices to be true and not offset or otherwise compromised. He called every commercial bank, finance company, and other lending organization within a 60-mile radius of Pittsburgh to inquire whether the coal company had any outstanding credit. (This is a legitimate pursuit of credit information called *fishing.*) The analyst further did a title search of liens filed against the company by obtaining from the local county clerk a list of all the uniform commercial credit code (UCC-1) filings against Pittsburgh Coal. He matched these against the various loans shown on the books of the company to make sure that the company had reported every outstanding debt.

These activities were focused on giving credibility to the financial statements that had been supplied to obtain credit. This is undoubtedly the primary purpose of the audit. In this case, the process enabled the bank to have confidence in the unaudited financials and make a million-dollar loan, backed by equipment collateral.

Credibility

Another principle of accounting that lends credibility is the concept of **full and complete disclosure.** This principle states that nothing will be withheld from the financial statements and that they are complete as presented. It works in coordination with another credibility principle—consistency. As a matter of course, if any change in accounting policy occurs in a particular year, the firm must go back to the previous year's statements and restate them as if the policy had been in effect at that time.

In the instance of acquisitions and dispositions, a similar accounting reworking is required of historic documents. In the case of a merger accounted for as a **pooling,** the acquirer must restate his business as if the two firms were one for the years contained within the current financial statement. This eliminates variations in performance records and could intimate that the firm is doing better when the improvement is solely due to the merger. Unfortunately, there is another method for acquiring a company: the **purchase** of assets. Here the assets are moved to market value, if the total price paid is in excess of book equity and the balance is then added to the *goodwill* account of the financial statement of the acquiring firm in the acquisition year. The sales and earnings information in previous income statements is not changed; this can be misleading to someone reviewing the financial statement who sees the sudden jump in assets and sales (and possibly earnings) and assumes the company is growing rapidly under skilled management guidance.

A final element within this credibility area is that of **materiality,** which means not reporting on everything that happens but only those things that are significant. This is a limit to the idea of full disclosure, although it is a very practical one. It is not essential for a firm to maintain a count of paper clips within its employees' desks so that an accurate inventory can be recorded. An attempt to keep track of such a small item would probably result in costs in excess of the value of having the information. If an item is not material it is merely consolidated into some other item. Paper clips are expensed as soon as they are delivered, excepting the case of a stationery store, which resells them.

Going Concern and Estimates

Estimates are particularly complex when it is necessary to measure incomplete transactions in order to produce a statement of the firm's condition without having to end its life. Relevant principles include **going concern** and conservatism. The going-concern concept requires that the historic value of a particular asset be the value to appear on the financial statement. (Using the current value would imply that an acquisition had recently taken place.)

This is somewhat unfortunate since bankers have viewed the balance sheet as a liquidation value document for many years, that is, they scrutinize the balance sheet attempting to forecast a back-way out for debt repayment. Most debts are granted with the anticipation of repayment in the normal course of the firm's operations. Nevertheless, bankers realize that normal operations are not always what happens and that liquidation may be necessary. The accountant makes no attempt whatsoever to get at liquidation value, which is defined as the opposite of market value, that is, the value given to an unwilling seller. (Appraisals refer to liquidation values as auction values.) They are inevitably the lowest values around.

If potential buyers get word that a financial institution has taken over these assets, the resale value will drop substantially. The going concern concept chooses not to take this worst view. Instead it assumes that the firm will continue to operate, and therefore, that the values originally paid for the assets and adjusted by depreciation are the most fair estimate of worth.

Conservatism means that bad things must be immediately anticipated but that accounting for good things must wait. The concept of the *lower of cost or market* is central to conservatism. According to this concept, a purchased asset appears on the balance sheet at the historic market value. If the value of the asset declines later on, the decrease must immediately be accounted for in the financial statements. This is true even though there is no immediate intention to sell the asset. It is also true even if the asset's value may later go back up, even if it is well known that the asset is a volatile commodity. On the other hand, if the asset increases in value, and assuming there is no immediate intent to sell, the value cannot rise above its historic cost. (This was market value at the time it was placed on the financial statement.)

Technically, conservatism also applies to the income statement. Therefore, if there are two ways of calculating net income, conservatism would tell us that the method that produced the lower income would be preferred. The idea of conservatism might be viewed positively from the point of view that this is the accountant's counterbalance to management's perennially optimistic view not only of the future but also of past events.

Revenue and Expenses

The principles most frequently considered for the income statement are realization, revenue and expense matching, and the accrual method. **Realization** records a sale and recognizes revenues not at the point of receiving cash, not at the point of receiving an order, and not at the point of signing a contract, but only at the point of delivery of the product or service by the seller. Only when the service or product has been delivered to the client has a sale occurred. A written contract or cash changing hands is not required and cannot cause a sale to take place before delivery.

The concept of **matching revenues and expenses** is defined as the procedure that any expenditures incurred to produce inventory are accounted for as merely transfers of assets from the cash account to the inventory account. There is no processing of the expenditure of funds to the expense accounts on the income statement, even though it is clear that funds have left the company. This movement from the cash account to the inventory account is called **capitalization.** In effect, the expenditures incurred to produce products are capitalized onto the balance sheet as inventory. These expenditures are held until the product is sold. Then, the costs accumulated in the inventory account are set against the sale proceeds (revenues) on the income statement.

Of course, there are expenses that the firm incurs whether it is producing anything or not. Generally, the salary of the president is not capitalized into the value of the inventory. Instead it is accounted for as an administrative expense as it is incurred.

The third principle affecting the income statement is the **accrual method.** The accrual method is an accounting for what you know to be taking place even though there may be no cash outflow. There may not even be an invoice arriving in the treasurer's or controller's office of the firm.

Start-up, Inc.

Assume that Start-up, Inc. is short of cash and that Joe, the president, agrees to wait until cash is available to receive his paycheck. It is clear that the firm has, nonetheless, incurred some expense in having the chief executive.

Big Receivables, Inc.

The accrual method is behind the recognition of sales based on the delivery of products or services, independent of payment. For example, when Big Receivables, Inc. delivers some products, the sale price is duly recorded in the accounts receivable section of its balance sheet and in the revenues account of its income statement. To match expenses with revenues the capitalized cost is removed from Big Receivables' inventory account on the balance sheet and included in the expenses section on the income statement. This is independent of any cash being received, although, usually as a practical matter, an invoice has been mailed to the customer.

Millerton Supermarket

Here is an extreme example: Sam, the president of Millerton Supermarket, has a legal problem and calls Jim, senior partner of a law firm; they then have a one-hour conversation. Knowing full well that Jim has written down on his notepad that one hour of that day was consumed talking to Millerton Supermarket, Sam calls his accounting department and advises them about the one-hour conversation. The bookkeeper knows that the rate of the senior partner of the law firm is $150 an hour; therefore, he creates a source document that records this conversation, charges legal expenses, and increases the accrued expense account until the law firm's invoice is received and the posting is moved to the accounts payable account. This expense will thus appear on Millerton Supermarket's next income statement, independent of either the arrival of an invoice from the law firm or the payment of cash for such a service.

In summary, the accrual method attempts to closely track a firm's success in generating wealth. *It takes into account what is known about revenues and expenses, not the flows of cash.* Unfortunately, this method is a double-edged sword that tends to create a considerable variance between the amounts recorded in preparation of the income statement and cash inflows and outflows. The more sophisticated the application of the accrual method, the less likely it is that the income statement or balance sheet will give *any* indication of the firm's actual capacity to pay its bills as they come due.

Executory items

Executory items are facts that are not on the financial statements. An example might include one of the more interesting accounting discussions at business schools: the value of personnel training. How does an outsider evaluate the labor-management relations within a particular company? These issues are of critical importance when evaluating a service company.

Lotus 1-2-3

An illustration of this is Mitchell Kapor, a programmer at VisiCorp, the distributor of the original computer spreadsheet program. He left the company in the early 1980s because he felt that VisiCorp was not progressing fast enough in updating a new version of the software. He became the principal programmer and founder of another company called Lotus Development Corporation. While VISICALC was the breakthrough spreadsheet product written by Daniel Bricklin, LOTUS 1-2-3 rapidly made inroads since it was written to take advantage of the new IBM computer. In January 1983, VISICALC was selling about 40,000 copies a month; by January 1984, VISICALC was down to 5,000 copies a month compared to LOTUS 1-2-3's rate of 40,000 copies.

Apple Computer

A further even more perplexing example compares the balance sheets of Apple Computer and IBM in 1980. It would have been difficult to guess that Apple Computer could create a market share for itself (with incompatible computers) in the personal computer business competing with IBM. After all, IBM had bested General Electric and RCA; even the first computer manufacturer, Sperry Univac, had been forced to merge with Honeywell's domestic operations in order to survive. The high levels of individual creativity—not shown on the financial statements—permitted Apple to achieve success.

Another executory item that is not evaluated on the financial statements is that of contracts made in the course of doing business. Some analysts look at a company's order backlog to estimate future sales. This assumes that the company can perform the contract as initially bid and make a profit. It does not address the fact that the low delivery price promised in many contracts may create enormous problems for the company.

Houston Crane

As an example, two individuals with crane operation experience started a business with a crane dealer providing the original financing in 19X0. The dealer introduced them to USI Credit upon completion of Houston Crane's second year of operations. In the first year the company made a small profit, roughly $20,000. In the second year, the company lost $20,000. The third-year forecast was to make about $100,000.

When questioned on the second-year loss, the owners reported that they had anticipated a $40,000 profit, but had underestimated costs on one contract by $60,000. Because business was so good and the new partners valued their reputation, they determined to complete the job despite the error and without pressing the customer for the difference (which would have been a possible alternative). During "oil patch" booms, owners felt mistakes would just be made up the next year.

The partners fired the previous estimator and hired a new one with more experience. This approach was unimpressive; mistakes in estimates happen, and the real problem was an immature firm that was not maintaining its margins sufficiently. If sales were to grow even more in the coming year, Houston Crane's new estimator might underestimate even more than one job, which the narrow margins would not cover either.

This case critically demonstrates that the financial statements did flash warning signs. It may have been questionable to consider lending, even on a secured basis, to a company with a one- or two-year track record, with a loss in the second year. Nevertheless, it was the company's contractual arrangements that caused the problem and future bad contracts would not show on the financial statements until it may have been too late.

There are some executory items that are quite appropriate to leave off the balance sheet, including the obligation to make future interest payments. Any debt on the financial statements consists merely of the original principal less any repaid portion. This is known as the present value of the debt, the theoretical amount that would have to be repaid at the present moment in order to satisfy the obligation. Therefore, even though stipulated repayment terms may conflict with this idea (e.g., prepayment penalties), it is still preferable to apply the going-concern concept and exclude from the balance sheet the interest that may be contractually due in the future.

Timing (Allocation) Estimates

The financial statements may be produced and distributed to outsiders at possibly arbitrary times. At and during these periods, transactions halfway completed must be assigned monetary values so that the financial statements can be fashioned. While the accountant is particularly wary of estimates, and will stick to historically validated information even in the face of new inputs, the financial analyst cannot take this luxury. Making a new investment, as in preparing a capital budget, means attempting to bring to market value all assets. Only by knowing current alternatives can a new investment be logically considered.

The Auditor's Opinion

After examining the financial statements of management, auditors must express an opinion on the quality of the statements. An **unqualified opinion** means that they receive the highest accolade in "presenting fairly the financial position and results of operations and changes in financial position" for the period involved. It is clear that the operating word within this sentence is *fair*.

Fairness itself is most frequently used in polite conversation to describe activities involving games and sports. It is rarely used to describe either the behavior of businesspeople or the motivations that drive them. Management prepares the financial statements with the primary aim to look good. They get to pick the time of the year when the statement will be prepared and make other major decisions on its appearance. The auditors compare the statements as presented with their lists of principles and policies promulgated by the Securities and Exchange Commission and by the Financial Accounting Standards Board in Stamford, Connecticut. Into this relatively muddy mix auditors stir the hope that they may continue to be the accounting firm for this particular business. It is discernible that the result is more than adequately described by the word *fair*. The word financial analysts would like to see, *accurate*, would be asking too much.

This produces some predicaments. The list of unqualified opinions of financial statements during the 1980s includes cases where, it later turned out, there were substantial deviations from the truth included in the statements. Here are some unearthed fair financial statements examples originally reported by O. P. Kharbbanda and E. A. Stallworthy [*Corporate Failure*, 1985]:

- In 1982 Stauffer Chemical reduced its earnings by 25% as a result of a post-audit review of its financial statements.
- AM International Incorporated in 1980 changed its earnings from a $10 million profit to a $190 million loss shortly after its financial statement was issued with an unqualified opinion of a major accounting firm.
- Ernst & Whinney gave an unqualified opinion to the United American Bank of Knoxville in January 1983. Within three weeks of the release of the financial statements the bank declared insolvency, setting off a chain reaction that hurt many other financial institutions that had deposits with United American.
- In 1982, Touche Ross was censured by the SEC for allowing Litton Industries to postpone losses from cost overruns on Navy contracts from 1972 through 1977—five years later.

It is clear from these reports that reliance only on audited statements will not prevent a bank from investing in a company that may have significant problems. The audit itself does not prevent management from lying. In conclusion, the accountant's job is a complicated, maybe even impossible, one. There are many regulatory authorities that attempt to keep financial reporting to investors at a high standard. Nevertheless, the financial statements need to be approached from a wary perspective.

One enlightening option is to read a few of the actual FASB *Statements of Financial Accounting Standards*. By reading the introductions to each announcement and the dissenting opinions of various board members, you can get an authentic depiction of the controversy that surrounds each of these accounting compromise standards. People in the accounting field do not speak with one voice and the debate surrounding each opinion is a clear demonstration of the subjectivity involved in actually coming to their decisions.

Conclusion

Validation of the reputation of the business firm and its management may require private investigation and analysis of past associations. These types of inquiries may seem obnoxious and unnecessary, but not having them can lead to a dismal fate. Certification of third parties includes not only the reputable auditor's unqualified opinion of the financial statements but also current appraisals of the value and confirmation of the presence of physical assets. Lastly, the clients must be asked to sign a statement recognizing their ability under federal laws not to supply fraudulent documents to a financial institution in an effort to borrow money. Without fail the financial institution must be willing to pursue legal remedies in the event of attempted fraud. (The reluctance of financial institutions to pursue such legal remedies—supported on the contention of avoiding embarrassment to the fraud victim—has encouraged companies to attempt to get away with as much as possible.) Only by aggressively attempting to halt fraudulent practices will the lending industry preserve the integrity of its own raw material, the financial statements.

What about the use of other or unaudited financial statements? The best alternative source of financial information is the income tax return submitted to the Internal Revenue Service. While some clients play down the accuracy of these returns (they will probably err on the conservative side), you are at least dealing with statements prepared for an entity that will prosecute fraud. If the firm claims that the income is actually much greater than that reported, that should resolve the issue of supposed character faster than a private investigation service! Assuming the best, there is significant information in the tax return, which should be certified as a *conformed* copy. It is definitely usable for the work ahead.

Financial institutions that take statements other than those above are not just relying on character but on lack of uniform rules and fuzziness even beyond what this chapter has pointed out. Many external factors affect the preparation of financial statements. Analysts must be aware of these factors in making their decisions. Therefore, the analyst needs to reconcile the statements for his own use. Preparing the spreadsheet, which is discussed in the next segment, is the means for making these adjustments.

The analyst must scrutinize the accounting statements to *identify trends in and relationships between the various elements* to prepare a solid foundation so that a convincing forecast of the firm's future performance can be projected. Predicting the future is a baffling proposition fraught with possible failure. It is, however, reaching toward the essence of the financial analyst's mission.

Weather Forecast Metaphor

The analyst forecasting financial statements is similar to a weather forecaster basing her predictions on historic relationships. For example, if it is raining in Philadelphia in the middle of July, the weather people know the likelihood that it will be raining in New York five hours later. These statistical relationships are stored in computers. Never mind the statistics, the principal thing we want from such forecasters is the temperature and the rainfall prediction: Do we wear a coat and take an umbrella?

Similarly the financial forecaster is attempting to estimate the future success or failure of a firm in which investment is about to take place. The analyst's responsibility is to determine which relationships in the financial statements are the ones that can be counted on to forecast the future.

Key Points: In order to better forecast the future debt repayment capacity of the firm, review the financial statements for:

1. Overall integrity—honestly relating business activity,
2. Earnings and cash flow constancy—evidence of stable trends, and
3. Financial position solidity—confirmation of the ability to weather difficult times, and the underlying causes for any divergence.

Chapter 2

Spreading Assets—The Basics

Most frequently, financial statement analysis begins with scrutinizing each account on the audited statements and placing the information into a format used for all investment analysis within the firm, that is, the spreadsheet. It is important to bear in mind that the financial statements provided to the investment analyst by a prospective borrower do not necessarily show the only picture of the firm's financial health. Why is this so? The firm's accountants create the financial statement for all the stakeholders: owners, managers, employees, and customers, each of whom may have very different purposes for reviewing them. Moreover, for obvious reasons, a public company's management will want to make the financial statement look *as good as possible from their perspective*.

Thus, the balance sheet and income statements should be viewed as presenting the analyst merely with one source of information. To accomplish the job, determining the debt capacity of a prospective borrower, the analyst must be prepared to disassemble the financial statements supplied to achieve two interim objectives:

1. Calculate the *breakup value* of the firm, assuming the worst, that management fails in its goals and that the assets will be sold to satisfy the liabilities.
2. Calculate the cash flow generating capacity of the firm, assuming the most likely course, that management succeeds sufficiently in its goals to enable the firm to repay its debts and remain as a functioning unit.

The issue of revaluation is a debatable one, especially since much of the comparative industry and prior-year information available for use has not been so adjusted. This problem has led some groups of analysts in the following direction.

Major New York Bank

A major New York bank uses a computer procedure to prepare spreadsheets for analysts working on public corporations. A computer uses reports updated on a regular basis and filed with the Securities and Exchange Commission that assign numbers to every known financial statement account. A spreadsheet is produced automatically when any analyst types the stock call letters into a nearby terminal. The computer people feel it is a time-saving device for the analyst to be handed a finished spreadsheet, completed in the bank format. But an unfortunate consequence is that the analysis necessary to performing this chore would never be part of their credit function again. While the last line of the computer printout advises the analyst to obtain the financial statement and examine the footnotes carefully before proceeding with analysis, it is clear that the preprinted computerized form predisposes everyone to look at alterations as having lesser validity than the straight balance sheet and income statement SEC numbers.

A former lending officer of this institution confirmed this reaction of analysts within the bank. He himself was concerned about the acuteness with which the credit officers examined the comments within the credit write-up. This officer felt that adjusting the financial statements using the footnoted information would give the bank's officers an advantage in detecting companies that would not be able to repay their loans.

Trying to fulfill the needs of proper analysis while also producing a finished report readable by senior management is a puzzle that may be partially solved by resorting to a personal computer format. Optionally available with this book is a template based on Lotus Development Corporation's LOTUS 1-2-3 spreadsheet program for use on microcomputers. With the computer, it is possible to use multiple columns of a spreadsheet to reorganize the information for the analyst's purposes while also producing the more standard, unadjusted spread information. Exhibit 2-2 and several other worksheets to follow are available on the optional floppy disk. Spending some time with these templates will quickly pay for itself many times over and free you from tedious tasks of number crunching. The mechanical side of the analysis is simplified by the spreadsheet template; thus, instead of worrying about arithmetic, the focus of the analysis can be on the interpretation of the footnotes. There are no macros in the spreadsheet, so you must know something about the program to operate it intelligently. These popular alternative programs can use these templates unaltered.

1. Borland International's QUATTRO
2. Computer Associates' SUPERCALC, version 5 and up
3. Microsoft's EXCEL
4. Lotus Development Corp.'s LOTUS 1-2-3, version 2 and up
5. Any spreadsheet that claims to use the .WK1 file structure of LOTUS 1-2-3, version 2

This presentation assumes that you are conversant with spreadsheet programs. The more advanced templates—like Exhibit 12-6—at the end of the book require the program you use to be able to perform basic statistical analysis. Whatever method you choose, by hand or by personal computer, the basic rules to follow in developing a spreadsheet from a borrower's financial statement are as follows:

1. *Round off numbers to four digits.* This practice will simply make the spreadsheet easier to read. For instance, if financial statement entries are in

billions, round them to millions for the spreadsheet. If financial statement entries are in millions, round everything to hundreds of thousands for the spreadsheet. The point of the spreadsheet is that it allows the analyst to review several years of financial performance at once. It is thus important to avoid multiple-digit numbers.

2. *Spread annual statements and interim statements separately.* Interim statements should be compared only with interims of the same date from previous years. If you are fortunate enough to obtain regular quarterly statements, you should have multiple spreadsheets that contain fiscal years, first quarters, second quarters, third quarters, and fourth quarters, unless the firm has absolutely no seasonal business pattern.

3. *Read the footnotes before beginning the analysis.* Since the first footnote generally details the basic conventions used to construct the financial statements, it is essential that it be read before spreading the statement. Footnotes concerning executory and contingency commitments should be read next. (These include information about potential lawsuits, warranties, and events that take place after the statement date.) All footnotes contain important information from the auditors describing their estimating process. For the analyst to be well informed, a careful reading of the footnotes allows the making of judicious adjustments to the spreadsheet from the original financials; these refinements better reflect the analyst's mission when preparing the spread.

4. *Consider the effects of inflation.* The use of inflation-adjusted accounting to improve the proper recording of assets and income is now quite difficult since SFAS (Statement of Financial Accounting Standards) #33 has been made optional. Since GAAP no longer requires the information in the footnotes, separate items below will give alternatives for obtaining and using it. It is important to consider the issues that gave rise to SFAS #33 (to be discussed in the spreadsheet chapter) because inflation-adjusted accounting is useful in reviewing a company's long-range performance.

5. *Examine intangibles.* Intangibles must be identified and researched, and evaluated.

6. *Adjust asset values when necessary.* Following item 4 above, the historical cost of assets is usually the only value now shown for the fixed assets on the balance sheet. To prepare a valid analysis, it is definitely worthwhile to obtain independent third-party appraisals that provide realizable (generally market) as well as liquidation values.

7. *Start with the balance sheet and move next to the income statement.* Balance sheet analysis is generally viewed as the key to understanding the borrower's character. Lenders look favorably upon firms with liquid investments (such as marketable securities), substantial stockholder equity, and small liability accounts. There is a widespread assumption—but not necessarily a correct one—that if high liquidity and low debt characterize a borrower's balance sheet, there is less likelihood that management's character will be tested. The ability to determine the status of a firm's liquidity requires a thorough understanding of all balance sheet entries. This segment is primarily designed to instruct you on

how to thoroughly examine a borrower's balance sheet (in preparation for preparing the spreadsheet) and to use it to identify the proper questions for management.

8. *Spend more time on lower-quality accounts.* As you progress through the financial statements, it will become evident that it is worthwhile to spend more time on certain entries. In Exhibit 2-1, for example, the entries that indicate the highest asset risk categories are goodwill and deferred charges. These entries are discussed in greater detail later in this chapter.

Spreading financial statements is only the first step in investment analysis. Eventually, the analyst should conduct a trend analysis using the spreadsheet to compare information found on the current financial statement with that of previous financial statements to assess how the firm has progressed over time. Trend analysis is explained in detail in Chapter 10. The analyst should also conduct a comparative analysis to determine how a firm's financial condition compares with that of its competitors. The comparative analysis is also discussed in Chapter 10. Nevertheless, both for a prospective corporate raider as well as during an involuntary (to management at least) liquidation for the benefit of stakeholders this initial spreading can be useful for determining the **breakup value** of a firm—*looking at market values focuses our attention on the back door out of an investment transaction: liquidation of the assets.*

Exhibit 2-1.

RISK OF REALIZATION OF ASSET VALUES

ITEM TYPE	RISK
Cash	Low
Current Receivables from Trade	Low
Long Term Notes Receivable	Medium
Receivables from Affiliates	Medium to High
Work in Process Inventory	Medium to High
Raw Material Inventory	Low
Finished Goods Inventory	Medium
Investments in Unconsolidated Subsidiary	Medium
Land Fixed Assets	Low
Plant Fixed Assets	Medium
Equipment Fixed Assets	Medium to High
Goodwill	High
Patents or Franchises	Medium
Deferred Charges	High

Asset Revaluation Analysis

The analysis of the balance sheet (Exhibit 2-2A) begins with the examination of asset accounts. Recall that assets are both expenses waiting to happen and purchases made with the intention of later resale at a profit. The latter point indicates that assets are investments in the sense that they are expected to produce future revenue streams. Therefore, asset acquisitions can be evaluated using the techniques mentioned herein, since they are investments. Assets can become obsolete and unable to produce revenue despite their apparent strenghts. The analyst must consider unexpected variations in an asset's future revenue stream when determining what value to place on the spreadsheet. Assets should be reviewed in terms of their marketability (ability to add to the firm's liquidity).

Oil Rigs

The Texas recession offers an illustration of how seemingly strong assets can fall in value. The number of oil exploration rigs operating in the Gulf of Mexico rose from only 600 in 1972 to roughly 4,500 in 1982. The enormous expenditure required to manufacture these new rigs was financed by major financial institutions, aggressively leveraging shareholder equity under the assumption that oil prices would never again drop below $30 a barrel. The plunge in oil prices sharply curbed exploration, leaving only about 650 rigs operative as of the late 1980s. The other rigs were idled and thus unable to generate income streams. As a consequence of the overly optimistic investment analysis, some financial institutions that financed this equipment failed and shareholders lost their investment.

Finally, a review of assets should also determine whether they are free-standing (not specifically pledged to other lenders). Although liens do not affect asset quality, they do affect a lender's ability to have recourse to the asset if necessary. The following sections survey the traditional assets in both the current (converting to cash in less than one year) and fixed (long-term) categories. Two more difficult items, inventory conventions in use and leased assets, are discussed two chapters later in Chapter 4.

Current Monetary Assets

One of accounting's chores is to reduce all business transactions to monetary value. Current monetary assets are relatively easy to analyze since cash, marketable securities, accounts receivable, and prepaid expenses are already in monetary form. They are part of the **current assets,** which will be ordinarily converted to cash during the current year. Calculating these items is frequently as easy as looking at the checkbook journal for the cash balance. Although for the other current monetary asset accounts the auditors may want to make certain adjustments, the degree of estimation is usually low. Thus, merely transferring these assets from the financial statements to the spreadsheets is frequently acceptable, but problems can still occur.

Cash {1}*

At first glance, it might seem that the accountant need only call the bank and check the account balances to verify the cash entry on the financial statements. However, since the bank's books do not reflect the most recently written checks, the value of the cash entry is determined from the company's books. (A bank with a loan in jeopardy, however, has the right to set off any balances in the borrower's checking account against the loan. The right to set off entitles the bank to funds that the firm has already ordered to be paid to others.) Moreover, although the borrower's book balance reflects all checks written against the account, it does not reflect the fact that checks deposited might be returned. That is, the company's book balance is credited for deposits that have not necessarily cleared with the bank, possibly from a defunct customer.

The major problem with the cash account entry is the *potential restriction on the company's use of its own cash* arising from, for instance, a compensating balance agreement. The Securities and Exchange Commission now requires firms that have compensating balance agreements with their banks to indicate in the footnotes that cash balances must be maintained at a certain average level.

> **Key Points:** Investigate any restrictions on the company's use of its own cash and bear in mind that the cash account may include deposits that had not yet cleared with the bank when the balance sheet was prepared.

Marketable Securities {2}

Marketable securities are commonly comprised of short-term government bills, commercial paper of corporations, and bank certificates of deposit. Repurchase agreements may also be found in this category. Since these securities are short-term, it is unlikely that their value will change significantly between purchase and collection of the principal. Nevertheless, *they are valued at the lower of cost or market at the time* the balance sheet is prepared. Any reduction in value from the original cost at the time of the new statement must be reflected on the income statement. Any subsequent increase in value can be returned to the balance sheet up to the original cost on the date of a later financial statement, with the income statement account adjusted accordingly.

The major problem with marketable securities is collection risk. The securities are the obligations of other institutions. The degree to which they are collectible depends on whether the firm has taken an aggressive investment posture and has invested in less than investment grade securities. Problems can occur, however, even with investment grade securities. Let's look at an example.

Penn Central

When the Penn Central Corporation collapsed in 1969, many firms had substantial blocks of Penn Central commercial paper in their portfolios. No

(Text continued on page 45.)

*Numbers in braces correspond to line items in Exhibit 2-2A.

Exhibit 2-2A.

BALANCE SHEET: TREND ANALYSIS AND BREAKUP VALUE

WORKSHEET 1A

Company Name:

Balance Sheet Date:	31-Dec-89		31-Dec-90		Dec-90 BREAKUP VALUE	
Rounded to: millions (000,000's)	$	%	$	%	$	%
ASSETS						
1 Cash						
2 Marketable Securities						
3 Accounts Receivable - Trade						
4 Inventories: Raw Materials						
5 Inventories: Work in Process						
6 Inventories: Finished Goods						
7 Subtotal Inventories						
8 Prepaid Expenses						
9 Other Current						
10 **Total Current Assets**						
11 Property, Plant & Equipment						
12 "Capital" Leased Equipment						
13 "Operating" Leased Equipment						
14 (Less Depreciation)						
15 Subtotal Net Prop, Plant & Equip.						
16 Investments and Advances						
17 Long Term Marketable Securities						
18 Affiliate & Sundry Receivables						
19 Net Assets/Discontinued Operations						
20 Other Noncurrent Liabilities						
21 Intangibles (Patents & Rights)						
22 Goodwill (Resulting from Mergers)						
23 **Total Fixed Assets**						
24 **TOTAL ASSETS**						

LIABILITIES

#						
25	Notes Payable					
26	Accounts Payable - Trade					
27	Taxes and Accrued Expenses					
28	Other Current					
29	Current Portion L-T Debt (Operating)					
30	**Total Current Operating Liabs.**					
31	Current Portion L-T Debt (Remaining)					
32	Deferred or Unearned Income					
33	Long Term Debt - Unsecured					
34	Long Term Debt - Secured					
35	Capital Lease Obligations					
36	Present Value of Operating Leases					
37	Other Noncurrent Liabilities					
38	**Total Senior Term Debt**					
39	Subordinated Debt					
40	Unfunded Pension Obligations					
41	Deferred Taxes (Debt Portion)					
42	**TOTAL LIABILITIES**					

EQUITY

#						
43	Deferred Taxes (Equity Part)					
44	Minority Interest					
45	Preferred Stock					
46	Common Stock					
47	Retained Earnings					
48	(Treasure Stock & Other Reductions)					
49	**Net Worth**					
50	**TOTAL FOOTINGS**					

Exhibit 2-2B.

BALANCE SHEET RATIOS   WORKSHEET 1B

Company Name:			
Balance Sheet Date:			
ADDITIONAL INFORMATION			**Brkup Value**
1 Estimate of Contingent Liabs.			
2 Sales			
3 Cost of Goods Sold			
4 Market Value of Equity			
5 Returns of Merchandise			
6 Earnings before Interest and Taxes			
7 LIFO Reserve			
8 Reserve for Accounts Rec. Losses			
BALANCE SHEET RATIOS			
LIQUIDITY			**Brkup Value**
7 Current Assets/Current Liabs	X	X	X
8 Quick Assets/Current Liabs	X	X	X
9 Sales/Receivables (Turnover Times)	X	X	X
10 Receivables Turnover (Days)	Days	Days	Days
11 Reserve for Loss/Gross Accts. Rec.			
12 Returns of Merchandise/Sales			
13 Long Receivables / Total Receivables			
14 Net Working Capital			
15 Tot Inventory Turnover (Days)	Days	Days	Days
16 Inventory/Current Assets			
17 Raw Materials Inv. Turnover (Days)	Days	Days	Days
18 Work/In/Progress Inv. Turnover (Days	Days	Days	Days
19 Finished Goods Inv. Turnover (Days)	Days	Days	Days
20 Cost of Goods Sold/Payables (Times)	Days	Days	Days
21 Payables Turnover (Days)	Days	Days	Days
22			
CAPITAL STRUCTURE			
23 Debt (Total Liabilities)/ Net Worth			
24 Long Term Debt/Total Capital			
25 Fixed Asset Turnover (S/FA)	X	X	X
26 Sales/ Current Assets	X	X	X
27 Total Asset Turnover (S/TA)	X	X	X
28			
Altman's Zeta: Bankruptcy predicted if % column <=1.87, Best if > 2.99			
	%	%	%
37 Working Capital/Total Assets			
38 Retained Earnings/Total Assets			
39 EBIT/Total Assets			
40 Mkt Val Equity/Total Debt			
41 Sales/Total Assets			
42 TOTAL			

funds were recovered for several years, and any recovery that came was at a fraction of the purchaser's original cost. In certain cases, the commercial paper holders suffered substantial losses and lost the invested liquid assets.

Certificates of deposit can also be problematical if they have been issued by commercial banks (or thrifts) on the verge of bankruptcy. Although time deposits of up to $100,000 are insured by the Federal Deposit Insurance Corporation (FDIC), the funds will not necessarily be available upon the security's maturity. Moreover, since the quasi-governmental organizations do not guarantee interest, some loss could occur.

Again, it is important to examine the footnotes for any additional information. If a substantial block of funds is invested in marketable securities, the analyst should inquire about their composition. Since the balance sheet is apt to be at least two months old by the time the analyst receives it, he should also find out whether the securities are still being held.

> **Key Points:** If investments in marketable securities are substantial, inquire about their composition. Collection risk is the major consideration and even high-quality or insured investments can result in a loss.

Accounts Receivable: Trade {3}

Accounts receivable result from the firm selling products on credit to customers. The first consideration in the analysis of accounts receivable is the likelihood of collection. Generally, the weaker the firm, the higher the collection risk. This is unfortunate since weaker firms must depend on accounts receivable for financing capability. When a firm has difficulty selling its products, however, salespeople are often instructed to sell aggressively without considering the credit capacity of the customer. Another tactic a weak firm might employ to generate sales though weakening the accounts receivable is to offer excessively extended payment terms.

One test of accounts receivable quality is reviewing the company's loss reserve. If the firm's experience in collecting accounts receivable has not been good, the auditors should compel management to set up reserves based on a percentage of outstanding receivables that previous experience shows will not make payment. If the reserve represents a significant portion of total accounts receivable (for instance, greater than 5%), the stated value of the entire receivables account should be questioned.

Accounts receivable are presented on most financial statements as a net figure and they are kept net on the first page of the worksheet. However, on the second page of the balance sheet worksheet (Exhibit 2.2B) is a list of additional information including the receivables' reserves found in the footnotes. The allowance for bad debts should be separately shown in line {8} on the second page of spreadsheet 1, Exhibit 2-2B. This practice will allow readers to make their own assessment of whether the reserve for bad debts is excessive.

Assuming additional investigation is warranted, the analyst should obtain an *aging report* on the accounts receivable from the firm. Exhibit 2-3 shows an aging report. Briefly, it shows the time of billing for individual customers and the status of the customer's payment. The aging report enables the analyst to review not only late payers but also customer concentration. Selling to only one customer can produce marketing savings and can allow the firm to concentrate on manufacturing to steady orders. However, it can also mean serious problems for the firm if that one customer stops ordering merchandise or encounters financial difficulties.

Sears, Roebuck & Co.

Sears, Roebuck & Co. historically had developed a number of clothing suppliers with whom they worked closely to assure high quality and the lowest cost possible. The suppliers developed new styles and manufacturing standards to Sears's specifications, and received, in turn, market prices without marketing expense. When Sears got into financial difficulties in the early 1980s, many of these same suppliers went out of business because they had no marketing skills or alternate customers—they were like a new firm with just production capability. There is risk in lack of customer diversification.

A review of the aging report can also uncover any disputes on specific shipments. The aging report shows the billing and receipts by specific date. For instance, if a customer has paid for a shipment that was received 30 or 60 days ago, but has not paid for merchandise that was shipped 90 days ago, there is probably a dispute about the earlier shipment. Although obtaining the aging report can be difficult—it is confidential and will almost never be offered as part of the general financial statements—the analyst should nonetheless be vigorous in procuring it.

Another possibility for a firm short of working capital is eliminating credit risk by dealing with a **factoring company.** Factoring firms (which buy a firm's accounts receivable and thus help its cash flow) constantly scrutinize the condition of accounts receivable. Frequently, the factor's client may not ship without prior approval since the factor wishes to control its outstandings to any one obligor. On the other hand, for a firm that does use a factor but has receivables remaining on its books, these may have been unacceptable to the factor and, thus, may be of questionable value to any fund's source.

Finally, the option exists to pledge the accounts receivable to a financial source against short-term borrowings. This is generally referred to as **commercial financing** to distinguish it from factoring. This pledging removes the receivables from general assets any lender might look to as a back door out of the transaction. On the other hand, the confining controls on receivables exercised by factors is lacking in the instance of a commercial finance arrangement. Therefore, unfortunately, if the receivables are bad in a financial collapse, the commercial finance lender will join the other lenders for the balance of its exposure after it takes any losses on the receivables.

Diamond Industry

The diamond business exemplifies this problem that can arise in accounts receivable financing. In the diamond trade, most dealers know each other (and

Exhibit 2-3.

Harry's Diamonds Company, Inc.						
Accounts Receivable Aging Schedule						
				Month of: June, 1990		
Customer Name	This Month	30 Days	60 Days	90 Days	120 Days	Over 120 Days
Stanley's Diamonds	$50,278	$45,890	$88,137	$53,580	$80,137	
Bloomingdales	$80,137	$75,090	$50,270	$25,750	$45,090	
Cartier	$53,580	$65,543	$52,580	$80,137	$50,270	
Bergdorf's	$25,758	$92,500	$30,782	$15,689	$32,126	
Tiffany & Co.	$15,689	$15,067		$12,357	$14,579	
Van Cleef & Arpels	$30,782	$28,432	$32,500	$21,120	$45,090	
Michael C. Fina Co.	$12,625	$15,067	$25,750	$17,987	$15,589	
Fortunoff	$15,067	$10,864	$15,689		$15,067	
Georg Jensen	$32,508	$32,123	$30,782	$45,890	$40,359	
Marcus Jewelers	$28,432	$15,689	$25,759	$15,689	$31,782	
Bergdorf Goodman	$45,890	$50,276		$53,580	$32,122	$45,258
Saks Fifth Avenue	$32,123	$30,702	$32,500	$28,432	$15,057	
TOTAL	$422,869	$155,115	$52,580	$187,297	$32,122	$45,258

may even be related to each other) and they tend to help each other out. Because diamonds and customers may be unique, trading often takes place in two directions. Thus, the firm making the sale that it wants to finance may also have a payable to the purchasing firm. This could create a setoff risk. Specifically, Firm A would trade merchandise with Firm B, creating receivables for each firm. Firm A would then finance Firm B's receivable with a commercial finance company. If Firm A failed, Firm B would set off its payable to Firm A with the receivable from Firm A, leaving the financial source with a loss. To avoid this situation, financial institutions require accounts receivable aging reports from all clients of the diamond dealer being financed to verify the one-way relationship with their clients.

In conclusion, receivables are very important assets because (1) the liquidity they represent and (2) because their direct connection with sales tempts management to exaggerate them. Collectibility is less of an issue for the analyst if the company's loss reserves are low and its client list is comprised of well-known or financially sound firms.

Key Points: If the company's loss reserve is greater than 5%, question the stated value of accounts receivable. Obtain an aging report for information on account concentration, payment history, and shipment disputes. Show gross accounts receivable, reserves for bad debts, and net accounts receivable on the spreadsheet.

Prepaid Expenses {8}

Prepaid expenses generally represent an advance payment for such current necessities as utilities and real estate rental. Typically, however, analysts re-spread prepaid expenses as a long-term asset. Although this practice is con-servative, it is difficult to justify since the firm would have to continue paying for these necessities even if it were in financial distress. These prepayments should therefore properly be carried as a current asset. The principal factor that makes prepaid expenses possess a longer-term nature is that they are often mixed in the same account as—and thus indistinguishable from—sundry receiv-ables. These sundry receivables can include such items as loans to officers, which may be in the form of a 90-day note, but are likely to be invariably renewed and difficult to collect if financial problems erupt (see below).

> **Key Points:** If prepaid expenses can be separated out from sundry receivables, they should be carried as current on the spreadsheet. Other-wise, carry them long-term.

Non-Current Monetary Assets

In addition to current monetary assets, there are a few non-current monetary assets. These include long-term (i.e., longer than one year) investments in marketable securities, notes receivable, dividends receivable from affiliates, and bond and note discounts or premiums, which are sometimes carried as deferred charges.

Long-Term Marketable Securities {17}

Long-term holdings in marketable securities carry the same default risk as short-term securities. However, long-term securities also carry the risk that interest rates will fluctuate and cause considerable shifts in their market value over time. Long-term investments, which sound similar, are not discussed here because many of those investments do not have a value that is constantly and readily made by the market. The assumption is also made that this discussion involves ownership interests that are less than 20% of the owned company.

A loss in value on a long-term security is handled differently from a loss in value on a short-term security. If a loss occurs because the value of a long-term security has fallen, the security's reduction in value on the financial statement is permanent. The security's value cannot be increased even if there are future gains that bring the security's market value back to its original cost.

While this is of dubious value for the financial analyst trying to determine breakup value for possible liquidation, the income statement is left unchanged because losses on long-term securities are posted directly to the net worth accounts. Thus, fluctuations in the bond or stock market will not affect a firm's net income. When the security is sold, the reduction in net worth previously taken is reversed and any loss or gain is recognized on the income statement. To prevent management from manipulating income after the fact, accounting rules do not permit moving current marketable securities to non-current account status without simultaneously recording any loss on the income statement.

Although this treatment of marketable securities prevents some manipulation of the balance sheet, it does not prevent the transfer of the long-term security that has regained its original value to the current portion of the balance sheet in which the gains can be recognized. This manipulation of the balance sheet can be monitored only if the analyst receives detailed schedules. Obviously, if these accounts are not significant, it is not worth pursuing receipt of such schedules.

> **Key Points:** Long-term marketable securities carry both default and interest rate risk and may be carried at less than market value. If investments in long-term securities are significant, obtain a detailed schedule of the investments.

Affiliate and Sundry Receivables {18}

Typically, a firm has current receivables other than trade receivables. These receivables might include loans, advances, or receivables due from stockholders, employees, or even related companies. Such receivables are frequently carried in the same account as prepaid expenses under prepaid expenses and sundry receivables. If it is possible for the analyst to separate the sundry receivables, enter them in the non-current portion of the balance sheet.

The reason for this is that if the company runs into problems, shareholders, employees, and officers will probably repay their loans only under pressure and in a slow fashion. Moreover, if the firm is in good shape financially, there would typically be no pressure on these borrowers to keep payments current. Although the common practice of officers borrowing on a demand note basis technically allows these loans to be carried as current assets, the firm's demanding payment in the short term is highly unlikely. Thus, even demand loans to officers should be carried as long-term assets.

> **Key Points:** Sundry receivables should be carried long-term on the spreadsheet.

Trade Notes Receivable {18}

Notes receivable need careful inspection since, on occasion, accounts receivable that the firm could not collect when due are carried in this category. Frequently, when a customer has acquired more debts than it can conveniently pay off, the seller will accept a signed note that enables the buyer to make small payments over time and enables the seller to earn some interest. This practice is not restricted to smaller firms. General Motors, Ford, and Chrysler, for instance, all provide extended-term financing for their vehicle customers through captive finance companies. When interest rates are high, they may even offer low rates, subsidized to boost sales.

The danger is the interest rates on notes receivable, which may be below market, reducing their market value. For example, if a business provides mortgage financing at a rate below current market rates, the present value of the note is considerably less than its face value. In effect, the company is subsidizing the holder of the note. In such instances, the analyst might consider reducing the value of the note when transferring it to the spreadsheet.

> **Key Points:** Notes receivable sometimes represent accounts receivable that could not be collected when due. If the interest rate on a note receivable is low, consider reducing the value of the note before transferring it to the spreadsheet.

Dividends and Interest Receivable {18}

Dividends and interest receivable from affiliates are usually carried by analysts as either a current asset (if it is due from a separate entity) or as a non-current asset (if it is due from an affiliate). For the same reasons as mentioned in the sundry receivables account above, most financial institutions prefer to spread these in the fixed-asset section.

The percentage of the firm's ownership interest in the affiliate determines how these items appear on the balance sheet. While discussed in more depth below, briefly, if the ownership interest is less than 20%, the net income of the affiliate is never recognized; only dividends are recognized as income when the affiliate declares them. This is based on the belief that having an insignificant minority interest through the security investment means that there is little management control over the affiliate. Therefore, income generated is not to the credit of the parent (investor) management. Only when dividends are declared can any benefit be construed to be received as a result of the investment.

> **Key Points:** A large balance sheet value for dividends and interest receivable warrants further investigation. The greater the firm's percentage of interest in the affiliate, the more control it has over the dividends it receives.

Other Non-Current Liabilities {20}

When selling notes or bonds, a business may incur commissions and other issuance fees. Accounting principles do not permit these fees to be immediately expensed. Instead, they are considered **deferred charges** and capitalized onto the balance sheet to be later amortized over the life of the bond issue. They are frequently carried as other non-current assets since they are relatively small. Nevertheless, since these deferred charges offer no breakup value to the business, the analyst should deduct them from both assets and net worth accounts.

Another deferred change is bond premiums; these arise when a firm acquires a bond with a coupon discount rate that is greater than the current market rate. Since such bonds sell at a premium over face value, which will not be returned as principal at the bond's maturity, the firm must amortize the premium it paid over the face value during the life of the bond or note. The amortization slowly reduces the bond's value to its face value amount on the balance sheet and is also an expense against income, offsetting the premium interest being received.

Other examples of deferred charges include moving expenses, merger expenses, and promotional costs; each represents an expenditure of funds that was initiated to improve future income. In keeping with the principle of matching revenues and expenses, these costs are capitalized onto the balance sheet and expensed later. The problem for the analyst, however, is that *it is impossible to track the earnings benefit that results from such costs.* Cases in which deferred charges might be justified are those in which a firm's expenses are directly involved in the production of revenue, such as drilling costs or exploration expenses for an oil company.

> **Key Points:** Because they have no breakup value, bond and note discounts, bond premiums, and other deferred charges should be deducted from the assets and net worth portion of the balance sheet and not transferred onto the spreadsheet.

Non-Monetary Asset Revaluation

The following asset categories are not stated monetary obligations due to the firm as are the monetary assets. Instead these are physical objects or intangible rights whose value is subject to constant and considerable change. The breakup value of these belongings is contingent on the economy, technology, inflation, and market vacillation. Therefore, the only value that can be placed onto the balance sheet is an estimate of the *true* value. In a well-borne-out trepidation of management's will to bend the financials to its own ends, GAAP swings away from market value, which it feels can be manipulated, and requires that historical costs be the basis of conversion to dollar values. Thus, the analyst is left severely handicapped in determining a breakup value balance sheet. (Later in Chapter 6, the equally severe impact on the income statement will be explored.)

Inventories {4}, {5}, {6} and {7}

Inventory consists of

1. **Raw materials** (generally purchased in the market and also valuable to other producers or consumers)
2. **Finished goods** (manufactured or converted to salable products to consumers without further modification)
3. **Work-in-process** (materials or services that are partially completed and useless for resale either back to the raw materials market or directly to consumers)

In general, the stated value of raw materials on the balance sheet is valid, the exception to this rule being volatile commodities and raw materials requiring costly or long-term storage. Similarly, the analyst can place a fair amount of reliance on the balance sheet value of finished goods inventory, except for products that are slow-moving or faddish in nature. Recall that the finished goods have a good chance of being sold at a profit, meaning that their being carried at cost on the balance sheet may be an understatement of their value; it is feasible that even another party could sell the item at cost in a breakup. The genuine dilemma is estimating the value of work-in-process. If a firm fails, work-in-process will most likely be of no value.

Because of the above, firms highly dependent on fashion trends, such as garment companies, are more likely to be able to finance accounts receivable than inventory. Although in some of these cases basic raw materials such as greige goods and plain fabrics are accepted as loan collateral, in general, lenders are reluctant to consider either work-in-process or finished goods as collateral. That is not to say that the analyst should completely discount the value of work-in-process and finished goods, but rather that he should closely examine the composition of inventory. If finished goods and work-in-process appear to comprise a greater portion of inventory than in the past, the analyst should find out why. Normally, inventory components should change proportionally with sales from year to year.

Using year-end inventory to calculate various ratios (which will be discussed in Chapters 8 and 9) may possibly generate spurious results. Most texts call for the use of average inventory, calculated as the sum of inventories at the ends of the last two years divided by two. However, since inventory is often at a low point at the end of the fiscal year, the result of the above calculation will not be the average inventory over the entire year. Thus, in addition to posting the inventory number to the spreadsheet, the analyst should refer to quarterly interim statements (preferably monthly statements) to calculate an average inventory value to be used in ratio analysis. This practice is unnecessary if the firm is not seasonal. The existence of seasonality, however, can be tricky to determine; for example, toilet paper manufacturers have two peak demand periods: one at Christmas and one at Easter!

The principle of conservatism requires that assets be recorded at the lower of cost or market value. Therefore, if the market value of inventory drops below the value of inventory resulting from any cost convention, the lower market value must be recorded on the balance sheet. Let's look at an example.

Retirement Estates, Inc.

Consider the operations of a Florida residential real estate developer. It has planned a subdivision based on an assessment of the marketplace and its ability to sell houses. The development is going to be built from scratch. There are many steps to this process: first, acquiring the land; second, obtaining the proper government approvals; third, putting the streets and sewerage into place; fourth, building houses on individual lots—starting with foundations, then moving up to the framing and roofing, and finally finishing the inside of the house.

Costs are incurred throughout this period. Costs that continue throughout the process include the interest expense involved in debt incurred to acquire the land for the subdivision and real estate taxes. As construction goes forward, the firm needs more money and may borrow in order to complete the individual steps described above. The accounting convention discussed in the first chapter concerning the matching of revenues and expenses calls for this interest and real estate expense to be capitalized into the financial statement, to be considered an expense upon sale of the property. Doubtless, it is a part of the cost of constructing the fixed asset. The principal point is that *an additional test of the value is required: net realizable value. This limits the cost allocations to not more than the property could be sold for at completion.*

A market standard is essential so that the value assigned to the inventory does not exceed the end product's price in the open market. Correctly, accounting principles require that the market value of the inventory of houses be periodically appraised to assure that cost does not exceed market. One alternative solution to the inventory valuation problem, especially when the average inventory cost convention is in use, is to require that any analysis subject obtain appraisals from approved independent third parties to establish a correct market value.

> **Key Points:** Quality is the main consideration for inventory. Although the stated value of raw materials and finished goods is generally reliable, it is difficult to value work-in-process. If any category comprises a larger portion of inventory than in the past, find out why.

Fixed Assets {11}, {12} and {13}

The next assets to be examined are called fixed assets, meaning long-term assets. The dominant portion of an operating firm's long-term assets are the plant, property, and equipment (PP&E). With the popularity of joint ventures, investments and advances to affiliates are also significant. Finally, intangibles, especially goodwill, are also increasing in importance. Current waves of corporate acquisitions using the purchase method of accounting are generating goodwill through the cost being in excess of the value of the assets acquired. Further, the conversion of the economy into one dominated by service businesses rather than manufacturing ones is generating intangible assets that accountants and financial intermediaries have yet to properly evaluate.

Plant, Property, and Equipment {11}

One of the most difficult aspects of evaluating PP&E is that the value that appears on the balance sheet may have very little basis in reality, meaning *the market*. This is because assets are listed at their book value (i.e., the original purchase price of the asset or its historical cost) less depreciation rather than market value.

Historical Cost Alternatives

CPI. Inflation is a constant presence in the U.S. economy. The problem of incorporating the effects of inflation into asset valuation analysis is extremely complex because the inflation rate varies not only from time period to time period but also from industry to industry. For example, the easiest possibility for adjusting the book values of assets to reflect inflation is to index financial statements to the consumer price index (CPI), a standard formulated by the Department of Labor that measures the increased dollar cost to maintain a middle income standard of living. The change in the CPI might be applied to various assets on the balance sheet to partially reflect the changing yardstick by which accountants measure business transactions. It is especially attractive since the CPI's determination is outside of management's wiles, if subject to those of politicians.

Unfortunately, although the CPI is external to businesses and thus provides some objectivity, the inflation rate for a basket of consumer goods may not be a relevant measure to apply to either manufacturing or service businesses. More-over, applying the CPI across the board produces ludicrous results in highly technological industries such as data processing and telecommunications. In these industries, equipment rapidly becomes obsolete, falling rather than in-creasing in value as the rising CPI would suggest.

Third-party estimate. Another alternative to using the original market value for PP&E on the balance sheet is to obtain an independent third-party estimate of the value. Auditors, however, fear that management will take advantage of this process and report misleading information. (In fact, management realizes that revaluing capital assets upward is a double-edged sword because future depreciation expense would increase if assets had higher values. Therefore, management would likely approach such revaluations with caution.)

One of the peculiarities of generally accepted accounting principles is that any value that changes on the balance sheet must simultaneously flow through the income statement. Thus, the GAAP income statement records all modifica-tions in wealth and how these alterations result in revisions in retained earnings.

It is interesting to contrast GAAP accounting to the accounting practices that individuals intuitively use. When an individual's home increases in value, the increase would not be recorded on that individual's tax return as income. Nonetheless, she would be able to receive a home equity loan based on the increased value of her home. Thus, it would appear that financial institutions are willing to make real estate loans based on appraised values. Similarly, when an individual contemplates the purchase of a physical asset, investment advisers recommend that an appraisal be obtained. In fact, appraised values for both physical and intangible assets are generally accepted as actual values for those assets—but not in GAAP. It might be argued that it is unreasonable *not* to allow businesses to change the value of their assets annually as the situation warrants it and to reflect that alteration in net worth *directly*, bypassing the income statement. Management should be held accountable for the operations of the firm and for responding to changes in the marketplace that will eventually impact the operations of the firm. *The practical question is: Should changing market values of physical assets impact management decision making when confronted with more than a several-year-old decision about the purchase price of that asset?* The answer is *yes;* that is what management does in the planning process to survive.

If the analyst fails to make similar adjustments to the book value of PP&E, his forecast of the future is likely to be lacking important prediction informa*'*on.

U.S. Steel

In 1962, the U.S. Steel Company (now USX Corp.) attempted to raise prices on steel products. Most of the plant had been built during the 1940s and had since been depreciated to nearly zero book value. At present profit levels, U.S. Steel would be very hard-pressed to replace the equipment that was wearing out, because the cost of new equipment had increased so substantially; unfortunately, this replacement was needed if the firm was going to compete against the growing dynamo of the recently (1950s) modernized Japanese steel industry. German imports had already taken a substantial chunk of the U.S. market and productivity issues were prominently on the minds of the industry. Moreover, by applying the full market value of the firm's PP&E to calculate returns on assets, it was clear that U.S. Steel's profits were inadequate at current price levels. The reasoning behind the proposed increase was that the value of the corporation's PP&E was significantly higher.

The Kennedy Administration, concerned that a price increase by U.S. Steel would trip off a round of inflation, discouraged U.S. Steel from imposing the increase, claiming that the company's GAAP calculated returns were adequate without it. The increase ultimately was not instituted.

U.S. Steel continued to make substantial book profits. It continued to pay substantial dividends and high executive bonuses and to grant ample wage concessions. But by 1979, U.S. Steel had liquidated itself by using up its undervalued fixed assets to make these disbursements. *GAAP accounting had failed to disclose that the steel industry had not been increasing its wealth each year but rather was pretending that the process of wearing out assets had a cost based on a yardstick 30 years old with the result that the accounting profit produced was really a fraud.*

This is not to suggest that more advanced accounting methods alone would have resulted in a permanently more robust U.S. steel industry, but rather to point out that the U.S. government and the industry itself might have faced the problems of adjusting to a declining steel industry long before it did. If the market value of assets had appeared on the balance sheet of U.S. Steel in 1962, it would have been obvious that returns were woefully inadequate.

Key Points: Because of the historical cost accounting convention, PP&E is often grossly understated. Understanding assets can cause a company's returns to appear to be much higher than they are.

Current Cost Accounting

To make valid financial comparisons between firms or industries, some consistent asset valuation method that reckons inflation is necessary. The financial statements supply the analyst only with the value of assets at the moment of their purchase. Thus, two companies that started similar businesses at different times can show different values for their equipment—even though the equipment is of exactly the same age. Let's look at an example.

Late Start, Inc.

Assume Late Start, Inc. commences operations five years after Early Bird Corp. and stocks its factory and truck fleet with used equipment and vehicles that are precisely the same age as Early Bird's. Because of inflation, Late Start will have paid a significantly higher amount for these assets than is showing as net undepreciated on the books of Early Bird.

In such situations, it would be impossible for an analyst to make a reasonable comparison of the performance and wealth-generating capacity of the two firms. Valid comparisons of such measures as return on equity and return on assets would also be impossible. For example, a firm with lower net undepreciated historical cost values will appear to be using its capital much more efficiently than a firm that has purchased its assets (even if old assets) more recently at the higher (inflation-induced) market prices.

In 1976, the Securities and Exchange Commission's Accounting Series Release #190 required that **inflation-adjusted accounting** be provided in the Form 10K reports of major public companies. In 1978, the Financial Accounting Standards Board (FASB) issued SFAS #33, requiring companies above a certain size to provide additional information about the current value of their assets in their financial statements. SFAS #33 was controversial: Some felt that the cost of supplying the additional information was too high relative to its potential value. Others felt that the information would be too complicated for most analysts to understand. These objections, particularly the latter one, prevailed. In December 1986, SFAS #89 was released, rescinding the requirement to supply current cost information.

SFAS #89 Dissent

It is instructive to read one of the SFAS #89 *dissenting opinions of a Generally Accepted Accounting Principles board member found in the FASB booklet:* "Mr. Mosso dissented. . . . He believes that accounting for the interrelated effects of general and specific price changes is the most critical set of issues that the Board will face in this century. The basic proposition underlying Statement 33—that inflation causes historical cost financial statements to show illusory profits and mask erosion of capital—is virtually undisputed. Specific price changes are inextricably linked to general inflation, and the combination of general and *specific price changes seriously reduces the relevance, the representational faithfulness, and the comparability of historical cost financial statements."* [emphasis added]

Although the lack of required current cost information leaves the analyst at a disadvantage, SFAS #33 had not had a great impact on the analysis activity of many financial institutions because it primarily affected large public corporations; these frequently borrow directly from the public via commercial paper or bonds. The analysis of the smaller corporations that borrow from financial intermediaries was inhibited because loan officers (1) received their credit training before SFAS #33 came into existence when inflation was relatively low and (2) doubted that financial statements were a main consideration in lending in contrast to their faith in their ability to evaluate the character of the borrower. Nonetheless, for a proper evaluation of a firm's financial condition, the analyst must know the current cost and replacement value of its assets.

Key Points: Find out the current cost and replacement value of fixed assets, through a fire insurance appraisal if necessary.

The Importance of an Appraisal

In most cases, lenders can ask borrowers to have their fixed assets appraised by a qualified appraiser. A fixed asset appraisal enables the lender to enhance his ability to evaluate the company's breakup net worth, a potential back door out of a loan. Among the services that any plant and equipment appraiser should offer are the following:

- A review of the sale of equipment and facilities similar to those being appraised
- A detailed listing of each item appraised, including age and manufacturer's reputation
- A determination of how much diminution in value will be caused by the company using the equipment
- An estimate of the facility's remaining economic life under the company's management

Exhibit 2-4 is an example of the kind of letter a lender might request the appraiser to prepare. Since appraisal is an inexact science, the more precise the instructions that are given to the appraiser, the more likely that the information developed will be useful to the analyst.

For some equipment, alternatives to the custom appraisal are available. These include the *Green Guides* [Chicago: Commerce Clearing House, published annually] for construction and materials handling equipment and *blue books* for used vehicles and other transportation equipment. These guides typically have the equipment serial number assigned by the manufacturer during certain dates of production. This allows the analyst to identify or verify the age of equipment in the customer's hands.

Key Points: If possible, request an appraisal of fixed assets prepared by a qualified third party.

Investments and Advances {16}

An asset that may be an important percentage of fixed assets is investments in **affiliates,** business entities over which the parent may not have complete control. The rules for handling the accounting include two methods that do not involve consolidation and include the securities method and the equity method as follows:

(Text continued on page 61.)

Exhibit 2-4.

APPRAISAL FORMAT
                    (Letter Written by the Appraiser to Client)
Gentlemen:

At your request, we have made an appraisal of:

_____
(Manufacturer, equipment type, model designation and serial number)

The purpose of the appraisal is to express an opinion of the economic life of
this equipment, its fair market and forced liquidation values at various
points of time up to and including the end of the lease term which you have
informed us is _____ years. In addition, you have asked us to make
reasonable inquirries into the reputations of the manufacturer, the user, the
reliability of the equipment in similar utilization and the maintenance
records of such equipment.

I. Definitions and Limitations

Economic life is defined as the anticipated period of time over which the
property may be profitably used in its original or related functions. It is
assumed that maintenance and repair policy will be that of a reasonable
user. We have taken into account that, historically, long term economic
expansion has increased the value of capital goods while technological
advances have reduced the value of older equipment as changes bring
increases in productivity and advances in design or operating
characteristics. In certain cases, governmental regulations such as
environmental or safety acts can affect the expected life. Therefore,
economic life is derived from a combination of past experience and current
analysis of similar property.

Fair Market Value is defined as the price at which the property would
change hands between a fully informed, willing buyer and a willing seller,
without compulsion as to time period to sell.

Liquidation Value is defined as the price, net of selling expenses which
could be expected if the property were foreclosed by a financial institution
and placed with a qualified broker or dealer, and if he is allowed to find a
willing buyer within a three to six month period.

    The use of the equipment will be by:

_____
(Name of User and Location of the Equipment)

Our discussions with this firm, during our investigations, have informed us
that they will use this equipment in their regular business of:

_____
(Business Activity and SIC Code) (Number of Shifts, if Applicable)

Even with proper preventive maintenance, including lubrication, cleaning
and replacement of component parts as required by the original equipment

manufacturer, the equipment will eventually show signs of wear requiring possible service from a minor overhaul to a major rebuild. The duration between these periods of downtime is a function of maintenance, working conditions and overall equipment design, limiting our maintenance estimates to a range.

II. **Investigations**

For this appraisal, we have reviewed the equipment specifications together with their estimated cost. We have conferred with manufacturers, dealers, brokers of used equipment and with users of similar equipment concerning the nature of the equipment and the type of service in which the equipment will be useful.

[If equipment is old:] We have made a personal inspection of the equipment in the field and attached our survey report herewith. [If equipment is new:] We have inspected similar equipment in the field and have reviewed the equipment specifications, attached. At your request, the factors of physical deterioration, functional and economic obsolescence were investigated.

Finally, our findings are based on in-depth discussions with supervisory and operating personnel, manufacturing representatives and consultants. We also reviewed auction and sales bulletins, trade publications, used equipment services and our files containing detailed specifications and condition reports for comparison of similar vintage equipment. We attended sales and auctions.

III. **Findings**

Our investigation and prior knowledge, while limited, of the **user firm** confirms them to be reputable, and we know of no specific cases wherein they utilized equipment to the detriment of a lender.

The manufacturer is a company which is well known in its industry as an innovator in design and engineering, materials application, maintenance and technological advancement. Our investigation and prior knowledge, while limited, of this firm confirms them to be reputable and we know of no specific cases wherein they manufactured equipment which proved to be defective to the detriment of a user and made no settlement.

With proper maintenance and operational care, this equipment should conttnue to perform the service for which it was designed in an adequate manner.

Besides the use which is planned, this equipment has (many, several, few) **alternative uses** including:

_____

_____

From this investigation, we have some familiarity with several

(continued)

Exhibit 2-4. *Continued.*

> **comparable sales** of similar equipment during the last two years. These
> include:
>
> _____
> _____
> _____.
>
> **In conclusion**, we advise you that, in our opinion:
>
> (a) Without including any increases or decreases for inflation or deflation
> during the term, and after subtracting any costs for removal and delivery of
> possession of the equipment, the value are as follows:

At End of	Liquidation Value as Percent of Original Cost*	Market Value as Percent of Original Cost*
1 Year		
3 Years		
5 Years		
7 Years		
9 Years		
11 Years		

> *If used equipment, state all values in dollars.
>
> (b) The useful life of the equipment is at least: _____.
>
> **IV. Certification**
>
> We certify that to the best of our knowledge and belief, the statements and
> opinions set forth herein are true and correct and made in accordance with
> actual findings on this date. We certify that as independent appraisers, we
> have no affiliation with the company referred to herein, nor do we have any
> interest in said company or in the above mentioned equipment. We have
> made no investigation of title or liabilities against the equipment appraised.

---

1. **Insignificant minority**—less than 20%; use **security** investment, that is, carry at lower of cost or market with only declared dividends recognized as part of parent income.
2. **Significant minority**—equal to or greater than 20% but less than 50%; use **equity** method with earnings of affiliate recognized as earned and added to investment value; receipt of dividends reduces investment. The statement of cash flow reverses the above, reducing earnings to the dividend (cash flow) level.
3. **Majority**—greater than 50%; consolidate all assets and liabilities, with net, except for minority interest, showing as shareholder equity.

The choice of the above is blurred by the additional subjective issue of the extent of control. If control exists, through membership on the board or participation in policy making, even though there is less than 20% ownership, the equity method may be allowed. If control is lacking, the parent can show that significant influence does not exist—perhaps of a foreign subsidiary where local politics may exert control, the equity method may be allowed, even though ownership is over 50%.

Prior to the issuance of SFAS #94 in October 1987, an additional large portion of investments placed in this category were subsidiaries that were involved in a business "different" from the parent. Previously, captive finance and real estate company subsidiaries often were accountable for substantial assets and related debt, but these were recorded only in the footnotes to the parent firm's balance sheet instead of being consolidated. (The problems pertaining to this practice will be discussed in more detail in the liability section in Chapter 3.) SFAS #94 now requires that subsidiaries that are majority (greater than 50%) owned must be consolidated regardless of their business. This continues to be a potential dilemma at the present time because of joint ventures whereby each venturer owns exactly 50% of the undertaking.

Since GAAP statements dated after December 31, 1988, are subject to SFAS #94, the principal matter of contention regarding affiliate investments has become how they are recorded when the parent holds a minority interest. Referring to the discussion of a firm's owning marketable securities, recall that such securities must be marked down to market value if, as of the balance sheet date, market value is lower than original cost. Because of the volatility in public securities markets, management often prefers that its long-term investments in affiliates, even if less than a 20% interest, be evaluated on the basis of the affiliates' reported net income performance rather than their stock price.

The initial posting of an investment using the equity method is based on the historical cost of the investment, and all further charges in the value of the investments are based on the income and dividends received. Thus, management usually prefers to carry its investments in affiliates on the equity basis.

Joseph E. Seagram & Sons

An illustration of the considerations that affect a company's choice of method for carrying an investment can be found in the Joseph E. Seagram & Sons Inc. and E. I. Dupont de Nemours & Co. takeover fight to acquire Conoco, Inc. Dupont won Conoco, but Seagram ended up having an insignificant minority block of Dupont stock. How should Seagram account for this investment on its balance sheet? If it chooses the securities method, any fluctuations in the market value of Dupont stock would affect Seagram's net worth. In addition, the earnings of Dupont would not be recorded as an enhancement of Seagram's financial statement; only when Dupont declared dividends would Seagram recognize the earnings from its investment.

Indubitably, Seagram chose the equity method. In fact, it acquired a position on Dupont's board of directors to assure itself of evidence of control. (To evidence this as control is a bit farfetched since it was only 1 person on a 20-person board of directors!) The good part is that Dupont's dividend decisions do not affect Seagram's earnings. Instead, Dupont's earnings are reflected as revenues in Seagram's income statement and increase the value of the investment on the balance sheet. When dividends are received, the investment account is reduced by the amount of cash collected.

An accessory benefit of the equity method is that if the affiliate experiences a series of losses, the firm can write its investment in the affiliate down to zero—*but not below zero.* Thus, after a certain point, losses will not be recorded on a parent's financials although they are occurring on the affiliate's. Although unusual, this could occur if the affiliate had substantial assets hidden from the accounting process (e.g., previously depreciated or amortized films, books, or real estate) and not recognized before the purchase, allowing the price paid for an interest by the parent to be less than the eventual value; these assets would allow it to continue experiencing losses without becoming insolvent.

If an investment in an unconsolidated affiliate represents a substantial percentage of the total assets, then the financial statements of that entity must be obtained to verify the book value of the investment.

Depreciation {14}

The next issue regarding fixed assets is depreciation. Depreciation refers to the distribution of the expenditure for the assets into costs attributed to the products produced for sale. That is, depreciation expense is deducted from sales proceeds in the determination of the company's profits. The value for fixed assets listed on the balance sheet is thus their historical cost minus depreciation. Prior to 1954, before accelerated depreciation was permitted by the IRS, all companies used straight-line depreciation, meaning that upon acquisition of an asset, management estimates the years over which the asset will be in use by the firm; then, the number of years is divided into the cost of the asset, with the result becoming the expense to be charged to the depreciation account each year.

Useful life estimates. Useful economic life applies to a piece of equipment's intended economic use. For instance, if there is a plan to donate some equipment to an equipment museum, the equipment's tenure in the museum would not be part of its useful economic life. A further complication to the useful economic life estimate is salvage value. A company must estimate not only how long it intends to use a piece of equipment but also what it expects to obtain for the equipment when it finally disposes of it.

Often, a company applies estimates previously calculated by a third party (like the IRS Asset Depreciation Range Guidelines table) to any new equipment it buys, and little or no effort is made to examine whether its own use or the extent of customization of the asset validates the initial estimates. Fortunately, the objectivity accounting principle comes into play in this area. Any management estimate of useful economic life and salvage value is subject to confirmation by an independent third party. In the event that auditors conclude that the useful life or salvage value is too high or the depreciation rate is too low, adjustments are made. Unfortunately, the lower-of-cost-or-market rule does not allow for values to be adjusted upward if useful life has been understated, and the depreciation is too fast.

Turboprop

A helpful example of the importance of correctly estimating useful economic life and salvage value can be found in the airline industry. By the early 1950s, passenger traffic was growing and it was clear that new planes would be needed. The proven technology at the time was the turboprop, a combination of jet engines and propeller. Since nothing superior was available and the airline industry needed planes, it outfitted its fleets with turboprops. When the pure jet-engine Boeing 707 was introduced in 1958, it caught on rapidly. The fixed assets of the airlines thus became rapidly obsolete; planes only ten years old plunged in value, causing an industry-wide capital crisis. Useful economic life estimates and salvage values had been too high.

Fuel-Efficient Jet

Looking at the new crop of commercial jet liners, a similar potential problem could emerge, if the strong growth in passenger travel does not continue to mask it. Consider the Boeing 767: It was built in anticipation of $2.50-per-gallon fuel costs. With its much more fuel-efficient but costly engine, its residual value may be less than anticipated. It may be lower as a percent of original cost than the residual value for less efficient but cheaper aircraft. The managers who arranged for the purchase of these aircraft may be inclined toward too high an estimate for their companies' balance sheets.

> **Key Points:** Regardless of the depreciation method chosen, estimates of useful economic life and salvage value are crucial. If the firm being reviewed is in a high-tech industry, make sure that these estimates are conservative.

Depreciation Method—Straight-Line vs. Accelerated

In 1954 after the IRS (and shortly thereafter the Accounting Principles Board) permitted accelerated depreciation, companies shifted to this method for both tax and financial reporting purposes. (See Chapter 5 for an explanation of how the different methods, including double declining and sum of years digits, work.) While these methods were created relatively arbitrarily, the basic idea was to provide the following solutions:

1. Accelerated depreciation would allow a rapid expensing of fixed asset acquisitions for tax purposes; this would assist businesses that were willing to acquire new capital equipment, theoretically creating more jobs, boosting the economy, and making the country more competitive with foreign producers.

2. Financial analysts cheered accelerated depreciation, claiming that the quality of reported earnings was higher since companies were taking high depreciation during the maintenance-free period in the equipment's early life, but that over time, maintenance costs would increase. Thus, taking more depreciation early on would even out net income computation from the asset over the equipment's useful economic life.

Cost Assignment by Usage

Another depreciation method is cost assignment by usage. It is based on clocking the number of hours a machine has run to determine the wear and tear that will be expensed. Construction firms regularly use this method. The trucking industry also uses this method by keeping track of the number of miles vehicles travel. This is generally a satisfactory method assuming the estimated useful life in hours, or whatever, is accurate.

The depreciation method chosen can be optional for management. *When a firm's management makes the choice of depreciation method, it does so with complete awareness of its effect on the financial statements.* For instance, a method that increases the amount of depreciation expense will reduce net income. Unlike inventory reporting, in which the same convention (i.e., LIFO or FIFO) must be used for both tax and financial reporting statements, depreciation methods can be different for tax and financial reporting purposes. Thus, with respect to depreciation, management has, for the most part, the best of both worlds: It can take the most accelerated depreciation method for tax reporting and take a slower (perhaps unrealistically slower) depreciation method for financial report-ing. (The Tax Reform Act of 1986 created some problems for managers, however. Preference items included in the Alternative Minimum Tax could, depending on a company's circumstances, penalize it for reporting different depreciation to shareholders than to the IRS.)

Today, unfortunately, most companies have returned to straight-line depre-ciation because it increases "apparent" net income. Straight-line is probably not satisfactory to the analyst.

Consistency plays a role in the choice of depreciation method. A firm is not permitted to change methods for a piece of equipment over time. For example, a bakery could use straight-line depreciation on its ovens and usage depreciation on its delivery trucks, but it would not be able to switch between usage depreciation and straight-line on its delivery trucks once it had established a precedent.

The selection of depreciation *method will affect both net income and the debt to net worth ratio.*

Consider the following choices:

1. Use an accelerated depreciation method.
2. Use a short estimated life.
3. Use a low salvage value estimate.

Now assets will be carried at a relatively low value on the balance sheet. Thus, net worth will be low, and the radio of debt to worth will rise. On the other hand, the opposite choices will cause a firm to seem less leveraged, since net worth will be higher.

The depreciation method a company has used can be found in the first footnote to the financial statements. This footnote should be read carefully and a rough approximation of the company's useful life assumption should be calculated by dividing the depreciation for the year into the gross fixed assets. The result should be compared with other companies in the same industry or discussed with management to check its validity.

Key Points: The company's choice of financial depreciation method will affect both its total assets and its net worth.

Intangibles (Patents and Rights) {21}

The next category of assets the analyst needs to examine are the intangible assets. As their name suggests, the value of such assets can be difficult to determine.

Research and development. A company's research and development (R&D) expense represents a particularly problematical area for the analyst. Prior to the issuance of SFAS #2 in 1974, abuse of R&D was common.

Sibany Manufacturing Company

An example of these abuses is the actions of Sibany Manufacturing Company. This firm issued stock, raising slightly more than $1 million in each of 1967, 1968, and 1969. The funds generated were plowed into R&D. The company had a substantial net worth because all R&D expenses were capitalized (in other words, they were deferred and carried as an asset on the balance sheet, never reaching the income statement as an expense). Sibany developed and patented a portfolio of more than 12 inventions over this three-year period. Unfortunately, by 1970 it had not been able to bring any of its inventions to commercial viability. Despite its net worth, the company was completely out of cash. Without the ability to generate income and cash flow from sales, Sibany was not a good loan prospect. Yet for a time, its viability as an investment was limited only by the imagination of the stock's promoters and by the skills of the engineers.

SFAS #2 requires that all R&D expenditures be expensed immediately. Investments in facilities for multiple research and development projects may be capitalized only if they have a future alternative use. That is, if the facilities are to be used only for the project in question, they must be charged off. Unfortunately, the accounting rules for R&D, which were instituted to prevent abuses, preclude an analyst's trying to match up R&D expenses and revenues flowing from the resulting projects with any reasonable accuracy. This violates the matching principle central to accrual accounting.

There are several inconsistencies in R&D accounting. One involves the treatment of patents. If R&D expenditures result in a patent, the only costs that may be capitalized are the legal expenses associated with recording the patent. If another firm acquires that patent, however, it may capitalize the entire amount of the patent acquisition based only on the premise that it paid cash for it.

Another inconsistency involves R&D contracts and opens a loophole of which many firms now avail themselves. If a firm is conducting research and development under a contract, it may capitalize the research and development expenses that go into fulfilling that contract. In effect, this accounting convention encourages the splitting off of companies' R&D departments. It has encouraged a rash of joint ventures between partners that would have otherwise undertaken research directly. Obviously, by capitalizing these expenses onto the balance sheet, the income statement has fewer expenses; therefore, net income is higher.

The computer software industry represents a special case for R&D accounting and has brought on yet another specific alternative to the zealous SFAS #2. SFAS #86, released in 1985, focuses on how a firm should capitalize the costs of developing software. It requires firms to analyze the software writing process to determine **technological feasibility,** which is defined as the point at which uncertainties that might remain concerning novel and unique functions and technological innovations are eliminated. Once technological feasibility is established, a firm can capitalize software R&D expenses, matching them to revenues when received. Costs that must be considered part of R&D include planning, product design, and detail program design. The costs of testing and coding software are swing variables that may or may not be capitalized.

When new software is tested, the research and development phase is considered complete. As the final coding and testing begins, the firm enters its production mode and can capitalize additional expenses. These rules are only a step in the direction of coping with the windfall profits that would result from expensing all R&D up front.

Accounting inconsistencies are found in the treatment of other intangible assets as well as R&D. Other intangible assets that can have significant value include trademarks, franchises, and various licenses.

Franchises

The obvious problem of calculating a franchise breakup value is illustrated in the following example:

Radio Station

No financial institution can finance a radio station without giving consideration to the value of the license from the Federal Communications Commission. This license can be revoked by the commission for various causes including challenge by public groups in the local community; nevertheless, such revocations are almost unheard of. Therefore, the franchise that the license provides to the radio station to develop an audience is quite valuable. The number and the wealth of listeners who tune to the radio station is very important in determining the value of the license. However, any development cost that goes into creating this license may not be capitalized onto the balance sheet, thereby preventing the demonstration of some store of value or possibility of future revenue stream.

Key Points: Although some patents and franchises are appropriately cut down by GAAP and in statement analysis, others can have significant value.

Goodwill and Other Intangible Assets

When a firm buys a company, it often pays more than the market value of its net physical assets. It may, for instance, pay a premium for a trademark, or for a product's reputation, or for the rapport that the seller has established with customers over a long period of time. Goodwill represents the difference between the market value of tangible assets and the actual dollars paid to acquire them. It is, perhaps, the most maligned of all intangible assets.

It is clearly difficult to put a value on such factors as customer recognition and product reputation. Bankers typically eliminate such intangibles entirely from the balance sheet. Even if they are included on the asset side of the spreadsheet, they are excluded from tangible net worth. This practice implies that physical assets, regardless of their quality (e.g., questionable accounts receivable), are more valuable than any intangible. Obviously this is not always true.

Seven-Up

Let's look at an example of the staunchness of consumer loyalty and the difficulty of attaining the status of leading products, both of which are represented by goodwill. In 1957 the Seven-Up Company stopped advertising its products for three years. By 1960 the market share of Seven-Up had dropped from 14% to 10%. Seven-Up then resumed advertisements, stemming the fall in market share, but it never regained its 14% share.

In the early 1970s, Philip Morris, a company well known for its excellent marketing campaigns, took a regional brewer, Miller Brewing Company, to the position of second largest national beer seller in the United States. In the late 1970s the company decided to try its hand at a soft drink. Seven-Up was selected, and after buying it, Philip Morris launched a mammoth advertising campaign aimed at increasing the soft drink's market share. Within a few months, virtually everyone in the United States knew of or had seen the "The UnCola" campaign. Whether the campaign was skillfully constructed or merely made people want to drink more cola instead of Seven-Up is an issue for marketers. What is clear, however, is that Seven-Up's market share did not increase. For several years, Philip Morris tried mightily to raise Seven-Up's market share through advertising. It failed to establish any additional goodwill value in Seven-Up, however, which it eventually sold.

Evaluating goodwill is difficult. Evaluating tangible assets, however, can also be difficult. For instance, consider aircraft residuals. Money spent for aircraft, which can rapidly become obsolete, appears on balance sheets as a tangible asset. On the other hand, advertising expenses, which can have considerable success in convincing people to do certain things, does not appear on the balance sheet at all—unless the company is sold. It is inconsistent that a firm cannot capitalize expenses such as advertising and R&D until an interested third party deems that these expenses have created value. Then, if a patent is bought, the cost of the patent can be amortized over its life. If the company is bought, the goodwill that resulted from the advertising can be amortized over a long period.

The analyst can hire an appraiser who will attempt to put some value or price on the goodwill. Investment bankers or merger and acquisition specialists are possible sources. An appraiser is needed when the return on assets is out of line with what would normally be expected. Specifically, if a company has a

Exhibit 2-5.

PHILIP MORRIS COMPANIES INC. and consolidated subsidiaries

Consolidated Balance Sheets as of December 31	1986	1985
		In millions
ASSETS		
Cash and cash equivalents	$73	$156
Trade receivables, net	1,878	1,797
Leaf tobacco	1,899	1,882
Other raw materials	755	761
Finished product	1,182	1,184
Total inventories - LIFO (with a current cost of 1986 -		
$4.5 billion and 1987 - $4.4 billion)	3,836	3,827
Other current assets	127	113
TOTAL CURRENT ASSETS	$5,914	$5,893
Land	$474	$399
Buildings	2,629	2,391
Machinery and equipment	5,071	4,461
Construction in progress	312	267
Property, plant and equipment, at cost	8,486	7,518
Less, accumulated depreciation	(2,249)	(1,834)
Property, plant and equipment (net)	$6,237	$5,684
Investments in and accounts with unconsol. subs	$1,067	$1,099
Goodwill and other intangible assets	**3,988**	**4,457**
Other Assets	436	296
TOTAL FIXED ASSETS	$11,728	$11,536
TOTAL ASSETS	$17,642	$17,429
LIABILITIES		
Notes payable	$864	$595
Portion of long-term debt due within one year	103	83
Accounts payable	813	946
Accrued liabilities	1,967	1,862
Income taxes	557	362
Dividends payable	178	119
TOTAL CURRENT LIABILITIES	$4,482	$3,967
Long-term debt	$5,945	$7,331
Deferred income taxes	994	872
Other Liabilities	566	522
TOTAL LONG TERM LIABILITIES	$7,505	$8,725
TOTAL LIABILITIES	$11,987	$12,692
Stock and Paid-in Capital	$543	$523
Retained Earnings	5,344	4,456
Currency translation adjustments	(103)	(242)
Cost of Treasury stock	(129)	
NET WORTH	**$5,655**	**$4,737**
TOTAL EQUITIES	$17,642	$17,429
TANGIBLE NET WORTH	***$1,667***	***$280***
TOTAL LIABS. TO TANGIBLE NET WORTH	***7.19***	***45.33***
	to 1	***to 1***

return on assets over 15% after taxes, there may be substantial intangible value in the company.

Philip Morris

The Philip Morris Corporation again provides an illustrative example of the importance of goodwill. Philip Morris acquired General Foods in 1985. Exhibit 2-5 shows the balance sheet of Philip Morris at the end of 1985. Goodwill totaled $4.5 billion. If this figure is subtracted from the company's net worth, net worth falls to $280 million and debt to worth is more than 45 to 1. Obviously, the lenders that financed this acquisition evaluated goodwill favorably. They probably estimated the future revenue (in other words, cash flow) stream that could be derived from goodwill or any intangible just as in their evaluation of any asset.

Key Points: Determine what future revenues will result from goodwill or any other intangible. This determination will enable you to make a proper decision about the value of goodwill on the spreadsheet.

Chapter 3
Spreading Liabilities—
The Basics

Liability Revaluation Analysis

The liability section is the next balance sheet section to be examined. Particularly, the items include current liabilities and long-term debt as the traditional obligations, the items making up the debt in determining debt repayment capacity. There are several other accounts that are currently spread as debt by some analysts, but actually may have a quasi-equity nature, because the requirement to repay them may not exist. These latter items include deferred and unearned income, pensions, deferred taxes, and minority interests. Another interesting group includes **executory agreements** that have obligations connected to them such as leases, receivables, sales, and contingent liabilities. Some of these less traditional liabilities are discussed in this chapter, but some are reserved for Chapter 4.

Most traditional balance sheet liabilities are monetary in nature. The monetary nature of these liabilities makes them somewhat easier to analyze than the plethora of non-monetary assets. Two accounting conventions, however, can create problems. First, the conservatism concept can distort the market values of different long-term obligations (as well as what the firm is obligated to repay) when inflation is high. Second, the objectivity requirement can make it difficult to obtain a demonstrable potential cost of contingent liabilities.

Seniority

Seniority is to liabilities what liquidity is to assets. Liabilities are listed on the balance sheet in order of their seniority. Going down the balance sheet, the seniority of unsecured liabilities is about equal until we reach subordinated debt. That is, unsubordinated lenders have approximately equal rights to recovering funds in the event of a bankruptcy.

Some creditors find this hard to believe. For instance, suppliers are frequently surprised to learn that even though they supplied most inventory, they do not receive any special treatment with respect to the distribution of proceeds from raw materials sales during a liquidation. On the other hand, any creditor that has an outstandng payable to the insolvent firm can set it off against the receivable from that firm. Thus, bankers can set off the liability of a company against the company's checking account balance.

Factoring companies that purchase account receivables from liquid firms occasionally are short-changed as a result of suppliers exercising their right of setoff. If, for instance, a supplier were concerned about the deteriorating financial condition of its customer, it might take back some merchandise in payment for raw materials.

Bankruptcy laws, however, are extremely particular with regard to creditors' attempts to get repaid immediately prior to the demise of a company. There is a section of the bankruptcy code stipulating that any unusual payments made within 90 days of bankruptcy (the **preference period**) may have to be relinquished if the bankruptcy judge decides that the payments were not in the course of regular business. For instance, a lender may ask for a partial prepayment if it is worried about the survival of the borrower. However, if the payments required under the borrower's repayment plan (or even the borrower's past payments) are less than the amount requested, the judge may rule that the lender's demand for a greater-than-usual payment precipitated the insolvency.

There is little a supplier can do to obtain unusually large payments that would not be considered out of the ordinary course of business. Usually suppliers have a markup percentage that is substantially greater than the interest spread earned by a creditor. When a firm fails, the supplier loses not only receivables but also a client. Thus, suppliers often stay in a risky situation until the bitter end, in the hope that their customer can turn around.

With respect to seniority, the subordinated lender is in a junior position to the other creditors. The preferred stockholders' position is junior even to the subordinated lenders. Common stockholders come last in order of seniority, although different classes of stock may provide different rights.

There are other rules that bankruptcy judges may enforce. Occasionally, owners who have made large subordinated loans to companies may have these loans converted into equity by the bankruptcy judge, in view of the fact that the stockholders and subordinated lenders are one-and-the-same. This action would deprive the stockholders of a superior position in the liquidation of the firm. In other cases, the bankruptcy judge may feel that creditors did not show due diligence. (**Due diligence** under the law requires that lenders take a sophisticated approach to financing. That is, rather than casually lending funds, analysts must prepare an analysis that justifies the lender's participation through thorough examination of data that a reasonable and prudent person would normally obtain in order to make an investment decision.) In this latter case, the lender may find that its loan is considered an equity investment by the bankruptcy court, eliminating its seniority, similar to that situation faced by the subordinated-lender stockholders just mentioned.

United Merchants and Manufacturers

In the case of United Merchants and Manufacturers, the bankruptcy judge decided that the lenders had not made sufficient due diligence, and he penalized them by approving a liquidation plan that gave stock in the newly structured firm to stockholders when lenders felt their payout of cash, debt securities, and stock did not fully compensate them. That is, the lenders and old shareholders both ended up holding stock in the company controlling the assets that were left, basically the Toys'R'Us retail toy chain. The lenders objected to the shareholders getting anything, since they did not feel fully compensated with the stock. The judge replied that the Toys'R'Us stock was more valuable than the lenders thought, but the clear result was that small shareholders got something beyond what they might have anticipated from their equity investment because the lenders were careless.

Increasing Proportion of Debt Capital

Another general topic that concerns liabilities is the increasing use of debt capital to finance business. Prior to the Great Depression, there was less debt outstanding among businesses than there is today. It was the dependence of business firms on both (1) the equity markets and (2) short-term lending from commercial banks that created severe financial stress during the depression. The 1929 collapse of the stock market was a tremendous blow to many hundreds of new businesses seeking additional capital to expand. Banks had extended short-term credit against future issues of new stock, which issues never transpired; thus, the commercial banks were faced with undercapitalized firms, causing the banks to nervously contract their credit extension. The chain reaction, including resulting bank and business firm failures, cooled the booming economy, contracted the bond market, provoked the government to restrain spending, and caused the depression.

As the capital markets rebounded during the 1940s and 1950s, lenders were more creative in structuring new ways for companies to borrow funds. Examples of liability products created during that period include debt instruments that allowed principal to be repaid in uneven schedules, as well as convertible debt. **Convertible debt** is subordinated debt that can be converted to equity at a preset price; when the share price rises above the conversion price, most holders convert to equity in order to improve their profits. Since equity markets were slower to develop new financing instruments, demand for debt grew faster than that for equity.

Another major factor behind an increase in demand for debt was the advent of corporate income taxes during World War II. Quickly corporate treasurers recognized that interest expense's deductibility made borrowing a less expensive source of capital, after taxes, than equity with its nondeductible dividends.

The Glass-Steagall Act of 1933 separated the markets of the commercial and investment banks, and probably also has contributed to the aggressiveness of the debt markets. After Glass-Steagall, only investment banks could underwrite stock, but both commercial banks and investment banks could supply debt to the marketplace. Competition from investment banks culminated, during the 1960s, in a great financial innovation, namely, commercial paper. **Commercial paper** permits companies to borrow substantial amounts on a short-term basis directly from individuals and institutions without SEC registration. With the advent of this borrowing instrument, commercial banks lost an important portion of their prime borrowers to the investment banks. As a result, commercial banks became more innovative in their pursuit of income sources, including a relaxing of their credit standards, especially in the market for mid-size companies.

Provident Tradesmen's National Bank

An example of the increasing use of debt financing by corporations can be found in a comparison of leverage ratios during the 1960s versus leverage ratios today. At the Provident Tradesmen's National Bank in Philadelphia in the 1960s, a customer with a balance sheet exhibiting a ratio of total debt to net worth in excess of 1:1 was not welcome as a prospective borrower. At that time, Provident Tradesmen's own liabilities to net worth ratio was approximately 7:1. Today, according to Standard and Poor's, the total *liabilities to tangible net worth exceeds 1:1 for the average industrial company rated AA and lower.* In fact, single B-rated firms have an average debt to worth ratio of 2.4:1. Moreover, most commercial banks have a liabilities to net worth ratio of approximately 20:1.

Finally, the 1980s increased the demand for corporate debt with intensified corporate acquisition and the somewhat related leveraged buyout activity. In many corporate acquisitions and leveraged buyouts, most of a company's equity is replaced by debt. In a paradox of defense against an unfriendly acquisition, some corporate managements have acquired substantial debt to make themselves less likely as a takeover candidate. This tremendous growth in debt has meant that the equity markets have not been a supplier of net new capital for nearly 20 years. Whether this situation will change is a matter of speculation.

Key Points: Ideas about why leverage is more important:

1. Avoid unfriendly takeovers
2. Help finance sustantial capital equipment/plant requirements
3. Increase return on shareholders' equity
4. Shortage in cash flow to sustain
   a. growth—debt all right here since returns will catch up to the investment
   b. no growth—just to stay abreast of technology or competitors— debt bad since risk and the variability it creates can cause future shortfalls
5. Stable earnings require less equity—rational for LBOs

Irving Trust Company

At an officers' dinner at the New York Hilton in January 1980, the senior lending officer of Irving Trust Company told me that, in his opinion, the 1980s would bring a tremendous turnaround in which leverage ratios would drop significantly and the stock markets would return to their original function of supplying massive amounts of capital.

This Pollyanna's vision has not occurred: Businesses continue to acquire more and more debt, and lenders must sharpen their analytical tools and loan negotiation skills (to say nothing of developing a facility for evaluating potential collateral) to defend themselves in an environment that promises increasing risk.

Off-Balance-Sheet Financing

Perhaps the most problematical change for financial statement analysts in the past 20 years has been the increasing use of off-balance-sheet financing by corporations. Three major factors were behind this increase: (1) the acquisition or creation of captive finance and real estate subsidiaries; (2) the acquisition of less than a 50% interest in or joint venturing of affiliates; and (3) the growth of the equipment leasing industry. With the implementation of SFAS #95, captive "other purpose" subsidiaries have been eliminated as a form of off-balance-sheet financing as of December 1988. A company, however, can still form up to a 50%-owned joint venture with another party, have the new firm borrow funds and account for the joint venture on an equity basis since it does not hold a majority interest. Thus, unconsolidated affiliates of companies can still be a source of off-balance-sheet financing. **Operating** leases (under SFAS #13) of equipment and real estate are still popular and also create the potential for substantial off-balance-sheet financing. Ancillary analytical problems of totally off-balance-sheet financing include earnings-maintenance agreements for joint ventures and other unconsolidated affiliates; since these agreements are considered *contingent*, they do not appear on the balance sheet.

Financial statement analysts should expect off-balance-sheet financing to increase. Recall that the corporate manager prepares the financial statements to look good. The analyst's responsibility is to get a reasonable idea of the amount of debt on and off the balance sheet, and to understand its repayment terms and purposes. Thus, analysts should *examine closely each element of the firm's funding structure* rather than just transfer numbers from the balance sheet to the spreadsheet.

Current Liabilities

Current liabilities are fairly easy to analyze, primarily because they are in monetary terms and relatively straightforward compared to other liabilities. Following are four prominent ones: notes payable, accounts payable, accruals, and current portion of long-term debt, with only the last being a puzzle concerning its position as a current liability.

Notes Payable {25}*

Notes payable, especially if they are captioned on the balance sheet as *notes payable to others*, may include commerical paper. If available, it is useful to obtain

*Numbers in braces refer to line numbers in Exhibit 2-2A.

credit agency ratings on commercial paper. With respect to the notes payable to banks, the analyst should determine the purpose of the short-term borrowing. In general, it is unusual for a firm to borrow funds at its fiscal year-end, since typically the fiscal year-end has been selected by management as a time when reduced current asset needs allow short-term bank borrowings to be fully paid, in turn making the firm look more liquid. More importantly, short-term notes at year-end may be an indication that the firm is planning to borrow on a long-term basis. Especially in times of falling interest rates, firms frequently attempt to delay a long-term financing by borrowing on a short-term basis until the lowest fixed rate can be obtained. At what point in time rates will be lowest is obviously a subjective judgment, and often firms can strain their cash flow by borrowing excessively on a short-term basis when long-term financing is really required.

> **Key Points:** If notes payable include commercial paper, obtain a credit agency rating of the commercial paper. If they consist of short-term bank notes, find out why the firm is borrowing short-term at fiscal year-end.

Accounts Payable: Trade {26}

The second major caption on the liabilities side of a balance sheet is accounts payable. Accounts payable represent funds owed to suppliers. Typically, suppliers offer discounts for prompt payment to their customers. If this account is large relative to the previous year, it may be that the discounts are not being taken. If the account is small relative to the previous year, other problems may be at fault. It is possible, for instance, that a comptroller may have placed bills aside and unopened for the remainder of the month/quarter/year to create the illusion that the company has fewer liabilities at the time of financial statement preparation. Any questionable variations in the figures should be investigated by requesting an accounts payable aging report and calling suppliers to verify amounts due.

> **Key Points:** If the accounts payable is excessive, the firm may not be taking advantage of trade discounts. If the accounts payable is high or low relative to the prior year, request an aging report and call suppliers to verify amounts due.

Accrued Expenses {27}

Accrued expenses generally consist of salaries, taxes, and other items the company has incurred, but for which it has not yet been billed. Accruals can be subject to considerable manipulation on the part of the firm since they are difficult for the auditors to verify. It is impossible to know whether everyone in the firm has been recording actions that cause funds to be owed.

> **Key Points:** A decline in accruals is a red flag for potential trouble; investigate it.

Current Portion Long-Term Debt {29} & {31}

Regarding the current portion of long-term debt, this account is carried as a current liability because it is payable within 12 months of the balance sheet date. Occasionally, firms hide these borrowings by renewing them at the end of the year using 53-week notes. (This technically forces the borrowing into the long-term debt category.) These 1-year-and-1-week loans abuse the concept of current liabilities. For the purpose of analysis, this type of obligation is no different from a 52-week note. Because its term is slightly longer than 365 days, however, management is able to carry this debt long-term and create the illusion that it is not a current liability. Information on the term of the note should be located in the footnotes, and should be reviewed by the analyst at the time the transfer to the financial spreadsheet is made.

> **Key Points:** Before transferring the current portion of long-term debt to the spreadsheet, review the footnotes. If the footnotes reflect that any note is actually a 53-week obligation, carry the entire amount current.

Long-Term Debt {33} & {34}

Three issues are of critical importance when analyzing long-term debt: (1) the maturity schedule, (2) the structure, and (3) the impact of inflation. The **maturity schedule** of long-term debt is a crucial datum for forecasting whether a company can repay its debt. Since this schedule does not appear on the balance sheet, the analyst must once again refer to the footnotes. (Even the schedule in the footnotes, however, may be incomplete. The footnotes generally provide a breakdown of each individual piece of legal debt. There may not be a precise breakdown of the total debt payments that will be required by each piece.)

The analyst needs to clarify whether the firm will, because of a bulge in its debt maturities, be forced to refinance merely to make its scheduled payments. Historically, when non-amortizing debt was common, bonds were issued on a 20- or 30-year repayment cycle. One or two years prior to maturity, a firm would issue a new set of bonds and simultaneously repay the old set for a small prepayment penalty. While this is not impossible today, market volatility can make maturity bulges uncomfortable times for both borrowers and lenders. It would be best to see an even maturity schedule, but more about this later. The footnotes generally state in words next to the individual piece of debt the required principal repayments for a least each of the next 5 years. From this information, the analysts should prepare their own schedule.

> **Key Points:** Refer to the footnotes for information to construct a schedule of all long-term debt payment due during each of the next 5 years.

Secured Debt {34}

There are many different ways to structure long-term debt. These include debt that is collateralized, subordinated, convertible to common stock, and debt that involves the sharing of risk through either leasing or joint ventures.

Secured debt represents a more extreme form of lender participation in the company's operations than unsecured debt. In a secured loan, the creditor holds first rights to the liquidation value of the collateral. Curiously enough, although the presence of collateral puts the lender on safer ground, secured debt has historically been associated with weaker firms unable to obtain unsecured financing. Thus, traditionally, secured debt is more expensive for the borrower than unsecured debt.

The secured loan generally carries with it an amortization schedule that bears some relationship to the life expectancy of the assets being financed. As an example of how the secured lender plays a closer role in the firm's operations, consider that unsecured and unamortizing lenders cannot regain their principal if the loan's original purpose was completed ahead of schedule. They thus have no control over the borrower's using the funds for another purpose that they may not have wished to finance.

Some bond covenants require that some amortization of the principal take place, but do not require that creditors be repaid until maturity. The borrower may thus invest this segregated pool of funds, called a **sinking fund,** until the maturity date. Unless bonds are retired with sinking fund proceeds, the full amount of the debt will show up on the borrower's balance sheet without offset. Thus, firms inevitably use the sinking fund to retire some bonds in order to reflect the reality of lower debt on the balance sheet.

Subordinated Debt {39}

From the point of view of a senior lender, subordinated debt, which usually includes all convertible debt, carries with it nearly the same obligations as stock. All senior lenders will be fully repaid before subordinated debt holders receive any funds. Subordination and convertibility are combined so that convertible debt holders may trade their interest-paying paper into equity if the firm prospers. Thus, this instrument bridges the gap between the limited return of the lender and the returns of the equity holder.

How should convertible debt be carried on the spreadsheet? One of the best answers is to consider conversion value relative to the current stock price. If the current stock price is near the conversion value, it is likely that holders of convertible debts will convert their debt to stock and the borrower will never have to repay the funds. For example, if the convertible debt can be exchanged for 20 shares of common stock prior to splits, it is likely, other things being equal, that each $1,000 bond will be exchanged when the stock prices goes above $50. (Obstacles to conversion may include lack of dividends on the common or volatile price movements on the common.) At $100 per share, the 20 conversion units are in effect worth $2,000. Therefore, lenders will not request repayment from the borrower, but rather will convert the debt to equity and sell the stock.

In closely held corporations, owners frequently lend to their own firms using subordinated debt. This method of putting capital into the firm gives them interest payments instead of dividends; this allows their firms to have the advantage of an interest expense tax deduction. Most analysts view this subordinated debt as the equivalent of equity. They should *not* make that assumption, actually, *unless the lender holds the subordinated notes,* because the owner cannot repay himself without the note. Such repayment would be clear evidence of fraudulent intent. Thus, in a bankruptcy, the financial institution would be able to access the assets of the owner.

> **Key Points:** Secured debt carries an amortization schedule that generally matches the life of the assets being financed. Convertible debt should be carried as equity if the stock price approximates the conversion value. In privately held firms, subordinated debt should not be considered equity unless the lender holds the notes.

Unearned Income {32}

Unearned income can represent two possibilities:

1. An offset to cash payments received for services or products that have not yet been delivered to the client (e.g., magazine subscriptions)
2. An offset (contra) account to a receivable that has been billed to the client, but whose revenue status is not yet earned because services or products have not yet been delivered

A good example of showing unearned income as a liability is the financial statement of commercial banks. They like to show as large an asset base as possible for industry-ranking purposes and, thus, carry installment loan assets as the product of the dollar amount of the monthly loan payments times the number of payments due. Clearly this method overstates the interest so far earned and requires an offsetting liability (that others may prefer to show as a contra account on the asset side of the balance sheet) of unearned income. This practice has been troublesome, especially for finance companies, because the receivable net of principal is not obvious, or even discernible. The problem is that the financial institution may have recognized more income on the receivable asset than the borrower is responsible for in the view of a bankruptcy judge.

Baldwin School

> Recently the Baldwin School, a private preparatory school, filed for bankruptcy because it spent all of its operating funds to renovate a new building. As part of a reorganization plan to enable the school to obtain a new building mortgage, the original lenders agreed to be paid out without any penalty on the basis of the simple interest method of recognizing income. It is conceivable that these institutions had already recognized some of the unearned income to be derived from any prepayment, using some accelerated method or merely charging direct costs associated with booking the original mortgage (e.g., legal fees) against the unearned income. (The precise accounting entries would be to recognize equal amounts of direct costs and unearned income. This has the same effect on income as capitalizing a bond underwriting fee and amortizing it over the life of the bond, but on the balance sheet it eliminates the deferred charge from the asset side and also lowers the unearned income liability.) If the

financial institutions involved had charged off these direct costs in anticipation of the mortgage running to maturity, then they would have suffered some principal loss as a result of this premature recognition of unearned income.

Unearned income can be abused by managements attempting to produce higher income levels. If the unearned income is earned too rapidly (i.e., the liability account is reduced), the asset account will remain extremely large relative to the future stream of payments. Management justifies recognizing earnings early on the basis that the receivable was costly to (1) find, (2) process through the credit department, and (3) book through the legal department. Thus, from their perspective, since most loans are paid over the intended period of time, it is valid to take more earnings up front. Nevertheless, assets exist on the balance sheet to indicate future earning streams. When the future earning stream has been compromised, then the asset value on the balance sheet is conceptually incorrect and absolutely incorrect for the analyst's breakup value analysis. Therefore, an unearned income account requires further investigation under all circumstances.

> **Key Points:** Seek a full explanation of the source of unearned income and the rationale behind the way it is recognized. If unearned income is recognized too quickly, it can distort the value of the asset from which it resulted.

Deferred Income {32}

The deferred income account is similar in nature and possibly interchangeable in usage with the unearned income account. However, it has come to be identified with the delay of revenue recognition because of some risk of collection. Unlike the unearned income liability, deferred income is closer to being a reserve account in the equity section.

Florida Land Sales

> The most popular example of deferred income has to do with Florida land sales. Land developers in Florida typically install the streets, sidewalks, and sewers at a small cost, for instance, $500 per lot. The lots are sold through the medium of purchase-money mortgages by salespeople who earn high commissions for convincing middle class workers that they should retire in Florida. It may cost as much as $2,000 per lot sold to compensate these salespeople for their work. This would elevate the cost of the property to the developer to $2,500. If land is sold to the purchaser at a price of $10,000, the developer earns a $7,500 profit. However, $10,000 is not received at the time of the sale. Instead, for a relatively small down payment, perhaps $500, the developer takes back the purchase-money mortgage of $9,500 to be paid over the next 20 years. Because of the hard-sell sales technique and the extremely long time intervals involved, collection is subject to substantial risk. In the past, a developer would account for this sale by recognizing the $10,000 as revenues.
>
> It developed in numerous cases that the purchaser would stop making

payments. Then the developer would sue the purchaser under the mortgage, a document carrying the official Florida Mortgage Tax Stamps and properly filed by the developer's attorney in Florida; the developer had a good legal stand. Nevertheless, judges frequently threw out the claim, stating that the purchase was nothing but a sham. Many developers, to the surprise of shareholders and creditors who had been reading glowing audited financial statements, went bankrupt.

Now, a specialized Statement of Financial Accounting Standards, namely SFAS #66, controls the recognition of land developer income. Issued in September 1982, it specifies the options available for income recognition in the retail land sales area. Given the parameters specified in the above example, the developer would gradually progress through the deposit method, the installment or percentage of completion methods, and finally, the full accrual method.

Under the deposit method, required if the down payment is extremely low, the development company continues to carry the real estate as an asset and the cash received only as a deposit (or deferred income) liability offsetting the cash received! The deposit method can be used for any transactions in which the down payment is considered insufficient to hedge the uncertainties surrounding the collection of the sale price, but is required here.

After the deposit grows sufficiently, the developer can account for the sale using the installment method in which profits are recognized to the proportional extent that the buyer's actual cash payments exceed the seller's cost of the property sold. Therefore, in this particular case, revenue is recognized only upon receipt of cash, not by the normal standard of delivery of goods or services. (Of course, most of these initial payments will consist of interest with the principal declining only later in the transaction.)

Clearly, the more payments that are made, the less risk there is that the purchasers will disavow the agreement. Generally, after 40% of the funds have been received, the seller can recognize the sale on the accrual method. There could be a considerable time lapse between the real estate closing and the receipt of that great a percentage of the purchase price.

Most analysts agree with the accounting treatment for the retail land sales area. The uncertainties regarding the collection of funds is great and carrying deferred income makes the risk more apparent than the prior practice of immediately recognizing income from a sale when little cash is received. Here, in contrast to so many areas, cash flow has been deemed important to income determination.

Percentage of Contract Completion

Another, perhaps less enlightening, example of the use of deferred income is in percentage of contract completion accounting. Briefly, the submission of a bid on a particular job implicitly carries with it an estimate of the profit to be earned by the contractor. If the contractor should complete the project for less than the originally anticipated costs, actual profits will exceed planned profits. Accounting requirements stipulate that profits in excess of those budgeted be carried in a deferred income account until the project is entirely completed.

This requirement attempts to prevent the contractor from either overestimating the percentage of completion at the contract's beginning or from profiting from circumstances (or luck) that helped the project at its beginning but could change before the end. This requirement can be particularly onerous for contractors that work for federal or local governments. Frequent changes in the stipulations extend the contracts and delay final approvals. Significant funds can thus be held in a deferred income account for several years, making the balance sheet of the contractor look extremely debt-laden. When approval is finally granted, this deferred income liability becomes revenue with no offsetting costs! Debt converts directly to net worth.

The deferred income account in the above example has merely become a reserve account similar to that set up by manufacturers for servicing of warranty claims. In effect, the contract specifications have already been provided to the government. In this case, being familiar with the track record of the contractor is more important to the analyst's decisions than the accounting rule.

Abuses concerning deferred profits have been less prevalent than those concerning retail land sales. In the Florida land sales example, corrective action was clearly indicated. In the government contractor example, however, the accounting requirements may be too strict.

> **Key Points:** Treat most unearned income accounts as a liability, especially if it results from, for instance, a property sale in which the seller takes back a purchase-money mortgage rather than cash proceeds. Further investigate deferred income that results from unexpected profits on government contract work, since, if the contractor's reputation is good, this debt might justifiably be recognized as net worth.

Unfunded Pension Obligations {40}

Most pension plans are filed with and regulated by the federal government. They create a legal, contractual obligation with employees, and the federal government has taken steps through the Employee Retirement Income Security Act of 1974 (ERISA) to ensure that these obligations are upheld. ERISA gives workers some recourse if a firm goes out of business having neglected the funding of its pension plan. Under the law the IRS can seize 30% of a firm's assets to complete the funding of a registered pension plan that is not fully funded when a company files for bankruptcy or goes out of business. Therefore, pension obligations can represent a significant liability if they are underfunded.

At the end of 1985, the Financial Accounting Standards Board made a significant move toward recognizing the obligations involved in employee pension plans. SFAS #87 requires that a company's pension liability be calculated and shown on the balance sheet.

Calculation. How are typical pension obligations calculated? First, actuaries calculate the amount of funds the firm must pay out to employees upon retirement. These calculations are based on the number of present employees, their average age, and their average salary. Assumptions are made about how old employees will be when they retire and what their salaries will be at that time. For the first calculation it is assumed that the employees' salaries will not increase. An assumption is also made about the rate of earnings of the investment fund that will be used to pay the pensions. The calculation is not quite straightforward because the corporation must also assume obligations for employees who had been working for the company prior to the announcement of the pension plan. This previously earned pension benefit is considered a **prior service cost.**

In fact, the calculation of the pension plan obligation is a relatively conservative figure, rarely exaggerated. It is nonetheless a genuine obligation of the employer to employees. If the firm were to go into bankruptcy, then employees would be considered creditors in every sense because the pension itself is a contract registered with the U.S. government.

The next step is to calculate the fair market value of the plan assets. When the market value of plan assets is less than the pension obligation, a net liability exists. In the past this net liability was treated as an off-balance-sheet item and a program for amortizing it was utilized to reduce its unfunded portion in the future. Other factors can also change pension fund liability. For instance, volatility in the stock and bond markets will change the value of the pension fund assets, assuming they were invested in these markets. In addition, the firm may reduce the size of its operations, in which case a smaller benefit might be paid to employees who had vested plans since their term of anticipated service will be shortened.

Hidden liability. Because numerous factors could affect pension fund liability, accountants felt that it was better to keep any net liability, resulting from underfunding or poor market (investment) performance, off the balance sheet. Although the pension liability is somewhat akin to a contingent liability in that the future amount due and the time of payment are not known with certainty, its absence from the balance sheet nevertheless did obscure the fact that some funds would be due in the future.

Hidden asset. The flip side of this situation is represented by the firm that responsibly funds its pension expense and a good investment performance results in an overfunded pension fund. In effect, the shareholders of this firm have a hidden asset that is not on the balance sheet. Observant analysts would recognize from the footnotes that the company could sell off its pension obligation to an insurance company for a cost substantially less than the market value of the plan assets. This would result in a net gain. This type of transaction was completed by Emery Air Freight in 1987, and it resulted in a net gain of $24 million after taxes. Gains could be significantly higher than this, however; for example, at the end of 1986, the pension plan of Philip Morris was more than half a billion dollars overfunded. A corporate raider could harvest substantial cash by purchasing an insurance company annuity for the employees at a cost less than the fair value of the assets presently in the pension fund. Many shareholders are probably not aware of this hidden asset since Generally Accepted Accounting Principles does not report it on the balance sheet.

SFAS #87

The issuance of SFAS #87 represented a significant improvement in pension accounting. First, the following definitions must be considered:

1. The **accumulated benefit obligation** is the present value of amounts forecast to be paid (including turnover, mortality, service to date, and current compensation). The issue here is how high a present value rate is used, because high rates imply that the market value of plan assets will grow at that rate.
2. The **projected benefit obligation** is the accumulated benefit obligation based on expected future salaries. (This is not required to be disclosed.)
3. The **annual pension expense** is a result of
   (a) benefits earned,
   (b) earnings in the plan based on the present value estimated rate,
   (c) the actual return, and
   (d) an amortiztion and deferral slush fund to net out to pension expense.

In short, the standard mandated that the obligation be stated; but it is shown on the asset side of the balance sheet as a deferred expense called *unfunded accumulated benefit obligation.* (Hence, the expense is not even seen in the income statement.) This permits the recognition of income and its reporting in the retained earnings account, which really belongs to the employees—a result of the principle of the going concern.

Moreover, the deferred expense is calculated by taking the accumulated benefit obligation net not only the plan assets but also prior service liability. Instead, the unamortized prior service costs are slowly amortized into the pension expense each year until they are completely funded.

Only when the net pension liability exceeds the unamortized prior service cost is the deferred charge asset offset by a reduction to the stockholders' equity account. The contra account to the stockholders' equity is called *excess of unfunded accumulated obligation over prior service cost.* Notice that a freestanding liability (similar to a bond debt) is not created by this accounting, which is a compromise solution helping managers to look better.

A significant overfunding is capable of limiting pension expense to a small amount over the coming years. This should be regarded by the analyst as a significant strength for a firm relative to its competitors. GAAP does allow reducing the annual pension costs so that eventually the overfunding will be eliminated and, thus, it helps prevent dramatic swings in pension expense from year to year. Since the analyst's task is to prepare a forecast of future earnings and cash flow, smoothing an expense that is partially affected by outside market forces is helpful.

> **Key Points:** Underfunded pension funds can represent a significant liability for a firm. Fortunately, this liability does appear on the balance sheet in accordance with SFAS #87. Overfunded pension funds represent for a firm a source of financial strength that may not appear on the balance sheet.

Quasi-Equity

Minority Interest {44}

If a firm owns less than 100% of a consolidated subsidiary, it has fiduciary obligations to other shareholders of that subsidiary. The minority interest account represents these obligations. Because of minority interests, a parent company may not simply move funds from one subsidiary to another, if, for example, the other subsidiary is financially distressed.

The major issue for the analyst to consider with respect to minority interests is the size of this account relative to the net assets of the consolidated affiliate. A significant minority interest may imply that the parent is really a holding company and therefore is riskier to lend to than operating companies. Holding companies are merely owners of stock in their subsidiaries and essentially have no tangible or intangible assets under their control. If the holding company runs into financial problems, the strong subsidiaries will likely be the survivors. The shareholders of these subsidiaries, however, would not be pleased if their company's assets were depleted to sustain weaker entities. Indeed, virtually any bankruptcy judge would support them and act to reverse such a situation.

Evidence of significant minority interest is a cue to lend to the affiliates directly rather than the parent. In the event of bankruptcy and liquidation of the subsidiaries, creditors of the subsidiaries would be paid in full before the parent company received anything on its stock interest.

The issue is not whether minority interest is a liability. It is not a liability because it has none of the aspects—such as mandatory interest and principal repayment—of a liability. Usually if the minority interest is small its existence is unlikely to have a significant impact on the corporation's ability to repay debt.

> **Key Points:** Minority interest may be cause for concern if it is large relative to the net assets of the consolidated affiliate. In addition, significant minority interest as a percentage of equity may indicate that the parent company is actually a holding company and that loans made directly to it are risky. On the other hand, if minority interest represents a relatively small amount, its existence as part of the firm's equity should not be of concern.

Deferred Taxes {41} & {43}

While some consider the deferred tax account to be a true liability, it has many aspects of an equity reserve account. Especially with reference to the contingency nature of the claims that the IRS may have, the analyst may possibly consider giving it an equity category. This area is discussed more fully in Chapter 4.

Off-Balance-Sheet Liabilities

Whether quasi-equity accounts should be treated as liabilities is subject to question. On the other hand, a company may have significant liabilities that do not appear on the balance sheet. These include:

- Debt obligations connected with SFAS #13 Operating leases
- Contingent recourse relationships concerning the sale of receivables to independent third parties

- Other contingent liabilities, specifically warranty problems and those connected with product safety

Operating Leases

Equipment and real estate leasing have affected the financial statements of many companies. Let's look at the retail industry as an example.

Department Store Industry

Since the 1960s, most large downtown department stores in cities like Philadelphia have been closed and replaced by the suburban shopping mall. Major shopping malls are owned by limited partnerships, not by the stores themselves as the downtown stores usually were. In a departure from past practices, when retailers owned their own stores, they now lease floor space on a long-term basis from the developers. Frequently, these leases contain a contingency clause specifying that the base monthly rent includes a percentage surcharge of the store's volume. Thus, the merchant shares the developer's risk in site selection.

But unlike the earlier period when retailers owned their stores, modern retailers carry no real estate and related debt on their balance sheets. Nevertheless, the retail store still uses the assets of the developer in its business.

Historically, real estate was included in the calculation of return on assets (net income divided by total assets) for the retailer. Since historical cost conventions in accounting do not permit the recognition of increases in fixed asset values, store managements have incentive to rent space rather than to own fixed assets. The debt that would have been incurred in order to fund the fixed assets is also eliminated. It is the elimination of this debt with which the analyst must be concerned.

Debt has certain specific characteristics that affect the operations and cash flow of any entity that incurs it. Specifically, debt represents fixed charges that must be paid each year regardless of earnings performance. Any debt creates a risk of insolvency, and obviously, the higher the debt, the greater the risk. *A firm that has no debt will never go bankrupt* because it has no obligations to meet. If such a firm is unprofitable, it will merely wind down operations, liquidating its assets and paying off the shareholders.

If a firm can keep debt-equivalent obligations off its balance sheet, it can present the illusion that it is less risky and has performed better.

Sherwin-Williams Company

In 1979 when John Breen became chairman, president, and chief executive officer of the Sherwin-Williams Company the firm was in considerable disarray. Several divisions were losing money and the company appeared to be highly leveraged with a debt to total capital ratio of about 50%. In 1984, the financial statement reported that, "The ratio of debt (including capital leases) to total capitalization was 29.5% at the end of 1984, . . . improved from 48.6% at December 31, 1978." The report continued: "The improvement in this ratio since 1978 resulted from improved profitability, debt repurchases, conversions of 6.25% debentures into common stock and other reductions in long-term debt."

If this information had been complete, it would have indicated significant improvement in debt repayment capacity. However, the footnotes showed that Operating lease obligations of Sherwin-Williams had increased $69 million in 1984 alone. As you can see, the increase in Operating leases was not mentioned as a contributing factor to the proportional decline in long-term debt.

In fact, the present value of the future Operating lease obligations totaled approximately $150 million. When this number is added to long-term debt and included in the calculations, the debt to worth ratio becomes 44%, representing a considerably smaller improvement than indicated by the 29.5%.

Review of the financial statement *analysis* of Sherwin-Williams by a prominent bank showed that the analysts had indeed been beguiled by the text in the annual report. They joined management's own report touting the improved creditworthiness of Sherwin-Williams as a result of the "reduction" in long-term debt.

Whenever management congratulates itself on its performance or blames poor performance on someone or something else, the analyst should be suspicious.

SFAS #13 specifies the conditions under which a leasing transaction must be capitalized onto the balance sheet (equipment on the asset side and long-term debt on the liability side). If the lease is not capitalized, it is carried only in the footnotes as an Operating lease. Most firms prefer Operating lease status because they wish to present a cleaner balance sheet, without the assets and associated debt on the liability side, as required by the Capital lease classification.

SFAS #13 focuses on how leasing transactions affect the risk of ownership. In a short-term lease, the leasing company's total return depends to a significant extent on the proceeds of selling the equipment at the end of the lease: the residual value. It retains the risk on at least that portion of the equipment's cost rather than transferring it to the lessee. On the other hand, the commitment to use a shopping mall space via a long-term lease is tantamount to assuming many of the risks of owning that real estate.

The requirement to *continually* make payments for use of the real estate creates the aspect of a liability. Like some other liabilities, leases give rise to recurring fixed charges that cannot be avoided. A bankrupt company may find a leasing obligation more difficult to settle than, for example, a secured debt obligation. (A debt usually finances an asset that the debtor owns.) The snag in discontinuing a lease is that the bankrupt lessee may have to pay rent for up to three additional years and still not retain any rights to the property. Unfortunately for the analyst, this contingent liability for three years of rental payments does not appear on the balance sheet.

A firm that is facing weak market demand may wish to break its lease obligation to reduce its operating overhead. Regrettably, it is precisely the lack of demand that will make breaking the lease costly. It will be difficult for the lessor to find a new lessee, thus cutting its losses, especially at the old lessee's rate. Since the lessor will be faced with a considerable loss, it will likely require the original lessee to make up the difference. In this respect, the lessee is taking a significant risk in either real estate or equipment leasing that is not being recorded.

The cure for this lack of information on the balance sheet is to capitalize the Operating leases onto the balance sheet to achieve an appropriate level of assets and liabilities. The information necessary for accomplishing this is in the footnotes of all audited financial statements; the technique is discussed in Chapter 4 because it is somewhat difficult. Nevertheless, try not to be tempted to work with a rental factor method of capitalizing leases, promoted by well-meaning but misinformed generalists. Every firm signs leases of different terms and rates and for different equipment. Using a generalized rental factor times the annual rental cost as a solution may well produce worse results than doing nothing.

Unconsolidated Captive Subsidiaries {33}, {34}, {35}, {36}, {39} & {40}

Unconsolidated captive subsidiaries also have the effect of removing assets and liabilities from the balance sheet. Before the issuance of SFAS #94 in October 1987, GAAP did not require that non-homogeneous affiliates be consolidated onto the parent company's balance sheet. The reasoning was that businesses like real estate or accounts receivable financing were so distinct in their operations that consolidation with a parent operating company would mask important financial issues. The real problem was financial intermediaries and analysts had preconceived ideas about the debt to worth relation which firms in different businesses could carry. These preconceptions did not allow for the fact that all firms have some assets like receivables and real estate that can be highly leveraged. To work around the analysts' blind spot, management of many firms set up special-purpose subsidiaries and transferred to them selected assets that could be highly leveraged. This allowed some firms substantial off-balance-sheet financing with only footnote disclosure.

General Electric Credit Corp.

Creating the illusion of low leverage by carrying debt on the balance sheet of an unconsolidated captive finance company is not a new idea. Consider General Electric Credit Corp. (now GE Capital Corp.), founded in the 1930s. The electric refrigerator was expensive relative to traditional kitchen appliances. It replaced ice boxes, but it cost hundreds of dollars. Potential distributors needed financing (called **floor planning**) to carry the inventories of these expensive appliances. Further, General Electric recognized that to sell millions of refrigerators it had to offer consumers a plan that could compete with daily payments to the iceman. Thus, it financed both the dealers and consumers. General Electric Credit Corp. was set up to service this need because General Electric did not want to carry these long-term receivables on its books.

Subsidiaries that did not have to be consolidated included those to which the parent company sold its accounts receivable and real estate and through which it carried self-insurance and even leased equipment. All of these entities restrict their assets to either paper (monetary) obligations or real estate, both of which are then highly leveraged.

The Limited Stores Inc.

An example of how unconsolidated subsidiaries can affect financing options can be found by reviewing The Limited Stores Inc.'s acquisition of Lane Bryant, a women's clothing retailer that had a $325 million consumer receivable account balance at the time of its purchase. Hypothetically, let's say financial analysts like to see retailers with less than two to one leverage. (That is, the relationship of debt to worth must be no more than two to one.) Therefore, for this retailer to carry on its balance sheet $325 million in receivable assets, it could borrow up to $217 million and then must get from sales of stock or retained earnings about $100 million in equity. Exhibit 3-1 shows what was required to support the Lane Bryant receivables.

What could be the alternative? The Limited Credit Corp. was born since a new credit institution may be postulated to be permitted five to one leverage, meaning that the total equity investment credit needed to carry the $325 million portfolio would be reduced from the $108 million to $18 million. Here is how:

1. Limited parent sells to Limited Credit the receivables for $54 million in stock and $271 million in cash.
2. Limited Credit has obtained the cash by approaching financial intermediaries and commercial paper rating analysts and convinced them that since its only asset is accounts receivable, it should be allowed to leverage itself five to one. Then it borrowed the $271 million based on Limited parent's equity investment of $54 million.
3. Then Limited (parent) would carry the $54 million on its balance sheet as an equity investment in an unconsolidated subsidiary. Since this investment in an unconsolidated subsidiary could be leveraged on the two to one basis permitted to a retailing firm, the parent can continue to borrow $36 million on that asset, reducing the commitment of equity capital only $18 million.

The $90 million savings in costly equity capital is a temptation that is difficult for an acquisitive management to resist. Generally, a much higher leverage ratio is permitted for a finance company with a more diversified portfolio of credits than a clothing retailer. This is because finance company receivables need only be collected; nothing needs to be purchased, processed, or sold to the consumer.

Questions and SFAS #94

1. Why didn't lenders simply finance The Limited directly? If the ratio of debt to worth is valid, should it not be different for divergent assets as their proportions appear on the financial statement?
2. Did Sherwin-Williams have an unconsolidated real estate subsidiary? Yes, with debt of $40 million.

3. Why were these subsidiaries kept off the balance sheet when conglomerates mix business types from transportation (high capital intense) with service industries (low capital) and manufacturing with publishing, retailing, and wholesaling? The reason is clear, that knocking debt off the balance sheet made corporate managements look good.

With the issuance of SFAS #94, the Financial Accounting Standards Board finally ended this means for achieving the illusion of low leverage. SFAS #94 required that all majority owned subsidiaries be consolidated onto the balance sheet.

The most abusive aspect of the unconsolidated subsidiaries was the *covert guarantee*. Before financing a captive finance subsidiary, creditors wanted assurance from the parent company that the amounts owed to the parent by third parties were bona fide. If the parent provided full recourse for the subsidiary's debt, then that debt would have remained on the parent's balance sheet. Instead, an **income maintenance agreement** was drawn up between the parent company and the unconsolidated subsidiary. It promised the subsidiary creditors that the parent would ensure that the earnings of the subsidiary were at least 1.25 times the fixed charges of the subsidiary's debt. It turns out that this multiple was necessary in order to achieve a credit rating that allowed the subsidiary to sell its commercial paper to insurance companies and other corporate investors who required an investment grade rating.

Accountants and management argued that this agreement fell short of being a complete guarantee. For example, if the subsidiary and its parent ran into problems at the same time, a bankruptcy judge for the parent could decide that this was an executory agreement that could be abrogated during bankruptcy. In that case, the finance company creditors would have only the receivables, the assets in the subsidiary they had been financing.

On the other hand, since it is rare that these collapses occur suddenly, the higher likelihood is that the subsidiary would start having problems before the parent, because of the notorious practice of selling to weaker credits in tough times, as was mentioned in Chapter 2. With the income maintenance agreement the parent company would have to keep pumping additional funds into the subsidiary until the subsidiary's income climbed to the amount covertly guaranteed. If this situation continued, nervous creditors could abandon the situation. Similarly, creditors who were already advancing funds to the parent company would likely either refuse credit or increase interest rates. Thus, for all intents and purposes, the income maintenance agreement is really a guarantee.

A close look at the practices that were permitted before this recent change demonstrates the need for constant modifications in accounting and illustrates how analysts can be misled by accepting the current Statement of Financial Accounting Standards as "truth."

Key Points: The issuance of SFAS #94 requires that all majority owned subsidiaries be consolidated on the balance sheet. View income maintenance agreements between parent firms and subsidiaries as guarantees.

Exhibit 3-1.

ACCOUNTING FOR AN UNCONSOLIDATED FINANCE SUBSIDIARY

Immediately prior to the merger, the firms financial statements appear as follows:

Acquired company's abbreviated financials:			Retailer permitted
		000,000's	Leverage ratio:
Lane Bryant			
Assets	**Liabilities**		**Debt**
Accounts Receivable	Debt	$216.7	**Net Worth**
$325.0			=
	Net Worth	$108.3	2
Total Assets $325.0	Total Equities	$325.0	1

Acquiring company's abbreviated financials:			Retailer permitted
		000,000's	Leverage ratio:
The Limited Stores Inc. (Before)			
Assets	**Liabilities**		**Debt**
Accounts Receivable	Debt	$216.7	**Net Worth**
$325.0			=
	Net Worth	**$108.3**	2
Total Assets $325.0	Total Equities	$325.0	1

The Limited Stores sells its receivables to a new finance company, Credit.
Credit, buys Limited's receivables with the cash which it raises from lenders.
The net equity ($54.2) appears on Limited's balance sheet, and it may use
the receivable proceeds to pay off its debt and make further acquisitions.

New finance company's abbreviated financials:			Financial Inter-
		000,000's	mediary permitted
The Limited Credit			Leverage ratio:
Assets	**Liabilities**		**Debt**
Accounts Receivable	Debt	$270.8	**Net Worth**
$325.0			=
	Net Worth	$54.2	5
Total Assets $325.0	Total Equities	$325.0	1

New parent company's abbreviated financials:			
		000,000's	
The Limited Stores Inc., (After)			
			Retailer permitted
Assets	**Liabilities**		Leverage ratio:
Accounts Receivable	Debt	$54.2	
$0.0			**Debt**
Investment in Unconso-			**Net Worth**
lidated Subsidiary	**Net Worth**	**$18.1**	=
$54.2			2
Total Assets $54.2	Total Equities	$72.2	1

Contingent Liabilities

Contingent liabilities are executory, implying a contract established in the ordinary course of business. Historically, contingent liabilities arose only through lawsuits. The firm's lawyers estimated the possible monetary ramifications of the lawsuit, and this information was included in the financial statement footnotes. Since the exact cost of the liability and the date of payment were unknown, accounting conventions did not require that the information be carried on the balance sheet. Attorneys protected their clients' interest by not indicating to the plaintiff even a vague dollar liability. Indeed, footnotes frequently stated that in the opinion of the firm's attorneys the potential liability would be immaterial.

Typically, corporate lawsuits involved patent infringement, failure to complete production or the delivery in the required amount of time, or causing consequential damages to the customer. Less frequently, lawsuits involved the firm's refusal to satisfy a warranty.

The nature of lawsuits against corporations changed with the publication of Ralph Nader's book *Unsafe at Any Speed* and the subsequent birth of the consumer rights movement. Consumer rights ushered in a new element for manufacturers to contend with: the implied warranty. Activists argued that by producing a product, the firm made a representation to any potential buyers that the product was safe. Serious problems have arisen for manufacturers of automobiles, and most recently, for asbestos producers.

Johns-Manville Corp.

One of the most dramatic cases of bankruptcy resulting from an unrevealed contingent liability is that of Johns-Manville Corp., a building products maker and one of the most successful companies in the United States. It manufactured asbestos used to insulate metal in large structures.

It was discovered that asbestos particles inhaled into human lungs could cause cancer. The first victims were laborers who manufactured the product and installed it, but victims also included children in school buildings, and so on. Using the implied warranty argument, lawsuits were filed against the company by attorneys working on contingency fees. Johns-Manville was confronted with having to fight disputes in many jurisdictions across the United States.

It would have been difficult for Johns-Manville, a *Fortune* 500 firm, to win a case in a local community. Many multimillion-dollar awards to plaintiffs of asbestos suits could, in fact, wipe out Johns-Manville's net worth. That is, a threatened problem could financially destroy a company that management and their accountants claimed was a healthy, ongoing organization in good financial condition.

Johns-Manville's executives approached a federal bankruptcy judge and presented their case: If the early suit winners depleted the corporation's net worth, then later victims would get nothing. Moreover, concerned creditors might withdraw their support from Johns-Manville, thereby causing its premature collapse.

To protect the plaintiffs, the bankruptcy judge allowed Johns-Manville to file for bankruptcy. Then he consolidated all pending asbestos cases into a single case to be tried in the Denver district. All of the stock of Johns-Manville has been placed in a trust to create a fund for those injured. The shareholders have essentially lost everything as a result of a contingent liability. The creditors have been protected in order to maintain the viability of Johns-Manville. However, recent news suggests that the trust may run out of funds before the cases are all heard. The creditors may also lose out eventually with the sale of J-M assets to satisfy requirements of the trust—the result of a hidden liability.

Key Points: Examine contingent liabilities thoroughly, especially legal liabilities. Carry such liabilities onto the spreadsheet by estimating a value from the information provided in the footnotes. Be aware of industry events and pending government regulations.

Addenda

Although the topics have reached the bottom of the balance sheet part of the spreadsheet, some of the materials have been pushed into Chapter 4. If you are advanced in analysis or have a particularly difficult analysis, you should read Chapter 4. Otherwise it is permissible to skip it; you may go directly on to the spreading of the income statement. The analysis of the above balance sheet items will aid in understanding trends within the firm and comparative analysis with others in the same industry, to be discussed in the chapters on analysis to follow. The constant reference to accounting assumptions and methods just completed is complex and difficult, but is necessary to ferret out a picture of the financial health of an entity from camouflage presented by management. The tools and methods used to spread the larger audited comanies can also be used for asking questions to the managements of smaller companies. These smaller entities have the same problems as their larger brethren and they can and should be investigated just as thoroughly.

Chapter 4

Spreading the Balance Sheet—
The Hard Stuff

Accounting is a language; as such, it has developed over time and is less adaptable to changes in management practice and corporate finance than analysts might like. The effort to provide interim information about business operations even on an annual basis is a compromise; therefore, to reduce the compromise, an assumption is made that the firm is a *going concern*. This avoids resolving many of the problems of an interim report. Unfortunately for analysts, firms tend to get into unexpected financial difficulty in the middle of their lives; thus, the interim statement must be taken seriously. For the lender, the worst situation is to participate in a creditor's committee over a liquidation of the failed firm. In this instance, the revaluing of the balance sheet to determine the breakup value of the firm as the back door out of the debt repayment scenario is mandatory.

Chapters 2 and 3 reviewed the assets and liabilities, respectively. Each account on the firm's balance sheet was studied to determine if it provided information allowing the analyst to derive breakup value. In particular, the plant, property, and equipment account came in for substantial criticism; here, the *historical cost basis obstructs the analyst*. Without SFAS #33, one of the few alternatives, besides a potentially expensive appraisal, is obtaining the fire insurance/casualty value of the part of the firm's fixed assets.

There are six other items where the clarity of the insights into the firm's liquidation value is important to a successful analysis:

1. Inventory accounting methods
2. Operating leases and off-balance-sheet financing
3. Defeasance and the inflationary impact on long-term debt
4. Pooling or purchase accounting of acquisitions
5. Deferred taxes and its quasi-equity nature
6. Foreign exchange accounting

While some have been touched upon in Chapters 2 and 3, they are somewhat difficult to understand and consequently are carefully reconsidered here.

LIFO and FIFO Inventory Conventions

Most businesses calculate their ending inventory values using conventions, a procedure used for convenience and cost-saving rather than accuracy. The three most popular conventions are first-in-first-out (FIFO), last-in-first-out (LIFO), and average cost inventory methods. **FIFO** calculates the ending inventory position based on the flow-through notion that materials are used in the order that they are bought, that is, the oldest materials are used first, leaving the current cost inventory on the balance sheet. **LIFO,** on the other hand, calculates the ending inventory position based on the converse notion that materials bought last are used first in the production process; the benefit is that current costs are used in the income statement. A third method, **average cost,** averages the old inventory's existing cost to the cost of new inventory each time merchandise is delivered. While its bookkeeping is more complicated, the average cost method is generally used by companies that would prefer to use LIFO, but whose inventories vary substantially in size from one period to another, a circumstance that makes the LIFO method produce spurious profits in the liquidation phase.

Balance Sheet vs. Income Statement

Basically, FIFO has the advantage of causing the most recent inventory costs to be reflected on the balance sheet whereas LIFO causes current costs to be reflected on the income statement. Thus, when FIFO is used, the inventory value on the balance sheet is extremely close to market value. On the other hand, LIFO results in a balance sheet value that is closer to the cost of inventory when the firm first adopted LIFO accounting, assuming (usually legitimately) that inventories stay close to previous levels or grow slowly over time. The average cost convention results in a balance sheet value that falls somewhere in between those resulting from FIFO and LIFO.

A recent study [Foster, 1986, p. 144] found that FIFO is currently predominant in the telecommunications, computer, cosmetic, and apparel industries and LIFO is predominant in the retailing, textile, chemical, oil, gas, and steel industries. The air transportation industry uses the average cost method.

As an aid to the analyst calculating the breakup value of the firm, accounting guidelines require that LIFO users include a footnote to their financial statements indicating what the difference in inventory value would have been had FIFO been used: This is called the *LIFO reserve* and is based on the idea of hidden value. Since the LIFO understates inventory value on the balance sheet, in inflationary times, the analyst should consider *transferring the reserve value to the spreadsheet and adding the difference (between the FIFO and LIFO values) to net worth* to bring the balance sheet back into balance.

In conclusion, valuing inventory is fraught with problems. The numbers that appear on the balance sheet are largely estimates of value using various conventions. While the accountant is struggling with balancing the accounting principles and needs of other potential users of the financial statements, lenders may have to grind their own axes.

Key Points: If the firm uses LIFO, consider transferring the FIFO value of inventory to the spreadsheet (and adjusting net worth accordingly) since it more closely approximates market value of inventory.

Operating Leases and Off-Balance-Sheet Financing {13} & {36}*

The leverage ratio used by analysts divides the outstanding debt of a company by either total capital or net worth. The higher this ratio (lots of debt relative to either capital or net worth), the less likely the company is to receive a good credit rating. Typically, historical cost valuation of fixed assets understates them (thus understanding net worth [assets minus liabilities]—the denominator), causing this ratio to appear worse than it would be using current costs. Let's look at an example.

Department Store

One of the major changes in the retail department store business since the 1950s has been the advent of the shopping mall. The idea of the grand downtown store is, in many cities, dated. Real estate partnerships generally own shopping malls and lease them to the department stores. This has enabled the department stores to get the fixed assets off their balance sheets. These assets do not contribute in any way to the value of the firm according to GAAP historical cost rules.

Thus, by entering into an Operating lease for real estate or equipment, a company can avoid reporting either the value of the fixed asset or the liabilities incurred to finance it. The leverage ratio is thus improved, since the liabilities do not appear on the balance sheet. In fact, it has been suggested that the Operating lease is management's rejoinder to historical cost valuation of assets.

Capitalizing Operating Leases Onto the Balance Sheet

Through SFAS #13 the accounting profession mandated strict rules for determining whether a lease should be capitalized onto the balance sheet. SFAS #13 also requires that a firm present in the footnotes to its financial statements all other non-cancelable lease obligations on equipment and real estate for the next five years, with a single value for the subsequent years.

It is common knowledge that it is possible for management to evade the spirit of the SFAS #13 test to create the appearance of less debt by writing leases specifically to qualify for Operating lease status. The complexity of the whole area has caused some incautious analysts to look for an easy way out: the **rental factor multiplier.** Several articles have been written about easy ways to capitalize onto the balance sheet the liabilities and assets manifest in Operating leases. Apparently the most popular procedure takes the rental payments, either for the prior or current year, and multiples them by some universal fixed factor. Such a factor, which achieved popularity in the early 1970s, was eight times the

*Numbers in braces refer to line numbers in Exhibit 2-2A.

total rental stream and was until recently used by Standard & Poor's. With the increase in interest rates, because of the 1970s market and inflationary vacillations, to a relatively high present plateau and with an additional trend in the marketplace toward shorter leasing terms, the eight-times factor now appears exaggerated. A more current article [Houlihan and Sondhi, 1984] suggests that a more reasonable factor is six. These universal factors are hazardous because they can seriously over- or underestimate the value to be placed on the balance sheet.

Moreover, it is unnecessary to choose a rule of thumb since, with the information given, it is possible for the analyst to more precisely capitalize onto the balance sheets the assets and liabilities of an Operating lease using present values. Exhibit 4-1 shows how this can be done using the footnote provided in the Sherwin-Williams Company annual report for 1984. Sherwin-Williams was the example given in Chapter 3 about moving all debt financing to Operating lease status.

The actual footnote information is shown in Exhibit 4-1 as the "First Section." It contains both of the subsequent years' unconditional obligations to pay rents under all leases. First, **Capital leases** are more like financings and are already capitalized onto the balance sheet by SFAS #13. Second, the **Operating lease** obligation looks more like a short-term rental to SFAS #13 and is not presently on the balance sheet. Let's do a comparison of the factor methods with the present value method. Using both suggested universal factors above would produce the following results on the Capital leases for Sherwin-Williams:

Capital Lease Next Year Rental	Factor	Result	Amount Shown by Auditors
$5,588	6 ×	$33,528	$15,700
$5,588	8 ×	$44,704	$15,700

Note: All numbers for this example are in millions. These factor results are really way off! Using the factor approach with the Operating lease rental of $42,317 would create a result almost equal to or even greater than the total obligation of $235,092—an inconceivable outcome.

For calculating a present value, a discount rate is required. Unfortunately in this footnote, the auditors did not provide the discount rate they used to discount the Capital leases back to $15,700. Where it is shown, the analyst should use it to discount the Operating lease minimum lease payments. The following goes through all the steps.

1. The first step is to back into (discover) the discount rate used by the auditors for the Capital leases. Under the minimum lease payments is the information showing how the Capital leases have been capitalized onto the balance sheet by segregating the *financing charges* portion of the rental from the *principal*. Especially important, if the footnote does not give the present value rate at which the rentals are discounted, is the *present value of the minimum lease payments*. Using a present value calculator or a personal computer program, the *present value of the minimum lease payments* becomes the net present value of the flow of payments due in future years, solving for the interest (discount) rate.

Exhibit 4-1. CALCULATING THE PRESENT VALUE OF OPERATING LEASES

From the December 31, 1984 Annual Report
of The Sherwin-Williams Company
(Rounded to 000's)

ANALYSIS

FIRST SECTION

Year	Capital Leases	Operating Leases
1985	$5,588	$42,317
1986	$3,635	$37,394
1987	$2,600	$30,808
1988	$2,379	$25,106
1989	$2,186	$19,022
Later Years	$11,649	$80,445
Total	$28,037	$235,092

Amounts representing:
Interest ($10,792)
Executory costs ($1,545)

Present Value of minimum lease payments $15,700

SECOND SECTION

Here the "Later Years" from the First Section have been "Stretched Out"

Year	Capital Leases	Operating Leases
1985	$5,588	$42,317
1986	$3,635	$37,394
1987	$2,600	$30,808
1988	$2,379	$25,106
1989	$2,186	$19,022
1990	$2,186	$19,022
1991	$2,186	$19,022
1992	$2,186	$19,022
1993	$2,186	$19,022
1994	$2,905	$4,357
Total	$28,037	$235,092

THIRD SECTION

Present Value Factor @ 14.77%	Present Value Operating Leases
0.85	$36,068
0.73	$27,165
0.62	$19,076
0.53	$13,250
0.45	$8,556
0.38	$7,293
0.33	$6,216
0.28	$5,298
0.24	$4,516
0.20	$882
Total	$128,320

Find the internal rate of return using the payment stream from the Stretched Out Capital lease "Second Section" directly above, using the present value number to the left as an investment in "time period zero." This calculates to the 14.77% rate used in the "Third Section" to discount the Operating leases to present value.

This is an internal rate of return (IRR) problem because the search is for the discount rate that will reduce the payments to the present value amount.

Unfortunately from the footnote itself, the flows per year are only available for the first five years, a serious disadvantage where long-term leases are involved. Therefore, the exhibit makes an approximation of the real flows by pretending that the *later years'* flows continue the last named year flow.

In effect, the remaining obligation after the first five years of the lease is extended. These calculations are shown in the section labeled "Second Section." The example extends both Capital and Operating lease payments: The footnotes indicate that $11,649 of Capital and $80,445 of Operating lease obligations are remaining after the first five years of the lease. Make a rough, but not absurd, assumption, that the firm will have to pay the fifth year's rental payment— $2,186 and $19,022, respectively—every year until the entire $11,649 or $80,445 is paid. Both expire in five years (in 1994), a good indication that the lease terms are similar for both SFAS #13 categories, indicating that only SFAS #13 is making much of a distinction between these groups of leases. The present value for the IRR equation would be the $15,700 present value of minimum lease payments disclosed in the footnotes. In the exhibit the IRR for the Capital lease is 14.8%.

2. The second step is to use the 14.8% to discount the Operating lease payments to present value. Calculating them individually, as in the exhibit, or feeding them into a present value calculator or to a lotus template will produce the same answer. In the "Third Section" of the example, the present value factors due for the next ten years are listed and then multiplied times the actual obligations from the "Second Section." When the results are summed, the present value appears to be $128,320 for the Operating leases.

Curiously, the analyst would have had to be using a universal factor of 128,320/42,317 or only 3 to come close on Sherwin-Williams. Essentially each firm's leasing obligations are structured to meet the needs of that firm, and universal factors are worse than useless.

3. The present value of Operating lease payments is entered on the spreadsheet as an additional fixed asset {13} and, since the company does not own any part of this asset, the same number is entered as debt {36} in the long-term liability section of the spreadsheet. In Exhibit 4-1 the value entered on both sides of the balance sheet is $128,320.

This exercise gives the analyst a much clearer picture of the equipment actually used by the company. An understanding of the firm's total liabilities is also enhanced. The analyst should bear in mind that the leases reported in the footnotes are only the non-cancelable ones and the payment shown is only the required payment. The footnotes do not include any contingent rentals that might have to be paid depending on certain levels of usage or sales nor do they include any short-term month-to-month rentals that may as a practical matter be renewed over and over for a long term.

Key Points: Transfer the value of the assets and liabilities of an Operating lease onto the spreadsheet.

Defeasance and Inflation

Virtually all home buyers are willing to agree to a mortgage payment that straps them financially during the initial years of the mortgage. Their expectation is that as years go by, their increasing earning power resulting from inflation will enable them to make the required payments with less effort. At the same time, inflation will cause their home to rise in value and therefore will increase their wealth.

Inflation and Bond Values

Lenders incorporate the inflation rate into the rate of interest they charge for financing. Assuming a lender wishes to have a *real* rate of return of 4%, and inflation is expected to be 6%, then the *nominal* rate charged on the fixed-rate financing will be 10%. When expectations of inflation grow, nominal interest rates tend to increase, and when inflation is expected to be low, nominal interest rates should fall. However, because expectations can get out of step with reality, after subtracting the inflation rate from the cost of debt financing during the 1970s, it turned out that the real interest rate for borrowing money was actually negative, meaning that it cost borrowers nothing to incur debt and that lenders actually lost money. In the 1980s, the situation reversed itself. Inflation dropped to relatively low levels and real interest rates soared to new highs, reflecting the fact that loan pricing kept prophesying a higher level of inflation than actually occurred.

By causing interest rates to fluctuate, inflation also affects the market value of long-term obligations. The movement of interest rates is *inversely* related to the market value of long-term fixed-rate bonds.

Market Rate Risk

As an illustration of the effect of inflation on bond values, consider a 30-year bond with a 5% coupon. The bond pays $50 in interest for every $1,000 in face value. If interest rates suddenly increase to 10%, new bonds issued in the market will have to pay $100 in interest for every $1,000 in face value. If an investor can obtain $100 in interest annually from investing $1,000 in a new bond, he certainly would only be willing to pay $500 for a bond that pays a $50 return. *Therefore, the old $1,000 bond will drop to a market value of $500.*

Inflation and Net Worth

Do the fluctuating market interest rates have any practical impact on the firm *after* it has issued the bond? Yes. Referring to the above example, the differential, between the 5% that the first borrower would pay in interest and the 10% that its later borrowing competitors would pay (all other things equal) for money, will be reflected on the income statements; the initial firm will have a lower interest expense and will be able to offer a product for less on the market, thanks to its below-current-market financing. In contrast, the balance sheets of the two firms will not reflect the first firm's debt as diminished in market value.

The current lack of reduced market value evidenced on the balance sheet might imply that the firm will have to pay off the face value of its bonds, which it will if the bonds go to maturity. (The lower of cost or market rule applies only to assets.) But unmistakably on the other hand, the company could go out into the marketplace and pay off all bonds by laying out only half as much money as it had originally generated by issuing them. The bondholders will then suffer a capital loss.

Most likely, to get the funds to replace the bonds on the financial statement would require the firm to issue new bonds for half the amount originally issued and then use the proceeds to retire the old bonds. Obviously the interest expense to the firm does not increase. Even though interest payments on each bond double, the firm is able to replace the old bonds by issuing only half as many new bonds. The result is that the firm has the exact market value of its bonds on the balance sheet. In the leverage calculation of the ratio of debt to net worth, the *accurate* bond value would be this market value.

If this method were the only way to achieve this result, investment bankers and the IRS would be the big winners. The investment bankers not only charge an issuance fee for the new bonds but also charge a brokerage commission for buying up the old bonds. For the Internal Revenue Service, the removal of old bond liability at a cost of half of their original proceeds value constitutes a capital gain on which the firm would have to pay taxes.

> **Key Points:** Inflation causes the market value of bonds to fluctuate. As rates rise, bond values fall, suggesting that firms that have outstanding bonds that carry lower coupon rates than going market rates may not have to repay the full amount of their debt.

Defeasance Implemented

There is, however, another method that permits the firm to carry its debt on the balance sheet at current market values: defeasance. This was originally a method that addressed a type of *debt extinguishment*, initially spelled out in APB Opinion #26, issued in October 1972. The opinion states that a borrower may establish an irrevocable trust for the debt, called an **in-substance defeasance.** The borrower places in a trust assets that will generate sufficient principal and interest over their lives to fully pay off the principal and interest obligations owed under existing debt. The existing debt is also placed in the trust and is considered *extinguished* from an accounting point of view.

How Defeasance Works

> The borrower issues new market-rate bonds in an amount reflecting the old bonds' current market value, now reduced below the face value because of inflation. These new funds are then invested in qualified assets, which are generally bonds issued by the government of the country in whose currency the original obligation is owed. These government bonds are then placed in a trust in sufficient amount to repay all principal and interest of the original outstanding bonds of the borrower. The original set of bonds is also placed in the trust. The

net accounting result is that the borrower has transferred the old obligation off of its books and can either amortize the capital gain for accounting purposes over the life of the old debt issue or can recognize it immediately as an extraordinary item.

APB Opinion #26 has since been amended by SFAS #76, issued in November 1983. SFAS #76 generally tightened the requirements for the in-substance defeasance as described above. It should be noted that from the IRS's standpoint, no taxable event has occurred, since, in contrast to the previous extinguishment of debt, nothing has changed because there is still a legal obligation of the borrower to repay the debt in the very unlikely event that the government goes bankrupt. Therefore, in-substance defeasance is not a taxable event.

General Motors

Defeasance was somewhat abused by corporations. An example of this occurred in the early 1980s, when General Motors (GM) planned a plant expansion in Spain. GM issued Eurobonds denominated in Spanish currency at an interest rate that was actually lower than that being paid to the Spanish government. It then invested the money in a smaller amount of Spanish government bonds to repay the principal and interest on the Eurobonds. Both sets of bonds were placed in an irrevocable trust and General Motors recognized a multimillion-dollar gain as income in 1983. This action prompted the Financial Accounting Standards Board to issue *Technical Bulletin #84-4* in 1985 that prohibited firms from taking advantage of defeasance to realize an accounting benefit within the immediate time frame of the original bond issuance.

Although the analyst might feel that accounting modifications were justified to prevent the abuse of defeasance, GM's action actually was not so different from typical banking activity, as illustrated:

Bank Loan Risks

Banks acquire funds at relatively low rates from depositors and invest them in assets that may be more risky and thus pay higher interest rates. Furthermore, banks have the accounting luxury of not having to record declines in the market value of their assets on financial statements. (If this were not the case, many thrifts would have shown zero or negative net worths by 1983.)

The necessity of engaging outsiders to create irrevocable trusts and buy government bonds in order to reflect market conditions on the balance sheet makes no sense unless one recalls the accountants' concern for conservatism and their distrust of market values in the face of the going-concern concept. *In any event, spreading outstanding bonds at their market value, rather than their face value, will produce a financial statement that more closely reflects economic reality and the likelihood of future repayment.*

Differences in the value of bonds arising from falling interest rates are generally not as extreme as those arising from rising interest rates. Most bond issues contain only minor time restrictions on the firm's ability to repurchase the bonds at little more than face value. Frequently, *call* protection exists for a maximum of five years. After that, the firm may retire its outstanding obligations by issuing new bonds at the lower interest rate and may use those funds to retire the older issue. Since the higher-rate issue can be retired before maturity, the market will not bid up its price nearly as much as it bid down the price of the low-rate bonds.

> **Key Points:** Defeasance allows a firm to extinguish its debt by placing the lower than market rate bonds in a trust along with other bonds that generate enough principal and interest to repay them. In general, the analyst should consider the market value of a firm's debt. Falling interest rates do not cause bond market values to rise as much as rising rates cause them to fall because most bond issues can be retired (called) by the issuer well before maturity.

Purchase and Pooling Accounting

The raft of mergers and acquisitions by corporations over the last two decades makes at least a brief discussion of purchase and pooling accounting a necessity. Among other dilemmas, the restatement of financial statements after such a collision of corporate cultures is a tragically inadequate measure to take, especially since the restatement is usually only for two years of balance sheets.

Pooling

The accounting is simplicity itself for the pooling approach: *just add everything together*. Pooling is conceived of as primarily an exchange of stock approach, leaving the original firms relatively intact! Net worth per share is not really reflected on the balance sheet to start with; therefore, acquiring another firm merely adds its assets, liabilities, and net worth to the acquiring firm. If either firm was paid a substantial sum for intangibles, the shareholders of the firm with less intangibles may notice that their book net worth per share may have dropped substantially after the merger.

Market values of acquired firms' assets are not taken into account. Thus, this transfer at historical cost *allows the new management to sell off assets and show handsome income*, as they are very likely to do. Rates of return on assets and equity are likely to be higher under pooling, since the combined firms retain their old historical cost values.

Purchase

The higher the proportion of the acquisition is made with cash, the more likely this method is to be used. This method must be used in an all-cash deal. Here, the accounting treats the transaction as if the acquired firm's assets and liabilities had been *purchased* rather than as if a combination of the two firms had taken place, as under pooling.

Therefore, to the extent limited by the price paid, the purchased firm's assets are appraised to market value and then the balance sheet is combined as follows:

1. Add the physical assets at market value.
2. Calculate the change in the deferred tax account for the depreciation deductions, which cannot be taken for IRS purposes because acquisitions are almost always treated as poolings for tax purposes: If the tax rate is 34%, then multiply that percentage times the increase in the value of the assets acquired (market value minus book value).
3. Add to the net worth account the difference between the market value assets and book value liabilities, net the addition to the deferred tax account calculated in step 2.
4. Add the difference between the market value of the physical assets and the sum of additions to liabilities, net worth, and deferred taxes to goodwill, sometimes euphemistically referred to as *excess of cost over value of assets acquired*.
5. Reserves may be set up during the first year of the acquisition, estimated to cover future losses on lawsuits or product warranties.

The analytical problem here is not the technique of adding any two firms together but the problem of using the simple combination as a good base to forecast into the future. If senior management of both firms is staying, then the merger may be primarily for capital needs only and the simple combination may work for at least the immediate future.

However, the likelihood is that management changes will occur in the relatively near future, and the experience of existing management or the relationship between the two corporate cultures may say more about the result than the accounting calculations. *Thorough interviews with management of the merging firms and review of any contracts of performance or nonperformance are necessary to reassure the analyst about the new financial statements.*

Deferred Taxes {41} & {43}

The next subject concerns the most nettlesome area in the accounting profession: income taxes. The **deferred tax** account results from timing differences between paying taxes based on earnings calculated by U.S. tax law and *reporting taxes* based on GAAP earnings.

The Depreciation Issue

The 1950s introduction of accelerated depreciation in IRS accounting caused many firms to employ accelerated depreciation for shareholder reporting. The accounting profession reluctantly accommodated the change in shareholder reporting; therefore, *in the 1950s many firms reported the same net income to the Internal Revenue Service as they did to their shareholders.*

When inflation rates began to soar during the late 1960s, businesses felt a profit pinch in an economy that was suffering from supply bottlenecks. During the 1970s, virtually every firm that had once used accelerated depreciation switched back to straight-line depreciation for shareholder reporting to *look good* to the stockholder audience. The composition of shareholders was rapidly shifting from individual investors who were willing to hold stock for longer terms to mutual fund and other market managers who felt pressed to produce short-term gains and, thus, sought to invest in companies that were performing well in the short term. A focus on short-term gains does not favor accelerated depreciation, which penalizes current earnings but boosts the prospects for enhanced future earnings.

Exhibit 4-2 shows the difference in income that results from using straight-line depreciation rather than the current method, which is the modified accelerated cost recovery system (MACRS). The actual tax due is the tax computed using the MACRS. For obvious reasons, the chief executive of a firm would like to report to shareholders the lower tax actually paid; therefore, net earnings after taxes for the firm would be higher than calculations would indicate using standard tax rates. However, the accountants take the position that the standard rate should be reported to shareholders with the difference placed in a reserve account.

As Exhibit 4-2 indicates in the fifth year, depreciation under MACRS is relatively exhausted, and the amount of taxes due, assuming the same level of operations, climbs significantly. To even the net income reporting out, the accountants take the differential identified and reserved in the early time period ($6,120–$2,040 in the exhibit), store it in an equity reserve account (called deferred taxes on the balance sheet) and then parcel it out during later periods. Unfortunately, although depreciation is the most common source of inflow to the deferred tax account, there are other causes that affect the net income calculation through provision for income taxes in excess of the cash tax due. These differences are enumerated in Chapter 5 in the income taxes section.

Liability or Equity?

Is deferred tax accounting a good approach to handling these timing differences? It has its particular problems because most analysts consider the deferred tax account to be a *liability* rather than an *equity reserve*. What is the difference?

1. First, consider that the IRS does *not* recognize there to be a *future liability* for firms that pay taxes based on a proper calculation of accelerated depreciation, dividend recognition, or other divergences. That is, deferred taxes would be one of the few liabilities whose dollar amount the analyst cannot verify.

2. Many *growth contingencies can affect this implied liability*. For example, a firm could continue to buy more expensive equipment each year (a common occurrence in an inflationary environment). As a result, it could always take greater accelerated depreciation. Under this scenario, as long as the firm grows,

Exhibit 4-2.

COMPARISON OF DEPRECIATION METHODS

Table of depreciation methods with a $100,000 piece of equipment with an economic life of 5 years

Year	GAAP Books		IRS Books	
	Rate	$ Amount	Rate	$ Amount
	Straight Line Depreciation		Modified Accelerated Cost Recovery	
1	20.0%	20,000	20.0%	20,000
2	20.0%	20,000	32.0%	32,000
3	20.0%	20,000	19.2%	19,200
4	20.0%	20,000	11.5%	11,520
5	20.0%	20,000	11.5%	11,520
6			5.8%	5,760

Second Year Income Statements to Stockholders and to the IRS

	GAAP Books Straight Line Depreciation	IRS Books Modified Accelerated Cost Recovery
Sales	$120,000	$120,000
Cost of Goods Sold	72,000	72,000
Depreciation Charge	20,000	32,000
All other expenses	10,000	10,000
Net Income Bef Tax	$18,000	$6,000
Tax	6,120	2,040
Net Income	$11,880	

The difference between the two tax amounts ($6,120 and $2,040) [shown in the "Second Year Income Statements..." (above)] of $4,080 is carried on the Balance Sheet [not shown] as Deferred Taxes, *and the company reports the GAAP Tax amount to shareholders.*

Fifth Year Income Statements to Stockholders and to the IRS

	GAAP Books Straight Line Depreciation	IRS Books Modified Accelerated Cost Recovery
Sales	$120,000	$120,000
Cost of Goods Sold	72,000	72,000
Depreciation Charge	20,000	11,520
All other expenses	10,000	10,000
Net Income Bef Tax	$18,000	$26,480
Tax	6,120	9,003
Net Income	$11,880	$17,477

The difference between the two tax amounts ($6,120 and $9,003) [in the "Fifth Year" (above)] of $2,883 [note the reversal in which method produces the larger figure from the "Second Year"] is recovered from the Balance Sheet Deferred Taxes account, and the company reports the GAAP Tax amount to shareholders.

the deferred income tax account will grow. In fact, this type of firm is most likely to need financing since it is expanding, and the conservative earnings are in error.

In contrast, consider the firm that has stopped buying new equipment and, with lower depreciation, has started paying taxes that can be accounted for through its deferred tax account. This firm is extremely *unlikely* to borrow since it is actually shrinking. Therefore, this firm is less likely to be the subject of financial analysis in the first place. Lenders are most concerned with firms that are growing and therefore need debt financing.

Finally, U.S. taxes may never be paid as long as a firm maintains its investments overseas and never repatriates its profits. This is an extremely likely scenario with the growth of multinational firms and the strongest growth occurring overseas.

3. Another reason the deferred tax account can obscure a firm's financial picture involves the dollar terms in which it is stated. In contrast to other balance sheet liabilities, which are carried at their present value (no interest that will be paid over the life is shown on the statement), *the deferred tax account is carried at its future value*. The value on the balance sheet represents the deferred taxes that will actually be the dollar value paid out at some unknown time, perhaps as long as 10, 20, or 50 years into the future when the firm stops growing. Indeed, the fundamental premise behind accelerated depreciation is the notion that paying for something in the future is cheaper than paying for it today. Governments are, in effect, giving the firm an interest-free loan for the taxes due on the difference between the depreciation timing of accelerated cost recovery and the actual depreciation of the equipment. At minimum the analyst would be better served to use some hypothetical payment period and rate for discounting deferred taxes to their present value.

4. One of the primary reasons for examining the liabilities so closely is to bring awareness to the problem of determining who will have a claim on assets in case of a liquidation. Clearly, the deferred tax account is unlikely to provide the IRS with this entitlement because in a liquidation the assets are in trouble in consequence of not producing a sufficient cash flow to make a profit. Indeed, *in liquidation it is likely that the IRS's accelerated depreciation was a more accurate accounting of the true situation*. The assets will sell for what the IRS thought they were worth and the deferred tax account will self-destruct.

Those Changing Tax Rates

The final accounting problem for deferred taxes is changes in the tax rate. When the tax rate moves down, as it did when it dropped from 46% to 34% in 1986–1987, the deferred account now has too much in storage. For example, MACRS helped cut taxes during the 46% tax rate period and taxes were added to the deferred tax account in anticipation of having to pay at that same rate at some later point. However, with the lower 34% tax rate that will apply when required tax payments increase and amounts are called for from the deferred tax account, the deferred tax account will never be depleted.

This problem caused the Financial Accounting Standards Board to issue

SFAS #96 in December 1987. While many aspects of SFAS #96 have been kept optional because its unexpected complexity prevented its framers from determining all of its consequences on different firms, it has allowed corporations to adjust their deferred tax accounts to reflect lower tax rates, remarkably allowing them to reduce their deferred tax accounts by the 25% reduction in the corporate tax rate.

General Electric Corporation

In response to SFAS #96, the change in the General Electric Corporation's deferred tax account permitted an increase in income in the amount of $800 million. Not only could the deferred tax account be reduced by this amount but General Electric would be allowed to recognize any reduction in the deferred tax account as part of its net income for 1987; thus, this would finally find its way into GAAP net worth. The effect of these accounting adjustments on income created numerous options for management to engage in income smoothing. For instance, General Electric's decision adding $400 million to income from the deferred tax account nearly matched a $450 million loss that GE wished to recognize by writing off a previous investment. GE retained a significant portion of the allowable increase in income with the excuse that it was based on tax planning for future earnings. The result of this planning was a substantial pool of remaining unrecognized earnings.

Then, the analyst should be asking himself: What would happen if the corporate tax rate increased in the future? This represents another situation in which running all balance sheet adjustments through the income statement can be problematical; *a one-time direct adjustment to GE's equity account would have made the prediction of future income less uncertain.*

If corporate income tax rates begin changing on a more regular basis in the future, financial statements will be extremely difficult to analyze. It is conceivable that swings in deferred tax accounts, especially for capital-intensive companies, could create artificial earnings, or conversely, wipe out earnings on a regular basis. Although such changes may be correct from the point of view of accrual accounting, they have nothing whatsoever to do with whether or not a company can repay its loans.

Key Points: To make the decision of whether to carry deferred taxes as equity or debt, consider:
—the growth rate of the company;
—the probability of changes in the tax law;
—the probability of the company having taxable profits in the future; and
—the desirability of discounting the deferred tax as a compromise reduction.
If a company is shrinking and its product is generating cash for which there is little opportunity for reinvestment, it is unlikely that the deferred tax account will long remain at its current levels. In this case, spread the deferred taxes as a liability. In other cases, add to the net worth section

of the shareholders any amount that you discount from the net amount of deferred taxes provided by the GAAP books.

Foreign Exchange—SFAS #52

Foreign exchange accounting is an area of great difficulty and complexity; it is only important when substantial subsidiaries exist in foreign countries. The accounting varies considerably depending on whether the U.S. dollar or a foreign currency is the functional one for each subsidiary. Therefore, access to senior management is essential to sort out the various results. The dollar is the functional one if:

- Receivables, payables, and debt are denominated in dollars.
- Prices of the products produced are influenced by worldwide competition.
- There are many inputs of parts and services from the United States as well as extensive parent/subsidiary interrelations. (Many South American subsidiaries are carried here because of high inflation rates present in their economies.)

Although there is further discussion of this topic in Chapter 6 concerning the more complex income statement issues, particularly the impact on the income statement and its meaning to forecasts, here are some balance sheet basics:

1. When a *foreign currency is the functional one*, the balance sheet is translated at the end-of-period rate with gains and losses posted to a separate shareholder equity account.
2. When the *functional currency is the U.S. dollar*, monetary items are translated at new currency rates and gains and losses are recognized in net income; non-monetary items are translated at historical cost exchange rates, not impacting net income.

Management usually prefers to have the functional currency be a foreign one because of the limited impact on the income statement. As a consequence, management may have decentralized the foreign unit with more autonomy or minimal remittances moving directly to the parent to qualify for this treatment. Sometimes, remittances are sent to another foreign subsidiary that clearly qualifies to have a foreign currency as its functional one. In this case, the balance sheet carries values more nearly current than the dollar currency option does.

Decision Errors

Two fundamental errors can be made in any investment decision. The *type one* error is investing money in a project or a firm that does not repay. Frequently, investment officers are warned by senior management to totally avoid these errors. But in attempting to avoid a type one error, another error can be made. A *type two* error results from declining an investment or request from a borrower that would have repaid the investment. If the LIFO value for inventory is merely transferred to an analysis spreadsheet without any adjustment, inventory—and the company's net worth—may be so grossly understated that the lender will wrongly conclude that no money should be lent to or invested in the business. The investment officer will thus commit a type two error. The paradox is that saying no may appear safe but may be an error of equally difficult consequences, especially over the long run.

Key Points: It is possible to be too conservative in investment analysis and thereby refuse a loan to a creditworthy company.

Review of Completed United Enterprises Spread

To recapitulate and summarize the balance sheet revaluation and analysis spreadsheet section of the book, Exhibit 4-3 presents the United Enterprises, Inc. (UEI) financial statements (originally shown as Exhibit 1-1) filled into a copy of the balance sheet Worksheet IA (originally shown as Exhibit 2-2A).

First, the financial statements of UEI have been directly transferred to the first two columns of the worksheet with only modest changes to accommodate its more universal asset and liability names. Cases in point are:

- The inventories have been subdivided into raw materials, work-in-process, and finished goods.
- Property, plant, and equipment have been initially recorded *gross* from the company's own footnotes before showing the deduction for cumulative depreciation.
- Special preference stock, paid-in capital, and retained earnings have all been lumped into common stock, because the distinction is irrelevant to the lender.

A change in appearance has resulted from rounding the numbers to millions, rather than the thousands used in the financial statement. However, major changes have resulted in the presentation in the third column to the right. The notes which follow relate to the third column numbers in Exhibit 4-3.

Note 1: Marketable Securities

Footnote K (Exhibit 1-1) describes the subsequent event of acquiring Master Lighting for $41.7 million. This event took place effective January 1, 1991, just a few hours after the date at the top of the statement. It is clear that UEI had accumulated funds to complete the transaction on the 31st of December; carrying these funds in the current section of the balance sheet (row 2) causes the marketable securities account to be higher than the funds really available for current asset purposes. The proceeds in the Time Deposits account will undoubtedly be applied directly to the purchase of Keystone.

The analyst should carry the $41.7 million as an additional investment in subsidiaries {16} reducing the combination of cash and marketable securities to the amount present in the previous year. Since reducing the marketable securities produces an insufficient amount, the analyst would have to assume that UEI would borrow an additional $10.7 million under the revolving credit, long-term debt {33}.

Note 2: Accounts Receivable Trade

In examining accounts receivable the analyst needs to scrutinize the quality of these accounts. The fundamental question that is addressed in this examination is "What is the likelihood of collection of these accounts?" In investigating these accounts the analyst should look for the provisions for bad debts or an aging report of accounts receivable.

Not having access to an aging report for United Enterprises, Inc., examine the allowance for bad debts. This allowance is equal to about 2% of the total amount of accounts receivable. This is an insignificant portion in comparison to the whole and it has not grown over the two years; therefore, no adjustment is necessary for accounts receivable.

Footnote G also shows that some of the receivables are not due within the current year. Nevertheless, the amounts due beyond 1991 are only $2.8 million, probably not worth making an issue of.

Note 3: Inventory

The valuation for inventories is directly related to the concept of the going concern. While raw materials can usually be resold for nearly their original cost (assuming no rapid commodities price changes), work-in-process and finished goods are a different matter. Their value frequently depends upon the viability of the firm and its control over inventory accumulation. Footnote A (3) gives us a feeling of reliability, since it shows inventories falling with sales; the spreadsheet shows inventories at only 25% of total assets in 1990, less than the 27% registered in 1989. Furthermore, the current cost of fixed assets on page 4 of Exhibit 1-1 states that "At the end of 1990, the current cost of inventory was $168.0 million." This number is extremely close to that reported by GAAP and is clearly a result of the UEI decision to report inventories on the FIFO basis, which carries current cost on the balance sheet. The converse would be a LIFO valuation, which would have to be adjusted by the so-called LIFO reserve stated in the footnotes.

There is still an issue remaining that concerns the composition of inventory, work-in-process. Based on estimates of the employees with a vested interest in having the number be as high as possible (because of the standard cost accounting systems in place in most organizations), it is almost impossible to know what the value of work-in-process is. If UEI fails and is forced into liquidation, work-in-process will more than likely be of little value. What good is an item that is neither a finished good or raw material? How will it be valued?

(*Text continued on page 113.*)

Exhibit 4-3.
BALANCE SHEET: SPREADSHEET & BREAKUP VALUE

Company Name: United Enterprises, Inc. and Consolidated Subsidiaries

Balance Sheet Date:	31-Dec-89		31-Dec-90		Dec-90 BREAKUP VALUE		See Notes
Rounded to: millions (000,000's) ASSETS	$	%	$	%	$	%	
1 Cash	$9.8	1%	$4.9	1%	$4.9	1%	
2 Marketable Securities	$5.0	1%	$31.0	5%	$10.0	1%	1
3 Accounts Receivable - Trade	$120.9	18%	$111.0	16%	$111.0	15%	2
4 Inventories: Raw Materials	$59.2	9%	$52.5	8%	$52.5	7%	
5 Inventories: Work in Process	$50.9	7%	$40.4	6%	$20.2	3%	3
6 Inventories: Finished Goods	$77.7	11%	$74.8	11%	$74.8	10%	
7 Subtotal Inventories	$187.8	27%	$167.7	25%	$147.5	20%	4
8 Prepaid Expenses	$38.7	6%	$34.4	5%			
9 Other Current							
10 Total Current Assets	$362.2	53%	$349.0	52%	$273.4	37%	
11 Property, Plant & Equipment	$321.3	47%	$343.1	51%	$546.7	75%	
12 "Capital" Leased Equipment							
13 "Operating" Leased Equipment							
14 (Less Depreciation)	($137.0)		($157.1)		($250.3)		
15 Subtotal Net Prop, Plant & Equip.	$184.3	27%	$186.0	27%	$296.4	41%	5
16 Investments and Advances	$21.0	3%	$25.0	4%	$66.7	9%	1
17 Long Term Marketable Securities							
18 Affiliate & Sundry Receivables					$34.5	5%	4
19 Net Assets/Discontinued Operations	$62.8	9%	$55.8	8%	$47.3	6%	6
20 Other Noncurrent Assets	$14.2	2%	$13.4	2%	$13.4	2%	
21 Intangibles (Patents & Rights)							
22 Goodwill (Resulting from Mergers)	$44.3	6%	$47.3	7%			7
23 Total Fixed Assets	$326.6	47%	$327.5	48%	$458.3	63%	
24 TOTAL ASSETS	$688.8	100%	$676.5	100%	$731.7	100%	

	31-Dec-89		31-Dec-90		31-Dec-90 BREAKUP VALUE		See Notes
LIABILITIES							
25 Notes Payable	$16.0	2%	$18.3	3%	$18.3	3%	
26 Accounts Payable - Trade	$55.7	8%	$45.5	7%	$45.5	6%	
27 Taxes and Accrued Expenses	$90.6	13%	$83.5	12%	$83.5	11%	
28 Other Current							
29 Current Portion L-T Debt (Operating)	$16.8	2%	$13.2	2%	$13.2	2%	
30 Total Current Operating Liabs.	$179.1	26%	$160.5	24%	$160.5	22%	
31 Current Portion L-T Debt (Remain)							
32 Deferred or Unearned Income							
33 Long-Term Debt - Unsecured	$56.5	8%	$75.6	11%	$90.3	12%	8 & 1
34 Long-Term Debt - Secured							
35 Capital Lease Obligations	$14.9	2%	$14.1	2%	$14.1	2%	8
36 Present Value of Operating Leases							
37 Other Noncurrent Liabilities							
38 Total Senior Term Debt	$71.4	10%	$89.7	13%	$104.4	14%	
39 Subordinated Debt							
40 Unfunded Pension Obligations							
41 Deferred Taxes (Debt Portion)	$12.1	2%	$26.1	4%	$14.5	2%	9
42 TOTAL LIABILITIES	$262.6	38%	$276.3	41%	$279.4	38%	
	31-Dec-89		31-Dec-90		31-Dec-90 BREAKUP VALUE		
EQUITY							
43 Deferred Taxes (Equity Part)					$11.6	2%	9
44 Minority Interest							
45 Preferred Stock							
46 Common Stock	$156.5	23%	$165.2	24%	$165.2	23%	
47 Retained Earnings	$276.4	40%	$284.6	42%	$325.0	44%	3, 5, 6, 7 & 8
48 (Treasure Stock & Other Reductions)	($6.7)		($49.5)		($49.5)		
49 Net Worth	$426.2	62%	$400.3	59%	$452.3	62%	
50 TOTAL FOOTINGS	$688.8	100%	$676.6	100%	$731.7	100%	

These questions may be vital to individual valuation and are always extremely difficult to answer. The solution chosen here is to reduce the value by half.

Note 4: Sundry Receivables

Sundries are usually carried in the long-term side of the balance sheet because while these items—such as loans to executive officers—have note terms of less than one year, they are not expected to be collected in less than a year. Since sundry receivables cannot be separated from prepaid expenses {8}, the total prepaid expenses and sundry receivables must be carried in the long-term sundry account {18}.

Note 5: Plant, Property, and Equipment

On United Enterprises' balance sheet, these fixed assets are currently valued on an historical cost basis. Thus the values given do not accurately reflect the replacement cost or market value of these particular assets. In lieu of current cost accounting data, the analyst could attempt to index these assets to the annual percentage change of the Consumer Price Index. The CPI is available in publications of the Bureau of Labor Statistics, U.S. Department of Labor [Washington, D.C., updated annually]. Nevertheless, applying the broad shopping-basket weighted prices of the CPI to the industrial manufacturing assets of UEI is a deceptively simplistic approach. This could only be justified as a last resort in the absence of current cost information (page 4 of Exhibit 1-1) or lack of fire insurance appraisals directly obtained from the firm.

The Current Cost restatement {15} in the third column is largely drawn from footnote D, page 4 of Exhibit 1-1. It tells us that "At the end of 1990, the current cost of . . . property plant and equipment (net) was $296.4 million." While the wiles of management may be at work here to boost this number to a high value, there is a penalty to pay for having it higher than GAAP. That penalty to net income is reviewed in Chapter 6.

Since there is insufficient information to determine gross assets or the current cost depreciation reserve, they have been estimated. First, find the proportional relationship between the 1990 GAAP values of gross property plant and equipment and the net property plant and equipment, as well as the relationship of the depreciation reserve and the net property plant and equipment. Next apply them to the current cost net property plant and equipment building backwards to the generated gross property plant and equipment and the depreciation reserve.

Note 6: Net Assets of Discontinued Operations

If assets are put on the selling block, the asking price is usually negotiable; United Enterprises' footnote B obfuscates the issue. Its language hides the information an analyst would need to come to an independent appraisal of the value. To decipher the results of the sales of the 14 operating divisions, analysts must set up their own calculations:

Item	Amount in Millions
Initial loss reserve	$ 86.1
Operating losses subsequent to June 1989	11.4
Remaining reserve after nine dispositions	46.8
Apparent loss on disposition of nine units	$ 27.9
Cash and notes received on dispositions	$ 23.9
Estimated original book value of dispositions	$ 51.8
Proportion of original book value received	46%
Currently reported net assets held for sale	$ 55.8
Remaining reserve after nine dispositions	46.8
Original book value of remaining assets	$102.6
This analyst's estimate of actual proceeds to be received (approximately 46% of $102.6)	47.3

In summary this analyst believes that in any sales effort, the best stuff with the most realistic prices go first. The leftovers have been overpriced and will need a reduction to be moved; UEI will probably take an additional loss of at least $8.5 million.

Note 7: Excess of Cost Over Net Assets of Purchased Businesses

UEI is in industrial goods markets, not brand-loyal consumer markets. Therefore, it is difficult to see how goodwill should be carried. The value of goodwill in a breakup normally represents items such as trademarks, patents, franchises, or a customer list. It is extremely difficult to put a value on such intangible elements as customer recognition and product reputation. Further, industrial goods are usually purchased on the basis of specifications, not past reputation. Unless UEI controls markets with high entry costs, goodwill is suspect.

Moreover, footnote A (1) states that "Amortization is taken to the extent that, in the opinion of management, there has been a decline in the value of the asset." And, no amortization is taken of a regular basis on $38 million, as noted in their footnote A. Without substantial justification to the contrary—for example, evidence of patents or trademarks—the analyst must delete goodwill {22} from the balance sheet. Of course, this requires reducing the retained earnings account {47} to allow the balance sheet to balance.

Note 8: Long-Term Debt

Reviewing the long-term bonds outstanding against UEI, it is clear that some of these are at lower-than-market interest rates. Opening the opportunity for defeasance, if the current rates for the $31.3 million Sinking Fund Debentures due June 1, 2005, and the $8.6 million Other Debt due June 1, 2007, are 10%, then the market value should be lower by approximately 20%, or $7.9 million, before deducting nearly $1.9 million for the present value of the capital gain at maturity. Therefore, the long-term debt {33} should be reduced by $6.0 million and the capital lease obligations {35} of $14.1 million segregated. (Retained earnings should be increased by the $6.0 million.)

Note 9: Deferred Income Taxes

The deferred tax account has many characteristics of an equity account, and the analyst must make some determination for carrying a value for this account under the debt or equity sections. Sometimes the analyst's firm is willing to consider the deferred tax account as neither debt nor equity, but this is a simplistic statement not observing the facts.

Footnote E shows that UEI saved substantial taxes by investing in a tax shelter program, not just from accelerated depreciation. The tax shelter items should be carried in the debt portion because they will have to be repaid at the expiration of the shelter; conversely, the assets generated may have to be written off. The remaining part of the deferred tax account is carried as equity, since UEI is clearly acquiring capital assets at least as fast as it is depreciating them. Carrying on their normal course of business will continually add to the deferred tax account, thus leaving behind a portion of this amount indefinitely.

If a company is shrinking its physical assets or has just built a massive new plant and is not expecting to spend as much on capital goods in the near future, it is conceivable that the deferred tax account may have to actually be paid to the IRS. It is clear that UEI is at least replacing its capital goods on a basis equal to or greater than its depreciation amounts. Therefore, it is likely that a part of the deferred tax account is really a segregated reserve account within the equity section {43}, not a debt {41} that would have to be repaid.

Chapter 5

Spreading the Income Statement—The Basics

Introduction

Asset and liability revaluation analysis of modern firms has shown that the traditional analyst's belief that the balance sheet is sound only if it exhibits high liquidity and low debt is too simplistic. High interest rates militate against the luxury of high liquidity and cheaper and more innovative debt markets have simultaneously encouraged firms to borrow more and also to hide it from investors and lenders. This forces the analyst to look more deeply into the other financial statement components.

Cash Flow vs. Income

Turning to the income statement, there is another widely accepted view that also may be erroneous, namely that net income is an indicator of future debt-paying capacity. This commonly held belief is that creditors are paid with profits just as dividends are paid from profits. Thus, the argument goes, by reviewing a couple of years of income statements, an analyst can garner sufficient information to predict future performance. Actually, rumors to the contrary notwithstanding, *debts and dividends are both paid for with cash*. Since the analyst usually will not be permitted to look at, let alone analyze, the cash journal, income will become a prime component of the cash flow used to pay debts and dividends.

Therefore, this chapter will look at net income primarily for its insights into cash generation—and wherever the accrual concept becomes the paramount accounting position, the chapter will sound a note of despair. Meanwhile, management has focused a considerable amount of its attention on shaping the income statement to its wiles, with the auditors gamely resisting. Not only does management want to look good relative to competitors but for internal and external purposes high earnings are vital.

- Earnings bring financial and non-monetary rewards to top management.
- Earnings give suppliers the motivation to keep prices low and quality high.

116

- Earnings provide assurance to customers that the firm will prosper in the future, continuing to supply quality goods and services.
- Earnings afford a basis for future capital infusions if the firm grows.

In the traditional assessment of the statement of income, the proportions of cost of goods sold, other operating expenses, and interest expense are compared to revenues. This approach is superficial in that it (1) emphasizes absolute relationships between the various components of the income statement and (2) is based on the assumption that the accountant has made the proper estimates in expense matching and accrual of income.

The fact is, the statement of income shows the accrual approach to wealth generation. It reflects the accountant's view about how much the company has improved during the fiscal period. Moreover, the notion that every aspect of a company's operations can be summed up in a single number, net income, is clearly oversimplified. If, in the past operating period, a strike or a failure of a major client or supplier took place, the lender must analyze the impacts on normal operations and use the information to predict future results. Despite all of the emphasis that is attached to it, net income is the remainder after a number of estimated expenses, the result of many steps that potentially are composed of risks.

Sustainable Earnings

The analyst's objective is to assess the firm's ability to sustain earnings. Reliable future projections of earnings require a dependable base on which to begin the forecast. The forecast is essential since every investment and loan is predicated on a forecast that the money invested will be repaid. *The job of the analyst and this section, then, is to examine the quality of the income statement components* including sales, cost of goods sold, depreciation, and other expenses. Some of the more complex effects on income, including results of foreign operations, extraordinary items, and discontinued operations, are included in Chapter 6. Some of the initial problems include the following:

- The income statement is commonly prepared covering an arbitrary time period.
- Revenues include sales that have not yet been collected, but remain in accounts receivable.
- Work in process percentages are particularly difficult to estimate, since the suppliers of the estimates cannot necessarily be depended on for accuracy.
- Values of cost of goods sold result from collecting and capitalizing the costs of production using conventions like FIFO and LIFO, which are estimates themselves. (This is discussed in Chapter 6.)

Introduction to Income Statement vs. Operating Cycle

A crucial analytical point in question concerning the usefulness of any income statement is its relationship to the operating cycle. Reflect that the annual income statement attempts to determine the profits in a company such as Chivas Regal whose manufacturing process takes 12 years; plainly they are only a rough estimate. In contrast, a one-year income statement would give more than good grasp of the profits of the typical restaurant. A shorter time period might be sufficient, but some restaurants' business is seasonal, causing a quarterly report to be deceiving. Exhibit 5-1 shows a simple diagram of the operating cycle—the time involved in converting raw materials to cash. It typically consists of four steps, each of which carries significant risk, inducing uncertainty into the estimation of net income:

Step 1. Raw materials and manufacturing facilities are purchased.
Step 2. The materials are converted to a product or service.
Step 3. Next, the product or service is sold, creating accounts receivable.
Step 4. Finally, the receivables are collected and converted into cash.

Each of these highlights an important part of estimating (rather than calculating) income. Think of how complex the first step can be, as shown in the following example.

Investing in a New Factory

Acquiring manufacturing capability is an important cost element of the profit estimation process for the reason that in constructing a new factory or office building the costs become part of fixed assets for future depreciation—a charge

Exhibit 5-1.

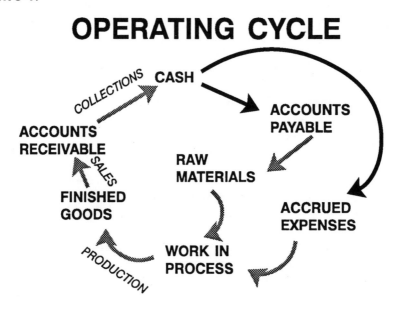

OPERATING CYCLE

against income. Consider the risks of miscalculating costs in each of the following initial parts of the construction process:

1. The firm hires an architect who converts the specifications of floor space, lighting, number of employees, and a given budget and zoning code into structural drawings.
2. The drawings are approved by the company and the local community in which the building will be constructed.
3. After considering a number of bids, the firm accepts the lowest bid, thereby choosing a contractor.
4. The contractor begins acquiring building materials and hiring supervisors, workers, and subcontractors.
5. And so on . . .

Most expenditures appear first as capitalized assets on the balance sheet—in the case of step 2 of the operating cycle, the capitalized expenditures appear as inventory. Only eventually do they appear as expenses in the income statement. The risks in step 2 of the operating cycle, manufacturing products, is illustrated by the firm whose workers are unionized and whose management–worker relationships are tense. If a strike brings production to a halt, the effect on the entire business would be catastrophic.

Another example of the risks inherent in estimating net income can be found in step 3, that of selling the product or service. Consider the previous example (Chapter 2) of the overdependent supplier to Sears, Roebuck & Co. Since Sears may purchase a substantial amount of the supplier's product, the supplier would most likely emphasize quality production at a low cost, rather than marketing. However, if for reasons beyond that supplier's control Sears were to suddenly reduce its purchases, that supplier might be unable to continue in business. The rewards and risks of dealing with primarily one customer are great in a business downturn.

These risks inhibit the development of knowledge about the interim status of any business before it is terminated. It causes us to consider the **period of the operating cycle** along with the annual or quarterly income statement in producing this base forecasting period. The operating cycle is the time it takes to complete the four steps above (albeit, not building a new plant). Some analysts call this the cash-to-cash cycle and there will be more focus on it in Chapter 7.

Spreadsheet Computer Template

As noted in Chapter 2, trying to fulfill the needs of proper analysis while also producing a finished report readable by senior management is a puzzle that may be partially solved by resorting to a personal computer format. With the computer, it is possible to use one column of a spreadsheet to reorganize the information for the analyst's purposes while also producing the more standard, unadjusted information. Exhibit 5-2A is another worksheet included in LOTUS 1-2-3 format on the floppy disk available with this book.

(Text continued on page 123.)

Exhibit 5-2A.

INCOME STATEMENT AND CASH FLOW: TREND ANALYSIS & ADJUSTED VALUES

WORKSHEET 2A

Company Name: _____

Statement Dates: _____

Rounded to: millions (000,000's)

INCOME STATEMENT	$	%	$	%	$	%	ADJUSTED VALUES $	%
1 **Net Sales (Revenues)**								
2 Cost of Goods Sold (Less Dep)								
3 Depreciation Expense								
4 **Gross Profit**								
5 Selling Expense								
6 General & Admin. Expense								
7 Officers' Compensation								
8 Other Operating Expenses								
9 **Operating Income**								
10 Other Non-Operating Income								
11 (Interest Expense)								
12 Interest Income								
13 (Other Non-Operating Expense)								
14 (Plant Closings & Writedowns)								
15 Earnings on Equity Investments								
16 **Profit Before Tax**								
17 Income Tax								
18 **Income Fr Continuing Operations**								
19 Net Profit fr Discont Operations								
20 Gain (Loss) on Sale of Operations								
21 **Income (Loss) Before Extraordin.**								
22 Extraordinary Income (Loss)								
23 **Net Profit**								

CASH FLOW STATEMENT			
24	Net Income Fr Continuing Operations		
25	Depreciation & Amortization		
26	Change in Deferred Taxes		
27	Adjustment to Reconcile Net Income		
28	**Funds Flow From Operations**		
29	(Increase in Accounts Receiveable)		
30	(Incr. in Inventory & Other Cur. Ass.)		
31	Increase in Accounts Payable		
32	Incr. in Accurals & Other Cur. Liabs		
33	**Net Cash Provided By Operations**		
34	Fixed Asset Sales		
35	(Net Capital Expenditures)		
36	(Purchase of Companies/Assets)		
37	**Funds After Investments**		
38	Increase in Long-Term Debt		
39	Issuance (Purchase) Own Stock		
40	(Dividends)		
41	**Net Change In Cash and Equiv.**		

NOTES:
1. Positive number = a Source of Cash, and a Negative number = a Use of Cash
2. You may have only enough information to just complete the current year cash flow

Exhibit 5-2B.

INCOME STATEMENT AND CASH FLOW RATIOS

Company Name:			
Statement Date:			
ADDITIONAL INFORMATION FOR RATIO DERIVATION			**Adjusted Values**
1 Interest Expense Capitalized			
2 Effective Tax Rate			
(Provision for Taxes net Deferred Taxes) / (Profits Before Taxes)			
3 Accounts Receivable, net			
4 Accounts Payable			
5 Inventory (including LIFO reserve)			
6 Total Fixed Assets			
7 Operating Lease Rentals			
8 Current Portion Long Term Debt			
9 Total Term Debt (including CPLTD)			
10 Net Worth			
LIQUIDITY RATIOS			
11 Times Interest Earned (EBIT/Int.)			
12 SEC Earnings Coverage			
(Earnings From Operations before Taxes and Interest Exp. + + Op Lease Rent / Interest + Op Lease Rent)			
13 Receivables Turnover (Days)			
14 Tot Inventory Turnover (Days)			
15 Payables Turnover (Days) (ACP)			
DEBT REPAYMENT CAPACITY			
16 Funds Available for Fixed Chgs			
(Funds Flow From Operations + Taxes Paid + Interest Expense + Operating Lease Rentals)			
17 Debt Repayment Capacity Coverag			
(Funds Available for Fixed Charges) / (Interest + Op. Ls. Rentals + Cur. Por. Long-Term Debt)			
18 EBIT/Earn Bef Taxes (Leverage)			
19 Funds Flow fr Operat. / Cur Mat LT			
20 Funds Flow / Capital Equip Exp			
21 Funds Flow / Dividends			
22 Funds Flow/Cur. Portion LTD			
24 Capital Equip Exp/Depreciation			
25 Term Debt/ Cash Flow			
OPERATING PERFORMANCE			
(Common size analysis in Spread Sheet section)			
26 Operating Cycle (Days)			
27 Net Operating Cycle (Days)			
28 Fixed Asset Turnover (S/FA)			
29 Return (Repeatable) on Assets			
30 Return (Repeatable) on Equity			

Sales Revenues {1}*

The accounting profession has accepted the legal definition of when a *sale* occurs. For legal and accounting purposes, a sale *occurs when products or services are delivered*. It is totally unconnected to cash generation, although in some instances cash may be involved. For instance, a grocery store purchase is typically complete when cash is exchanged for groceries.

A department store purchase, on the other hand, is different. Department store sales are often paid for through store charges or credit cards. With respect to the latter, the financial institution that issued the credit card will reimburse the department store. Reimbursement aside, generally accepted accounting principles require that the sale be recognized at the time the merchandise is taken from the store.

Health Club

A health club is an example of a business in which delivery of products and services may not always be straightforward. Upon joining a health club you are encouraged to pay for the entire membership up front. (Paying in advance, explain health club managers, helps build a commitment to exercise.) If you are unable to make the full payment at once, you will be encouraged to sign up on a monthly payment plan—typically a contract that stipulates that you owe the health club money even if you never enter its doors again.

How should the health club account for the sale? Is service going to be supplied by the health club over some period of time into the future?

- No new equipment will be put into the health club.
- Lights will not be kept on longer.
- More people will not be hired.

It turns out there is nothing to prevent the health club from immediately recognizing the earnings generated from the customer's signing the contract except continuing to operate the business, which brings more contracts and more revenues. So, in the past, the health clubs sold the accounts receivable, the year-long payment plan to which the customer had agreed. The membership contract typically stated that if it were assigned to an independent finance company, the customer had to pay the full amount due regardless of any claim against the health club. This clause was an attempt by the health club to make the contract negotiable to the finance company. It meant that the customer would have to pursue any case against the health club separately without involving the finance company that had acquired the contract. It was a good arrangement for all involved except the consumer.

*Numbers in braces refer to line numbers in Exhibit 5-2A.

European Health Spas

In the late 1970s when the health clubs took consumers to court to enforce the terms of these contracts, many judges declared the contracts unconscionable and unenforceable because they knew of the hard sell approach to convincing consumers to sign such contracts. European Health Spas was so hurt financially by these court rulings that its parent company had to sell off the individual clubs to other investors. Moreover, the parent company's captive finance subsidiary, USI Credit, which had acquired much of the European Health Spas' paper, also suffered substantial losses and had to assure creditors that it would not buy uncollateralized receivables from affiliates in the future.

Despite the seeming legality of the contract—and thus the accounting recognition of a sale and validity of the book value of the account receivable—the health club's arrangement seemed unreasonable from the start. Thus, the analyst should bear in mind that if a practice seems excessive, others, namely judges, may agree.

Income Recognition at Banks

Interest recognition is a current problem for bankers. The convex curve in Exhibit 5-3 shows the level of interest income as it is traditionally recognized on a loan of equal payments. Income determined by the so-called **gross yield method** is highest at the front of the loan based *solely* on the amount of principal outstanding. This income recognition method assumes that there is no credit risk in the loan and that the only consideration for the recognition of income is the amount of principal involved. Although this method is straightforward, it has little basis in reality. To further illustrate the point, look at this case:

Exhibit 5-3.

$1,000 Loan with interest at 10%

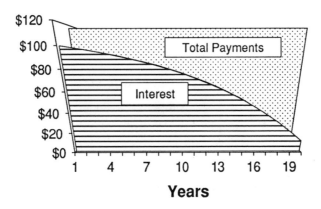

Years

Bank Income Recognition

Assume that a bank has made a new installment loan with even payments of principal and interest being made each year until full amortization of the principal: Refer to the cash-flow line in the following exhibits. (The horizontal line at the $170 mark shows the yearly cash flow.)

A. Level Payments

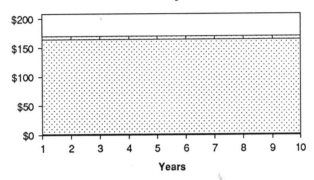

Now, envision a hypothetical meeting of three bank officers who, for the sake of argument, have to determine how to recognize this loan's income. The bank chairman wants to look good to the shareholders by generating high earnings. He urges that all income on the transaction be recognized from early loan payments and all principal payments come from the later loan payments. His notion of income is indicated by the front-ended income chart.

B. Front-ended Income

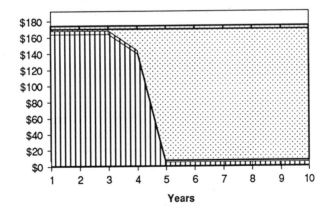

The senior credit officer strongly disagrees. He urges that principal be recovered from the initial payments and income be recognized only after the entire principal is repaid. His view of income is represented by the principal recovery first chart. All moneys received to the left will be considered principal payments, and all payments to the right are interest. The senior credit officer and the bank president have exactly opposite views.

C. Income After Principal Recovery

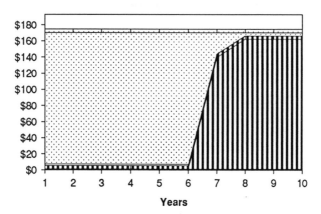

The vice-chairman suggests a compromise. He suggests taking a fixed proportion of the loan payment as income in each year of the transaction. The vice-chairman's suggestion is represented by the horizontal line at about the $60 mark.

D. Level Income

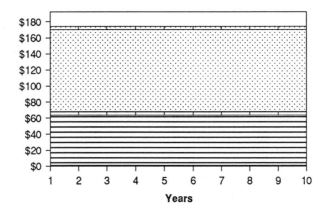

Which opinion is closest to the way the income is recognized by generally accepted accounting principles? Although none of the patterns match precisely, the generally accepted accounting principles method shown in Exhibit 5-3 most closely matches the line representing the chairman's suggestion!

The gross yield method ignores risk of default. All that is necessary is an accounting and allocating of the repaid funds based exclusively on the amount of loaned funds outstanding. Borrower solvency is assumed even when payments are not made for four to six months; then, the loan must be written off in summary fashion against an all-too-frequently insufficient loan loss reserve. Earnings on a loan cannot really be known, however, until all principal is returned. Recognition of inflows on any long-term loan is thus only an estimate of profit.

With regard to Latin American loans made by American banks throughout the 1970s, if the senior credit officer in the example above had had his way about the income recognition only *after* the principal was recovered, the major banks would have been less profitable over the 1970s and early 1980s, but they would have avoided the stupendous losses exemplified by Citibank's $2.5 billion write-off in 1987. If the bank reflects on the repayment risks on any loan, it would not recognize the earnings strictly based on the amount of principal outstanding. Here is another case in point where *accountants are just estimating what the earnings are.*

Key Points: The most common method of income recognition on loans and bonds often ignores risk aspects of the security.

Alternate Income Recognition for Contractors

Because of the extended period over which their jobs are completed, contractors recognize income using two methods: (1) the completed contract method and (2) the percentage of completion method. Under the **completed contract method** the contractor capitalizes all expenses onto the balance sheet as part of contracts in progress. If the contract called for progress payments, they would be carried as a liability account—either as deposits or payments under contracts in progress. The assumption behind this method is that the completion time for the contract or its final cost is subject to too much uncertainty to make any interim calculations. Unfortunately, many income statements must be prepared before contract completion, and using this method provides the analyst with no approximations of how expectations of expenses and revenues match each other.

In the **percentage of completion method,** an initial budget is drafted that designates a profit percentage. As under any progress payment plan, representatives of the buyer and seller meet periodically and negotiate the percentage of completion number on which the customer's invoice will be based. Then, the proportional costs are allocated against the revenues. If costs are below what was initially budgeted, the budgeted cost amount is expensed and a deferred income account is set up on the liability side of the balance sheet. The hypothesis is that the contractor was lucky at the beginning of the contract, coming in under the expected costs, but compensating bad luck will occur later in the contract. Percentage of completion is a conservative approach to income recognition and can give the analyst a much clearer idea of what is taking place on a period-to-period basis than the completed contract method.

Key Points: Contractors recognize income using either the completed contract method or the percentage of completion method. The latter is the one that gives better estimates of the firm's operations.

Income Recognition for Equipment Rental Firms

Firms in the equipment rental business include rental car companies such as Avis, and office equipment companies such as Xerox and IBM. When they operate on a short-term rental basis, the cost of the equipment for these companies is carried as rental fleet on the balance sheet, and depreciation is expensed against rental payments. This accounting practice provides significant information to the analyst concerning contract performance, the firm's success in negotiating lease contracts, and its servicing capability. In this respect, it is similar to a percentage of completion method of income recognition. If the estimates on the equipment life are incorrect, then the renter will return the equipment before sufficient funds have been received to fully pay for it. Conceivably, generally accepted accounting principles might suggest that the completed contract method be used by equipment lessors. That is, any recognition of income would be delayed until the lease was completed and the used equipment was sold. Another alternative would be to recognize the full revenues at the time the lease is signed, as in the health club example, or to possibly offset the revenues by unearned income. As the analyst can discern, leasing company income statements would look quite naked for their initial years if the completed contract method were required of them.

Key Points: Although there may be easier conventions to use from an accountant's perspective, the percentage of completion income recognition method is the most useful one for financial analysis of nearly every type of firm.

Universal Problems Regarding Sales Recognition

Income smoothing issues. Some selling practices have significant risks associated with them. Consider delayed billing (also called dated billing), for example. A firm nearing the end of its fiscal year may be concerned about meeting certain sales or earnings objectives. It may thus make arrangements with a customer to accept delivery of goods in exchange for delayed billing. In general, delayed billing is not proper. It can be a method for smoothing income and creating the illusion that there is an upward trend. By requesting and reviewing an accounts receivable aging report, the analyst can determine whether the firm is delaying billing.

Returns and allowances. Another potential problem area in sales recognition is returns and allowances, which can be hidden if the firm discloses only its net sales. The lender should ask for the gross sales figure and then calculate the returns and allowances.

Contingency sales. Sales with a right to return present another problem for the analyst. Contingency sales or sales on consignment are especially common in the high fashion business. The risk is that the goods will be returned and revenues will have to be reversed.

Atari

An example of return problems occurred with Atari Corporation, which sold video game cartridges to distributors for approximately $15 each. Atari's cost was probably 50 cents per cartridge; the distributors in turn sold the cartridges to stores for $20; the stores sold the cartridges to customers for $29. As competition heated up, prices fell. Atari cut its price from $15 to $10. In doing so, it lessened the value of the inventories held by its original distributors because new distributors could acquire inventory at a lower price. The relationship between Atari and its original distributors could have been chilled. In order to placate these distributors, Atari offered them a $5 accounts receivable credit per cartridge for the inventory they had on hand.

The distributors, apparently feeling more loyalty to their stores than to Atari, took advantage of the fact that Atari was not requiring an audited inventory count for the accounts receivable credit. The distributors contacted their major stores and offered them the same discount. Thus, the inventory counts they submitted to Atari included merchandise that had already been shipped. The result was that Atari had to take a $400 million writedown on its accounts receivable. This writedown caused an enormous loss for the company for the year.

In this case, Atari was not even selling on consignment. Atari feared losing its market. The wisdom of its strategy, however, is subject to question. In contrast, a primary competitor, Commodore Corporation, within the next two years had a severe problem with its distributors because it cut prices and did not protect them with credits. Commodore's sales fell for a brief time, but Atari's action was especially disruptive from a financial statement analysis point of view because it raised questions regarding the integrity of accounts receivable.

Sterling Homex

An extreme case of income recognition being faulty but difficult to detect can be found in Sterling Homex. SH built modular housing; it had obtained a few contracts for the sale of its modular buildings and it decided to begin construction under some contracts. The acquirers of the modular housing elements experienced building code problems; they asked SH to delay the intended shipment date. The slowdown in shipment caused a liquidity crisis for SH.

To forestall the inevitable, SH engaged in a fraud: It created invoices indicating that modules had been delivered and that a sale had occurred; meanwhile, it shipped modular homes out into the middle of the desert. Now the inventory was reduced and accounts receivable were created. Sterling Homex management correctly believed that it would be easier to continue borrowing funds from the banks if these institutions could see from the statements that sales were occurring, deliveries were being made, and receivables were germinating.

The analyst must verify, especially for medium-size concerns, that customers are satisfied with merchandise coming from the borrower. Although it is difficult to obtain a firm's customer list, *the value of speaking even briefly with a borrower's customer cannot be exaggerated.* Since it is the future that interests the analyst, the expectations of customers regarding future purchases are critical to any analysis. A single customer reference check in the case of Sterling Homex would have saved the reputation of the credit officers who depended on the accountant's opinion too much.

> **Key Points:** In general, be suspicious about a firm that engages in delayed (or dated) billing. If the gross sales figure does not appear on the income statement, find out what it is and calculate returns and allowances. Find out the company's policy regarding returns since it can significantly affect the value of accounts receivable.

Conclusion

SFAS #48 addresses the recognition of revenues issue and set forth six conditions that must be met before a sale can be recognized.

1. The sales price must be known at the sale date.
2. The buyer must have paid for the product or have an obligation to pay that is not contingent on resale.
3. The obligation of the purchaser must not be altered by theft or physical destruction.
4. The purchaser's organization must have real economic substance.
5. The seller must have no significant obligation to bring about a resale.
6. The amount of any future returns must be reasonably estimated.

Discernibly, whether these conditions are met may not be readily apparent to the auditors.

Direct Expenses

Cost of Goods Sold {2}

Cost of goods sold represents the *direct* expenses involved in producing a product or service. For a manufacturing company it includes the cost of raw materials, direct labor, and depreciation of the plant and equipment used in the production process. For the retailer, cost of goods sold represents the purchases of finished goods to be sold in stores. (Stores carry all other expenses as selling and administrative expenses since they are not involved in a direct processing activity that changes the goods in any way.) These direct costs are transferred to the income statement from the balance sheet where they represent part of finished goods inventory.

The method used for calculating the cost of goods sold involves considerable estimates. Cost of goods sold is calculated by:

1. Beginning inventory
2. Add all purchases
3. Subtract out ending inventory

The estimated items are the levels of beginning and ending inventory. These ending inventory levels, you might say, are physically counted and are a fairly certain number. The certainty is challenged when it comes to obtaining a "count" of the work in process, which the following example makes clear.

The Ambitious Foreman

Consider the foreman who wants to show how successful his department has been and, thus, overestimates the work in process percentage. A high work in process value results in a high ending inventory number. This in turn results in a lower cost of goods sold. When subtracted from the revenues, this low cost of goods sold results in a high operating profit. All other things being equal, this high operating profit will translate into a high net profit. On the other hand, consider the owners of a small firm. They want to pay as little in taxes as possible each year. Therefore, they will want any ending inventory number to be small. This is accomplished by underestimating the percentage of completion of the work in process inventory. Finished inventory can also be lowered in value. The resulting low ending inventory value will make the cost of goods sold high relative to the calculation using the foreman's estimate. Thus, net income and related taxes will be lower.

Key Points: The cost of goods sold is calculated by adding purchases to beginning inventory and then subtracting out ending inventory. Firms can change the cost of goods sold by improperly estimating ending inventory.

LIFO vs. FIFO Costs

The formal estimates that are part of the calculations for ending inventory are affected by inventory accounting conventions like LIFO and FIFO. Most firms use either first-in-first-out (FIFO) or last-in-first-out (LIFO) inventory methods. As mentioned in Chapter 4, FIFO calculates the cost as if all the merchandise that was originally acquired is fully consumed before any new merchandise is tapped. The LIFO inventory calculates the cost as if the base inventory stays in place and that new inventory flows across the top being skimmed off in the production process.

Accounting courses encourage FIFO as a more "natural idea" of the way inventory progresses through the company's warehouse. It does have logic: Inventory that comes in first is used first. Especially in areas of continuous process businesses, such as chemicals and oil, the idea of dumping raw materials in one end and getting finished goods at the other end apparently points to the FIFO convention as an analogy to what actually happens. The following is a true, illustrative story.

The Lazy Waitress

A bank has a private dining room facility. While a restaurant on another floor in the building sends food up in a dumbwaiter, the local branch personnel serve the food and clear the table. Ann, whose primary job is filing checks, dons a waitress uniform about 11:00 A.M., sets up the private dining room, and proceeds to serve lunch to the officers and their clients or prospects.

One of Ann's duties is to refill the condiment containers. It is over this task that she and the operations manager of the branch conflict. At one point he comes into the pantry as she is setting up the day's lunch and sees that she is "topping off" the condiment containers. He carefully explains to her that it would not do for an important bank customer to dip his spoon into the sugar bowl and end up with some sugar that might have been lying around on the bottom for three months. In the manager's opinion some procedure is necessary to keep track of when Ann puts sugar in each bowl. His concern over this issue eventually becomes a fetish, and other officers realize that he is making a great to-do over nothing.

This example shows that FIFO is just a convention, not truth. It allows the company accountants to account for inventory without having to track each grain of sugar, each nut and bolt. Supply bins are used in many assembly areas today. While some bins are conceivably constructed so that the bottom opens and the parts originally brought first to the factory are used first, this is by no means universal. LIFO is also a reasonable approximation of many real-life cases. All conventions are just that—approximations.

What remains to be investigated is the impact these conventions have on net earnings. The proposition to be proved here is that *LIFO results in a truer picture of income* if the inflation rate changes from year to year whereas FIFO inherently distorts income when price levels change.

Quality of Income

Exhibit 5-4 shows how the effect of inflation on income differs depending on whether LIFO or FIFO is used. The first column of Exhibit 5-4 represents the base year in which a firm sells a certain number of products at a profit. This schedule could be prepared to help the firm choose between two options: FIFO and LIFO. For the first year after the present (base) year, assume that the inflation rate averages 10%. Unit sales in that year are level with the base year's and the dollar sales figure has increased only as a result of inflation. Normally, purchases (cost of goods sold) will increase proportionally with inflation as well.

The ending inventory varies depending on whether LIFO or FIFO is used. Under FIFO the old inventory is theoretically completely sold and the firm is left with an inventory of newly purchased units and a 22% profit increase! Therefore, the firm earns a significant profit on the beginning inventory that was on the balance sheet at the old, pre-inflation cost. *Under LIFO,* the firm theoretically uses up all the new inventory first. It is thus left with the old inventory in place. As Exhibit 5-4 shows, this eliminates the holding gains from

Exhibit 5-4.

LIFO VERSUS FIFO INCOME RECOGNITION

	# UNITS	BASE PERIOD $	YEAR 1 10% INFLATION FIFO	LIFO
SALES	10	$1,000	$1,100	$1,100
BEGIN INVENTORY	5	$350	$350	$350
PURCHASES	10	$700	$770	$770
END INVENTORY	5	$350	$385	$350
COST OF GOODS SOLD	10	$700	$735	$770
NET INCOME		$300	$365	$330
CHANGE IN NET INCOME			21.67%	10.00%

	# UNITS	YEAR 2 15% INFLATION FIFO	LIFO	YEAR 3 5% INFLATION FIFO	LIFO
SALES	10	$1,265	$1,265	$1,328	$1,328
BEGIN INVENTORY	5	$385	$350	$443	$350
PURCHASES	10	$886	$886	$930	$930
END INVENTORY	5	$443	$350	$465	$350
COST OF GOODS SOLD	10	$828	$886	$908	$930
NET INCOME		$437	$380	$421	$398
CHANGE IN NET INCOME		19.79%	15.00%	-3.81%	5.00%

	# UNITS	RECAPITULATE YEAR 3 5% INFLATION FIFO	LIFO	YEAR 4 5% INFLATION FIFO	LIFO
SALES	10	$1,328	$1,328	$1,395	$1,395
BEGIN INVENTORY	5	$443	$350	$465	$350
PURCHASES	10	$930	$930	$976	$976
END INVENTORY	5	$465	$350	$488	$350
COST OF GOODS SOLD	10	$908	$930	$953	$976
NET INCOME		$421	$398	$442	$418
CHANGE IN NET INCOME		-3.81%	5.00%	5.00%	5.00%

inventory and results in an operating profit that increases 10% *in tandem with the 10% inflation rate.*

Turning to the second year, notice that the inflation rate has increased to 15%. LIFO income again increases by 15%, keeping up with inflation since there is no growth in unit sales. When the inflation rate moves higher still, FIFO continues to pump dramatic 20% gains (higher than the level of inflation) into profits because it considers as cost of goods sold the old inventory value.

These profit gains are called *inventory holding gains;* they arise because the firm holds inventories that keep increasing in value during inflationary times, *not because the firm is operating efficiently.* Forecasting from this exaggerated base is difficult. LIFO causes the current cost of inventory to be reflected in the income statement and carries the lower inventory value on the balance sheet, as discussed in Chapter 4.

It is often said that FIFO earns more profit in inflation and LIFO earns more profit in deflation. Unfortunately, this aphorism is misleading and largely irrelevant since (1) firms cannot switch cost conventions back and forth at will and (2) deflation is a truly rare event. In fact, the IRS does not permit firms to use different inventory conventions for tax purposes than are used for shareholders under GAAP. Nevertheless, let's look at what happens when the rate of inflation falls, a more likely event.

Falling Inflation: FIFO Income Becomes Illogical

In the third year, the rate of inflation has fallen to 5%. *When the rate of inflation falls, FIFO profits drop, sometimes dramatically*—in the example, the fall from a 15% to 5% inflation rate caused FIFO profits to drop 4%. While any positive rate of inflation exists, FIFO profits still remain higher than LIFO profits. The worst part of it is the erratic income pattern under FIFO. FIFO does not result in the sort of base model an analyst would want to use for forecasting future income. Turning to year 4 in Exhibit 5-5, you can see that if the United States were able to keep the rate of inflation stable from year to year, both FIFO and LIFO would produce the same change in the net income. FIFO depends on a stable monetary unit to determine net income. LIFO does not; it contributes the most current cost of inventory to the income statement as an expense.

Key Points: LIFO income fluctuates more closely with inflation than FIFO income. It is difficult to forecast from a base of FIFO income.

LIFO Liquidation

Many accountants are concerned that recognition of inventory holding gains is not restricted to FIFO. LIFO liquidation permits a firm that has used the LIFO convention for several years during inflation to engage in income smoothing toward the end of the year by running down its inventory. As a firm uses its extremely low-valued inventory, which was on the balance sheet as an early cost, income can be materially increased.

This issue raises two important points. The first is the *prudent way to correct the loophole for manipulation of income is that GAAP should require firms to increase the inventory on the balance sheet to current cost (FIFO) value, reflecting the difference in a reserve account in the net worth* section. This would have the effect of continuing to run the most current costs through the income statement (like LIFO) without permitting a firm to enjoy income smoothing later as a result of liquidating inventories carried on the balance sheet at extremely low costs.

The second point is that firms that need credit are not the same firms that are calmly liquidating inventory. Generally, firms in need of financing are experiencing a growth in sales and could not afford to liquidate inventory. The conclusion is that it is less dangerous for the financial analyst—who is trying to project income—to have firms all using LIFO than using FIFO since the expanding firms are the ones coming in to borrow.

> **Key Points:** The analyst must somehow separate the profits a firm makes into profits from operations and profits from inflation to perfect his projection of debt repayment ability.

Depreciation {3}

Depreciation is the allocation of fixed asset acquisition costs into the products or services the firm produces. It is generally not separated out on the income statement and must be obtained from the cash flow statement. See Chapter 2 for a preliminary discussion of the concept and meaning of depreciation. While straight-line and usage methods are fairly intuitive, declining balance and sum of years digits methods are not. In general, the analyst will not be involved in calculating depreciation because straight-line and usage methods are invariably those in use today by public corporations. Further, the analyst can be sure that management rarely underestimates the useful life of a piece of equipment for GAAP reporting purposes. In fact, an example to come explores how management contrives to restate prior years' income by deciding, ex post facto, that the original useful life estimate was too short and by recalculating all past years' depreciation charges downward.

For the non-public firm that reports accelerated depreciation because it just keeps one set of books, and they are by necessity tax books, the analyst may be curious about the methods. The other methods are substantially different than straight-line and the difference that can be made in net income by sticking to straight-line are clear by looking at the two most popular conventions.

1. The declining balance method can be of different percentages. The most popular are the 150% and the 200% declining balance methods. The tax law enacted in 1986 brought the 200% method to prominence in the name of modified accelerated cost recovery system (MACRS). Because of complexities related to the first year half year convention (only six months of depreciation is taken), the IRS publishes tables stipulating the rate of depreciation. The following is an example for a piece of equipment qualifying for the *five-year class.*

Useful Life Year	MACRS Amount
1	20.0%
2	32.0
3	19.2
4	11.52
5	11.52
6	5.76

The double declining balance **MACRS method** is ascertained mathematically by first calculating the straight-line amount, which is 20% per year. Next, multiply that amount times the declining balance percentage, which is 200% in this illustration. Thus, the first year's depreciation would be 100%/5 years equals 20% rate, times the 200% equals 40%, but because of the half year convention, this is reduced to 20% again. For the next year, take the straight-line 20% rate times the remaining balance of 80%; this equals 16%; now multiply times the 200% for 32% of the original amount. The next year is calculated by multiplying the 20% straight-line rate times the balance of 48% times 200%, and so on. However, the law stipulates that the taxpayer may take the balance on the straight-line method, should it prove greater. (This is done to allow the balance to be finally used up, since taking a percentage of a declining balance would never create zero.) Therefore, since for the last 1.5 years the remaining 28.8% divided by 1.5 is larger than the declining balance calculation, the higher straight-line amount is chosen for the remaining years (11.52% versus 6.91% in the fifth year).

2. The **sum of years digits method** is entirely different and is presently not legal for tax purposes. The useful life is first estimated and then all of the digits up to and including the estimate are summed. For example, a five-year life would lead to a sum of 15 digits (add 1 through 5). Now divide 100% by 15 for the interim multiple of approximately 6.5%. For each year, the digits in reverse order become the other multiple as follows (assuming no half year convention):

Year	% Multiple	Digit Multiple	Amount
1	6.5%	5	33.5%
2	6.5	4	26.5
3	6.5	3	20
4	6.5	2	13
5	6.5	1	7

Spreading depreciation onto the spreadsheet as a separate account requires that the analyst subtract it from some other expense category to avoid increasing total expenses. The problem is that fixed asset depreciation contributes to both direct (cost of goods sold) and indirect (selling and administrative expense) accounts. The depreciation amount listed in the statement of cash flow is not designated to either cost category.

Barclays Bank's spreadsheet instruction booklet advises the financial analyst to subtract the depreciation from the selling, general, and administrative expenses account. The rationale is that the manual's British writer perceives businesses from the point of view of "the nation of shopkeepers" rather than of manufacturers. In stores, most fixed assets are devoted to the selling part of the operations, not to the direct cost of goods sold part. In the United States, however, manufacturing is still an important activity, and it would be better to break out the depreciation from the cost of goods sold since probably the bulk of the depreciation expense is derived from manufacturing machinery.

In other types of operations, especially mineral extraction, a similar cost, that of amortization, is also charged to cost of goods sold. **Amortization** generally refers to the expensing of cost items that have been capitalized onto the balance sheet such as the acquisition of a patent, with a number of years to run before expiration, or the exploration for a mineral extraction site and its development. Amortization and depreciation may be lumped together in the statement of cash flows so that you may not be able to break them out separately.

Before SFAS #33 was rescinded, current cost information was provided in sufficient detail to enable the analyst to decide to which area the depreciation should be charged. Unfortunately, this information is not longer required, and the analyst is thus unlikely to identify it. (There is further discussion of SFAS #33 in Chapter 6.) Depending on the analyst's relationship with the subject firm, it might be possible to obtain depreciation subtotals for both accounts. Otherwise, depreciation should be subtracted from the larger-cost account to create the minimum distortion, usually cost of goods sold.

By separating depreciation from other expenses on the income statement, the analyst can examine differences in the annual amounts of depreciation that corporations deduct from net income. Since *depreciation is an expense that has no cash consequence,* it is the first major item that can, depending on the allocation method used, create problems for the analyst and *demonstrate how using unadjusted income statement estimates may obscure debt repayment capabilities.*

> **Key Points:** Find out what depreciation expense for the statement period was from the cash flow statement. Include depreciation expense on the spreadsheet; adjust cost of goods sold or selling and administrative expenses accordingly so you do not overstate expenses on the spreadsheet.

The lender should also compare a company's depreciation rate (percentage of gross fixed assets taken as depreciation) to that of its competitors.

Bethlehem Steel

> Bethlehem Steel announced in the mid-1980s that it was extending the estimated useful lives of much of its plant and equipment from a modest 12 years to a more liberal 18 years. Not only did this create earnings in the current year but by restatement it changed the prior year's loss to a profit! Although this dramatically improved the firm's income statement, the resulting change in depreciation was probably in the wrong direction from an analytical viewpoint.

Whether Bethlehem Steel had taken the incorrect route or not, it would be useful for the analyst to know what the useful life estimates employed by the competitors in the industry were.

> **Key Points:** Make sure a company's rate of depreciation is in sync with the rest of the industry.

Other Operating Expenses

There are a few remaining operating expenses—those that are not directly associated with the production process. In most companies, costs other than those tied directly to production are not even considered for capitalization into inventory. They are immediately expensed. Examples include selling and marketing expenses, administrative expenses, and depreciation of any fixed assets used for selling and marketing or administration. The primary issue in examining these indirect expenses for transfer onto the spreadsheet is the possibility of income smoothing.

Income Smoothing at Its Worst

Management may attempt to make performance look better than it actually is by avoiding some expenses that may have an optional, discretionary, or elective aspect, especially for a six-month to one-year period. Typically, *management attempts to smooth out anything that might detract from a steady growth in income.* Expenses connected with maintenance are much more easily delayed than direct expenses.

In the Heinz example, mentioned in Chapter 1, officers delayed sales and altered invoices and shipping documents to imply that growth in revenues and earnings had been even. Fulfilling the budget figures became a fetish of the senior management. Thus, middle management found itself doctoring records *en masse* to produce the expected result. To be considered below are the significant effects of smoothing on maintenance, research and development, and marketing expenses.

> **Key Points:** Firms sometimes delay the recognition of indirect expenses to smooth income (i.e., to give the appearance that income is growing at a steady pace).

Maintenance {8}

While frequently considered as a part of direct expenses of producing a product or service, maintenance can also fall into the other expenses area because its continued exercise may be unrelated to output, for instance, landscaping. The important issue is that its continuance on a regular basis is susceptible to management's desire to smooth income. Skimping on maintenance—and training—is a tactic to which management frequently stoops when difficult times strike a firm. Maintenance can be delayed without serious ramifications for only a limited period before operating expenses rise due to the inefficiencies caused by lack of maintenance. (Leasing companies frequently report dismay at the lack of maintenance performed on their equipment near the end of a lease contract; the user has little stake in maintenance immediately prior to turning the equipment back to the lessor. This is clear evidence of management's control over specific maintenance items and the concurrent ability to affect income through this expense category.)

Advertising {5}

Although a firm's halting advertising for an extended period can cause problems, advertising can be curtailed for short periods without long-lasting effects, just like maintenance. Reducing advertising expense will have the effect of increasing income in the short term. The drain on future earnings and increased expenses to recover lost ground will be modest.

On the flip side, a major marketing campaign (like automobile manufacturers' rebate plans) may boost short-term earnings. By increasing advertising expenditures, especially if billings are paid in advance (a frequent requirement for media placement), income can be smoothed downward, and the firm can effectively postpone the recognition of increased profits. Advertising expenses cannot be capitalized, and because of the advance payment schedules, it is difficult to always link the expenses to the proper period.

> **Key Points:** A firm's increasing advertising and maintenance expenses can have the smoothing effect of postponing profits; cutting back will boost short-term profits. Thus, both areas are ideal for smoothing activities. Watch for variations in these areas from year to year as evidence of smoothing, thus reducing the quality of earnings.

Research and Development {8}

Besides smoothing abuses, one of the problems with research and development costs is that they must be expensed as incurred. This can create windfall profits at a later time for the firm when revenues from research have no expenses to be matched against them. The problem with windfall profits is that they make it difficult to predict future earnings.

The Financial Accounting Standards Board's SFAS #2 fails to allow the experience of the managers and the company to play a role in capitalizing these expenses. There are newborn companies, founded by talents with no experience, that should have no capitalization rights, even if they meet some standard. On the other hand, some innovative firms—like Lotus Development Corporation—have earned the right to better match expenses and revenues.

With further reference to the software industry, once a product has been developed and has been accepted in the marketplace, the software manufacturer's income soars. The manufacturing cost of the program diskettes and instruction manuals is low, and volume can be considerable. *The main issue, however, is whether the income is sustainable.* Consider VisiCorp, for instance, a company in which insufficient research and development expenditures and lack of success in upgrading the product, VISICALC, led to the departure of the employee who later developed LOTUS 1-2-3, which ultimately dislodged VISICALC. VisiCorp's high revenues were short-lived, partially because management chose not to incur the expense required to upgrade its product. It is thus extremely difficult for a lender to assess a company with only one best-selling software program. The ability to maintain performance is certainly suspect, and the lender must be careful to verify the capability of the firm to produce additional programs and upgrades.

A curious trend has developed in research and development because of the ability to capitalize costs incurred under a contract. This has stimulated the formation of joint ventures and new businesses undertaken purely for research and development. These firms can avoid showing an expense until a project is completed, allowing the parent firms to also defer the expense until later.

> **Key Points:** In certain industries, such as the software industry, mismatching of expenditures on research and development to revenues makes prediction of future net income almost impossible.

Officers' Compensation {7}

Traditionally, this category was only used for private companies that might pay officers/owners high salaries rather than dividends, for which there is no tax deduction. Today, the ability and propensity of officers of companies of all sizes to take costly salaries, bonuses, golden parachutes, and so on is a danger for lenders. Therefore, obtaining this information either from the company directly or from published records for public companies (using the SEC Form 10K report) is important. Restricting this compensation until loans are repaid is also frequent in loan covenants.

Operating Income (Loss) {9}

Operating profit can now be determined by subtracting indirect expenses from the previous subtotal, gross profits. The operating profits (before taxes, extraordinary items, non-operating income, and taxes) is occasionally viewed as *the epitome of the operating performance of the firm.*

Non-Operating Income and Expenses

Besides their primary operations, firms are required to segregate expense items not directly related to the production of goods or the providing of a service. For example, paying interest expense is considered non-operating because debt is considered a non-essential for business operation; E. I. Dupont de Nemours & Co. was renowned for not having debt on its balance sheet. In the late 1970s, however, Dupont started borrowing; today it is almost inconceivable that a business would operate without debt at least to support expansion of plants. (Apple Computer still has no long-term debt.) Therefore, the characterization of interest as non-operating remains after the situation has changed. It is an anachronism that while Capital leases are accounted for as debt with interest expensed in the non-operating areas, Operating leases are considered operating expenses and carried in cost of goods sold or under another operating expense area.

Other examples of non-operating activities include renting out an unused facility and writedowns on plants and equipment. This latter item may cause some questions for its presence here rather than in the *extraordinary* expense area discussed in Chapter 6. Current developments of recurring writedowns, as U.S. industry goes through a major transformation caused by technology and international competition, eliminated writedowns as meeting the *non-recurring* test of the extraordinary category and relegate them to non-operating.

Interest Expense and Income {11} & {12}

Interest expense and income from investments generally appear in a separate section on the income statement. These items are taken as given and, although there may be some investment risk, they usually represent a small part of the total corporate activity. *If the firm is highly leveraged and borrows substantial amounts of floating rates, interest expense can fluctuate greatly due to market rate movements.*

In the discussion on sales it was noted that, if plotted, interest income on a loan for a bank would slope downward over time. The same thing is true for interest expense for the borrower. Interest expense on a loan gradually tapers off. Income will be depressed at the beginning of the loan and high at the end because of this downward sloping interest expense recognition. Unless the firm is constantly expanding and borrowing to finance it in a relatively even flow, this restricts use of past income trends to forecast future growth. For instance, the firm that has undertaken a one-shot financing of equipment and whose sales level and other costs remain unchanged may appear to produce more net income as time passes. The analyst should bear in mind, however, that this profitability may be due more to falling interest expense rather than improved operations.

Another potential problem area involves the issue of capitalized interest expense, discussed in the Retirement Estates case in Chapter 2. This is interest expense that the firm has paid to cover borrowings incurred to finance the production of a product that, in turn, has not yet been sold; therefore, the interest cannot be matched against an incoming revenue and must be held as an asset like a deferred charge. The contradiction of (1) carrying interest expense on the income statement under *non-operating expense* (this must mean it is not directly related to production) while (2) carrying it as a capitalized item on the balance sheet because the *related revenues have not materialized* has apparently not occurred to the accounting profession! When the conflict is between the accrual concept of income and classification, accrual wins out, much to the dismay of the cash-flow–focused analyst.

Capitalized interest expense can be high in some instances, especially, for example, if a company is involved in the development of real property, such as a public utility or motel chain. It is useful to examine these capitalized costs and determine the extent to which interest capitalization takes place from the footnotes. If other information shows that the value of the property is significantly in excess of the total capitalized costs, including interest, leave it capitalized; otherwise take the cash flow approach and expense the whole amount on the income statement.

Other Income: Rent and Earnings on Equity Investments {15}

Rental income can become a material amount for companies that build or own more than their immediate needs. Another reason is retaining formerly used real estate to defer the tax consequences of taking a capital gain on its sale—until possibly a low profit year! This income could tend to smooth the business cycle–determined flows of a production-focused organization.

Other income can include dividends from non-majority-owned non-consolidated subsidiaries (remembering SFAS #94) carried on the equity method. If these amounts are substantial, a question is raised concerning the nature of the subject company's operations: Is it instead a holding company? If so, it is not a proper borrower; rather the operating subsidiaries should be lent to directly.

Other income also includes any other revenues not previously mentioned including non-material amounts of fixed asset disposition profits and profits from non-operating investments.

> **Key Points:** If not substantial, take non-operating income and expense at face value on the income statement and transfer them directly to the spreadsheet. A company's interest expense on a loan falls over time; thus, make sure that improvements in profitability are not merely the result of lower interest expense.

Plant Closings and Writedowns {14}

In the early 1980s this heading would never have been found here; it belonged in the extraordinary items account. This was before the vacillation in commodity prices caused companies as strong as American Metal Climax to take substantial writedowns year after year as they tried to adjust to changing market conditions. In order to accurately forecast the future income of companies that have not properly allocated costs (through depreciation) of their fixed assets, or set up sufficient reserves to account for their market dependency, the plant writedown account has been brought up to the pre-tax area. (Extraordinary items shows everything in an after-tax mode that reduces its significance in the eyes of observers.)

Conclusion

Without doubt, these non-operating expenses (and income) items bring to the forefront the *importance of the analyst's judgment in proper evaluation.* When the early expensing of costs is too great—as in research and development areas—later windfall profits can occur, distorting present income and leading to overly optimistic forecasts of the future. The opposite may be said for capitalizing too much interest expense, only deferring the day of truth. Moreover, a cautious stance also needs to be taken in industries where profits are dependent on fluctuating demand and supply rather than on the operating skills of managers.

Profits Before Income Taxes {16}

This heading subtotal is placed here for uniformity with most spreadsheets; it adds little. The requirement to pay taxes is as certain as any expense, and this subtotal serves primarily to highlight the existence of taxes. It is also used in certain ratios that look to the total earnings available to pay interest expense; theoretically, if interest expense equals or exceeds income before interest and taxes, no taxes would be paid, since interest expense is deductible.

Income Taxes {17}

The next step is the presentation of the income tax expense. As discussed in the deferred tax section of Chapter 4, this expense does not equal the cash the firm pays the government. Instead, the accounting *tax expense is calculated based on the corporation's effective tax rate and the earnings as presented to the shareholders* using generally accepted accounting principles under SFAS #96. This is likely to be higher than the cash outflow since the operation of the deferred tax account reserves amounts for future payment of taxes on accelerated depreciation taken now. Following are the most common timing differences.

1. **Foreign affiliates**—One of the differences is GAAP recognition of taxes on overseas income, discussed in Chapter 6. Indeed, since actual taxes are levied only on repatriation of dividends, substantial sums can build up in the deferred tax account that can only grow larger if expansion, and the concurrent need for additional investment, occurs primarily in foreign markets and dividends are not declared.

2. **Acquisitions**—Another potential feed to the deferred tax account was mentioned in Chapter 4 in the acquisition accounting section. A purchase accounting transaction usually creates increased values of assets on the balance sheet that cannot be depreciated for tax purposes. Therefore, the deferred tax account is increased for the difference between the non-existent tax benefits arising from normal depreciation. It is slowly amortized as the book depreciation exceeds the tax depreciation over the remaining life of the assets.

3. **Capitalized interest**—A third example is different treatments chosen for capitalizing interest expense for GAAP purposes but expensing it for tax purposes. This is discussed fully in this chapter.

4. **Completed contract**—Using the completed contract income recognition method for tax purposes and percentage of completion method for stockholder purposes creates another divergence between the tax books and GAAP accounting. Similar is the use of the installment method of accounting for revenues for tax purposes and the accrual (immediate) method for GAAP accounting.

5. **Miscellaneous**—This category includes using various tax incentives for expensing mineral exploration, drilling, movie production, an so on for tax purposes but capitalizing them for GAAP purposes for amortization over future years.

Finally, there are several requirements for reporting under GAAP where the IRS does not recognize that anything has happened and the tax treatment ignores the charge. Therefore, the deferred tax account is allowed to decline without the normal step of payment of taxes.

1. **GAAP losses**—Restructuring charges or other GAAP losses may create the opposite effect since losses for IRS tax purposes may not be taken on an accrual basis but must be held in abeyance until the lost assets are legally disposed of.
2. **Amortizing goodwill**—A further example is the reduction in net income from amortizing goodwill, again not reflected in IRS handling. Therefore, GAAP income taxes are reduced, but IRS taxes must await resale of the assets at a loss to permit the sale to take place.

The financial statement footnote that reconciles the amount paid to the Internal Revenue Service with the amount listed on the income statement is the most complex of all footnotes. While analysts may improve their understanding of the firm's tax situation from the footnote, *taking note of the listing of the cash taxes paid from the statement of cash flow is sufficient* for most analytical purposes. The analyst may wish to substitute this cash outlay for the GAAP tax expense on the spreadsheet, given the Chapter 4 aversion to the accrual method used for calculating the provision for income taxes.

An even more advanced approach is to review the firm's deferred tax account over the last several years. If its balance sheet account is level, then the tax shown on the income statement is probably appropriate. If the deferred tax account is falling, then the income tax amount on the statement of income is less than that paid to the IRS. Finally, and most commonly, if the deferred tax account on the balance sheet is increasing, the amount by which it is increasing is almost precisely the amount by which provision for taxes on the income statement is overstated. You may want to review the discussion of deferred taxes in Chapter 4.

> **Key Points:** Tax expense on the GAAP income statement does not represent the cash that was paid out to the U.S. government for taxes. For the actual cash outflow, refer to the statement of cash flow.

Net Income From Continuing Operations {18}

Among most analysts this is the subtotal that has come to be most popular rather than the net profit total below, which takes into account discontinued operations and extraordinary items. This is the first numerical input used in the statement of cash flow (indirect method) to be discussed in Chapter 7. While not as focused on the operations as the operating profit subtotal above, it is a better overall appraisal of management's success at generating wealth from total corporate assets.

Net Profit {23}

The purpose of the income statement is to measure the wealth produced by the firm since its last statement. From the analyst's perspective, it does this job adequately if management has combined growing earnings with a balance sheet that has high liquidity and low debt such that the firm can effortlessly withstand any seasonal stress and generate any needed capital.

Maintaining these strong income statements and balance sheets typically earns a publicly owned firm the highest credit ratings, Aaa by Moody's Investors Service and AAA by Standard & Poor's. Currently, there are no more than 16 industrial firms in the United States that are so rated. For these highly rated firms, financial analysts can take the balance sheet and the income statement at face value since management is so conservative that even the inexperienced investor buys the firm's debt without analysis.

Beginners at financial analysis who are examining a highly rated company generally need only to find the previous financial analysis in the credit files and update it, mimicking the prior analyst's methods as closely as possible. This leisurely approach is appropriate because the chances of an analyst discovering something alarming in the financial statements of General Motors, for example, are close to nil. Another example is Texaco, whose financial condition and earnings potential before and after losing a multibillion-dollar liability suit were basically the same. *The analyst should better devote any painstaking analysis to companies that do not have such high liquidity and low debt.*

Net income is important to the publicly held firm. Regular increases in earnings keep shareholders happy and limit the potential for proxy fights and hostile takeovers. Privately held firms pay less attention to net income. Freed of demands from pension and mutual fund managers for strong short-term performance, management of privately held firms can take a longer-term view, although management may be self-focused in its long-term planning efforts. The question is: Is net income determination the concluding step before making a lending decision? The answer is that funds flow has become a more valuable analytical tool.

A Final Note

The net income figure is clearly the result of many estimates—and much controversy. The analyst needs to ask: If earnings are only 2% or 3% of revenues, is the number statistically valid given all the estimates used in the calculation? *If a firm shows a net income that is a low percentage of sales, whether it is actually making any money at all is questionable.*

Chapter 6

Spreading the Income Statement—The Hard Stuff

While essential for a complex credit, the following items are also more difficult to understand and they may not be important for all firms. They are:

1. Extraordinary items
2. Discontinued operations
3. Depreciation and inflation's impact on income
4. How Capital lease rentals can distort both income and cash flow
5. Foreign operations

Extraordinary Items {22}*

Extraordinary items are *non-recurring* in nature. For example, the losses resulting from the severe damage of a plant by a storm would be an extraordinary item. However, this category also includes gains or losses from other, less extraordinary events such as the profits from the sale of fixed assets by a firm that does not usually sell its assets. (In contrast, the losses are carried above in plant closings and writedowns {14} to penalize management for taking too little depreciation.) Sometimes this characterization is overly conservative. Let's look at two examples.

Louisiana Crew Boats

Louisiana Crew Boats, Inc. conveyed work crews out to drilling rigs in the Gulf of Mexico for major oil companies. The *modus operandi* of the owner was to acquire fast new vessels, built to specifications assuring that maintenance would be low. He operated the boats with relatively little maintenance for four years and then disposed of them usually at substantially over-book value, creating a profit. He faithfully turned over his portfolio of vessels at the rate of 25% per year, increasing the size of the fleet modestly each year. The accounting firm included the profits from the sale of the vessels in extraordinary earnings. Since

*Numbers in braces refer to the line numbers in Exhibit 5-2A.

146

this was an integral part of the owner's operation, the analyst might feel that these profits should be considered a part of net income before extraordinary items. There is no indisputable answer to this puzzle.

Moran Towing Corp. and McAllister Bros., Inc.

Another example of the complexities that can surround the recording of extraordinary items is found by reviewing how two tugboat companies, Moran Towing Corp. and McAllister Bros., Inc., dealt with an impending strike. In the late 1970s there was the threat of a tugboat pilots' strike in the New York harbor. The executives of McAllister Bros. purchased a business interruption insurance policy from Lloyd's of London for $350,000. Apparently, Lloyd's gamble was that Moran, not having this insurance, would attempt to push the negotiations forward and settle, thereby forcing McAllister either to accept the terms or risk permanently losing customers since the union would only strike against it.

As it turned out, Moran did not force a settlement and the union struck for six weeks. After the strike was settled, McAllister collected $6.5 million because of reduced revenues. The following questions had to be addressed:

- How should McAllister account for the insurance proceeds?
- Were McAllister's proceeds legitimately extraordinary income items? (The insurance merely covered the expenses—not profits—incurred during the six weeks.)
- How should the premium of $350,000 for the policy be carried on McAllister's financials? How can it be just a normal expense while the proceeds from the policy are extraordinary?
- How should Moran consider the loss of revenues that it suffered since it did not obtain the insurance policy? Should the drop in revenues be shown as an extraordinary loss?

GAAP accounting required the insurance settlement be carried as extraordinary revenues after tax and the policy fee carried as ordinary expense. The loss of revenues incurred by both firms was not accounted for at all, but the interest and maintenance expenses incurred during the strike were considered ordinary expense. The net result was that the operating income and profit before extraordinary items were both depressed for both companies.

The most important point from this case is the way it reflects on the managements of Moran and McAllister. As a lender the assessment of the managements would have to be that it is safer to finance McAllister than Moran. The non-recurring issue is not as important as the underlying process by which management protects its business.

Indeed, the analyst should investigate all extraordinary items for what they may reveal about management expertise. If the extraordinary item reflects on management's judgment about how to run a business, then *the extraordinary earnings should be converted into regular income* as this will provide a better cue about how management responds to difficulties.

Pacific Far East Lines

Pacific Far East Lines (PFEL) operated as a shipper between Australia, New Zealand, Japan, Hong Kong, and the West Coast of the United States. Unfortunately, a series of management miscalculations put PFEL in severe financial difficulties. One miscalculation was to build LASH vessels (for Lighter Aboard Ship), most useful for handling bulk commodities and working in ports not equipped for containerization. Ultimately, containerization would come to dominate trade between the U.S. West Coast and the Far East.

The firm was acquired by the Aliotos, the family of the former mayor of San Francisco. When Mayor Alioto's son took over PFEL's operation, he planned to convert three LASH vessels into container ships. The firm sought a $30 million loan for the conversion. The loan could be well collateralized since containerized ships were in demand on both coasts. The real issue facing creditors was the operating capability of the Aliotos.

Forecasting their ability based on a review of PFEL's financial statements was an uncertain proposition. Since the Aliotos had taken over, *all profits generated by the firm were extraordinary items resulting from sale of LASH vessels.* The new management had not been able to manage the existing business and make an operating profit.

Irving Trust declined financing based on the relative inexperience of PFEL's management and their inability to show a recurring profit other than by selling off vessels. Although a loss on default would have been unlikely because of the collateral, Irving's decision prevented a potential loan workout. Financing was obtained instead from Greyhound Leasing, McDonnell Douglas Credit Corp., and one bank, Continental Illinois. The $30 million was put into the conversion of the vessels, and six months after the vessels came out of dry dock, PFEL declared bankruptcy.

The creditors had to devote substantial time to the PFEL workout. Despite the fact that the income statement, particularly the extraordinary items, suggested that the firm was not operating any more efficiently, some financial institutions were willing to speculate on this loan because the collateral appeared to have a high value.

Making loans based on collateral value and ignoring management's ability to generate cash flow from the assets is more of a commodity speculation than a proper lending activity.

> **Key Points:** If the extraordinary item reflects good business judgment on the part of management, include the extraordinary earnings in regular income.

Discontinued Operations {19} & {20}

The discontinued operations account on the income statement shows a net after-tax profit or loss from operations that the firm has publicly announced it will discontinue. This does not mean that these divisions or subsidiary companies, which previously were consolidated, have been disposed of.

The decision to eliminate a division frequently results from a senior management change. Research in the field [Copeland and Moore, 1972, pp. 63–69] has confirmed that dispositions and discontinued operation announcements regularly occur when new management takes over. That is, senior management wants to sweep out the errors of its predecessor and increase the potential for smooth and strong growth in the future.

Look at Exhibit 1-1, Footnote B from the United Enterprises annual report for 1990: The footnote indicates that in June 1989, 14 divisions were discontinued. The company's extraordinary charge in 1989 included an allowance for the future losses that would be incurred by these divisions until they were sold. By December 31, 1990, half of the discontinued businesses and their assets were still owned by United Enterprises. The company had been unable to sell these divisions even on a discounted basis. Nevertheless, management was able to exclude the divisions from financial statement reporting: No sales or expenses were reported for the discontinued operations, only the net after-tax impact on income. (In this case, a reserve for future operating losses had also been recognized; therefore, no further losses needed to appear on the income statement.) This practice enables the parent company operations to be unaffected by the discontinued subsidiaries. Yet, legally, the discontinued operations are still under control of senior management and thus can affect the firm's loan repayment capacity.

The decision to hold rather than to dispose of discontinued operations reflects on the judgment of company management. The loss reserve may be inadequate to allow for sale of these entities or to carry their future losses for the long term. The analyst should make sure that discontinued operations will be shortly disposed of—or at least not cause significant problems for the parent.

> **Key Points:** If it appears that the reserve for discontinued operations is inadequate or that the company will not be disposing of the discontinued operations in the near future, consider taking an additional reserve against equity.

Depreciation and Inflation

Inflation (and time of acquisition of an asset) and the components of depreciation can dramatically affect the income statement. Consider this illustrative example.

Boudin Towing

Thomas Boudin left his job as a river pilot in 1910 and began a steamboat company. By the 1960s Boudin Towing was a large, well-respected firm in New Orleans. Suddenly in 1973, Thomas died, at the age of 90. He left two daughters, who were not involved in the business, and a son, Scott, age 55, who had spent his entire business life working for Boudin Towing. The net worth of the firm was roughly $60 million.

Thomas had made no provision for passing the firm on to his children before his death, so inheritance taxes came to nearly $40 million. His daughters did not want to keep their assets tied up in the company, so Boudin Towing was sold to a public utility for $40 million in cash—for the IRS—and $20 million in stock divided three ways among the children.

Scott decided to use his $6.5 million worth of utility stock as capital to start another towing company. The utility had not required Scott to sign a non-compete clause, so he was able to hire a dozen people who previously had worked for his father's company. To get back into the business, Scott had to purchase boats. All new tow boats would be too expensive, so Scott began acquiring a portfolio of used boats. Having purchased these vessels, Scott started calling on old clients, quoting competitive prices and doing business. He was shocked when he reviewed his new company's first income statement. His portfolio of vessels had all been accounted for at market value, and using traditionally conservative estimates of useful lives, substantial depreciation had been charged to the income statement: Scott was losing money. His bankers were discouraged. Even after several years of trying to nudge up prices and cut costs without losing all his clients, Scott's business was just breaking even.

The problem was that Scott's competitors were using fleets that had been purchased over a 10–20-year period, meaning that their balance sheet fixed asset values were much lower, since Scott's fleet was listed on the balance sheet practically at market value.

Although competitors with fleets purchased over many years might believe that their profits were adequate, in actuality, the *holding gains from owning the vessels over a long time were producing their profits rather than the day-to-day operations.* Despite the fact that Scott owned boats of exactly the same vintage as his competitors, the higher fixed asset values gave him much higher depreciation amounts. Given the competitive bidding for the business, he would only break even against competitors who based their bidding on lower depreciation expenses. Nevertheless, Scott believed that he was operating at greater efficiency than many competitors and that by the time they had to replace boats, they would be in trouble. The competitors' vessels were certainly more valuable than their financial statements indicated. Since they knew this, it is curious that they were not more concerned about the return on the market value of these assets.

By understating depreciation on valuable assets, expenses were lower and net income was an illusion; *the profits were the liquidation of these holding gains.* A metaphor for this is a widow living in inflationary times on the interest she is paid from her savings account. The low rate on her savings account is not even keeping up with inflation; she is really living on capital, with the purchasing ability value of her savings account becoming less and less each year. To add insult to injury, the government taxes the "interest" she receives.

The analyst's ability to make comparisons about efficiency between firms is almost eliminated in cases such as Boudin Towing's. The relative efficiency of operation is obscured by factors such as *how recently the firm purchased its equipment.* Although this may be somewhat of a mixed blessing for corporate management (showing generous profits is certainly a way of keeping shareholders happy and it produces substantial incentive bonuses), it certainly presents a problem for the lender who must determine a firm's ability to generate earnings in the future.

> **Key Points:** Inflation can cause fixed asset values on the balance sheet to be substantially below market values. The low depreciation expense resulting from these undervalued assets can result in high income. This high income, however, may be illusive, resulting more from the liquidation of holding gains than from operations.

Inflation-Adjusted Accounting

Concerns about the accuracy of depreciation date back to the early 1950s, when analysts became troubled by how depreciation charges were inadequate to reflect the inflation-induced value in fixed assets. (The concerns about FIFO accounting created LIFO.) There were some suggestions for replacement funding, that is, setting up a reserve to help pay for the inflation differential when purchasing replacement fixed assets. Under this plan increased depreciation would have gone into a reserve for the anticipated increased cost of fixed asset replacement—entered between the debt and net worth sections on the balance sheet. (Ship owners can do this for tax purposes.) In financial and economic terms this reserve represents the concept of opportunity cost since there may be no intention of selling the equipment, as required by the accounting profession to obtain revaluations. Ignoring a higher depreciation charge does not make it go away. Although replacement funding was debated for years, it was never adopted, being thought too radical a departure from the allocation of cost basis for depreciation charges.

In 1976, the SEC became impatient with the profession's unwillingness to act on the inflation issue. It issued Accounting Series Release #190, calling for required inflation-adjusted accounting in the *10K* report for major public companies. After two years of increased debate, the Financial Accounting Standards Board issued SFAS #33, committing auditors to showing the effects of inflation in the financial statements. SFAS #33 required firms to provide additional information as follows:

1. Each year appraisers had to assess the market replacement value of the fixed assets and inventory.
2. Using the new values, new depreciation amounts and new cost of goods sold were calculated. These inflation-adjusted values were displayed included in a separate schedule and also showed a recalculated income.
3. Because current costs were also calculated into inventory, the FIFO bonus could be identified and eliminated.

The problems associated with low depreciation expense have not escaped even the Treasury Department. Besides allowing ship owners the replacement reserve expense, the IRS's initial proposal for the 1986 tax code included depreciation based on inflation-adjusted equipment values. The consumer price index was to be used to increase the value of equipment each year so that, for tax purposes, depreciation expense could be higher. This remarkably permitted purchasers of fixed assets to take depreciation expense in excess of the original cost over the life of the equipment; it, however, was not adopted.

Demise of Current Cost

Unfortunately, in December 1986, the Financial Accounting Standards Board discontinued the requirement for inflation-adjusted financial reporting, in SFAS #89. The dilemma with SFAS #33 for most financial analysts was that many medium-size and smaller companies did not have to report the inflation information required. Moreover, research compared current cost data with historical accounting data; based on a review of hundreds of firms in varied industries, the research indicated that it made little difference in most cases whether historical cost or current cost data were used. In fact, the result of this *statistical* research was used to justify the elimination of SFAS #33.

The premise of this research, however, was at odds with the interests of the lender in specific companies rather than averages. Debt is supposed to be a lower margin, lower risk investment activity than equity investment. Lenders do not wish to turn companies away that will pay back loans, especially those willing to pay higher rates. The task is to identify and to avoid only those few companies that will go out of business without repaying their debts. Given that the analyst is trying to identify the "swing" or potentially defaulting company, the question of whether there is any difference between inflation accounting and historical cost accounting may be critical.

The solution to the asset valuation problem is to require bank customers that borrow substantial amounts to pay for third-party appraisals on a regular basis. With current cost appraisals in hand, depreciation values can be estimated based on the proportional relationship between the reported depreciation and the gross assets of the firm.

It should be noted that it is conceivable that the current cost value of the equipment will be lower than the GAAP value. Let's look at an example:

Federal Express

In fact, lower market value was the case on the 1985 financial statements of Federal Express. The firm's fleet of Boeing 737's had fallen dramatically in value as a result of several plane crashes involving 737's. Federal Express reported in the current cost section that the value of its fixed assets was less than their book value. The difference was not material, however, and no adjustment was required to be made on the books of the company by generally accepted accounting principles.

Key Points: Estimate the effects of inflation on depreciation by applying the firm's depreciation rate to third-party current cost appraisals of fixed assets.

Capital Lease Rents {2}, {5}, {6} & {8}

The accounting of lease rental expense for Capital leases is accomplished by expensing "interest expense," "principal" reduction, and "depreciation." Rent is a legally obligated cash outflow, but what are the accounting expenses? Exhibit 6-1 shows three different ways of accounting for the financing and use of a fixed asset. The firm may (1) borrow long-term funds to finance the equipment; (2) enter into a Capital lease to acquire the equipment; or (3) use an Operating lease (short-term rental).

Under the financing option (the buy and borrow alternative in Exhibit 6-1) the firm takes straight-line depreciation and charges the expense to cost of goods sold or selling, general and administrative expenses. In addition, it is required to pay an interest expense, using the gross yield payment calculation—incurring more in the early years and less in later years. Over time with other things being equal, *income rises under this option since interest expense is falling— more principal is being repaid.*

With a **Capital lease,** depreciation expense is calculated and charged as if the firm owned the asset (the firm must use the same depreciation method— usually straight-line—that it would use for similar assets). The *quasi*-interest expense is calculated by multiplying the firm's **incremental borrowing rate** (the rate at which the firm could arrange a similar term loan) by the value of the asset. Alternatively, if the firm knows the residual value expectation of the lessor, the **implicit rate** (the discount rate that equates the rental and residual value expectation with the equipment cost) in the lease must be calculated and used if it is lower than the incremental borrowing rate.

The use of the implicit rate for calculating interest under capital lease accounting causes problems for the analyst because of the implicit rate being unrealistically low since it ignores the tax benefits garnered by the lessor as part of its compensation for doing the deal. It is inevitably lower than the incremental borowing rate the company is really paying. Since the interest rate in the Capital lease transaction is lower, the income statement resulting from the Capital lease alternative will not be precisely aligned with the income statement resulting from the borrowing alternative. Exhibit 6-2 shows the difference between the two.

For the Operating lease alternative, *the income statement expense equals the actual cash paid out.* Therefore, the expense—and income—is level throughout the term of the lease. Operating leases result in a better income statement for predicting future earnings potential, just as the LIFO method of expensing inventories did. In summary, there are clear trade-offs in using the leasing alternatives, for instance:

1. If the treasurer wishes fewer assets and liabilities, choose the SFAS #13 Operating lease.
2. If the treasurer wishes to show growing earnings where sales are relatively flat, choose the Capital lease, especially with a low implicit rate, which produces a low "interest expense."

Key Points: A firm's using an Operating lease to finance equipment will result in an income statement that is more useful for predicting future earnings potential than an income statement resulting from a firm's using either a SFAS #13 Capital lease or a loan to finance equipment.

Exhibit 6-1.

FINANCIAL STATEMENT COMPARISON OF CAPITAL LEASES WITH OPERATING LEASES AND BUY AND BORROWING

One Year after Acquiring or Leasing Asset

BALANCE SHEET	BUY AND BORROW	OPERATING LEASE	CAPITAL LEASE
Assets			
Total Current Assets	47,695	47,280	48,596
Plant, Property and Equipment	100,000		
Equipment on Capital Lease			100,000
Less Accumulated Depreciation	(16,000)		(16,000)
Total Fixed Assets	84,000	0	84,000
Total Assets	131,695	47,280	132,596
Liabilities			
Current Portion Long-Term Debt	13,950		
Current Portion Capital Lease Payment			14,435
Total Current Liabilities	13,950	0	14,435
Long Term Debt	73,705		
Capital Lease Obligations			72,425
Total Long-Term Debt	73,705	0	72,425
Equity			
Paid-in Capital	30,000	30,000	30,000
Retained Earnings	14,040	17,280	15,736
Net Worth	44,040	47,280	45,736
Total Liabilities and Equity	131,695	47,280	132,596
INCOME STATEMENT			
Sales	180,000	180,000	180,000
Expenses			
Cost of Goods Sold	125,000	125,000	125,000
Lease Expense		23,000	
Depreciation	16,000		16,000
Operating Income	39,000	32,000	39,000
Interest Expense	13,000		9,860
Income Before Taxes	26,000	32,000	29,140
Income Tax @ 46%	11,960	14,720	13,404
Net Income	14,040	17,280	15,736

Assumptions:

1. Equipment = $100,000   2. 20% residual after 5 years

3. Loan alternative = $100,000 @ 13% with payments of $35,345 annually

4. Annual lease payments = $23,000; 20% Purchase Option; present value discount rates are as follows: Nominal rate=5%, Implicit (SFAS #13) rate=9.86%, Yield to lessor=13%

Exhibit 6-2.

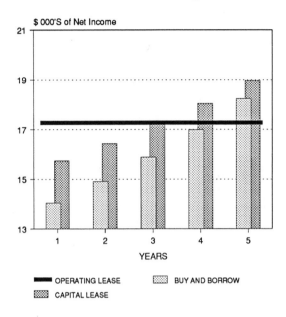

LEASE ALTERNATIVES
Effect on Accounting Income

Foreign Operations {10}, {13} & {15}

The subject of foreign operations is too complex to pursue in detail. However, lenders should be aware that in the late 1970s there was great controversy over the issuance of SFAS #8, the original pronouncement on foreign currency translation. SFAS #8 required companies to process all currency exchange rate gains and losses in foreign activities through the income statement, which was disruptive to the work of financial analysts. It exemplifies the inconsistencies in applying the principle of conservatism: refusing to account for changes in fixed asset values through the income statement, yet forcing unrecognized gains and losses to appear in the income statement as if the investments in overseas activities were closed out every year.

SFAS #52 was a partial solution, released in December 1981. It requires companies that have substantial investments in overseas operating subsidiaries and that use the foreign currency as the functional one to translate most assets— with the exception of items closely related to cash, such as marketable securities and accounts receivable, which are translated at current rates—at historical rates. (See Chapter 4 for more on functional currencies.) Liabilities must still, unfortunately, be translated at current rates. Then—the best part—the net worth picks up the differences in the balance sheet conversion with a reserve account. There is no direct effect on the income statement.

The income statement items are translated at the average exchange rate for the period. In contrast, exchange rate gains and losses in foreign currency positions involving purchases of assets, investments in unconsolidated ventures, and futures contracts are posted to the income statement as non-operating income or expense.

The requirement that liabilities be translated at current exchange rates provides a significant penalty to a firm investing in a country whose currency is appreciating against the dollar. Why should the firm be required to show the liability as current and payable within one year, but show the assets at historical cost? It might be argued that in this case the accounting concept of conservatism has gone too far.

Subjecting the firm's balance sheet and income statement to liability revaluations as a result of foreign operations has created a huge market in foreign futures. Although firms may have no need for the currency, futures are acquired and traded in an effort to keep accounting exposure on an international level continually balanced. (Hedges acquired to protect long-term investments in operating subsidiaries are included in the cumulative transaction adjustments account within the statement of changes to equity.) Posting the differences in currency values to the retained earnings account is a vast improvement over running these adjustments through the income statement. The inconsistency between the handling of fixed assets and long-term liabilities, however, makes SFAS #52 a less than perfect solution.

> **Key Points:** If a company has substantial foreign exchange losses in the statement of retained earnings or income, find out why.

Conclusion

As a finishing to the income spreadsheet section of the book, Exhibit 7-3 in Chapter 7 gives an example of the United Enterprises income statements (Exhibit 1-1), placed onto a spreadsheet, shown in its blank version in Exhibit 5-2A.

Summarizing, here is a checklist of GAAP options affecting net income:

1. *Foreign currency translation* affects net income in that it is mostly at the current exchange rate, but depreciation of any older fixed assets (non-monetary) is at rates in effect at the time of purchase.
2. *FIFO* increased income as a result of asset holding gains in inflationary times.
3. *Operating lease* rents are carried in the operating expense or cost of goods sold accounts while *Capital lease* rents are converted to artificial interest and depreciation.
4. *Percentage of completion* accounting smooths income reporting while the completed contract method makes income irregular.
5. *Bulk purchase* of a company or assets may result in future writedowns of goodwill, and *pooling of interests* in acquisitions may result in undervalued assets that can be sold to bolster net income with large capital gains.
6. *Securities* at lower of cost or market method affect income only if carried current, but the equity method will pass through subsidiary losses and gains.
7. *Straight-line depreciation* is used (along with optimistic economic life estimates) primarily to give the impression of greater income levels.

Chapter 7

Statement of Cash Flow

How Cash Flow Is the Crucial Variable

The day-to-day decisions of management do not focus on maintaining liquidity or avoiding debt, lender belief to the contrary notwithstanding. Short-term planning efforts are instead directed toward increasing sales and reducing costs. Along with supervision of marketing and production come administration of accounts receivable policy, inventory controls (and expansion), accounts payable policy, and sources of short-term financing. High liquidity may be exchanged for the prospect of increased sales. That is, credit policies may be liberalized, resulting in increases in accounts receivable, and abundant product inventory may be kept on hand to support consumer demand. Accounts payable policies focus on improving supplier relations and possibly on obtaining discounts for prompt payment. Almost every decision management makes involves the use of cash funds. Indeed, while the senior management of the firm may focus on smoothing income growth for improved shareholder relations, the *corporate treasurer is preoccupied with controlling cash.*

The treasury area also focuses its investment analysis tools on long-term cash deployment, especially for:

1. Capital investment outlays (both for maintaining the level of productive capacity and improving it).
2. Permanent increases to working capital caused by growth (expansion entails increases in accounts receivable and inventory).
3. Research and development expenses that may require significant time before revenues are forthcoming.

The sources of cash to pay for these long-term expenditures must be identified and investigated. Concurrently, the treasurer's responsibilities include negotiating debt repayment terms, interest, and principal to time periods when the firm can best afford them.

What Analysts Can Learn From Studying Cash Flow

Management decisions always involve the generation and expenditure of cash, except for worrying about how the reported accrual accounting results will impact (1) the stock price and (2) unsophisticated lenders. Thus, a schedule of cash flows would enable the lender to gain a better understanding of the firm's operations, and ultimately, of the firm's debt repayment capacity. A schedule of cash flows (aside from the revenues and expenses shown in the income statement) should provide answers to the following questions:

- Is capacity expanding and at what rate?
- Is the capital structure of long-term debt and equity improving or deteriorating?
- Are working capital assets being used to fund long-term assets or to pay off long-term debt?
- Is cash flow substantial enough to repay long-term debt maturities or is old debt being merely refunded?

Key Points: Since management decisions always involve the generation and expenditure of cash, and since loans are repaid with cash, a lender needs a schedule of cash flows to determine a firm's debt repayment capacity.

Why the Derivation of Net Cash Flow Is Vital

Firms cannot easily modify their cash outflows in all areas. For instance, it is difficult to effect major changes in cost of goods sold, interest payments, and other expenses without spending money in other areas such as production, employee training, and research and development.

Government Debt

The U.S. government offers an illustrative example of the *difference between required expenses and controllable ones*. The government has in recent memory had difficulties balancing its budget. The total government budget is approximately $1.7 trillion, and the deficit runs at about $200 billion. Since the deficit is only 10% or 11% of the total budget, balancing the budget should not be an insurmountable hurdle.

Consider this analogy: If your firm decides to reduce its costs in prudent preparation for a recession, management may decide to cut salaries by 10%. Although employees would not be pleased about the salary cuts, few would have to change their life-styles significantly as a result of the pay cuts.

Why then is the U.S. government unable to effect such budget cuts? The answer is that the vast bulk of U.S. government expenditures are fixed, almost untouchable by legislators. These expenditures include interest on the government debt, salary and housing expenses for the armed forces, social security, welfare, and Medicaid benefits. These items account for over a trillion dollars of expenditure, leaving only $600 billion susceptible for potential cuts. From this perspective, the $200 billion deficit is much more difficult to eliminate.

Extending the business firm cost-reduction analogy, the equivalent would be imposing a 33% pay cut, not 10%. Obviously, this would result in major life-style changes for the staff, with resumes being hastily pulled together.

The *distinction between required and controllable expenditures is, in effect, what is missing from the income statement.* Most expenses reported on the income statement cannot be controlled by management. (This generality needs to be hedged for firms that are in severe financial distress and that are open to a massive restructuring. A prime example is the Chrysler Corporation. In that case, the board of directors gave Lee Iacocca *carte blanche* to make changes that were needed to save the company.)

As liquidity declines and debt increases, creditors need more detailed understanding of a firm's cash flow. Inappropriate liabilities greatly increase a firm's chance of failure in the event of stress. The income statement is only focused on the operating cycle and ignores the flow of cash within the long-term assets and liabilities of an organization; the use of accrual accounting for reckoning wealth generation frequently disguises these cash flows even in the current asset and liability accounts. Hidden from the income statement are transactions in both the current asset and current liability accounts as well as on the long-term side of the balance sheet. For example, the income statement ignores an excessive buildup in the accounts receivable or inventories, capital expenditures, purchases of businesses, increases and decreases in debt, and new equity infusions.

Sources and Uses Statement

Initial endeavors to produce a cash flow statement involved calculating the net changes in the various balance sheet accounts between the two balance sheet dates; this is called a sources and uses analysis. Exhibit 7-1 takes the balance sheets of United Enterprises from the two years shown in Exhibit 1-1 and calculates the net changes in them. The notes in Exhibit 7-1 provide details about the calculations. The current (working capital) accounts are not included in the initial calculations since the resulting change in working capital is the figure to be derived and reconciled. Income statement results are factored in as part of the reconciliation of the changes in retained earnings.

From this statement of balance sheet differences, the analyst should be able to:

- Determine whether the operations of the firm are generating cash or using it up.
- Determine whether cash generation is sufficient to enable the firm to expand sales as rapidly as it might wish.
- Roughly calculate the increases in fixed assets and the depreciation.
- Determine how much long-term debt has increased.

The pitfall of the sources and uses method is that the statement of sources and uses is *comprised of net differences rather than gross flows.* For example, identifying changes in the fixed asset accounts does not distinguish between depreciation, purchases of new assets, and sales of used assets; sales of assets reduce both the gross asset and depreciation accounts, confounding the calculation of the gross changes. Without disclosure of fixed asset sales, which would

Exhibit 7-1.

TRADITIONAL (DERIVED) SOURCES AND USES STATEMENT
UNITED ENTERPRISES 1989-1990

Sources	In Millions
Income - from Income Statement	$31.2
Depreciation and Other Non-Cash Charges - Note A	34.1
Increase in Long Term Debt - Note B	18.3
Decrease in Fixed Assets besides Plant & Equip. - Note C	0.8
Total Sources	**$84.4**

Uses	
Increase in Plant, Property and Equipment - Note B	$21.8
Net Purchase of Stock - Note D	$34.2
Dividends - Note E	$23.0
Total Uses	**$79.0**
Increase (Decrease) in Working Capital	$5.4

Note A - Derivation of Depreciation and Other Non-cash Charges			
	Depreciation Account	Deferred Tax Account	TOTAL
1989	$137.0	$12.1	$149.1
1990	157.1	26.1	183.2
Derived	$20.1 +	$14.0 =	$34.1

Note B - Derivation of Increase in Long-Term Debt and Plant, Property & Equipment		
	Long Term Debt	Property, Plant and Equipment
1989	$71.4	$321.3
1990	89.7	343.1
Derived	$18.3	$21.8

Note C - Derivation of Change in Other Fixed Assets					
	Held for Sale	Goodwill	Investments	Other	TOTAL
1981	$62.8	$44.3	$21.0	$14.2	$142.3
1982	55.8	47.3	25.0	13.4	141.5
Derived	($7.0)	$3.0	$4.0	($0.8)	($0.8)

Note D - Derivation of Change in Stock Outstanding			
	Stock and Paid-in Capital -	Treasury Stock	TOTAL
1981	$156.5	($6.7)	$149.8
1982	165.2	(49.6)	115.6
Derived	$8.7	($42.9)	($34.2)

Note E - Derivation of Dividends	
Retained Earnings 1981	$276.4
Net Income 1982	31.2
Retained Earnings Should Be	$307.6
Retained Earnings Are	284.6
Derived Dividends	$23.0

also affect the depreciation reserves, this netting has made it impossible for the analyst to determine how much new capital equipment has been purchased. Further, unless depreciation is specifically identified, its exact identification has also become unattainable. Moreover, it is difficult to distinguish between whether the firm has merely added a small amount of new debt or both paid off old debt and acquired substantial amounts of new debt. The distinction may speak volumes about concerns of previous lenders being resolved by substituting new lenders or, conversely, whether the firm has the flexibility to adjust to new market conditions.

The sources and uses statement represents a good start in improving the understanding of management activities. The sources and uses statement does not, however, give the analyst a clear picture of how cash flows through an organization during the course of a year. Instead, it calculates net changes from one period to the next in various accounts. Nevertheless, the statement can provide the analyst with some useful information. For instance, the statement shows that an increase in the deferred tax account represents an inflow of cash for general corporate purposes in the sense that it represents cash not paid out.

> **Key Points:** The sources and uses of funds statement, although a step in the right direction in terms of cash flow reporting, fails to give a true picture of cash generated from operations since it shows only net difference in various balance sheet accounts.

Statement of Changes in Financial Position

The accounting profession acted to improve cash flow disclosure by requiring the statement of changes in financial position (SCFP) through Accounting Principles Board (APB) Opinion #19 in 1971. The APB preceded the Financial Accounting Standards Board and was an arm of the American Institute of Certified Public Accountants (AICPA). APB #19's primary aims were to require corporations (1) to disclose their various non-cash charges to income and (2) to report changes in the long-term asset and liability accounts.

The first disclosures would permit better estimates of the cash generated by companies' operations. The first input is *profits from continuing operations,* which excludes extraordinary items and income or losses from discontinued operations. Next are added back *non-cash charges* previously deducted in the income statement, such as depreciation and depletion and increases in deferred taxes; these items were previously recorded on the income statement as expenses, but in fact they do not involve cash outlays. The first subtotal is calculated and titled **funds provided by continuing operations**—hereinafter occasionally called **funds flow.**

Funds provided by continuing operations has more technical integrity than any information previously available to the analyst. With this first subtotal in the statement of changes in financial position adding back depreciation and changes in deferred taxes to net income and eliminating extraordinary earnings, the calculation gives the analyst a basis for comparing different companies. Otherwise their *divergent depreciation* methods and *dissimilar estimates of useful economic lives*—and thus different depreciation charges—on similar equipment (arising from purchasing the equipment at different points in time) make income comparison useless. This is the problem previously illustrated by the Boudin Towing case (Chapter 6). The funds provided by operations subtotal shows differences in performance success resulting from operating efficiency rather than the differences in the methods of estimating depreciation and tax expenses. Funds provided by operations also furnishes the analyst with an approximation of the amount the firm has available to repay long-term debt, **debt repayment capacity.**

Bethlehem Steel

> An example of the effect that changing the depreciation estimate can have on income can be found by looking at Bethlehem Steel. In 1984, Bethlehem Steel announced that it was increasing the estimated useful lives of its fixed assets to 18 years; this cut depreciation expenses and also reduced the firm's net loss for 1984, from $400 million to only $100 million. The ability of a company to make a change like this after years of operations might give one pause about how reliable the depreciation estimate is.

In effect, the statement of changes in financial position allows the analyst to eliminate some types of income smoothing. By focusing on funds flow from operations, analysts can ignore Bethlehem Steel's depreciation methods. They can also ignore the accounting requirement that increases in the deferred tax account should be deducted from net income. Funds provided by operations thus enables the creditor to better assess the company's potential debt repayment capacity.

Finally, as mentioned in the conclusion to Chapter 5, the net income figure is clearly the result of many estimates—if earnings are only 2% or 3% of revenues, is the number statistically valid given all the estimates used in the calculation? *The impact of accrual estimating procedures on net income from continuing operations is lessened by the substantial part that depreciation and the increase in the deferred tax account add to* the funds provided by operations, now an extremely good approximation of debt repayment capacity.

The next step in completing the Statement of Changes in Financial Position is to integrate the funds provided by operations with (1) the amount of debt that was paid off and the amount of new debt that was added, and (2) which assets, if any, the company bought and sold (e.g., plant and equipment, investments in other subsidiaries, etc.).

The third step is the integration of changes in working capital, usually caused by growth in firm revenues, but possibly caused by poor management of inventories and accounts receivable and payable. By adding any increases in the accounts payable account and other current liabilities (sources of funds) and subtracting increases in the current asset accounts (uses), the statement produces the change in the cash account.

APB Opinion #19 has yet to receive the attention it deserves. Until as recently as the early 1980s, most lenders were still not focusing on funds provided by operations as a critical number. One of the primary intents of a financial statement analysis, however, is to construct a full financial statement forecast of the company's future performance. The usefulness of this forecast in determining debt repayment capacity depends on how accurately it reflects the company's ability to regularly generate funds with which to repay debt. *The funds from operations is a better base for debt repayment capacity than net income, subject as the latter is to accrual estimates.*

> **Key Points:** The statement of changes in financial position, prepared by the firm's own accountants, is superior to the sources and uses statement, concocted by analysts with incomplete information. Moreover, it separates out funds provided by operations as a close approximation of debt repayment capacity.

SFAS #95

In November 1987, the Financial Accounting Standards Board released SFAS #95. It is one of the most important changes in accounting requirements in the 1980s. SFAS #95 requires, as part of the financial statements, the statement of cash flows (SCF), which diminishes the impact of accounting estimates. In its purest form the **direct method of the statement of cash flow** attempts to have companies disclose actual gross cash flows from operations—tabulation of the cash journal (checking account register). Fortunately, as a last-moment compromise with those who thought this information would be too costly to prepare, companies were permitted to report via the **indirect method**, which uses almost the same items, in slightly different categories, as the statement of changes in financial position.

Analysis Categories

SFAS #95 was issued in response to financial institutions' expressed need to analyze an enterprise's ability to meet its obligations. The SCF allows the financial institution to identify the differences between net income and associated cash receipts and payments. The SCF separates a company's cash flows into three categories: (1) operating activities, (2) investing activities, and (3) financing activities.

In view of the anticipated limited use of the direct cash flow method, Exhibit 5-2A shows an approximation of the indirect cash flow method. It bears sufficient relationship to the former statement of changes in financial position to make the analyst and credit manager feel comfortable, yet provides information that has been shown to be statistically reliable in determining debt repayment ability. Some examples may help clarify how cash transactions (cash receipts and cash payments) are classified.

Cash flows from operations {33} include cash flows arising from:
1. Activities normally involved in producing and delivering goods and services, including the *collection of accounts receivable* and both short- and long-term notes receivable from customers.

2. Acquiring materials and making payments to employees for services including *increases in inventories*.
3. Interest expense (in contrast with the income statement presentation).
4. *Unfortunately*, extraordinary items including lawsuit settlements and insurance claims.

Permitting various extraordinary items to be carried as operating activities is a problem. Consequently, the lender must adjust the subtotals in the SCF to determine the firm's recurring capability of repaying debt.

Cash flows after investments {37} include cash flows arising from any sale or acquisition of fixed assets.

Cash flows after financing include cash flows arising from:

1. Any borrowing or repayment of long-term debt, even if the debt was merely intended as a hedge on investment activities.
2. Any payment of dividends.
3. The issuance of equity or debt instruments of any kind and the payments of dividends or principal to any lenders.

In an effort to reduce redundancy on the spreadsheet this title has not been shown separately from the last, reconciling with cash, account.

Net change in cash and cash equivalents {41} indicates that short-term movements within the cash account itself do not need to be tracked. The cash account is defined to include all other kinds of accounts that are the equivalent of cash, including money market instruments.

These are satisfying subdivisions of cash flows for analytical purposes, related as they are to the planning process within the business firm.

> **Key Points:** The statement of cash flows discloses cash flows arising from the operating, financing, and investing activities of the firm.

Direct and Indirect Cash Flow Presentations

The FASB booklet clearly points out in the appendix that:

> A majority of respondents to the exposure draft asked the board to require use of the direct method. Those respondents, most of whom were commercial lenders, generally said that amounts of operating cash receipts and payments are particularly important in assessing an enterprise's external borrowing needs and its ability to repay borrowings.

It is conceivable, but probably a waste of effort, that an analyst could construct a direct method cash flow statement from (1) the traditional balance sheet, (2) the income statement, and (3) the indirect method statement of cash flow. This is a sadistic assignment for an intermediate course in accounting. The elimination of the accrual accounting estimates in each of the accounts is difficult.

Exhibit 7-2 gives an example of the type of manipulations that might achieve an informative result from the traditional statements.

Analysis of Item Changes in Cash Flow Presentation

APB Opinion #19's funds provided by operations (net income plus depreciation and other non-cash charges) has been eliminated in the statement of cash flow. **Net cash provided by operating activities** *now includes all changes in the current asset and current liability sides of the balance sheet*. This revised funds flow concept of net cash flow from operations is based on the assumption that accounts receivable, inventories, and accounts payable rise or fall (1) automatically (in spite of anything management may do to deter it) in response to an increase or decrease, respectively, in sales or (2) as a result of management's inability to properly control them. This assumption has reasonable aspects:

- More inventory is needed to supply more output.
- More accounts receivable are generated as more people buy on credit.
- More accounts payable are generated as more supplies are ordered.

Since these are true, some theoreticians had argued that the derivation of the APB Opinion #19's funds provided by operations was misleading. For a company whose sales are increasing, corresponding increases in the current asset accounts will most likely *not* be fully offset by increases in accounts payable and accrued liabilities. *Therefore, increased sales require additional cash*. The analyst, the argument goes, might view funds provided by operations as cash that is available for the repayment of debt or dividends, when in fact, some (or much) of this cash could be consumed by increasing current asset accounts.

The counterargument is that *there are many situations in which the corporate treasurer can control the current asset accounts*. Management can decide to invest additional cash into either inventory or accounts receivable to improve sales, support price increases, or manage an important new account. Similarly management may decide to buy low-priced inventories to boost profitability. The point is, increases or decreases in sales do not always create pressures on the current asset accounts that are out of management's control. Moreover, fixed asset investments may alter the relationship between current asset accounts and sales growth by improving credit collection and inventory utilization. Finally, and most importantly, in the event of a financial squeeze, the company usually has the ability to liquidate accounts receivable and inventories to meet required debt payments.

By holding off any subtotal of funds generation until after all increases in accounts receivable and inventories, the cash flow statement encourages a type 2 error: that a company reinvesting excess funds into potentially highly productive assets will be construed as losing control of current asset accounts. *For all growing companies, the result of this assumption about management control of current assets and liabilities will almost always be a negative figure for the first subtotal of the cash flow statement*. Indeed it is most likely that (except for unusually profitable firms) the only companies that will show a positive figure are those that are

(Text continued on page 170.)

Exhibit 7-2.

CONSOLIDATED STATEMENT OF CASH FLOWS -- DERIVATION

THIS EXHIBIT GIVES INSTRUCTIONS FOR DERIVING THE GROSS CASH
FLOW PRESENTATION

ITEMS REQUIRED FOR THE **DIRECT METHOD** OF PRESENTING THE STATEMENT OF CASH FLOW.	**INSTRUCTIONS** FOR PRODUCING THE REQUIRED ITEMS FROM THE **INDIRECT METHOD** OF PRESENTING THE STATEMENT OF CASH FLOW, INCOME STATEMENT AND BALANCE SHEET.

CASH FLOWS FROM OPERATING ACTIVITIES

Cash received from customers

Sales less any increase in Trade Receivables, including Long-term Trade Receivables (add back any provision for losses). Be careful not to include other items which may be a part of the so-called "Net Revenues," such as Equity in Earnings of Affiliates.

Cash paid to suppliers and employees

Add: Cost of Goods Sold, Selling Expense, General and Administrative Expenses and increases in Inventory and Prepaid Expenses
Subtract: Depreciation, Amortization and Other Non-cash Charges, increases in Accounts Payable and increases in Accrued Expenses.

Dividends received from affiliates

Usually can be derived by subtracting Undistributed Earnings of Affiliates from Earnings on Equity Investments.

Interest received

On loans and other debt instruments

Interest paid (net amount capitalized)

On loans and other debt instruments

Income taxes paid (cash)

Provision for income taxes less any increase in the Deferred Tax account and in Taxes Payable.

Other cash income

Cash receipts not arising from investing or financing activities; these include lawsuits and insurance settlements and refunds from suppliers.

Other cash expense

Cash payments not arising from investing or financing activities; these include lawsuits, cash contributions to charities and cash refunds to customers.

Extraordinary items cash proceeds

Not included in the two previous items.

NET CASH PROVIDED BY OPERATING ACTIVITIES

Subtotal (A positive indicates a **Source** of funds while a negative number indicates a **Use**.)

CONSOLIDATED STATEMENT OF CASH FLOWS -- DERIVATION, continued

ITEMS REQUIRED FOR THE **DIRECT METHOD** OF PRESENTING THE STATEMENT OF CASH FLOW.	**INSTRUCTIONS** FOR PRODUCING THE REQUIRED ITEMS FROM THE **INDIRECT METHOD** OF PRESENTING THE STATEMENT OF CASH FLOW, INCOME STATEMENT AND BALANCE SHEET.

CASH FLOWS FROM INVESTING ACTIVITIES:

Cash proceeds from sale of facility

Should be available on Indirect Statement of Cash Flows.

Payment received on note for sale of fixed assets with purchase money note

Should be available on Indirect Statement of Cash Flows.

Capital expenditures and assets acquired through capital leases.

Should be available on Indirect Statement of Cash Flows.

Payment for acquisition (net its cash)

Should be available on Indirect Statement of Cash Flows.

Remaining Changes in Fixed Assets

Changes in Goodwill and Other Assets requiring the use of cash.

NET CASH USED IN INVESTING ACTIVITIES

Subtotal (a Use of funds)

(continued)

Exhibit 7-2. Continued.

CONSOLIDATED STATEMENT OF CASH FLOWS -- DERIVATION, continued

ITEMS REQUIRED FOR THE **DIRECT METHOD** OF PRESENTING THE STATEMENT OF CASH FLOW.	**INSTRUCTIONS** FOR PRODUCING THE REQUIRED ITEMS FROM THE **INDIRECT METHOD** OF PRESENTING THE STATEMENT OF CASH FLOW, INCOME STATEMENT AND BALANCE SHEET.

CASH FLOWS FROM FINANCING ACTIVITIES

Net borrowings under current notes	Should be available on Indirect Statement of Cash Flows.
Principal payments under capital lease	Should be available on Indirect Statement of Cash Flows.
Increase in Current Portion of Long-term Debt	Calculate from Balance Sheet
Increase in Long-term Debt	Should be available on Indirect Statement of Cash Flows, less any addition made to previous item.
Proceeds from (cost of) common stock (Net sales and purchases)	Should be available on Indirect Statement of Cash Flows.
Dividends paid	Should be available on Indirect Statement of Cash Flows.
NET CASH PROVIDED BY FINANCING ACTIVITIES	Subtotal (Usually a source of Cash.)
NET INCREASE IN CASH AND CASH EQUIVALENTS	Add the subtotals from Operating, Financing and Investing Activities.
CASH AND EQUIVALENTS FROM THE BEGINNING OF THE YEAR	From the Balance Sheet
CASH AND CASH EQUIVALENTS AT END OF YEAR	Add two above numbers and compare with Balance Sheet.

CONSOLIDATED STATEMENT OF CASH FLOWS -- DERIVATION, continued

ITEMS REQUIRED FOR THE **DIRECT METHOD** OF PRESENTING THE STATEMENT OF CASH FLOW.	INSTRUCTIONS FOR PRODUCING THE REQUIRED ITEMS FROM THE **INDIRECT METHOD** OF PRESENTING THE STATEMENT OF CASH FLOW, INCOME STATEMENT AND BALANCE SHEET.

RECONCILIATION OF NET INCOME TO NET CASH PROVIDED BY OPERATING ACTIVITIES

Net Income	From Income Statement
Adjustments to reconcile net income to net cash provided by operating activities:	All of the following items are provided in the first section of the Indirect Method, Statement of Cash Flows:
a. Depreciation and amortization	A Source of Cash
b. Increase in Deferred Taxes	A Source of Cash
c. Provision for losses on Accounts Receivable	A Source of Cash
d. (Gain) or Loss on sale of facility	(A Use of Cash) A Source of Cash
e. Undistributed earnings of affiliates	(A Use of Cash)
f. Payments received on notes receivable	A Source of Cash
Changes in assets and liabilities net of effects from acquisitions	
a. Increase in Accounts Receivable	(A Use of Cash)
b. Increase in inventory	(A Use of Cash)
c. Increase in Prepaid Expenses	A Source of Cash

(continued)

Exhibit 7-2. *Continued.*

CONSOLIDATED STATEMENT OF CASH FLOWS -- DERIVATION, continued

ITEMS REQUIRED FOR THE **DIRECT METHOD** OF PRESENTING THE STATEMENT OF CASH FLOW.	INSTRUCTIONS FOR PRODUCING THE REQUIRED ITEMS FROM THE **INDIRECT METHOD** OF PRESENTING THE STATEMENT OF CASH FLOW, INCOME STATEMENT AND BALANCE SHEET.
d. Increases in Accounts Payable and Accrued Expenses	A Source of Cash
e. Increases in other Current Liabilities except Current Portion of Long-term Debt	A Source of Cash
TOTAL ADJUSTMENTS	Subtotal
NET CASH PROVIDED BY OPERATING ACTIVITY	Add Net Income and Total Adjustments

Supplemental schedule of noncash investing and financing activities:	
Fair value of assets acquired	Should be available on Indirect Statement of Cash Flows.
Cash paid for stock	Should be available on Indirect Statement of Cash Flows.
Liabilities assumed (ADD)	Difference between above two numbers

shrinking! Therefore, funds provided by operations can still be useful for solvency analysis.

Funds provided by operations. Exhibit 5-2A slightly reorganizes the materials from SFAS #95's statement of cash flow; in lines {24} to {27} it includes the items from the APB #19's statement of changes' first subtotal of funds provided by operations. By appending an interim subtotal, useful supplemental information is generated, specifically, *the funds available for debt repayment before changes in current accounts.* If funds provided by operations are negative, there is unquestionably a severe problem.

Senior credit officers typically dislike negative figures. The implication of negative net cash provided by operating activities is that the firm is unable to produce any cash. Inevitably, cash flows from investing activities will also be negative, unless there is a major asset disposition. It will thus frequently appear that cash flow from financing activities is the company's only source of cash.

The major difficulty in completing this section is line {27}, adjustment to reconcile net income with cash. This is the admission that net income is a poor starting point to calculate actual cash flowing through the organization. It includes a number of adjustments that made income and cash flow depart from each other in addition to depreciation and deferred taxes. It includes, for example:

- Changes in the provision for losses on accounts receivable
- Gains on sales of assets
- Undistributed earnings of affiliates
- Accruals in expenses for deferred compensation plans
- Gains or losses from discontinued operations
- Changes and reclassifications in the deferred tax account

Net cash provided by operations. The next subtotal including lines {29} through {32} takes the changes in current assets and liabilities into account. It also shows them in a way that is familiar to sources and uses experienced analysts. Clearly, a corporate treasurer should be questioned if, for instance, additional funds are being invested in accounts receivable and inventories, but sales are not increasing.

Net cash after investments. For lines {34} through {36}, the analyst must add in capital equipment expenditures and use of corporate funds to acquire *other* firms' stock or assets. Although the sale of fixed assets or previous investments may reduce the outlay, this section almost always produces a negative value.

Net cash after financing activities. Although not given a separate subtotal in the exhibit, the payment of dividends, issuance or repurchase of the company's own stock, and the acquiring of new long-term debt or paying off old debt are the items that bring a reconciliation to the cash and equivalents.

The SCF is an excellent tool overall. It represents a departure from concepts such as accrual accounting and revenue and expense matching—concepts that introduce so many estimates into the calculations of net income as to make it an unreliable gauge of the firm's debt repayment capacity in many cases. Permitting firms to report on a net cash flow basis is perhaps less of a problem in the near future than allowing extraordinary cash flow items to be carried as operating activities. Consequently, the lender must adjust the subtotals in the SCF to determine the firm's recurring capacity of repaying debt.

Key Points: The statement of cash flow is a useful tool that should provide the lender with more information about a company and more questions for the company's management. It represents a departure from accrual accounting and provides the lender with a good indication of the cash a company has available to repay debt.

Review of Completed United Enterprises, Inc. Spread

To summarize the income and cash flow spreadsheet section of the book, Exhibit 7-3 presents United Enterprises, Inc. (UEI) financial statements (originally shown as Exhibit 1-1) placed into the spreadsheet Worksheet 2A (originally shown as Exhibit 5-2A).

(Text continued on page 174.)

Exhibit 7-3.
INCOME STATEMENT AND CASH FLOW: TREND ANALYSIS & ADJUSTED VALUES

Company Name: United Enterprises, Inc. and Consolidated Subsidiaries

Rounded to: millions (000,000's)

	Statement Dates:	31-Dec-89		31-Dec-90		Dec-90 ADJ. VALUES		SEE NOTES
	INCOME STATEMENT	$	%	$	%	$	%	
1	Net Sales (Revenues)	$1,041.3	100%	$971.4	100%	$971.4	100%	1
2	Cost of Goods Sold (Less Dep)	760.1	73%	707.4	73%	709.4	73%	2
3	Depreciation Expense	23.3	2%	26.4	3%	37.2	4%	2
4	Gross Profit	257.9	25%	237.6	24%	224.8	23%	
5	Selling Expense	102.5	10%	106.7	11%	107.9	11%	2
6	General & Admin. Expense	73.7	7%	79.0	8%	79.7	8%	2
7	Officers' Compensation							
8	Other Operating Expenses							
9	Operating Income	81.7	8%	51.9	5%	37.2	4%	3
10	Other Non-Operating Income	9.1	1%	14.8	2%	7.5	1%	
11	(Interest Expense)	-14.2	-1%	-11.9	-1%	-11.9	-1%	
12	Interest Income							
13	(Other Non-Operating Expense)							
14	(Plant Closings & Writedowns)	-3.8	-0%	-3.1	-0%	-3.1	-0%	
15	Earnings on Equity Investments	7.0	1%	7.8	1%	7.8	1%	
16	Profit Before Tax	79.8	8%	59.5	6%	37.5	4%	
17	Provision for Income Tax	36.5	4%	28.3	3%	25.0	3%	
18	Income Fr Contin. Operations	43.3	4%	31.2	3%	12.5	1%	3 & 4
19	Net Profit fr Discont Operations	-10.6	-1%					5
20	Gain (Loss) on Sale of Operations	-95.4	-9%					
21	Income (Loss) Bef Extra Earn	-62.7	-6%	31.2	3%	12.5	1%	
22	Extraordinary Income (Loss)					4.0	0%	
23	Net Profit	-62.7	-6%	31.2	3%	16.5	2%	3

CASH FLOW STATEMENT					ADJ. VALUES		
24 Net Income Fr Continuing Operations	43.3	59%	31.2	44%	12.5	18%	2
25 Depreciation & Amortization	23.3	32%	26.4	37%	37.2	55%	6
26 Change in Deferred Taxes	7.2	10%	20.6	29%	20.6	30%	
27 Adjustment to Reconcile Net Inc	-0.9	-1%	-6.5	-9%	-2.5	-4%	
28 **Funds Flow From Operations**	**72.9**	100%	**71.7**	100%	**67.8**	100%	
29 (Increase in Accounts Receiveable)	-5.1	-7%	13.0	18%	13.0	19%	
30 (Incr. in Inventory & Other Cur Ass)	-25.9	-36%	29.5	41%	29.5	44%	
31 Increase in Accounts Payable	18.3	25%	-17.0	-24%	-17.0	-25%	
32 Incr. in Accruals & Other Cur. Liabs.							
33 **Net Cash Provided By Operations**	**60.2**	83%	**97.2**	136%	**93.3**	138%	
34 Fixed Asset Sales	-4.9	-7%	7.0	10%	7.0	10%	
35 (Net Capital Expenditures)	-38.2	-52%	-30.2	-42%	-30.2	-45%	7
36 (Purchase of Companies/Assets)	-22.1	-30%	-9.6	-13%	-51.3	-76%	
37 **Funds After Investments**	**-5.0**	-7%	**64.4**	90%	**18.8**	28%	
38 Increase in Long-Term Debt	-1.6	-2%	16.7	23%	27.4	40%	7
39 Issuance (Purchase) Own Stock	-1.3	-2%	-38.8	-54%	-38.8	-57%	
40 (Dividends)	-21.5	-29%	-21.2	-30%	-21.2	-31%	
41 **Net Change In Cash and Equiv.**	**-29.4**	-40%	**21.1**	29%	**-13.8**	-20%	7 & 8

Short FIFO Adjustment

NOTES:

1. Positive number = a Source of Cash, and a Negative number = a Use of Cash
2. You may have only enough information to just complete the current year cash flow

First, the income statements and statements of cash flow have been directly transferred to the first two columns of the worksheet with only modest changes to accommodate its more universal asset and liability names. Cases in point are:

- Depreciation {3} has been obtained from the Statement of Cash Flow and subtracted from the Cost of Products Sold to derive Cost of Goods Sold (Less Depreciation) {2}.
- Other income has been moved to the more appropriate category Other Non-Operating Income {10}.
- The two items representing sources of funds from the deferred tax account (one is a change and the other is a reclassification) are consolidated in a single number on the Statement of Cash Flow {26}.
- Two items have been consolidated into the Adjustment to Reconcile Net Income {27}: the Undistributed Earnings of Affiliates, a non-cash credit to income; and the unspecified "Other (net)" at the bottom of the Operating Activities section.

An additional change in appearance has resulted from rounding the numbers to millions, rather than the thousands used in the financial statement. However, major changes have resulted in the presentation in the third column to the right. The notes which follow relate to the third column of Exhibit 7-3.

Income Statement

Note 1: Net Sales

Sales occur when products or services are delivered. While the UEI Income Statement gives no information on returns of merchandise, it is assumed to be insignificant if no notes about it are present.

Note 2: Depreciation Expense

For depreciation, the Supplemental Information on Changing Prices (Exhibit 1-1, pp. 3–4) has been used to obtain the new depreciation expense of $37.2 million. Since revised values were given for the Selling Expense and General and Administrative Expenses (incorporating the change in them caused by depreciation), the reduction in the Cost of Good Sold (Less Depreciation) is greater than it should be. Nevertheless, the small inaccuracy is justified by seeing the relationship between the information from the Supplemental Information on Changing Prices and the Adjusted Value column.

Note 3: Other Non-Operating Income

Footnote F reports "$7.3 million ($4 million after tax . . .) associated with litigation settlements." This analyst is not about to consider proceeds of litigation settlements to be operating income for any firm other than a law firm. While perhaps insignificant in relation to Net Sales, the number could be significant when compared to the Net Income; therefore, $4 million is segregated into Extraordinary Income {22}, and the difference of $3.3 million is deducted from Provision for Income Tax {17}.

Note 4: Provision for Income Taxes

While the Provision for Income Taxes is not the cash flow actually being paid out by UEI, it has been left in its present state because the Statement of Cash Flow will add back any change in the Deferred Tax Account.

Note 5: Gain on Sale of Operations

While footnote B identifies sales of asset transactions, they are for discontinued operations that have been reserved against. Therefore, there is no effect on the Income Statement, even though there is clearly a cash flow involved that it would be useful to know more about.

Cash Flow Statement

Note 6: Adjustments to Reconcile Net Income

Besides the previous adjustments mentioned above, the extraordinary item referenced in Note 3 is also incorporated here.

Note 7: Purchase of Companies/Assets

The acquisition noted in Footnote K is incorporated not only into the Balance Sheet on worksheet 1 of the spreadsheet (Exhibit 4-3), but also into the Statement of Cash Flows by increasing the long-term debt by $10.7 million, increasing purchases of companies by $41.7 and decreasing cash and marketable securities by $31 million.

Note 8: Change in Cash and Equivalents

Besides the change in depreciation derived from the Supplemental Statement on Changing Prices, there is an unexplained difference between the change of $14.7 million in Net Income and the $10.8 million change in Depreciation. This difference of $3.9 million is a result of using the FIFO accounting convention for inventories. This increases the apparent income, and increases income taxes, but does not increase cash, because the inventory is replaced at the new higher cost. It is removed as a consequence.

Shown net change	($13.8)
Add back FIFO adjustment	3.9
Add back acquisition net adjustment	31.0
Total showing previous column	21.1

Chapter 8

Use of Ratios in Liquidity and Solvency Analysis

Purpose and Types of Analysis

Ratios are the primary tool of financial statement analysis. The most commonly used ratios in financial analysis are those that have been passed down by previous generations of lenders who found them useful. Newer ratios introduced by theoreticians have been slow to gain acceptance among lenders; still, they meet important analytical objectives. Although ratios are frequently used to discriminate between stronger and weaker companies or to estimate a company's financial vulnerability, the primary objective of ratio analysis should be to point out where additional information about a company's financial condition is needed. This is because ratios are merely combinations of numbers that are themselves estimates. In reconstructing the business activities of a firm from the accounting data, the analyst can use ratio analysis to supply the questions whose answers spotlight the management decisions that produced the result reported.

When analyzing ratios, the lender typically looks for two things. One is a deviation from industry standards (**comparative analysis**), and the other is a deviation from the firm's past performance (**trend analysis**). Ordinarily, firms within the same industry have similar ratios. Thus, industry averages are useful standards against which to measure an individual firm. Deviations from industry averages are an example of how use of ratios identifies a need for further investigation.

Trend analysis involves analyzing how ratios change over time within one firm. By observing trends, the lender can detect problem areas and question management about them. Such questions will not come as a surprise since management typically knows which of its firm's ratios are out of line with the industry average or the firm's previous history.

About the Ratios Used Here

Thirty-five ratios are presented in this segment so that the analyst may pick and choose among them. They are automatically calculated if you are using the

LOTUS 1-2-3 spreadsheet template that can be ordered with the book. They are on the second page of both the balance sheet (Exhibit 2-2) and income statement (Exhibit 5-2) spread. Every lending decision does not require every ratio. As a general rule, no more than a few ratios should be discussed in the write-up. While the computer can help calculate the more sophisticated ratios, the computer can also facilely figure dozens of complicated ratios that can produce unmanageable amounts of information for senior credit officers to digest.

Big Lotus 1-2-3 Spreadsheet

In one financial institution, a LOTUS 1-2-3 template was used for financial statement spreadsheet analysis. Although it was an intelligent use of 1-2-3, certain aspects of the spreadsheet were so restrictive that they marred the analysis. Instead of allowing the analyst to delete ratios that did not indicate anything abnormal, the template had to be printed out in full and presented as part of the credit review. The computer printout of the spreadsheet was *eight pages long!* With so many ratios and other derived numbers presented, senior credit officers were overwhelmed by information.

Thus, this potentially useful tool was improperly used by policies that refused to permit the analyst to judge what was important. Consider the suppositions that had already been made by the customer's management and their accountants while preparing the financial statement; consider as well judgments that had been made by the analyst in spreading the financial statements. A policy demanding the full presentation of all computer-generated ratios seems ludicrous. As it turns out, two years after the advent of this spreadsheet program, analysts felt more confident of their capabilities and started deleting chunks of the computerized spreadsheet so that could they present something that was more cogent. If an analyst earns the trust of the senior credit officers and has typically employed good judgment in written analyses, then this sort of discretion should be permitted.

Key Points: Although it may be possible to quickly calculate and review all ratios, not all ratios should be included in the credit review.

Ratios and Statistics

Ratio analysis is similar to statistical analysis in that both emphasize averages. Because a firm's ratios are good, it does not mean that during the course of the year management made no errors and fulfilled all of its expectations. Yet lenders often give the benefit of the doubt to the firm that exhibits good ratios and surmise that the ratios for the company will continue to be good. It is important for lenders to consider that ratios can be manipulated. Indeed, it is possible to use some obscure ratios to prove just about any preconceived notion about a firm—just like in statistics. Before highlighting a ratio as a red flag, the analyst should be sure that some analytical muscle is behind it.

A later section focuses on using ratios to predict the likelihood of bankruptcy. Many studies of this function have been undertaken, and the most famous was conducted by Edward Altman, a professor at New York University.

The reason for Altman's success is that he selected ratios grounded in theory. He was also careful to select ratios that, while empirically valid, supported practically every existing theory about how a firm should look financially. His ratios focused on liquidity, leverage, and performance, which are the three areas this segment will address. Understanding how each ratio substantiates a firm's viability or vulnerability in one of these three areas is essential to ratio analysis.

> **Key Points:** Selection of ratios can be manipulated to prove just about any point. Before highlighting a ratio as a red flag, make sure that it is more than an empty statistic.

Window-Dressing Ratios

Notwithstanding the purpose of ratios, lenders and investors tend to base their lending decisions directly on ratios; this encourages firms to "window dress" their financial statements. A company window dresses in order to improve the appearance of its financial statements. The corporate treasurer is well aware of the conventional ratios that lenders use to make decisions and thus makes every effort to ensure that the financial accounts of the firm are arranged to produce the most favorable image possible. Often window dressing is unsophisticated and can be easily detected. Less obvious means of window dressing, such as off-balance-sheet financing, are also commonplace, however, and the lender must be alert to them.

A firm is always in competition with other firms in the industry for funds from lenders and stockholders. If a company does not look good financially, funds are going to be difficult to obtain. In turn, suppliers, employees, and customers may also be difficult to obtain. Creditors, customers, and workers are attracted to competitors that have the strongest financial positions.

By focusing too much on ratios, lenders run the risk of committing both type 1 and type 2 errors. (That is, they are more likely to refuse credit to companies that would repay loans and lend to companies that would not.) Typically, companies with excellent ratios have their loan rates bid down by competing creditors to such a degree that the loans become only marginally profitable. In fact, the likelihood of making prudently profitable loans is slim for the lender that loans solely on the basis of ratios; this is because the firm whose overall position justifies a better rate frequently must pay for the sole reason of its weak ratios.

Admittedly there might be a problem for bankers in extending credit to firms whose ratios are below industry standards. Banking portfolio regulators (including the Federal Deposit Insurance Corp. and state and Federal regulators) are some of the worst abusers, slavishly seeking only good ratio performance during their loan portfolio evaluations. They also tend to form conclusions based on only partial information, and this intimidates bank lending officers.

Common-Size Ratios

Common-size analysis is a method for relating the various accounts within the balance sheet and income statement using percentages. For the balance sheet, all entries are expressed as a percentage of total assets, also known as total footings. Each entry on the balance sheet is divided by total footings to produce its respective common size. On the income statement, all entries are presented as a percentage of sales. Thus, the common size for total (or net) sales is 100%. Common sizes can also be used for the statement of cash flow.

Common-size calculations are helpful because, by reducing everything to two digits, it is easy to spot changes and trends and to see the relationships between various accounts. The calculations are easy to do and most spreadsheet forms (as Exhibit 2-2) include a column next to the dollar one in which to place these percentages.

While some may lump all common-size ratios in a separate table, the common-size calculations should be entered next to the raw numbers on the spreadsheet because common-size calculations by themselves can be misleading. During the early 1980s recession, the cost of goods sold as a percentage of sales rose dramatically for most firms. This increase made it appear as though companies were losing control of their costs and that productivity was falling. What was actually happening, however, was that companies were dropping prices in order to maintain sales and production levels. Price cuts depressed margins and percentages made it appear that cost of goods sold was increasing. In fact, cost of goods sold as a percentage of unit sales had stayed the same. Unit volume, however, had increased and sales prices were falling.

Examples of how cost of goods sold can change the common-size percentages in surprising ways include variations on the profit margin change hypotheses: (1) reductions in raw materials cost and (2) improved controls on costs and asset use, possibly evidenced by enhanced asset turnovers.

Moreover, other changes in profit margins can be caused by (1) sale of assets boosting revenues and (2) one-time tax adjustments.

Key Points: Common-size analysis represents balance sheet entries as a percentage of total assets (or footings) and income statement entries as a percentage of sales.

Analysis of Account Liquidity

Liquidity is the ability to raise cash. An asset is liquid when it can quickly and easily be converted to cash at a price near its market value. Treasury bills are the prime example of a liquid asset since they can be sold immediately at their market value by paying only a small commission. **Liquidity** has also been defined as the ability to meet short-term financial obligations without having to liquidate long-term assets and the ability to convert assets to cash. This latter definition is a good one. Recall that assets are listed on the balance sheet in order of their liquidity with the most liquid asset, cash, listed first.

Cash and Marketable Securities

Obviously cash is the most liquid asset followed by marketable securities and accounts receivable. Marketable securities can be pledged to secure loans. It is important to make sure that the apparent liquidity of various assets is not compromised by liens or other restrictions on their use.

La Quinta Motor Inns

An example of the importance of checking on the liquidity of assets can be found by looking at the motel developer, La Quinta Motor Inns. La Quinta maintains substantial balances of cash and marketable securities. Marketable securities are acquired with funds derived from local industrial revenue bonds (IRBs) issued to allow La Quinta to build motels in the Sun Belt, which is the company's marketplace. These funds are restricted for use only in constructing motels in the area in which the bonds were sold. La Quinta must keep very exacting records on how it uses these funds. These funds may not be commingled with other cash on hand nor can they be used to pay La Quinta's other bills. Thus, the cash account is not as available as it initially appears.

United Enterprises, Inc. (cont.)

Another example of assets that may be less liquid than they appear at first glance can be found by looking at the large cash and time deposit balances in United Enterprises' December 31, 1990 financial statements (Exhibit 1-1). United Enterprises planned to acquire a lighting fixture manufacturer on January 1, 1991 (see Note K in Exhibit 1-1). Although the acquisition required the outlay of $40 million in cash, the company did not segregate liquid assets in any way even one day before the closing! United Enterprises thus appeared to be extremely liquid. Yet, *all its cash and marketable securities were committed* to the transaction.

> **Key Points:** Make sure that the availability of cash and marketable securities is not restricted in any way.

Accounts Receivable

The liquidity of accounts receivable can be difficult to assess. For example, when a company's sales are declining, its managers may be tempted to reduce credit standards and take any potential sale on credit with little screening. The temptation would be especially compelling for the firm that sells items at a high markup.

High Markup Shoe Importer

As an example of how a company might accept marginal credits, consider a shoe importer. The firm buys shoes abroad for $7.50 a pair and wholesales them for $30 a pair to retail stores that in turn charge consumers $50. The sales division dominates the administration of the shoe importing company and each salesperson reports directly to the president. The controller has the responsibility of approving credit for any potential customers. If the controller turns down a credit request, the salesperson would likely go straight to the president's office to complain. Naturally the president has to resolve the dispute between the salesperson, who thinks every customer is as good as gold, and the controller, whose *Dun & Bradstreet Report* (a private credit reporting agency) shows the customer paying late or not at all.

(Among other general bibliographical information supplied on any firm, the *D&B* report gives the payment history as relayed to it by suppliers of the firm in question. Thus, the status of its accounts payable is reported in a list on the front page. Looking at this page with dozens of "slow," "past due," and "in litigation" labels, it is comparatively easy to draw the conclusion that most new suppliers will have an accounts receivable problem with such a client.) Instead, the controller compromises by requiring of customers a 25% down payment on the shoes. This way, the company can cover its costs and have only the profit at risk.

Another potential problem with accounts receivable is that a financially distressed company is apt to slightly compromise the quality of its goods by cutting corners. The extent to which quality has dropped can become an issue if the firm gets into serious financial difficulties. Commercial finance companies that occasionally assist firms in financial difficulty have found that rumors of bankruptcy cause customers to slow their payments.

Bankrupt Receivables

If a firm files for bankruptcy, the tone of its obligors becomes uncompromising. Customers may refuse to pay their debts, explaining to the finance company who bought the receivables that it received a defective shipment. This is a difficult claim to refute. Since the finance company has little ability to judge whether the customer's shipment met the usual standards, it typically will seek some compromise to avoid the merchandise being returned.

Key Points: Accounts receivable may not be as liquid as they appear.

Inventory

Typically, a firm must obtain an appraisal before any financing of inventory can take place. Commercial finance companies typically are willing to finance about 50% of the appraised inventory value. The inventory's liquidity depends on the relative amounts of raw materials, work in process, and finished goods. We have already discussed the problem of estimating work in process. During a bankruptcy, the liquidity of work in process is low since the production process may have come to a complete halt. Usually raw materials are the most liquid component of inventory followed by finished goods.

Key Points: Raw materials are the most liquid of the components of inventory, followed by finished goods. Work in process is the least liquid component.

Fixed Assets

Fixed assets include real estate, an illiquid asset. At the other end of the spectrum, they also include equipment that is fungible, that is, equipment that many companies can use such as a corporate jet aircraft; being fungible, therefore, it has a certain amount of liquidity. In contrast, installations of equipment in which the building and the equipment are practically one and the same (for instance, a coal-washing plant) are illiquid since they are fixed in place and are not easily used by another firm.

> **Key Points:** In general, fixed assets are not very liquid. Some equipment, however, such as a corporate jet, can be used by different companies and therefore does exhibit liquidity.

Intangibles

Although intangibles may have considerable value, they are generally not liquid. There are exceptions, such as the New York City taxi medallion, which is readily marketable. A franchise like McDonald's, for instance, may also be readily salable.

> **Key Points:** Although there are some exceptions, intangible assets are generally not liquid.

Liquidity Ratios—Part I: Quantity Ratios

Liquidity ratios fall into two groupings: quantity ratios and turnover ratios. Exhibit 8-1 lists the quantity or balance-sheet-focused liquidity ratios and their definitions.

Exhibit 8-1.

QUANTITY RATIOS

RATIO NAME	RATIO DEFINITION	Traditional Lender Preferred Relationship
Current Ratio	$\dfrac{\text{Current Assets}}{\text{Current Liabilities}}$	$\dfrac{2}{1}$
Quick Ratio (Acid Test)	$\dfrac{\text{Cash + Accounts Receivable}}{\text{Current Liabilities}}$	$\dfrac{1}{1}$
Working Capital	Current Assets - Current Liabilities	HIGH

Current Ratio

Foremost among the balance sheet ratios is the current ratio. It is popular because it is easy to calculate—one need simply divide current assets by current liabilities. As a rule of thumb, traditional lenders like to see a current ratio of 2 to 1. The reason is that a 2:1 current ratio implies high liquidity and suggests that the firm will have the ability to meet current liabilities. Even if current assets are converted to cash less quickly than the accounts payable and accruals, 2 to 1 gives sufficient coverage to eliminate concern.

Another factor behind the popularity of the 2:1 current ratio is its value in predicting the cash proceeds of a liquidation. It is generally accepted that in times of trouble the way to move merchandise is to take 50% off its price.

United Merchants and Manufacturers—Part I

When United Merchants and Manufacturers, once the largest manufacturer of men's clothing in the United States, went bankrupt in 1979, the inventory of its large men's store chain, Robert Hall Clothes, was sold off for 47 cents on the dollar—including the racks. This is not 47 cents on the dollar of retail value but 47 cents on the dollar of cost: the capitalized expenditures to generate finished goods inventory on the books of United Merchants and Manufacturers.

This outcome has been repeated innumerable times, and financial analysts do not hesitate to reduce asset value by 50% if they anticipate liquidation. Auctioneers, whose goal is to effect a quick sale rather than to obtain market prices, perform liquidations. With this in mind, the philosophy behind the 2 to 1 rule is disernible: The 2:1 current ratio suggest that even compromising assets with a 50% "haircut," they would still generate enough cash to pay off all current creditors.

On the other hand, if the analyst's goal is to be certain that the firm has sufficient funds available to meet obligations, and if the current portion of the balance sheet lists assets and liabilities due within the next year, even a 1:1 current ratio would appear to be adequate.

In addition to being ruled by an overly conservative rule of thumb, the current ratio is at the mercy of window dressing. The first column of Exhibit 8-2 shows a firm's trial balance at December 30, one day before the closing of the firm's books for the fiscal year. The current ratio is only 1.5 to 1. Since the creditor will not be pleased, the treasurer must do something to improve it. He might, for instance, try to have a quick sale and get rid of some inventory (column 2). Unfortunately, this would merely move assets from the inventory to accounts receivable. (Although profit would be included, the increase in current assets would probably be insufficient to improve the current ratio.)

Alternatively, the treasurer might try very hard to collect the accounts receivable over the one-day period (column 3). Again this merely converts the accounts receivables to cash and does not change the current ratio in the slightest way.

The firm might order and take delivery of additional inventory (column 4). Unfortunately, this would increase both sides of the balance sheet and cause

Exhibit 8-2.

WINDOW DRESSING THE CURRENT RATIO

BALANCE SHEET		Each of the "Trys" is a variation of the first column.			
ASSETS	Initially	1st Try	2nd Try	3rd Try	Success!
Cash	$2,100	$2,100	$3,600	$2,100	$0
Accounts Receivable	2,000	4,500	500	2,000	2,000
Inventory	2,200	500	2,200	4,200	2,200
Total Current Assets	6,300	7,100	6,300	8,300	4,200
Fixed Assets	6,000	6,000	6,000	6,000	6,000
Total Assets	12,300	13,100	12,300	14,300	10,200
LIABILITIES					
Notes Payable	1,800	1,800	1,800	1,800	0
Accounts Payable	1,500	1,500	1,500	3,500	1,200
Accrued Expenses	900	900	900	900	900
Total Current Liabilities	4,200	4,200	4,200	6,200	2,100
Long Term Debt	3,000	3,000	3,000	3,000	3,000
Total Debt	7,200	7,200	7,200	9,200	5,100
Net Worth	5,100	5,900	5,100	5,100	5,100
Total Liabilities and Net Worth	12,300	13,100	12,300	14,300	10,200
RATIO CALCULATION					
Current Assets	6,300	7,100	6,300	8,300	4,200
Current Liabilities	4,200	4,200	4,200	6,200	2,100
	=	=	=	=	=
Current Ratio	**1.50**	**1.69**	**1.50**	**1.34**	**2.00**

the current ratio to fall below 1.5. This is an insight: It seems that increasing both sides by the same amount (assuming an initial ratio of more than 1:1) makes the ratio worse.

Perhaps, by reversing this process, the ratio can be improved. Column 5 of Exhibit 8-2 shows what happens when the treasurer uses cash on hand to pay off notes payable and some accounts payable. The current ratio increases to the 2:1 value required by creditors. Literally nothing has changed, but using up available cash to pay any current liabilities, as long as the ratio was initially at least 1:1, will always improve the ratio.

The Quick Ratio (Acid Test)

The quick ratio equals cash plus accounts receivable divided by total current liabilities. By eliminating inventory, which is typically the least liquid of the current assets, the quick ratio attempts to improve the validity of the test of the company's ability to pay its current liabilities. Traditionally, cash, marketable securities, and accounts receivable should be sufficient to cover current liabilities—that is, the quick ratio should be 1:1. One of the assumptions behind this rationale is that accounts payable and accounts receivable have matching maturity schedules. Therefore, with cash and accounts receivable equal to total current liabilities, the lender is safe.

Unfortunately, the quick ratio would not even show that the firm has just done some fast window dressing in Exhibit 8-2. The quick ratio is unchanged at 1:1 after the use of cash to pay off notes and trade payables. Lax accounts receivable policies are also not identified.

Net Working Capital

The term **net working capital** is almost always shortened to **working capital** by bankers; they calculate it by taking the difference between current assets and current liabilities. By itself, working capital is a useless number. It is only useful for comparison with values of previous periods.

General Motors

If, for example, one day the newspaper reported that during the last quarter General Motors' working capital had fallen $4 billion, you might be aghast, not realizing that General Motors was having so many financial problems. How relieved you might be to scan the first couple of paragraphs of the article and discover that the working capital of General Motors had been $7 billion and now had been cut to a mere $3 billion.

Often, a lender's review of financial statements is focused on obtaining confidence that obligations can be paid even if a firm encounters severe problems. If the preponderance of assets is in cash, marketable securities, accounts receivable, and inventory, lenders are less concerned about a company. Unfortunately, maintaining substantial assets in these categories may not be profitable for the company.

Traditional analysts also like to see low current liabilities. On the liability side of the balance sheet overall, the analyst prefers to see more net worth and less debt. The difference between the current assets and the current liabilities thus becomes an important number. It is intuitively obvious that if current liabilities are very low and current assets are very high, bills will be paid on time. But, if a firm in trouble is pushing inventory out the door to any company that will take it, the resulting low quality of accounts receivable will hurt liquidity just as much as if the merchandise had not been sold. Neither the current nor quick ratio will show this weakness.

Maintaining high levels of cash and marketable securities has its rewards: Opportunities exist for firms with ready cash. Such firms can take advantage of bargains available on the spot market for various commodities and they can make quick investment decisions. In short, companies with cash command a certain freedom of operation that does not exist for the companies that have to go to their lenders whenever an opportunity presents itself.

> **Key Points:** The current and other balance sheet ratios are susceptible to window dressing and these quantity ratios give more of a rough idea of the outcome of liquidations than any real indication about the firm's ability to repay debt.

Liquidity Ratios—Part II: Cash Conversion

The lender must understand two important points. First, a ratio that is valuable for liquidity analysis shoud show not only a firm's cash position but also the firm's ability to generate cash over the longer term, because that is when creditors expect to be paid. Second, firms exhibiting liquidity ratios that easily meet the rule-of-thumb standards are not representative of the critical situations in which analytical skill is required. For these potentially hazardous situations, the finer-tuning of operating cycle analysis is necessary. What follows is a series of illustrations of how the operating cycle affects liquidity needs in the future. *Without examining the interrelationship between the operating cycle and liquidity, it is almost impossible to make reliable lending decisions.* Consider close examination of the operating cycle an example of fine-tuning, like, for instance, this illustration:

Mensa Society

> The Mensa Society is an organization for people with IQs over 140. They are in the top 1% of the population in terms of IQs and have a standing complaint about standardized IQ tests. The Mensa Society claims that these tests are prepared to measure people with average IQs of 100. They acknowledge that the tests may be adequate for measuring one or two standard deviations from the mean, which includes IQs from 70 to 130, and includes 95% of the population. But the IQ tests do not discern well enough the differences in intellect among people with IQs of 140, 150, 160, 170, and so on.
>
> Although few people are curious about whether their IQs are 140 or 160, it is quite possible, and the Mensa Society has done this, to create a test to distinguish between people with 140 IQ and above. Therefore the test would not be good at distinguishing between those with 100 IQ and those with a 70 IQ.

The point of this example is that lenders must learn where to focus their credit analysis tests. Firms with above-standard quantity (see Exhibit 8-1) ratios have low risk and the primary purpose of analysis of their statements is creation of documentation for the bank examiners. The more complex task is for lenders (1) to analyze firms that need funds and (2) to distinguish between those that will pay the debt back and those that will not.

The firms that approach lenders for financing typically need money to support sales growth, or a research and development undertaking, or even an acquisition of another business. That is, they are planning to make a change that requires additional funds. It is extremely important for lenders to pay careful attention to firms that have high relative needs for funds. The ratios of these firms will provide little guidance to the credit officer, who should not compare them to firms that are flush with cash and thus require no loans.

The Operating Cycle Length

A firm's genuine need for liquidity will vary depending entirely on the length of its operating cycle. Recall that the operating cycle (see Exhibit 5-1) follows the following general pattern:

1. Raw materials are acquired and taken into inventory.
2. Labor is added and finished goods are produced.
3. Finished goods are sold; inventories are converted to accounts receivable.
4. Receivables are collected so that cash is available to pay the suppliers, labor, and stockholders. Moreover, a lender may have helped finance the conversion cycle and must also be repaid.

The interval during which this conversion of raw materials to cash takes place is a key to how much liquidity a firm requires. Let's look at a couple of examples of operating cycles and how the business activities of two different industries are affected.

Sebastian's Restaurant and Chivas Crown—Part I

A restaurant is a suitable example of a firm with a short operating cycle and, thus, little need for liquidity. In contrast, a spirits distiller has a long operating cycle and greater liquidity needs. Exhibit 8-3 shows two abbreviated, hypothetical financial statements, one of Sebastian's, a restaurant, and the other of Chivas Crown, a distiller. Assume that both firms pay wages on a weekly basis; thus, the accrued expenses of both firms will be limited to one week's wages. They acquire raw materials and make other expenditures such as advertising, which are proportional to their sales; therefore, their accounts payable will be proportional. The differences between the firms arise from the fact that Chivas holds some inventory for 12 years whereas the restaurant probably holds inventory for only 4 days. The conversion cycle of the restaurant is so short and its turnover of current assets is so quick that the owners do not need to have the money on hand even on Monday to pay wages due on Friday. The entire conversion cycle of the restaurant will turn over nearly 2 times before a wage payment is required.

In addition to the 12-year inventory, Chivas will supply 60 days of credit to its wholesale distributors, building up its accounts receivable. It is unlikely that any of Chivas's suppliers will offer terms longer than 30 to 60 days. The Scotch distiller must have considerable working capital to carry the inventory for 12 years and remain current with suppliers.

Key Points: The shorter a firm's operating cycle, the less its need for liquidity.

(Text continued on page 190.)

Exhibit 8-3.

OPERATING CYCLE COMPARISON

As of December 31

	Initial Situation		Part II	
	Sebastian's In Dollars	Chivas Crown In 000's of Dollars	Sebastian's In Dollars	Chivas Crown In 000's of Dollars
INCOME STATEMENT				
Sales	$1,236,700	$1,236,700	$1,236,700	$1,236,700
Cost of Goods Sold	$865,690	$865,690	$865,690	$865,690
General, Selling & Admin Ex	$185,505	$185,505	$185,505	$185,505
Net Income Before Taxes	$185,505	$185,505	$185,505	$185,505
Taxes	$63,072	$63,072	$63,072	$63,072
	$122,433	$122,433	$122,433	$122,433
BALANCE SHEET				
Assets				
Cash	$3,388 (1 day)	$23,783 (1 week)	$3,388	$23,783
Accounts Receivable	$10,306 (3 days)	$206,117 (60 days)	$10,306	$206,117
Inventory	$9,619 (4 days)	$865,690 (1 year)	$9,619	$865,690
Total Current Assets	$23,313	$1,095,589	$23,313	$1,095,589
Fixed Assets	$100,000	$600,000	$150,000	$600,000
Total Assets	$123,313	$1,695,589	$173,313	$1,695,589

Liabilities	Initial Situation		Part II	
	Sebastian's In Dollars	Chivas Crown In 000's of Dollars	Sebastian's In Dollars	Chivas Crown In 000's of Dollars
Notes Payable		$212,000		$212,000
Accounts Payable	$16,648 (7 days)	$72,141 (30 days)	$16,648	$72,141
Accrued Expenses	$3,567	$3,567	$3,567	$3,567
Current Portion L-T Debt			$25,000	$600,000
Total Current Liabilities	$20,215	$287,708	$45,215	$887,708
Long Term Debt	$20,000	$600,000	$45,000	
Total Debt	$40,215	$887,708	$90,215	$1,487,708
Net Worth	$83,098	$807,881	$83,098	$207,881
Total Liabilities and Net Worth	$123,313	$1,695,589	$173,313	$1,695,589
Working Capital Required	$3,098	$807,881	($21,902)	$207,881

RATIO ANALYSIS

	Sebastian's	Chivas Crown	Sebastian's	Chivas Crown
Current Ratio	1.15 to 1	3.81 to 1	0.52	1.23
Accounts Receivable Turnover	3 days	60 days	3	60
Inventory Turnover	4 days	360 days	4	360
Total Operating Cycle	7 days	420 days	7	420

Current Portion Long-Term Debt Dilemma

The current portion long-term debt, carried as a current liability, is the amount of long-term debt required by contract to be amortized within 12 months of the balance sheet date. Although the current asset and liability section of the balance sheet is set up to include anything maturing within a one-year period, this is *one of the few accounts that actually takes a full year to mature.* Accounts receivable and accounts payable are set by trade terms and very rarely extend beyond 90 days. Prepaid expenses and sundry receivables could extend out for a year, but it would be unusual. (Because sundry receivables are so difficult to pin down, most analysts carry them long—in the fixed asset section—anyway.)

Inventory is also an offspring of the operating cycle. Although production methods require that inventories of tobacco and liquor companies, for instance, remain in the raw material stage for periods significantly longer than one year, inventory is always carried as a current asset, due to historical precedent.

The firm's operating cycle gives a clear picture of the required payments and asset conversions to be made in the future. Although current liability accounts are self-renewing (new orders are placed with or near the time of payment for old orders), cash must be generated to repay the old items. As the operating cycle runs its course, the firm places new orders and the accounts payable balloons again. The work force continues working so that accruals rebuild as well.

If the operating cycle is longer than normal trade terms permitted by suppliers of labor and materials, additional funds will be needed to carry inventory and accounts receivable. These funds originate from the capital section of the balance sheet (below the current liabilities subtotal). Since the reason for using the current ratio as a liquidity test is to determine a firm's ability to make its required payments promptly, *the operating cycle should determine the portion of long-term debt that should be carried as a current liability.* Instead of carrying 12 months' worth of long-term debt payments as a current liability, only the portion of long-term debt related to the operating cycle of the firm should be carried current and included in the current ratio.

Sebastian's Restaurant and Chivas Crown—Part II

Referring again to Sebastian's Restaurant, suppose Sebastian's decides to place a new dishwasher and stainless steel counters in its kitchen. It obtains financing from its local bank—the full $50,000 cost to be paid over 2 years. If the loan is taken out on December 15, and Sebastian's fiscal year end is December 31, about one half of the total principal or $25,000, which normally would be repaid during the first 12 months, will appear on the current liability side of the balance sheet.

Refer to Sebastian's balance sheet (Part II columns) in Exhibit 8-3. Carrying this portion of debt results in an extremely low current ratio. If the first payment is due on January 1, Sebastian's current liabilities should reflect only that payment since it must be paid out of the cash account on hand within the 3-day conversion cycle of the firm. With this alteration, the current ratio reports something important and straightforward.

For Chivas Crown, the inclusion of long-term assets in inventory makes calculating a current ratio with only 1 year's worth of the (relatively larger) term loan payments showing as a current liability a meaningless exercise. Since not all of the inventory will be held for 12 years, the current ratio should be calculated by first calculating the average life of the inventory. Second, that factor should be multiplied by the total of GAAP current portion long-term debt plus long-term debt, proportionally increasing the new current portion long-term debt! (Exhibit 8-3 makes this adjustment, showing a great deal of the long-term debt of the distiller in the current account.) With this conformance, the current ratios of Sebastian's and Chivas will not be that different.

Actually, the more correct procedure might be to carry Chivas Crown inventories as the long-term assets they assuredly are.

In any case, the GAAP logic of carrying the entire amount of debt due within the next 12 months as a current liability is open to question. Current liabilities should correspond to the operating cycle. What causes liquidity to fall and how does a fall in liquidity hinder the scheduled repayment of the loan? One problem of financial statement analysis is that everything is relative. The convenience of absolutes (generalities or rules of thumb) is tempered by the fact that they are not applicable to every case. Declining liquidity in a restaurant, for instance, is less consequential than in a firm that has a long conversion cycle.

> **Key Points:** The portion of long-term debt that should be carried current should correspond to the firm's operating cycle. Otherwise, the current ratio will be misleading.

Liquidity Ratios—Part III: Quality Ratios

Since there are many problems with the quantity ratios, let's continue searching for additional assistance in solving the liquidity puzzle. Exhibit 8-4 lists the turnover ratios and their definitions. They include fixed assets, accounts receivable, inventory, and accounts payable turnovers. Basically turnover ratios determine whether an asset is stale. If inventory or accounts receivable have been in the firm's possession long enough to become stale, the probability that they will produce cash gradually becomes less and less. *Low turnover ratios can lead to the firm having liquidity problems more frequently than a low current ratio* (a prime example of a quantity ratio, the antithesis of the quality ratios). This is because if the quality turnover ratio indicates that current assets are stale, this *always* represents cash paid for assets whose value has fallen, whereas the significance of the current ratio is not changeless but bounded by the length of the operating cycle.

All turnover ratios are calculated from a balance sheet number and an income statement number. The income statement number adds a bit of dynamic flow to the analysis. The balance sheet, being completely static, often is a bad starting point for investigation of events that stretch over an entire year. By using information from the income statement and combining it with balance

Exhibit 8-4.

QUALITY RATIOS

RATIO NAME	RATIO DEFINITION	PREFERRED RELATIONSHIP
Asset Turnover	$\dfrac{\text{Net Sales}}{\text{Total Assets}}$	HIGH
Receivable Turnover (times)	$\dfrac{\text{Sales}}{\text{Accounts Receivable}}$	HIGH
Average Collection Period	$\dfrac{365}{\text{Receivable Turnover (times)}}$	LOW
Inventory Turnover (times)	$\dfrac{\text{Cost of Goods Sold}}{\text{Inventory}}$	HIGH
Average Days in Inventory	$\dfrac{365}{\text{Inventory Turnover (times)}}$	LOW
Accounts Payable Turnover	$\dfrac{\text{Cost of Goods Sold}}{\text{Payable}}$	HIGH
Operating Cycle	Average Collection Period + Average Days in Inventory	LOW

sheet numbers, it is more likely that the resulting calculations will be useful for making decisions.

Accounts Receivable Turnover

There are two different ways of expressing accounts receivable turnover. The first results from *dividing accounts receivable into sales*; this represents the number of times accounts receivable turns over per year. The second calculates the number of days in which receivables turn over on average, and is known as the **collection period**. The latter is calculated by *dividing number of times of turnover per year into 365*. For example, if you were to divide accounts receivable into sales and find that sales turned over 12 times a year, it would be easy to compute that accounts receivable were turning over once per month (30 days). Ideally, turnover times should be as large as possible and the collection period (in days) should be as small as possible. Either of these calculations indicates the receivables' liquidity and collectibility.

To be sure that the quality of the receivables is high, it is necessary to find out the payment terms that the firm offers its clients as well as the payment terms that are standard in the industry. If the firm's collection period is longer than it has been in the past, or longer that what is typically found in the industry, it is necessary to find out why. It is possible that the firm is extending credit to less creditworthy companies; it is also possible that the firm is carrying for an extended period a good customer who is in a cash bind. An extremely long collection period justifies requesting a detailed accounts receivable aging report as discussed in Chapter 2 (Exhibit 2-3).

Financing a customer's purchases is an excellent way of boosting sales. For the firm that decides to take this route (and its success would be evident in a rising sales figure) an increase in the collection period is not necessarily bad. Recall that using ratios in an absolute sense does not inexorably lead one to a correct credit decision. *It is important to understand why the ratio value has changed* rather than to assume that an increasing collection period means that management is not in control of the situation.

> **Key Points:** Accounts receivable turnover provides a rough indication of the age of receivables, a prime determinant of their quality.

Inventory Turnover

The inventory turnover ratio is not calculated by dividing inventory into sales, as is the case with fixed asset and receivables turnovers, because inventory is on the books at cost. Instead, this turnover should be calculated as *inventory divided into the cost of goods sold*, since most (if not all) of the flows to inventory proceeded through cost of goods sold. Some financial analysts do calculate inventory turnover by dividing inventory into sales. The problem with using sales in the calculation (in addition to the fact that because sales include profits, the number of times that inventory turns over would be overstated) is that firms have different levels of profitability. If one firm in a specific industry has a 20% net profit margin, and it is compared to a firm that has only a 2% margin, it will appear that the inventory in the firm with the higher profit margin is turning over more quickly. This in turn may erroneously lead one to believe that inventory turnover has something to do with profitability.

The number of times per year that inventory turns over can be divided into 365 to get the days of turnover per year, also known as the **inventory holding period.** It is preferred that a firm have as short a holding period as possible. A short holding period means that the inventory is turning over quickly. The rule-of-thumb for this ratio is that heavy-industry inventories should turn over about once every six months. It is rare to find a firm whose inventory is turning over more slowly than once a year, as the Scotch distiller exception. In fact, most production firms have inventories that turn over every 2 to 3 months.

If a firm's inventory turnover differs from its past performance or industry standard, management should be asked to explain the change.

Just-In-Time Inventory

An example of changing inventory turnover is the significant change in the auto industry: a shift to the just-in-time (JIT) inventory control system promoted by the Japanese. Previously, the car makers ordered new parts about every 4 to 6 months. They obtained bids from various suppliers and usually accepted the lowest bid consistent with quality. By ordering inventory this way, the auto manufacturers were creating expensive storage problems for themselves. They also created peak demand cycles for smaller suppliers, making efficiency for these smaller suppliers difficult and increasing their liquidity problems.

In the early 1980s, when interest rates and funding costs were high, the automobile manufacturers decided to reduce inventory to save money. By working more closely with suppliers, the auto makers enabled these smaller companies to operate more efficiently, even though they supplied in smaller quantities and on a more frequent basis than before. The manufacturers also realized considerable savings in not having to store and pay for inventory before it was needed.

A look at the financial statements of Chrysler immediately before and after its brush with bankruptcy reflects the significant difference that a change in inventory policy can make. Inventories were drastically curtailed at Chrysler. In fact, this new control was one of Iacocca's principal changes in Chrysler's operations. It improved liquidity and helped the company intitially to survive on a much smaller scale and to expand later without the need for additional working capital. The funds freed up from inventory were used to repay debt, and more recently, to help acquire other companies such as American Motors Corporation.

Key Points: Inventory turnover provides a rough indication of the age of inventory, a prime determinant of its quality.

Accounts Payable Turnover

Because payables are expenses that the firm incurs to acquire raw materials, cost of goods sold should also be used as the numerator for the accounts payable turnover ratio. Although not every expense in cost of goods sold flows through the accounts payable account, cost of goods sold reflects better the relationship to payments than do sales. Many suppliers offer a discount of 1% or 2% to encourage early payment of bills. The typical options are either to pay in 10 days and get a 2% discount or to pay the full amount in 30 days. If the firm pays early, it thus obtains a 2% price cut for only 20 days' use of its money. Twenty days is 5.5% of a year (20 divided by 365 days in a year); the 2% discount divided by 5.5% produces an annual rate of 36%. Prompt payments are well worth the effort.

Another point of interest, with an opposite conclusion, concerning accounts payable turnover is that suppliers tend to be easier to negotiate with than other creditors when the firm needs extended terms. Suppliers have a more substantial markup than commercial lenders and are amenable to helping a client out. Moreover, once the discount period has passed, the firm can, in effect, borrow from the supplier interest-free. For this reason, firms tend to lean on the suppliers when liquidity is low, as in a rising interest rate market. Most suppliers look at the accounts payable report in a *D&B* as a prime indicator of the firm's liquidity. The Dun & Bradstreet reports show how firms are paying on their suppliers' bills.

Key Points: Accounts payable turnover is a good indicator of a firm's cash availability.

Operating Cycle in Days

The operating cycle in days is an aggregate of the previous turnover ratios. The inventory holding period plus the receivables collection period indicates how many days it takes a firm, on average, to acquire raw materials, process them into finished goods, sell them, and collect the cash. The operating cycle can be further refined by subtracting out the accounts payable turnover in days. The resulting value is the **net operating cycle,** the number of days the firm will have to finance itself through long-term sources of capital or through short-term sources such as notes payable.

> **Key Points:** The operating cycle equals the inventory holding period plus the accounts receivable collection period. The net operating cycle equals the operating cycle minus the accounts payable turnover in days.

Fixed Asset Turnover

Fixed asset turnover is calculated by dividing fixed assets into sales. The fixed asset turnover ratio indicates the relative efficiency of fixed assets in use as well as their importance to the company. Companies with substantial fixed assets typically lack liquidity. For example, consider the American Telephone & Telegraph Company (AT&T). AT&T, especially before divestiture, had a huge quantity of fixed assets, all of which it rented out. Total fixed assets exceeded total sales each year, indicating a lack of liquidity in AT&T's operations.

In contrast, an accounting firm's fixed assets, that is, desks, chairs, and computers, would be small compared to total revenues each year. Therefore, a lack of liquidity in an accounting firm would not be attributable to its substantial investment in fixed assets.

> **Key Points:** Fixed asset turnover is merely a general indication of the firm's liquidity.

Growth, the Operating Cycle, and Liquidity

Although a growing firm may be profitable, it will have severe stresses and strains on its operations because of the growth. Exhibit 8-5 demonstrates how liquidity can deteriorate in the face of increasing and profitable sales. Chips and Cables is contrasted with an alternative firm (see Exhibit 8-6) that is losing its market and going down the drain, but Buggies and Whips is awash in liquidity.

Chips and Cables

The abbreviated balance sheet of Chips and Cables, a microcomputer supply firm, shows that:

1. Working capital equals $300,000.
2. The current ratio is 7 to 4, just shy of the 2 to 1 required by the lender.

Exhibit 8-5.

LIQUIDITY DETERIORATES IN FACE OF SALES IMPROVEMENT
CHIPS AND CABLES, INC.

FINANCIAL STATEMENT APPEARANCE					
Shown in (000,000s)	INITIAL	Days	SALES	SALES	SALES
BALANCE SHEET	PERIOD	Turnover	UP 100%	UP 100%	UP 100%
ASSETS					
Cash	$100	30	$200	$400	$800
Accounts Receivable	300	90	600	1,200	2,400
Inventory	300	135	600	1,200	2,400
Current Assets	700		1,400	2,800	5,600
Fixed Assets	400		800	1,600	3,200
Total Assets	**1,100**		**2,200**	**4,400**	**8,800**
LIABILITIES					
Accounts Payable	300	135	600	1,200	2,400
Notes Payable	100		300	700	1,500
Current Liabilities	400		900	1,900	3,900
Long Term Debt	200		400	800	1,600
Total Debt					
Net Worth	500		900	1,700	3,300
Total Footings	1,100		2,200	4,400	8,800
ANNUAL INCOME STATEMENT					
Sales	1,200		2,400	4,800	9,600
Cost of Goods Sold	800		1,600	3,200	6,400
Other Expenses (Net)	200		400	800	1,600
Net Income	200		400	800	1,600

RATIOS					
Working Capital	**300**		**500**	**900**	**1,700**
Current Ratio	**1.75**	**to 1**	**1.56**	**1.47**	**1.44**
Debt to Worth	**1.20**	**to 1**	**1.44**	**1.59**	**1.67**

3. The debt to worth ratio (which will be examined more thoroughly in the solvency section) is approximately 1.2 to 1.
4. On the income statement, the firm is earning profits of $200,000 on $1.2 million in sales. The net profit margin is 17%.

Consider the following scenario: Chips and Cables is a good bank customer that has been a borrower for several years. The owner, Mike Kaplan, calls on the bank and explains that, because of an upcoming increase in expenditures for advertising and the opening of additional markets, the firm needs to plan for

Exhibit 8-6.

LIQUIDITY IMPROVES IN FACE OF SALES DECLINE
BUGGIES AND WHIPS, INC.

FINANCIAL STATEMENT APPEARANCE					
Shown in (000,000s) BALANCE SHEET	Initial Period	Days Turnover	Sales Fall 50%	Sales Fall 50%	Sales Fall 50%
ASSETS					
Cash	800	30	2,100	3,500	4,200
Accounts Receivable	2,400	90	1,200	600	300
Inventory	2,400	135	1,200	600	300
Current Assets	5,600		4,500	4,700	4,800
Fixed Assets	3,200		1,600	800	400
Total Assets	**8,800**		**6,100**	**5,500**	**5,200**
LIABILITIES					
Accounts Payable	2,400	135	1,200	600	300
Notes Payable	1,500		0	0	0
Current Liabilities	3,900		1,200	600	300
Long Term Debt	1,600		800	400	200
Net Worth	3,300		4,100	4,500	4,700
Total Footings	8,800		6,100	5,500	5,200
ANNUAL INCOME STATEMENT					
Sales	9,600		4,800	2,400	1,200
Cost of Goods Sold	6,400		3,200	1,600	800
Other Expenses (Net)	1,600		800	400	200
Net Income	1,600		800	400	200

RATIOS					
Working Capital	1,700		3,300	4,100	4,500
Current Ratio	1.44	to 1	3.75	7.83	16.00
Debt to Worth	1.67	to 1	0.49	0.22	0.11

a sales increase of 100% over the next 12 months. Kaplan then asks if the bank would finance his firm's short-term receivables by increasing the short-term credit line from the existing $100,000. Since the bank has been comfortable extending credit to the limit of net working capital, the account officer agrees to advance Chips and Cables up to $300,000 if required.

The second column of Exhibit 8-5 shows what happens to Chips and Cables after sales double, such as

- The fixed assets of the firm also double. It takes roughly a proportionate amount of machinery in order to produce more products.
- Inventory doubles as more products are in the pipeline and no essential change in the production operation has reduced the amount of inventory required.

- Accounts receivable increase since more customers are buying the product on credit.
- The cash doubles as a result of increased amount of check-clearing time (float).
- Long-term debt doubles to help finance the new equipment required.
- Accounts payable increase since the firm orders more inventory and owes more suppliers money.
- Short-term debt jumps by 200%!

All the liquidity ratios have deteriorated. Yet, Chips and Cables has met its profit objective of $400,000.

Columns 3 and 4 of the exhibit show what happens if sales continue to double for the next 2 years.

It is clear that wealth production is not the same thing as the ability to pay bills. Debt to worth and the current ratio get progressively worse. (It is curious that the net working capital total that the bank uses to determine the amount of short-term financing it will extend continues improving.) If the bank depended on the current and debt to worth ratios to assess creditworthiness, it would refuse credit to this growing and profitable firm since both ratios are deteriorating.

Now let's look at the alternative, a shrinking firm.

Buggies and Whips

Referring to Exhibit 8-6, Buggies and Whips is a firm whose operations are contracting. Its sales are falling by 50% each year. Exhibit 8-6 starts with the last column from Exhibit 8-5, but moves in the opposite direction. Assume that the firm can dispose of fixed assets (mainly undepreciated land under fully depreciated plants) and inventories as sales fall. As revenues decline, the current and debt to worth ratios improve dramatically. Although hourly workers are laid off, management prefers to keep all salaried staff. The president of Buggies and Whips approaches the bank with a request for financing to buy, of all things, an oil company. Because of Buggies and Whips' highly liquid balance sheet, the bank agrees to help finance the purchase!

Clearly, high liquidity is not synonymous with management expertise. Using the current and debt to worth ratios without more extensive cash flow analysis is thus a dangerous way to make decisions. Although the Buggies and Whips example may seem outlandish, the banks' financing of the steel industry's acquisition of oil companies in the early 1980s was justified on analogous analyses. (Perceptive forecasters took this steel industry initiative as warning that the oil industry was next to have troubled times.)

Key Points: Growing firms typically have liquidity problems. High liquidity offers no indication of whether a firm is well managed.

Postscript on Liquidity Enhancements

Operating Cycles Revisited

Both Chips and Cables and Buggies and Whips had long operating cycles. Frankly this worked well as an example because longer operating cycles exaggerate the demands for working capital in the growing firm and magnify the surplus working capital in the shrinking firm.

For a firm with a short operating cycle, increasing sales will have little effect on the need for additional funds. Normal trade credit will largely carry the firm with a short cycle through production and collection. Therefore, significant new working capital will not be required to fund the current assets that build up when growth occurs. On the other hand, a firm with a longer operating cycle, as in the examples above, will show substantial capital needs in the future to accommodate the growth. Therefore, the calculation of a firm's operating cycle should be the first step in estimating liquidity problems.

Traditionalists define liquidity in terms of liquidation of balance sheet values. Yet, the credit analyst needs to go further. A focus on turnover ratios and investigation of how the operating cycle affects liquidity allows conclusions about how growth fuels a buildup in inventory and accounts receivable relative to sales and creates liquidity problems for the firm.

> **Key Points:** The longer the firm's operating cycle, the greater the need for liquidity in the growing firm, and the more magnified the working capital surplus in the shrinking firm.

Average Accounts Limitation

Before concluding the section, let's review a problem of turnover ratios for a seasonal company: average figures. In the balance sheet segment, we discussed the problem of managers picking dates for fiscal year-ends that will reflect a good balance sheet posture. R. H. Macy's fiscal year, for example, ends in June when inventories and accounts receivable are lowest. The buildup of inventories after Thanksgiving and the buildup of accounts receivable after Christmas would make both the current ratio and turnover ratios look terrible if the fiscal year-end were in December.

Some financial statement analysis texts suggest that the analyst take the inventory number of the previous year-end, add it to inventory for the current year-end, and divide by two, to get an "average" figure. This is a good method only for a firm that is not seasonal. For firms that are seasonal, like R. H. Macy, this method will not improve the accuracy of the calculation. Unfortunately, *an accurate calculation of average turnover ratios requires that the analyst obtain at least quarterly data.* Monthly data would be preferable, but in most cases quarterly data will be sufficient.

> **Key Points:** The use of average figures in turnover ratios presents a problem for seasonal firms. For more accurate results, use monthly or quarterly data to calculate averages.

New Funds and Cash Flow Ratios—An Improvement?

In Clyde P. Stickney's recent book [*Financial Statement Analysis: A Strategic Perspective*, 1990, Harcourt Brace Jovanovich, San Diego, CA], he tries to validate the funds flow subtotal by incorporating it into various ratios. First, look at how Stickney would present the statement of cash flow.

1. **Gross operating cash flow**—traditional *funds from operations* including adjustments subtracting non-cash income items and non-operating items like asset sales.
2. **Net operating cash flow**—net cash from operations including working capital cash adjustments.
3. **Non-discretionary cash required**—cash outflows from replacing worn-out plant and equipment (including cost effects of inflation) and required debt principal repayment. Calculate the annual replacing of plant and equipment figure as follows: Find the average life of assets, then find the future value of the replacement cost at the expected inflation rate and divide by the average life.
4. **Disposable net operating cash flow**—deduct non-discretionary cash requirements from net operating cash generation.
5. **Discretionary cash required**—plant and equipment expenditures for sales growth and any non-mandatory debt or equity reduction. Calculate as follows: Start with the replacement cost including the inflation adjustment above and subtract from the actual expenditure plus any expenditures on new joint ventures or subsidiaries.
6. **Net cash needs**—deduct discretionary cash requirements from disposable net operating cash flow.
7. **Non-operating cash sources**—new debt or equity and sales of assets.

Now review the following ratios relating to liquidity and their explanations; additional ratios are included in the solvency section later in this chapter.

1. **Net income/gross operating cash flow**—applicable for identifying cash flow (liquidity) trends specifically relating to interest costs and non-operating items.
2. **Net income/net operating cash flow**—factoring in working capital and liquidity problems as ratio approaches one.
3. **Net working capital/net operating cash flow**—efficiency of working capital management.
4. **Gross operating cash flow/current liabilities**—a potential replacement for the current ratio, the design includes the dynamic variable of cash flow, but in my opinion the current liability variable still has the problems mentioned above concerning the current portion long-term debt.

Most of the above ratios would probably be improved if they stuck with the gross operating cash flow figure (funds provided by operations). From a theoretical viewpoint, these ratios do not directly relate the expenditure or repayment requirement with the proper source of repayment. Moreover, to judge net working capital or current liabilities, numbers 3 and 4 above, the true issue is conversion of the current assets to cash; speculating on the net cash flow, an item previously identified with repayment of long-term debt, is not nearly as logical as comparing these former to total sales. Stickney justifies his support of number 4 above with the research of C. Casey and N. Bartzcak in "Cash Flow—It's Not the Bottom Line" [*Harvard Business Review*, July–August 1984, pp. 61–66], which found in an empirical study that a ratio of .4 or more was common for a "healthy" firm.

Other Questionable Ratios

Two popular ratios are of questionable value: (1) trade liabilities divided by net worth and (2) net sales divided by working capital. Although trade liabilities divided by net worth can indicate whether the supplier has more funds invested in the business than stockholders do, it is a useless ratio for indicating a company's debt repayment capabilities.

Similarly, net sales divided by net working capital is not very helpful. This ratio supposedly indicates how liquid the company is by comparing net working capital amounts to ever-growing sales. The assumption is that if working capital does not increase with sales, the company's liquidity is declining. For a company that previously had conservatively high working capital, this ratio would give a false warning. It would again give a spurious reading on a company that had moved to a just-in-time inventory control system and thus reduced its need for working capital.

Focusing on useless ratios can be just as ineffective as worshiping the current ratio which, for example, steers the decision in the wrong direction: liquidation instead of repayment. *The need for working capital and liquidity is solely based on the operating cycle of the firm* and directly connecting it to sales does not change that fact.

> **Key Points:** Ignore trade liabilities divided by net worth and net sales divided by net working capital.

Conclusion

Liquidity may be defined as the ability to raise cash, but its importance in determining debt repayment capacity has been seen to be on the *quality of the firm's assets*. Thus, concerns about liquidity again return the analyst to the balance sheet enigma: Is this a liquidation picture or not? For the lending analyst it is hard to deny this back door way out of financing. Therefore, liquidity analysis is a vital part of Chapters 2–4, which cover balance sheet breakup valuation.

Lending officers are in full knowledge of this idea and have used liquidity analysis especially in reviewing short-term loans. The capstone of this approach is Chapter 11 on cash budgeting; here, the financial analyst gets to forecast the precise inflow of the short-term funds to repay a note.

What is different here is the view that liquidity analysis can be useful for long-term lending, particularly in perfecting the liquidation approach.

Solvency Analysis

Solvency is the ability to pay bills as they come due. This section examines ways for the analyst to measure whether a company's level of debt is prudent based on its repayment capacity—funds provided by operations. Starting with the balance-sheet-focused leverage concepts, solvency analysis gradually branches out to look at funds provided by operations and used to repay debt. This section concludes with some corporate finance concepts about optimal capital structure so the analyst can understand how the corporate treasurer determines appropriate debt levels—they are surprisingly different than the lender's approach.

How Much Leverage?

Creditors are often under the misconception that corporate treasurers or controllers want to keep business debt under control. In fact, just the opposite is true. The treasurers and controllers are inclined to increase debt as long as the business can earn more on the borrowed money than creditors require for interest payments. Thus, debt financing has two advantages over equity financing:

1. The spread of earnings over the cost of funds can be an added return to shareholders.
2. During inflationary times, debt can be repaid with cheaper dollars.

The corporation used debt to finance physical assets (equipment, plant, and inventories) that probably appreciate in value during inflationary times. For some corporations, the assets may appreciate much more than the general price level. This encourages managers to speculate in assets. Speculating in assets the firm is planning to use anyway is not as ill-advised as speculating in assets for which the firm has no use. Nevertheless, unless the firm is a trading company, asset speculation can put the firm and the bank at greater than normal risk.

Books on financial leverage commonly take the position that, because of the fixed costs required by it, debt is a dangerous way for a firm to raise capital. Clearly, some conservative organizations in the last century or so have also taken that position. Dupont, for example, had no debt on its balance sheet until 1979.

Exhibit 8-7 shows how corporate treasurers might convince themselves that more debt is not a problem for the firm. Looking at the base year (first two columns), the high-leveraged versus low-leveraged firms are chiefly distinguished by the amounts of interest paid and the quantity of equity. The low-leveraged company has half the debt that the high-leveraged company has, 1 to 2 versus 2 to 1 debt to equity.

Although net income is lower in the high-leveraged company, return on equity to shareholders is almost twice that of the low-leveraged firm. As earnings increase (second two columns), net income remains lower for the high-leveraged firm, but return on equity retains its almost doubled position, thereby justifying the continued use of debt.

The standard academic example of the evils of leverage points out how fixed charges drag down earnings when a company's sale decline. However, the

Exhibit 8-7.

Demonstration of why Treasurers accept higher LEVERAGE

(Dollars in 000s)	BASE PERIOD		EARNINGS UP		EARNINGS DOWN	
ITEMS	High Leverage	Low Leverage	High Leverage	Low Leverage	High Leverage	Low Leverage
Net Income Before						
Interest and Taxes	1,000	1,000	1,500	1,500	750	750
Interest Expense	200	100	200	100	200	100
Net Income Before Tax	800	900	1,300	1,400	550	650
Tax	400	450	650	700	275	325
Net Income	400	450	650	700	275	325
Change in Earnings Be-						
fore Interest and Taxes	n/a	n/a	50%	50%	-50%	-50%
Change in Net Income	n/a	n/a	63%	56%	-58%	-54%
Long Term Debt	2,000	1,000	2,000	1,000	2,000	1,000
Equity	1,000	2,000	1,000	2,000	1,000	2,000
Total Liabilities and Equity	3,000	3,000	3,000	3,000	3,000	3,000
Return On Equity	40%	22%	65%	35%	27%	16%

fifth and sixth columns in Exhibit 8-7 show that even with a 25% drop in sales, the sharp reduction in net income for the highly leveraged firm still leaves it with a higher return on equity than the lower-leveraged firm. Corporate treasurers are interested in return on equity for shareholders and they will focus on this example to justify further debt. Thus, the lender should not rely on the corporate treasurer's assessment of how much debt is prudent.

Ohio Coal Company

Ohio Coal Company (OCC) grew rapidly during 1972 due to the increase in coal prices resulting from the increase in oil prices instituted by OPEC. OCC's net worth had climbed to $3–4 million; the company had outstanding debt of $2–3 million. OCC wished to set up a facility so that it could dramatically increase operations over the next three to four years. The company's equipment was pledged to various finance companies and the rates on its debt were quite high. Thus, OCC also wished to reduce its cost of funds. Based on an appraisal of the assets and an analysis of their operations, Irving Trust decided to grant OCC a revolving credit line of $10 million.

These funds were to be taken down over time to acquire other assets as well as pay off the existing outstanding term debt so that the liens Irving took on OCC's equipment would have priority. The company bought equipment for an expansion program in Missouri that required an initial takedown of about $6 million. Irving received regular payments from the company for the next nine months, but OCC drew down no additional funds.

Upon visiting the company to see what had slowed further takedowns, the corporate treasurer politely told the Irving officer that Citibank had granted the company a $25 million line in a syndication of Citibank, Chase, and Pittsburgh's Equibank. This company for which Irving had strained to justify a $10 million line had suddenly pried $25 million out of two of the largest banks in the country.

The assets, against which Citibank had a lien (via the bank's natural resource department), were the coal reserves (untouched, in the ground) held under contract or owned outright by Ohio Coal. The banks kept no control over how the money was spent, but the loan's ostensible purpose was to develop a massive new coal mining operation in Colombia, South America, and two large drag lines to expand its facility in Missouri.

Further, the company had broadened its scope of operations as it had extra funds and perceived the need. To cite an instance, when they mined a certain section, trees had to be removed. After selling the trees to loggers for several years, Ohio Coal decided to have its own logging and sawmill operation to reap the benefits. There were few steps between that and the company starting up its own home building operation, and so on.

The first payment on the $25 million facility was not for six months. The company was trying to decide whether to obtain a release from Irving's covenant (which tied debt to their cash flow) or to just pay Irving down on its loan. After the report was made on the new OCC loan facility, Irving, following the crowd, quickly agreed to release the debt restrictions so carefully negotiated.

OCC started having problems within the next six months. New federal laws that regulated the mining of coal were passed. Moreover, OCC's Colombia operation had problems and its other operations started to show the strain of lack of management attention. As the first Citibank loan payment drew near, the company notified its creditors that it was unable to make the payment as required. The situation deteriorated from there.

In the Ohio Coal Company case and many others, corporate bankruptcy problems can be traced back to eager bankers or financiers unwilling to stand up to their borrowers. (Another lesson of the OCC case is that a creditor should never be the last lender to a client. There should always be room left so that an additional lender can come in, if necessary.)

A lender can arrive at a credit decision by many different means. *Citibank's decision to lend to OCC was based on a liquidation analysis* of the firm's assets. The problem with this approach, however (as Citibank lenders discovered too late), is that asset values can be just as uncertain as intangible asset values and cash flow. Natural resource financing is a difficult field since the price of those commodities can fluctuate. Funds flows from operations would have justified a smaller, but safer, loan.

Key Points: The lender must determine how much leverage is prudent for a borrower. Basing a loan on asset liquidation analysis can be risky since these asset values can change.

Solvency Ratios

Lenders face a limitation on their percentage return from any particular loan, but no limit on their risk of principal. Therefore, for lenders, solvency analysis is more important than the performance analysis that interests the stockholder (to be discussed in Chapter 9). Through solvency analysis the analyst attempts to forecast the company's ability to:

- Meet current obligations
- Maintain asset quality
- Restrict the extent and character of liabilities
- Withstand possible setbacks from internal or external sources
- Most importantly, raise new funds when needed

Considering how rapidly asset values can change, it is surprising that anyone would base lending decisions primarily on the liquidation approach. However, the liquidation approach proved useful at times in the past when investments in plant and equipment were stable and technology changed slowly. Another factor that supports the liquidation approach is the fact that, on average, financial institutions with bad loans backed by pledged assets have been able to recover up to 70% of their outstandings. This track record focuses attention on the balance sheet and the riskiness of the assets as the prime consideration for approving loans.

The list of solvency ratios (and their formulations) to be discussed below appears in Exhibit 8-8.

Debt to Worth Ratio

A cliche, debt to worth measures the relationship between liabilities and owner's equity. The debt to worth ratio has several permutations, including total debt to either owner's equity or to total capital, as well as term debt to total capital.

Financial institutions sometimes look for maximum 1:1 relationship of debt (whichever kind) to worth ratio or 50% relationship between debt and capital. *The rationale behind these rules-of-thumb is that if assets can be sold for 50% of their book value, there will be enough proceeds to entirely pay out the lenders.*

The problem with relying on the accounting information about assets is that their historical cost—via generally accepted accounting principles—does not give a good prediction of liquidation value and therefore calculates net worth assuming *no inflation* in the value of these assets. (Remember, net worth is merely assets minus liabilities.) Furthermore, since the debt to worth ratio also uses liability account values equal to face value—again from the GAAP-based balance sheet—it does not reflect any differences in the market value of the debt. If interest rates have fallen since the fixed-rate debt was issued, the debt account values, carried at their original present value, are undervalued because bond values go up when interest rates fall. Conversely, if interest rates have risen, the fixed-rate debt balances on the balance sheet are overstated and net worth is being miscalculated again, this time from assuming no interest rate changes.

Key Points: The proper course of action in calculating debt to worth ratios is to revalue to market value the fixed-rate debt and assets.

Exhibit 8-8.

SOLVENCY RATIOS

RATIO NAME and alternatives	RATIO DEFINITION	PREFERRED RELATIONSHIP
Debt to Worth (Liabilities to Equity) alternatives include:	$$\frac{\text{Total Debt}}{\text{Net Worth}}$$	$$\frac{1}{1}$$ or less
Total Debt to to Tangible NW	$$\frac{\text{Total Liabilities}}{\text{Tangible NW + Minority Int.}}$$	$$\frac{1}{1}$$ or less
Long-Term Debt to Capital	$$\frac{\text{Long-Term Debt}}{\text{Long-Term Debt + Net Worth}}$$	$$\frac{1}{1}$$ or less
Interest Coverage (Times Int. Earned)	$$\frac{\text{Earnings Bef. Int. \& Tax (EBIT)}}{\text{Interest Expense}}$$	HIGH
Fixed Charges Cover. (Times Int + Rent Cov)	$$\frac{\text{EBIT \& Rents}}{\text{Interest + Rents}}$$	HIGH
Debt to Funds Flow	$$\frac{\text{Total Liabilities}}{\text{Funds from Operations}}$$	LOW
Long-Term Debt to Funds Flow	$$\frac{\text{Long-Term Debt}}{\text{Funds from Operations}}$$	$$\frac{5}{1}$$ or less
Debt Payment Coverage	$$\frac{\text{EBIT + Depreciation + Rents}}{\text{Interest + Rents + Current Portion LTD}}$$ at least $$\frac{1}{1}$$	

Interest Coverage (Times Interest Earned) Ratio

The interest coverage ratio is viewed as a most important debt capacity ratio for debt-rating agencies. This is the times interest earned ratio and it compares earnings before interest and taxes to interest expense. The rationale behind calculating this ratio with adding back taxes is that should pre-tax earnings fall to the level of interest payments, there would still be sufficient funds to make these interest payments, since interest is a tax-deductible expense and no taxes would be due.

In contrast to the debt to worth ratio, which does not give any real indication of a firm's ability to repay debt, the interest coverage ratio is more utilitarian in that it connects the concepts of wealth production (or profit) with that of outlays for interest expense and shows a rough availability of funds to pay for the use of debt capital sources. Times interest earned is thus a better diagnostic technique than the debt to worth ratio for financial statement analysis.

Fixed Charges Coverage (Times Charges Earned) Ratio

In view of the increasing use of equipment and real estate leasing to keep debt off the balance sheet, the interest charges a firm pays may not fully reflect its required annual outflows for the equivalent of debt payments. Therefore, the SEC requires a broader ratio to be calculated that *accounts for lease rentals*. This new ratio is called the fixed charge coverage (an enhanced times interest earned) ratio. In calculating it, rent expense is added to both the numerator and the denominator of the times interest earned ratio. In general, a firm is expected to exceed the minimum 1:1, which may be necessary for survival, as much as possible and certainly to be in alignment with others in their own industry.

Adjusted Leverage Ratio

Clyde Stickney includes income to examine the extent of leverage; his *adjusted* leverage ratio results from multiplying:

1. Common earnings leverage, derived by dividing net income by operating income before financing costs (i.e., the proportion of operating income allocable to common shareholders)

and multiplying the result by:

2. Capital structure leverage, in turn, derived by dividing assets by equity (the inverse would be the proportion of assets financed by shareholders)

Stickney thought that this ratio would help relate riskiness that shareholders are asked to engage in with returns on assets or equity. For example, if net income were half operating income and assets were twice equity (debt to worth of 1 to 1), the ratio would be unity. If net income became three quarters of operating income, the adjusted leverage would go to 1.5. Therefore, if income allocable to shareholders is greater than the asset/equity structure proportion, the ratio will exceed unity; if it is less, the ratio is less than unity. Comparing the two components is useful to see how close to unity the results are; being much under unity would imply excessive management risk taking.

Empirically, however, it turns out that the extent of leverage (measured by this ratio) does *not* seem to be correlated with ROAs or ROEs. What are the implications of this finding? Stickney suggests that borrowing is unrelated to shareholder risk/reward and is only an undertaking by management for their own purposes. Another alternative, closer to the judgment of this book, is that *funds flow from operations is the necessary element to determining debt capacity,* in turn dependent on the set repayment schedule; thus, *this focus on times interest earned has its limitations.*

Additional Cash Flow Solvency Ratios

Finally, consider several other Stickney *alternative* ratios using his new cash flow concepts; referring back to his cash flow definitions listed on page 200:

1. **Net operating cash flow/interest and lease rentals**—updated times interest earned ratio, with sensitivity to working capital uses of funds, if any.
2. **Disposable net operating cash flow/interest and lease rentals**—similar to the Securities and Exchange Commission's fixed charges coverage ratio, but taking into account replacement capital expenditures, working capital uses, depreciation, and other non-cash charges.
3. **Net operating cash flow/disposable net operating cash flow**—percentage impact of non-discretionary cash needs on net cash flow.
4. **Gross operating cash flow/disposable net operating cash flow**—percentage impact of non-discretionary cash needs on cash flow (the same as item 3) except that changes in working capital has been removed.
5. **Discretionary cash required/net operating cash flow**—percent of net operating cash spent on discretionary requirements; can show excessive growth.
6. **Net operating cash flow/assets**—using the new cash flow subtotal to calculate cash return on assets.
7. **Net operating cash flow/equity**—using the new cash flow subtotal to calculate cash return on equity.

Again, most of the above ratios would probably be improved if they stuck with the gross operating cash flow (funds provided by operations) figure used in item 4. From a theoretical viewpoint, these ratios do not directly relate the expenditure or repayment requirement with the proper source of repayment. For example, to deduct increases in inventories, which may be entirely optional, prior to calculating cash returns on equity (item 7) is questionable.

While these ratios can be helpful, especially with single-company trend analysis, their validity with regard to determining debt capacity remains to be empirically validated. Clearly the logical validation needs to be examined by theorists and the logical linkages between reason for the debt and the source of its repayment need to be refined as in items 2 and 4 above.

Debt Payment Coverage (Ultimate Time Charges Earned) Ratio

At the bottom of Exhibit 8-8 is this book's final move to true fixed charges coverage. The debt payment coverage ratio recognizes that much corporate debt is amortizing. The ratios discussed so far have not taken the required amortization (i.e., the amount accounted for in the current portion long-term debt) into account. By combining the maturities of long-term debt due in the coming year—preferably due in the next operating cycle—into the ratio, the analyst can obtain a *better gauge of the company's ability to pay its debt.*

Recall from the review of the statement of changes in financial position that there is a non-cash expense on the income statement: depreciation—usually the largest number added into net income to obtain funds provided by operations, hereinafter, funds flow. That is, although depreciation is expensed, no funds leave the company. This debt coverage ratio also takes this into consideration. Debt payment coverage equals:

$$\frac{\text{Net Income} + \text{Depreciation} + \text{Taxes} + \text{Interest} + \text{Rentals}}{\text{Interest} + \text{Rentals} + \text{Current Portion Long-Term Debt}}$$

One of the hurdles with this ratio is that credit officers cannot just figure it out in their heads the way they can the debt to worth ratio. The advantage of this ratio, however, is that it has some genuine implications regarding loan repayment capacity, not just liquidation capacity. It amasses all the outflows necessitated by debt and all the funds conveniently available to pay them.

While some may prefer to use the SFAS #95's net cash flow in the formula, there is adequate justification to using APB #19's funds flow definition—net income plus depreciation because

1. Funds flow is an easier and more standardized value to calculate than net cash flow.
2. A firm having trouble meeting its current debt requirements can sacrifice the growth in receivables, inventories, and fixed assets, which net cash flow deletes without questioning.

In any case, the company that is expanding rapidly without sufficient profits or capital will definitely see its debt payment coverage drop as earnings decline.

Long-Term Debt to Funds Flow Ratio

This ratio examines how many years a company would have to take to repay its long-term debt with funds from operations, assuming it focused its efforts on that alone. (Sometimes this ratio is shown as funds flow to long-term debt, the inverse of this one. To obtain the number of years from that ratio, the result must be divided into one.) This ratio is sensitive to industry norms. For example, a real estate firm will have net funds flow of only a small percentage of its long-term debt. The relationship of the ratio—long-term debt to funds flow—could comfortably be as long as the terms of their real estate mortgages. For most companies, a rule of thumb for term debt to funds flow is that it should be no greater than 5 to 1 (funds flow to term debt no less than 20%). This means that the company can repay its term debt in 5 years of devoted use of funds from operations.

To correct the ratio for companies with substantial operating lease obligations, the present value of total lease obligations can be added to the long-term debt numerator and rental expense from the current statement of income can be added to the funds flow number in the denominator. (See Exhibit 4-1 for determining the present value of an Operating lease.)

Let's compare the usefulness of these funds flow–oriented ratios with the balance sheet ratios (debt to worth and the current ratio) in assessing a firm's ability to handle debt already on its books. *The funds flow–oriented ratios provide more of an indication of the genesis for loan repayment capability than the liquidation focus of the current or the debt to worth ratios.* The plan is that the liquidation alternative will never take place. The funds flow ratios have meaning in and of themselves, regardless of industry norms or past company history. Their single drawback is they are more complicated to calculate than are debt to worth and current ratios. Nevertheless, the quality of information that these ratios provide makes the additional effort much worthwhile.

> **Key Points:** Funds flow–oriented ratios, such as debt repayment of long-term debt to funds flow, are more directly indicative in assessing a firm's repayment capability than balance sheet–oriented ratios such as debt to worth or the current ratio.

Optimal Capital Structure

We still have not answered the question: How much leverage should a firm be permitted? To arrive at a complete answer, a course in corporate finance is required. Yet, it may be useful at this point to mention the issues such a course might address.

Traditionally, managers and creditors have focused on rules of thumb to measure capital structure and to judge its validity. As firms' debt appetite grows, however, the old leverage rules and even the ratios themselves are no longer valid. The more practical analyst examines relationships within a particular industry and calculates the averages of these ratios. These industry averages are then used as a guideline. This approach takes on added significance in light of the implementation of the new FASB pension and consolidation of subsidiary statements since both of these statements will increase leverage ratios on an industry-wide basis.

Many theories have been combined to arrive at some theory of optimal capital structure. Since corporate treasurers are using this to make decisions about how much debt their firms should have, it may prove to be useful for the analyst. The two elements the analyst needs to calculate are the opportunity investment rate and the cost of capital (preferably the marginal cost of capital curve).

Opportunity Investment Rate

Firms have many investment opportunities they can take. Sometimes the potential returns are so high that the selection of alternatives is not an absolutely scientific matter.

Lotus 1-2-3

> Consider the example of a software company such as Lotus Development Corporation (Lotus). The management of Lotus must decide which of all the proposed programs will become the next $100 million seller. Clearly, the cost of developing any of the programs is significantly less than the potential gain.

(The situation is similar in the movie business. A box office hit can earn hundreds of millions of dollars irrespective of how much has been spent.) This is not to imply that money spent on these products has nothing to do with their potential success but rather that the potential returns can far exceed the cost.

A company such as Lotus always has many different programs under development and it wants returns to be high. In some cases, its returns on investment are in the range of 40% or 50%. The proposals in which these firms consider investing are presented to management with documentation to substantiate their ability to earn high returns.

If the firm has a broad range of projects, it can rank them as in Exhibit 8-9. The bottom axis indicates the dollar investment required and the vertical axis indicates the percentage of return the firm could expect to earn over the life of the investment.

Cost of Capital

The next step in the analysis is to calculate marginal cost of capital. In Exhibit 8-9 a hypothetical marginal cost of capital curve intersects the various project options for the firm. The project that the curve intersects furthest to the right is the last investment that the firm should make. It should endeavor to

Exhibit 8-9.

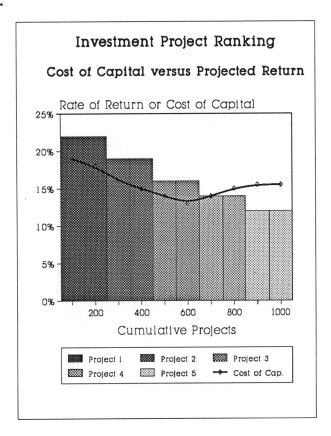

obtain the capital necessary to undertake all the projects up to that point because it can earn more on the investments than it will have to pay the suppliers of funds. The marginal cost of capital curve takes into account not only the cost of debt but also the cost of equity. It also accounts for the reaction of shareholders and creditors to increasing levels of debt. (Although the mathematical proof of this material is beyond the scope of this book, it is important that the lender be familiar with the way the firm makes investment decisions.)

Assume that a firm is able to construct a marginal cost of capital curve. Intuitively, you might sense that a marginal cost curve would have its low point in the middle. This is logical because, for example, if the firm were going to the stock market to issue only $500,000 worth of stock, the marketing costs per dollar of raised capital would be high. The firm's lawyers would still have to prepare a prospectus for the SEC and the firm's investment bankers would still have to contact many brokers to alert them that the sale was going to take place.

On the other hand, if the firm were to attempt to issue huge blocks of stock, raising tens or even hundreds of millions of dollars, investors may feel that there was unusual risk involved and would want to receive a commensurate return. IBM, for instance, would probably not have any trouble marketing a private placement of $100 million. It might have some trouble and it would definitely experience increased costs, however, if it tried to raise $20 billion. For highly rated firms that wish to raise a prudent amount of capital, a low rate is achievable.

Optimal Leverage

Several theoreticians, in particular, Modigliani and Miller [1958], have mathematically investigated optimal leverage. They initially proved that shareholders fear bankruptcy so much that they will offset the cost benefits of borrowing by demanding compensating higher returns on their equity (stock) investments, eliminating debt's cost advantage.

Fortunately for lenders, one of the assumptions in the model is that there are no corporate income taxes. When the corporate income taxes are included in the model, Modigliani and Miller showed that since interest payments are subsidized by the government, corporate management's most profitable course is to seek to finance the firm entirely with debt. Although the shareholders may make demands for compensating increases in expected returns, they do not overcompensate for the tax-break subsidy. For analysis purposes, *the point to understand is that corporate treasurers have incentive to borrow as much as the market will bear.*

The tax benefit to borrowing can cause potentially harmful disturbances within the economic and capital market structure of the country. Allowing corporations to deduct interest expense compels corporate treasurers to make decisions they otherwise might not.

Funds Flow Ratios and Leverage

Since theory justifies a corporate treasurer borrowing as much debt as possible, *lenders and rating agencies alone essentially control leverage levels.* If the

...tors use are reliable and if they correctly indicate the
...y debt, then the firm, the lender, and the economy
...nadequate or do not distinguish between companies
...at cannot, then the following ramifications result:

...ke a contribution but are not approved based on
...ad spend a lot of time looking for debt in vain.
...ay debt may obtain it based on faulty ratios and
...ankrupt.
...l the loan to the company that was creditworthy
...o profits.
... the loan to the company that was not creditwor-
...timately fail and be taken over by the FDIC.
... the difference in lost jobs and extra money for

...lated in this section are a quintessential means
...apacity to repay debt. The corporate treasurer
... calculation of this relationship. The treasurer
...intermediaries and investors charging higher rates as
the firm takes on more debt.

Leveraged Buyouts

A leveraged buyout is an extreme example of a firm's appetite for leverage.
In leveraged buyouts, the shareholders are replaced by lenders as the prepon-
derant suppliers of capital to the firm. The important point for analysts is that
regular, consistent, and *stable earnings and funds flow are necessary to justify
eliminating the stockholders' equity cushion from the lender's perspective.* Clearly, the
firm must be earning more on its assets than it pays for the borrowed money.
Otherwise, it would have to sell assets to pay the interest. Except for high
leverage, these entities are like any other borrower and analysis of their operations can be accomplished by following the normal guidelines in this book.

Using Ratios to Predict Corporate Failure

This section takes an empirical approach to ratios. Sensing that ratios are
excellent ways of detecting and encapsulating financial condition, researchers
have studied data available from the Securities and Exchange Commission files.
Using computers, they have experientially tried to distinguish ratios and patterns of ratios that predict something about the firm's future performance.

These analyses use the firm's declaration of bankruptcy as the definition of
financial failure. Bankruptcy is then linked to the ratios of the firm's previous
financial statements. The objective is to find correlations between specific ratios
and failure. The results of the search theoretically can then be used on other
firms to forecast success or failure.

Most of these studies produced no rules of thumb that could be used to determine whether a firm would fail or not. Moreover, most of them made no attempt to distinguish between firms that entered bankruptcy and successfully restructured and those that were hopelessly indebted and were liquidated in their entirety. There was also no effort made to identify marginally troubled firms that are of interest to lenders. Finally, the analyses did not address the problem of lenders classifying a company's loan as a "special mention" or "doubtful" well before that firm files for bankruptcy.

William H. Beaver

Beaver, a professor of accounting at Stanford University, broke new ground in the 1960s by running correlation analyses on dozens of ratios in an attempt to distinguish between firms that would fail and those that would not.

Beaver found that three ratios had value in predicting financial difficulties: (1) funds flow divided by debt, (2) net income divided by total assets, and (3) debt divided by total assets. Funds flow divided by debt and net income divided by total assets are both profitability ratios, whereas the debt as a percent of total assets ratio is a balance sheet ratio.

Although relying on these ratios may be highly useful for predicting type 1 errors, it can cause many type 2 errors. The analyst needs some way of distinguishing between firms that have poor ratios and lack the capacity to pay and firms that have poor ratios but will repay the loans. *The ratio that stands the test of both of the sides of the equation is the funds flow to term debt ratio.*

Beaver's research showed that when a firm's funds flow to term debt dropped below 0.2 (a relationship of 1:5—the source of the five times, debt to funds flow, rule of thumb mentioned above), the likelihood of failure increased substantially. While only 57% of the firms that eventually filed for bankruptcy had a weak term debt to funds flow ratio five years before filing, almost 78% did one year before filing. The range of type 2 errors committed by using the funds flow to term debt ratio as a guide was under 10% for all time periods.

The research also found a correlation between (1) net income to total assets dropping to less than zero and (2) financial failure. This is entirely expected since the only way for this ratio to be negative is for the firm to lose money; losing money is a ticket to financial problems. When debt as a percentage of total assets exceeds 50%, failure is also predicted. This finding would appear to give credence to the rule of thumb that debt to worth should be held to a one to one relationship. However, considering the increases in corporate debt with respect to net worth in the past 20 years, this finding suggests that nearly every firm in the United States is heading for failure. Additionally detracting from its usefulness, this ratio's misclassification percentage averages about 30% of the total.

Two other ratios were tested: (1) working capital as a percent of total assets and (2) the current ratio. These ratios showed that once working capital as a percent of total assets fell below 30%, failure was predicted. For the current ratio, once the ratio fell below 2.5 times, failure was predicted. Both of these ratios had percentages for type 1 errors (misclassification) of about 37%, rendering them useless.

strictly on mechanical ratios, and they insist that ratios play only a part in the comprehensive analysis leading to the determination of credit quality.

In 1977, the financial consulting group of Irving Trust Company prepared a correlation analysis and found which ratios had the most significant correlations to ratings from "AAA" to "BBB." Standard & Poor's ratings represent (in a very general way) the following—greatly paraphrased—capacity to repay:

AAA—capacity to repay is strong.

AA—slightly less strong than AAA.

A—strength high but susceptible to adverse economic changes.

BBB—adequate capacity to repay but more likely to be weakened by adverse economic changes.

BB—adverse business, financial, or economic conditions could impair its ability to repay.

B—now has capacity to pay, but vulnerable to change.

CCC—presently vulnerable to default unless conditions are favorable.

Exhibit 8-11 shows the results of the Irving analysis. If ratios change proportionally as ratings change from AAA to BBB, then there is a statistical correlation. This correlation does not mean that the ratio indicates whether debt repayment will be made (truth) but rather indicates what Standard & Poor's rating will be (opinion).

For instance, the steady decrease in the interest coverage ratio as ratings move from AAA to BBB suggests that this is an important ratio in determining a firm's rating (just as was suspected). If the changes are irregular or flat between ratings, then the relationship may be less significant. For example, the

Exhibit 8-11.

Average Financial Statistics for Rated Industrial Companies

Rating	AAA		AA		A		BBB	
Period	1975	1973	1975	1973	1975	1973	1975	1973
Number of Companies	20	17	43	42	102	92	33	35
RATIOS								
Average Total Sales ($ Billions)	12.8	9.8	2.4	1.6	1.4	1.2	1.5	1.0
Long-Term Debt Capital	20.10	17.70	26.40	21.20	30.50	27.30	37.00	35.60
Total Debt Capital & Short-Term Debt	23.60	21.40	30.60	25.40	33.50	31.70	42.00	41.90
Funds from Operations Long-Term Debt	111.40	166.50	75.50	112.36	52.70	62.00	38.00	37.50
Pretax Earnings Bef Int & Tax Interest Expense	17.60	18.60	9.80	13.50	6.20	8.80	4.00	4.70
Net Income Permanent Capital	12.40	14.00	11.40	12.20	10.20	10.80	8.40	9.20

Source: Irving Trust Company, Economic Department Newsletter, 1975, New York, NY

sales levels drop significantly from the AAAs to AAs. From AA to BBB, however, there is very little difference between the average sales levels. The conclusion is that S&P does not think all that much of sales levels as determining ratings.

Other positive correlations include the traditional term debt as a percent of total capital relationship and the funds flow to term debt relationship championed by Beaver. Curiously enough, return on capital does not have a high correlation with ratings—shareholders clearly have different interests than lenders. Return on capital probably would do better in a recommendation analysis prepared by a stock brokerage firm. All the ratios, in all grade levels, experienced a significant deterioration from 1973 to 1975. *This reflects the generic increase in long-term debt by all firms.*

After the late 1970s, Standard & Poor's began to publish on its own averages on rated firms in its magazine *CreditWeek*. Exhibit 8-12 shows some of the results from the report of November 16, 1990. Although not all ratios compare to the Irving Trust study, some do, and they confirm trends of increasing debt within the capital structure of business over the past 10 years.

Pre-tax interest coverage, now including rents from leases, fell in the AAA rated firms from 18.6 times in 1973 to only 5.6 times in 1989. Interest coverage at AA firms fell from 13.5 in 1973 to 5.5 in 1989, and the single A rated firms' coverage fell from 8.8 times to 3.6 times. These are significant declines and they reflect the fact that interest expense represents a much larger proportion of corporate earnings at the end of the 1980s than it did in the mid-1970s.

The Irving ratio of short- plus long-term debt divided by total capital plus short-term debt can be compared with the total debt divided by capitalization including short-term debt (including eight times rents) on the Standard & Poor's report. Including Operating leases, the ratio percentage has increased from 24% in 1975 to an average of 33% in the 1985–1989 period for the AAAs. For the BBB firms the ratio percentage increased from 42% in 1975 to 55% in the 1985–1989 period. The most important finding from these recent numbers is that the *total liabilities to tangible shareholders' equity has reached a 1:1 relationship in the AA firms,* and is higher in all firms rated lower than AA.

A study of the ratio analysis across the Standard & Poor's ratings indicates which ratios are the most important in determining credit ratings (see Exhibit 8-13). Interest coverage ratios would be expected to be the most significant. Indeed, there is a high correlation between ratings and interest coverage, funds flow to fixed charges, and interest coverage of fixed charges.* However, the interest coverage ratio excluding rents is a better match to the ratings changes than is the interest coverage ratio including rents (fixed charge coverage). It is fair then to draw an apparent conclusion: *Standard & Poor's gives less weight to the factor-derived value of lease obligations than to the book value of pure debt.* This is demonstrated because, in the third row, there is practically no difference in the fixed charge coverage ratios—including Operating leases—especially in the A to BB groups, indicating low correlation to the ratings' changes. Given that the ratio uses the notoriously inaccurate factor method to capitalize leases onto the balance sheet, this low correlation is a blessing.

The funds flow from operations categories also seem to step down smoothly

*This is represented in the exhibit by a smooth, sharply downward slope.

Exhibit 8-12.

Average Financial Statistics for Rated Industrial Companies

Rating	AAA		AA		A		BBB		BB		B		CCC	
Period (85-89 is averaged)	85-89	1989	85-89	1989	85-89	1989	85-89	1989	85-89	1989	85-89	1989	85-89	1989
RATIOS														
Earnings Before Int and Tax / Interest Expense	23.1	20.0	14.2	14.5	9.5	8.4	4.5	5.1	1.5	2.8	1.3	.8*	1.0	0.1
Pretax Fixed Charge Coverage Including Rents (x)	6.5	5.6	5.8	5.5	3.6	3.6	2.6	2.8	2.0	2.0	1.2	0.9	0.9	0.6
Pretax Funds Flow Interest Coverage	30.0	25.6	18.1	19.0	12.5	11.1	6.5	7.1	3.3	5.0	2.5	1.4*	2.3	1.1
Funds from Operations / Total Debt (%)	129.9	117.7	120.3	130.0	47.1*	70.2	42.6	50.6	16.0	10.5	9.2	4.5	9.0	0.0
Free Operating Cash Flow / Total Debt	46.4	42.5	43.3	25.5	81.9	21.8	28.0	9.2	-7.6	-4.9	-9.6	-0.9	4.8	-6.3
Pretax Earnings / Permanent Capital	26.4	25.4	22.6	22.6	18.3	18.4	14.7	15.9	12.2	13.0	8.9	7.8	6.2	3.7
Operating Income / Sales	21.8	22.5	16.9	17.4	15.8	16.2	13.6	14.1	14.4	14.6	9.6	9.9	11.3	11.2
Long-Term Debt / Capital	14.3	18.5	20.7	21.9	29.8	31.1	38.0	40.6	53.6	58.9	69.8	81.8	65.3	85.7
Total Debt / Capital & Short-Term Debt	22.7	27.8	26.9	29.3	35.0	36.6	41.6	44.5	56.6	62.0	71.8	82.8	68.3	93.2
Total Debt / Capital & Short-Term Debt + 8x Operating Lease Rnts	33.0	38.8	39.1	41.7	48.7	49.7	55.3	57.6	65.7	69.6	77.1	87.1	75.5	94.9

* Medians were used in these 3 cases because the averages were out of range.
Source: Standard & Poor's CreditStats, November 16, 1990, New York, NY

Exhibit 8-13.

Average Financial Statistics
of Rated Industrial Companies for 1989

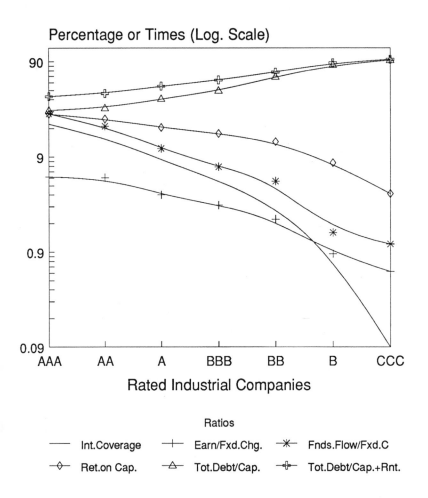

Percentage or Times (Log. Scale)

Rated Industrial Companies

Ratios

| — Int.Coverage | —+— Earn/Fxd.Chg. | —✱— Fnds.Flow/Fxd.C |
| —◇— Ret.on Cap. | —△— Tot.Debt/Cap. | —⊕— Tot.Debt/Cap.+Rnt. |

Source: Standard & Poor's CreditStats

at each rung on the ratings' ladder, although the AAAs are head and shoulders above the other firms. After the AAs and lower-rated firms, there is a moderately even progression. The unevenness in the return on permanent capital employed, as expected, verifies the distinction between the concerns of the creditor and the concerns of the stockholder. The same occurs with operating income as a percent of sales, or operating profit margin. These two ratios are used only slightly by Standard & Poor's to make its predictions. The various debt to worth or capitalization ratios continue to rank in the prediction of rating. However, all the various versions appear to move in too smooth a path from a low percentage for AAAs to a high percentage for the lower rating categories to be of much value in distinguishing between higher-rated firms.

In conclusion, it is evident that the rating agencies, primarily concerned with long-term debt, have focused their attention on interest coverage and funds flow ratios contrasted to the long-term debt and debt to worth ratios that many traditional analysts would have us believe.

> **Key Points:** The rating agencies, primarily concerned with long-term debt, have focused their attention on interest coverage ratios, funds from operations compared with long-term debt, and debt to worth ratios.

Survey Results

Some research reported by Charles Gibson [1983] provides a postscript. He surveyed commercial bank lending officers to procure their opinion on the analytical significance of ratios. Exhibit 8-14 shows the top ten rankings. As

Exhibit 8-14.
Commercial Loan Departments' Survey
Most significant Ratios and Their Primary Measure

RATIOS RANKED IN IMPORTANCE Description and Name	Primary Measure
1. Total Liabilities / Equity **DEBT TO WORTH**	Debt
2. Current Assets / Current Liabilities **CURRENT RATIO**	Liquidity
3. Funds flow / Current Maturities of Long-Term Debt **CASH FLOW TO TERM DEBT**	Debt
4. EBIT + Rents / Interest Expense + Rents **FIXED CHARGES COVERAGE**	Debt
5. Net Recurring Profits After Taxes / Sales **NET PROFIT MARGIN AFTER TAXES**	Profitability
6. EBIT / Interest Expense **INTEREST COVERAGE**	Debt
7. Net recurring Profits Before Taxes / Sales **NET PROFIT MARGIN BEFORE TAXES**	Profitability
8. EBIT / Earnings Before Taxes **DEGREE OF FINANCIAL LEVERAGE**	Debt
9. Cost of Goods Sold / Average Inventory **INVENTORY TURNOVER**	Liquidity
10. Sales / Average Accounts Receivable **ACCOUNTS RECEIVABLE TURNOVER**	Liquidity

Source: Gibson, Charles, H. and Patricia A. Frishkoff, *Financial Statement Analysis*, Kent Publishing Company, Boston, Mass., 1983, p. 436

would be expected, the debt to worth and current ratios are at the top of the list. But following closely behind are the funds flow to long-term debt (using here the current maturities of long-term debt), fixed charge coverage, net profit margin after tax, and times interest earned (interest coverage). This confirms that bankers are focusing more of their attention on ratios that involve funds flows from the income statement and statement of changes in financial position to make their decisions.

Chapter 9

Use of Ratios in Performance Analysis and Earnings Quality

Operations Analysis—Repeatable Earnings

Operations analysis serves two purposes. The first and most important is to determine whether current earnings performance can be continued into the future. The second is to assess the efficacy with which management uses assets and raises funds. The purpose of financial analysis differs from that of the accountant's historic "what happened." *The financial analyst is looking to the future; therefore, what will be and what will not be repeated is critical.* The transactions that the accountant has classified as extraordinary must be investigated to make sure they are non-recurring; if they will not alter the future because they were unusual, their influence on earnings should not be great. Instead, identifying recurring aspects of the firm's operations gives a better guide to whether current earnings will be repeated.

Performance analysis focuses on the following aspects of a firm's operations: profit margins, sales growth, return on assets, and return on equity. To assess a firm's ability to generate profits, the primary ratios used are those derived from the common-size analysis described in Chapter 8. Each entry on the income statement is represented as a percentage of sales. Exhibit 9-1 shows the various operating ratios. The operating profit margin and net profit margin are the ratios most used by credit analysts. The return on assets, equity, and capital are estimates of efficiency and good indicators of the future growth of the firm and of its stock price. They are consequently popular with equity investors, although growth is not a necessary condition of debt repayment capacity.

Profit Margins

Single-Product Firms

In some industries, the operating profit margin is the predominant means of assessing management's performance. This ratio is especially useful for firms that have a simple operating process and that must focus on managing volume and maintaining expense levels. An example of this is the trucking industry,

Exhibit 9-1.

OPERATING RATIOS

RATIO NAME	RATIO DEFINITION	PREFERRED RELATIONSHIP
Net Profit Margin	$\dfrac{\text{Net Income}}{\text{Sales}}$	HIGH
Operating Profit Margin	$\dfrac{\text{Operating Income}}{\text{Sales}}$	HIGH
Return on Assets	$\dfrac{\text{Net Income + (Interest Expense times (1-tax rate))}}{\text{Total Assets}}$	HIGH
Return on Equity	$\dfrac{\text{Net Income}}{\text{Net Worth}}$	HIGH
Return on Capital	$\dfrac{\text{Earnings before Interest and Taxes}}{\text{Capitalization}}$	HIGH

where the primary function is merely loading goods onto trucks and moving through to the destination. Historically it has been expected that an operating profit margin of at least 6% must be maintained. When operating costs rise above the 94% of revenue level, the likelihood of failure increases.

In other businesses, especially those with complex manufacturing operations, the cost of goods sold is the important figure. In heavy manufacturing, for example, the cost of goods sold tends to be the dominant expense, often reaching 70% of total sales. This results from both the capital intensity of the business and the high cost of labor and capital in the United States.

In contrast, the manufacturing costs for major computer supplies are a lower percentage of revenues. This is offset by the substantial risk in manufacturing computers: Products can become obsolete quickly, requiring retooling and redevelopment of new products. Thus, mainframe manufacturers have historically been able to charge ample markups over manufacturing cost. Manufacturing costs of some major computer producers reach a level of only 40% of total sales. For example, IBM has consistently been able to generate operating profit margins in excess of 50% of sales.

Cost structures provide information that can generate an industry standard, useful for intra-industry analysis. Moreover, knowing a company's past experience with cost control allows the analyst to see whether costs are rising or falling and thus to measure management performance efficiency.

Multiple-Product Firms

Even medium-size companies typically have more than one product. Thus, sales levels and the cost structures of most firms result from several divisions and several marketplaces. The Securities and Exchange Commission requires some financial data to be segregated by product or market. The company can decide how to present the separated information, however, and for the most part the results are less than useful for financial statement analysis (e.g., the business may merely be separated into consumer products and industrial products).

Federal Express

Federal Express has seen its profit margins slip because of competition. But with constantly rising sales, the main problem the company had was trying to expand into a new service, Zap Mail, same-day electronic delivery. The costs of facsimile machines fell rapidly to end users and Federal Express's revenue growth did not occur. In this case, management went to great pains in their reports to segregate the deleterious effects of Zap Mail. Thus, the analyst would be able to differentiate the main business of Federal Express—courier overnight mail—from Zap Mail to assess the company's prospects.

The Conglomerate

In a conglomerate, the variability of different marketplaces can be hidden by averages. Because they did not supply the specific information that would enable analysts to understand what was transpiring in the individual divisions, many conglomerates suffered from a loss of credibility. Conglomerate stocks have generally sold for significantly less than individual companies operating within specific industries. The stock market lost faith in companies that originally diversified into different businesses to reduce risks because it became apparent that few if any managers had the ability or skills to operate the many distinct activities of conglomerates.

This is not to say that there have not been some entrepreneurs who were able to make conglomerates work. Charles Bluhdorn at Gulf and Western, Inc. was an example. The analyst should take note, however, that with Bluhdorn's departure from Gulf and Western, the other executives immediately eliminated many of the divisions of Gulf and Western that did not appear to be part of the new image of the firm: publishing and entertainment. Instead, the funds from these dispositions bought additional subsidiaries, like Prentice-Hall, a publishing firm, hopefully strengthening Gulf and Western's position in its newly chosen field of concentration. In this way it hopes to convince analysts that it is no longer a conglomerate and it deserves a higher stock price multiple on its earnings.

Key Points: The use of common-size analysis of expenses is satisfactory for single-product or service firms. Unfortunately, averages obscure analysis of cost control for the multiple-product-line company. The best approach is to request a breakdown of the financial statements by division.

Sales Growth

Some firms experience rapid sales growth; while not a necessary condition to debt repayment capacity, it frequently stimulates borrowing, as discussed in Chapter 8. Forecasting for a firm that is growing rapidly is difficult because of compounding problems, growth on top of growth. For example, sales double every 5 years at only 15% and triple at 25% growth!

Total Growth Over Original Sales for 5 Years Compounded

Year	At 10% per year	At 15% per year	At 25% per year
1	110%	115%	125%
2	121	132	156
3	133	152	195
4	146	175	244
5	161	201	305

The assessment of a company's growth potential is a difficult one. In the past 30 years, several high-tech companies that began in garages have developed into major corporations. How can the analyst incorporate such growth into the analysis? First, let's look at some examples.

Xerox

Haloid Corporation acquired the xerographic patent from its inventor in 1949. After 10 years of research and development, the firm brought to market a machine that made offset printing masters in a process unparalleled in quality and speed. Haloid made the decision early to market the machines on a rental basis, initially charging by the copy. The company planned to price competitively with the then-popular wet copy processes. Haloid anticipated that its machines would recover their full cost within 2 to 3 years. After that, the machines were expected to turn a substantial profit.

When the machines hit the marketplace, a phenomenon that experts had not anticipated occurred. Demand for the ability to produce a *quick, plain paper copy* was far greater than anyone had expected. Haloid Corporation was able to recover the full $2,000 cost of manufacturing the machine within 6 months. In 3 years Haloid Corporation, now known as Xerox, became a *Fortune* 500 company with billions of dollars in sales and revenues.

Since that major breakthrough, Xerox Corporation has been hard-pressed to add to its product line. Although its copiers today are considered among the highest quality, Japanese competitors have taken more than 50% of the market, especially at the lower-volume end. Kodak has taken some of the high-volume end. Xerox has acquired other businesses and done research and development, especially in the computer and color xerography areas, but it has been unable to create enhanced products that shut out other competitors or to break into any new product areas. It has lost its growth rate.

Polaroid Corporation

Polaroid Corporation invented instant film, and after great initial growth into the *Fortune* 500, has been unable to expand into new product lines. It has been careful to control its development process patents and has moved into the area of color film production. Polaroid has developed numerous applications that use instant photographic results. It has fought down every competitor and managed to remain preeminent in instant photography, including an expansion into new industrial uses. Polaroid unquestionably has had missteps along the way—including instant motion picture film—and its growth has slowed.

Apple Computer

Apple Computer rose from total obscurity to *Fortune* 500 status in the early 1980s when VisiCorp's financial spreadsheet made Apple's personal computers popular with businesspeople. It has constantly striven to market new products that will enable it to compete with IBM and DEC in the business market. After a series of missteps in applying technology (originally developed by Xerox, which also never successfully brought it to market), it has finally produced a computer that appears to have caught the imagination of business, especially in graphics design: the Macintosh computer. Whether Apple will make dramatic inroads into corporate business and whether it will continue dynamic growth in the future is uncertain.

The ability to capture and maintain market share is critical to stability and profit growth. Although the examples above have depicted firms whose innovation was originally behind their success and sizable market share, holding onto that market share over the years is a true test of management skill.

Return on Assets

This element of operational performance focuses on the efficacy of asset use as measured by the return on assets (ROA) ratio. Commonly (and incorrectly) calculated by dividing net income by total assets, a firm's ROA is high when asset use efficiency is good or when there are few assets used in the business. The ratio is low when assets are used inefficiently or when there are substantial assets used in the business relative to sales. ROA is also useful for trend and intra-industry analysis. It has attained popularity in management's own internal reporting because it allows for the comparison of managerial performance between different divisions of the same company.

Unfortunately this formulation of ROA ignores leverage. Nearly all companies borrow funds as part of long-term capital. The interest expense on these borrowed funds is actually a return to investors of long-term capital funds configured as debt, not that dissimilar from the net income owned by equity investors. Since interest is deducted before net income is calculated, the first formulation ignores this return, which would have dropped to the bottom line if all capital funds had derived from stock. Interest should be added back into income before calculating ROA to allow comparison between firms of different debt/equity capital structures. To fully accommodate the equity metaphor, the interest expense must first be reduced by the amount of taxes that would be collected if this interest were really part of net income.

Another enhancement is to add back the minority interest income to the numerator of the ratio. When indicated, minority interest implies that the entire assets of the affiliate firm have been consolidated with the parent. Therefore, while the net income report is intended as a return to shareholders, calculating ROA uses all of these assets and should use all the earnings generated by them, which includes minority interest.

ROA should also be compared to the average interest rate on company debt. A company should earn more on its assets than it pays for its debt. If a firm is unable to earn more money on its assets than it must pay back to its creditors, then it is liquidating itself to pay interest expense. If it can earn more than the cost of debt, it will be able to give shareholders more value and thus compensate them for the risk involved in borrowing, namely that the firm may not be able to pay it back in a timely manner, which could lead to bankruptcy and loss of the shareholders' investment.

> **Key Points:** Add interest expense (net of taxes) back into income to calculate ROA. The return on assets should be compared to the cost of funds of the company; if it is lower, the company would be better off to sell its assets and pay down its debt.

Unconsolidated Subsidiaries

As discussed in Chapter 3, the problem of unconsolidated subsidiaries has largely been eliminated by the issuance of SFAS #94. Nevertheless, they demonstrate the interrelationships between the financial statement accounts, management aims to look good, GAAP accounting principles, and the calculation of ratios.

Refer to The Limited Credit case (captive finance subsidiary) in Chapter 3 (Exhibit 3-1). How does The Limited's activities affect its performance ratios? The answer is that by removing assets from the financial statement and by accounting for its subsidiary as an equity investment The Limited was able to improve its return on assets. While the spinoff eliminated credit card interest income along with interest expense from the loans used to finance the accounts receivable, finance companies have slim returns on assets; as independent entities, they are acceptable to shareholders because the market permits them high leverage ratios, providing an acceptable return on equity. As long as the return on assets of the finance company is more than the cost of borrowing, shareholder returns can reach adequate levels. Nonetheless, finance institutions' returns on assets are extremely low—generally less than 1%—after interest expense. By not consolidating its finance subsidiary, The Limited reported only net returns on an equity investment. Therefore, since only the finance company's reasonable returns on equity are averaged in, The Limited's return on assets looks good.

Real estate subsidiaries also have to be consolidated, but the owner/entrepreneur often personally owns the real estate. By leasing real estate to his businesses, the owner can extract returns from his company without incurring the double taxation that dividends would extract. Moreover, he can show the current value of the real estate on his personal financial statements. This is one reason why lenders regularly require guarantees from entrepreneurs. Nevertheless, since part of the return from real estate is the holding gain from inflation—the very thing that makes FIFO so distracting—the low net operating returns on real estate do not detract from the firm's return on assets, assuming they are held outside the business financial statements.

> **Key Points:** Unconsolidated subsidiaries can make a firm's performance ratios appear better than they would if the subsidiaries were consolidated.

Discontinued Operations

Another example of problems in calculating returns on assets is the income or losses from discontinued operations. These should be removed from the net income number in all the ratio calculations discussed. These businesses are being eliminated from the future operations of the firm. Their assets have already been eliminated from the balance sheet and the sales and expenses are not included in the income statement. Although these businesses are still controlled by the company, they should not be used to make forecasts.

> **Key Points:** Do not include income or losses from discontinued operations when calculating operating ratios.

Return on Equity (ROE)

The next ratio for evaluating operations is the return on shareholders' net investment. If this ratio is calculated by dividing net income by shareholders' equity, it may be overstated because net worth may be deflated by assets carried at historical cost. To obtain the realistic return to shareholders, the ratio should be calculated *by dividing the market value of the common stock at the beginning of the year into income.*

The shareholder buys stock not only for a dividend return but for a comprehensive return that includes the increasing value of the stock. If the return on net worth is low for several years, the stock price will reflect this low return. Shareholders focus on the growth rate in earnings per share. Return on balance sheet net worth is more of a curiosity and it is of little real value to any creditor.

Quality of Earnings

Earnings quality is a central issue in financial statement credibility. Much of the analyst's attention in the credit process centers on company performance and the ability to repay debt. The objective of performance analysis is to use the historic information to generate forecasts. Therefore, some managements choose accounting conventions that show high performance rather than give a more accurate indication of it; the result is low-quality financial statements. Spotting these connivers is critical to proper analysis; a firm can even acquire a reputation for producing an inferior earnings statement. This is a very difficult reputation to shed even with new management.

Earnings quality and credibility are correlated with dependability of performance, that is, stability. Lack of it (variability) is associated with high risk. Therefore, the lack of stability in the income and cash flow statements and high-risk assets on the balance sheet translate into higher interest charges from creditors and expectations of higher returns by shareholders.

This topic has been developed by a number of authors, notably Joel Siegel [Bernstein and Siegel, 1979]. The following checklist is partially derived from his work to help the analyst assess earnings quality. The advised procedure is to go through the list of 12 items with each subject firm and check for any occurrences that should create questions for management. A firm with many occurrences, a bad score on financial statement quality, may have excellent reasons for these accounting subterfuges, but like bad food in a restaurant, they should raise the analyst's concerns about how clean the kitchen is.

1. *Has the firm changed accounting policies?* Accounting policy changes that result in more income being recognized compromise earnings quality. For example, Bethlehem Steel, by changing its useful life estimate for plant and equipment, was able to reduce its depreciation expense by $400 million per year. This change did not just alter easily identifiable extraordinary earnings but actually increased the firm's regular profits for the previous two years, and into the future. Moreover, a change in depreciation methods is footnoted in the year of its enactment, but is never mentioned again. Therefore, it should be regarded as a mark against earnings quality.

2. *Does the firm use the FIFO inventory convention?* Generally, FIFO reduces quality. FIFO causes both the current and future income to be overstated since current costs are kept on the balance sheet. The analyst should prefer a firm to use LIFO, which causes current costs to flow through to the income statement. Inflation rate switches cause FIFO accounting earnings to fluctuate in even wider swings from year to year. These fluctuations create major problems for the analyst who is attempting to make a forecast. LIFO income causes perturbations only when inventory is reduced, chewing into low-cost materials.

3. *Does the firm engage in off-balance-sheet financing?* Although it may seem that off-balance-sheet liabilities and assets might not affect the income statement, pension liabilities can depress earnings far into the future. (Before SFAS #87, which required a firm's unfunded pension liability to be included on its balance sheet, the analyst's only alternative was to pick up the liability from the footnotes.) To alert analysts about this potential liability, the SEC required firms to include in their fixed charge coverage ratios interest expense equivalent to that which the firm would have incurred if it had borrowed sufficient money to fund the unfunded pension costs. Although such expenses do not appear on the income statement, since funds are not in the pension trust–producing earnings for the eventual payment of pension benefits, this hypothetical expense takes on more significance as a dormant expense that will affect earnings in future years.

Another off-balance-sheet booster of return on assets is the sale of accounts receivable to independent finance companies with recourse. The contingency risk arising from this recourse can be significant if the firm has been pushing sales to low-quality credits. Contingency liabilities resulting from recourse may be identified only vaguely in a footnote.

Since firms are no longer able to carry their majority-owned subsidiaries as equity investments, financial analysts should expect that, going forward, firms will enter into joint ventures with financial institutions and other entities to move their accounts receivable back off their balance sheets. If a firm owns 50% or less of a subsidiary, it is not required to consolidate it—a typical joint venture. Recourse on the sale of accounts receivable to subsidiaries in which the firm holds less than a majority interest will be hidden since the contingency contract may be interpreted as an executory agreement. In any case, earnings quality will be reduced because of the real and contingent liability of these off-balance-sheet obligations.

4. *Does the firm have any significant pending litigation?* Lawsuit settlements can greatly affect future earnings. The contingency footnote reviews potential outcome of litigation; however, lawyers are likely to provide a conservative estimate. This reduces earnings quality.

5. *Does the firm have extremely low profit margins?* A creditor should view a net profit margin of 1% or 2% on sales, for instance, as *no* indication at all of successful performance (with the possible exception of cases in which low margins are the industry standard). Occasionally, the profit margin, calculated using net income divided by sales, hides the fact that non-operating earnings are providing a sizable chunk of the net profit. Thus, in certain industries, transportation, for instance, the analyst should focus on the operating profit margin rather than on net profit margin.

6. *Does the firm have significant investments and advances to unconsolidated subsidiaries and joint ventures?* As previously mentioned, joint ventures, such as those providing feedstock for the inventory needs of the firm, enable a firm to increase its leverage. Among the prominent users of joint ventures are public utilities. Sharing the cost of building power plants reduces the financial impact of a disaster, such as failing to obtain an operating permit as in the case of the Shoreham nuclear power facility. Although there are advantages to joint ventures, utilities can hide aspects of their operations from shareholders and creditors by carrying these investments on an equity basis.

7. *Does the firm have substantial reserve accounts?* Reserves are no more than set-asides of net worth to buffer some potential future loss. Typically reserves are set up for warranty problems or pending litigation, but they can also be created during asset disposition. Any earnings or losses that result from a change in reserves should be considered extraordinary items.

8. *Have there been sharp reductions in discretionary expense items?* Discretionary expenses, such as advertising, maintenance, and research and development are subject to manipulation. Testing the validity of reductions and increases in these expenses includes calculating ratios that compare advertising, maintenance, and research and development to sales over several years. Maintenance expense

levels can be compared to total fixed assets since the age of the fixed assets is generally not known to the creditor. Research and development expenditures may increase sales in the future, but can also move in waves as products are released.

9. *Has there been unwarranted deferral of costs or premature accrual of revenues?* An example of expense deferral is not amortizing goodwill over a reasonable period of time. From a quality of earnings perspective, a failure to amortize goodwill is defensible only if management can provide specific information to support its contention that goodwill has value. Premature revenue recognition is a problem with firms that sell in a rapidly changing market and immediately recognize revenues. A rapidly changing market opens up the risk of returns and customer pleas for credits to offset falling prices or changing styles. New product introductions can be fraught with problems. A prime example is the computer software area, where nearly every publisher has had to invest significant time and money into correcting errors ("bugs") that were not discovered during "alpha" or "beta" testing. These errors required that corrected copies of software be sent to users at a nominal cost, sometimes at less than the production cost.

10. *Are extraordinary losses and gains recognized at the same time?* Selling a fixed asset that has appreciated in value at the same time that an ailing subsidiary is discontinued, for instance, should be a clue to the analyst that consolidated earnings in past years were exaggerated to permit the investments to stay in place. Having the two events occur simultaneously should raise the analyst's suspicion about management's real motives.

11. *Have there been sharp declines in fixed asset turnover?* A fall in fixed asset turnover implies that the assets may be risky or obsolete and they are not producing salable products at a competitive price. It could mean that the firm has acquired assets but has been unable to make them productive. An example would be Federal Express's investment in Zap Mail equipment. Having spent millions of dollars on the acquisition of equipment that is underutilized, fixed assets grow and sales will not. The ratio will fall: Efficiency is off.

12. *Are capital expenditures less than depreciation expense?* The depletion of capital assets is sometimes referred to as "milking" the company. Although earnings may not fall in the early years of this practice, costs eventually will rise as capital assets become less productive. Failure to replace fixed assets may be a result of management's inability to keep up with rapid technological change within the industry, or it may be an indication of management's compromising the future potential of the firm.

In addition to reviewing the firm's capital expenditures as a percent of depreciation over time, the analyst should review the technological changes within the industry and note the industry trend in depreciation expense as a percent of fixed assets or sales. Capital expenditures are determined from reviewing the Statement of Cash Flows.

United Enterprises, Inc. (cont.)

Referring to United Enterprises' 1990 Statement of Cash Flow, in Exhibit 1-1, it is evident that capital equipment expenditures are less than depreciation.

Because most of United Enterprises' equipment was long-lived, and there had been 10 years of rapid inflation prior to 1990, even maintaining the same level of fixed assets would have required expenditures substantially more than the amount depreciated.

The company's capital assets did not shrink in 1990 because of mergers and acquisitions. Unfortunately, this is symptomatic of the way in which United Enterprises managed businesses. At one point in the 1980s, the company had 150 major divisions, built up by acquiring companies from their entrepreneurial founders. By 1990, this number had dwindled to 30. Many of the acquired businesses had merely been milked, closed, and liquidated. Apparently management did not have the talent to strengthen and sustain any of the businesses it operated. Its method of growth was to acquire firms by giving the owner stock in exchange for the business. The acquisition focus of the company can be verified by looking at the Statement of Cash Flows and seeing that expenditures for acquisition of companies continued from year to year.

Non-Financial Factors Affecting Quality of Earnings

The following is a list of self-explanatory, non-financial factors related to low quality of earnings:

- A change of auditors
- Convictions of management or even allegations that management has engaged in dishonest activities
- Government regulation of the industry
- Faddish or trendy product line
- Highly elastic product demand (i.e., demand fluctuates with price changes)
- Single-market access

The Quality of Earnings and Inflation

Many companies are affected by increases in the costs of fixed assets and supplies. For firms such as retail stores, which resell largely unaltered items, most cost increases are correctly incorporated into cost of goods sold. However, for companies that do a considerable amount of processing and require material fixed assets, depreciation expense will be below what the actual cost of producing these goods on this machinery should be. Their costs are not being properly recorded.

United Enterprises, Inc. (cont.)

Business Week [May 2, 1983] reported that there were substantial discrepancies between the profits that corporations reported using GAAP and their profits after using inflation-adjusted accounting, SFAS #33. Although inflation in 1982 was only 6.1%, GAAP historical cost accounting indicated that, for the nation's largest corporations, net income dropped 22%. When inflation-adjusted figures for current costs were used, net income fell 60%. After accounting for the gain from holding net monetary liabilities, the results showed that *GAAP overstated profits by 50%*. This circumstance occurred with inflation at a low level; thus, it will continue even though inflation remains low.

Refer to Exhibit 1-1, the inflation-adjusted accounting data for United Enterprises' 1990 income statement. It shows how the firm reported the effect of changing prices on its profits. The first column carries the historical cost–based reporting numbers. The various expenses produced a net after-tax income of $31.2 million. The second column shows adjustments made for price changes. Net income in this inflation-adjusted or current cost column is only $16.5 million.

In tracking down the difference, notice that depreciation of $26.4 million reported under historical cost has jumped to $37.2 million under current cost accounting. This can be explained from the note at the bottom (D) stating that United Enterprises' fixed assets have a current cost (appraised value) that is 76% greater than their historical cost showing on the balance sheet ($296.4 million versus $168 million). The resulting depreciation differential is equal to $10.8 million, accounting for a large chunk of the $14.7 million difference in net income.

How should this additional depreciation be allocated to the expense accounts? First, look at the changes in the selling expenses and the general and administrative expenses from the first to the second column in the exhibit. For selling expense, current costs showed a $1.2 million difference. In the general and administrative expense account, a $700,000 expense difference is reported. The remaining $8.9 million in depreciation must be allocated to the cost of goods sold account.

The reason for the remaining $3.9 million difference in income is that FIFO inventory convention recognizes inventory holding gains. United Enterprises uses FIFO accounting, and therefore, during 1990 it was able to recognize $3.9 million of net income above what LIFO, and its current cost accounting, would have permitted. This gain was a result of the inflationary impact on the inventories' values. Considering that this difference amounted to 12% of net income, it was not a number to be taken lightly.

At the bottom of the exhibit, notice that United Enterprises is given credit for having more monetary liabilities than monetary assets, resulting in a $3.7 million paper gain for the year, and increasing inflation-adjusted net income to $20.2 million.

To examine this paper gain more closely, consider how lenders determine interest rates charged to borrowers. Lenders have a target inflation-free yield they wish to earn. Understanding that there will be some inflation during the year, the lender must add the expected inflation rate to the yield required to achieve that real return. This added inflation premium may be regarded as a penalty. This penalty is included in the interest rate charged to the client, referred to as a **nominal interest rate.** Consider that part of the interest payment is the recapture of principal that otherwise would be lost to inflation. Therefore, the nominal interest charge includes a prepayment of principal. Thus, not all nominal interest paid should be an accounting expense.

United Enterprises, Inc. (cont.)

Under generally accepted accounting principles United Enterprises had expensed something that was not an expense. Therefore, it is added back into net income as shown in the last couple of lines. That explains the $3.7 million paper gain shown on the company's statement of income adjusted for changing prices.

Business Week analyzed how current cost accounting affected the profits of several industries. The drug industry's GAAP result were closest to the inflation-adjusted results, with inflation-adjusted profits representing 82% of GAAP profits. The drug industry is subject to rapid technological obsolescence. Presumably, these firms are depreciating their assets at a faster rate than others, which brings their GAAP depreciation rate close to an inflation-adjusted rate. Other firms that had similar high correlations between inflation-adjusted profits and GAAP profits either had very little in fixed assets or were in highly technical areas such as publishing, leisure time products, and aerospace.

Those industries for which differences between GAAP and inflation-adjusted profits were most extreme included the following:

- Natural resources: GAAP profits increased 9%; inflation-adjusted profits *decreased* 17%.
- Appliance manufacturing: GAAP profits increased 3%; inflation-adjusted profits *decreased* 23%.
- Chemicals: GAAP profits increased 1% over the 1978–1982 period; inflation-adjusted profits *decreased* 25%.
- Paper manufacturing: GAAP profits fell 8%; inflation-adjusted profits fell 36%.
- A few industries have slightly higher profits under inflation-adjusted accounting including food processing, which reported a 9% GAAP profit increase and a 12% profit increase under inflation-adjusted accounting.

In conclusion, inflation-adjusted accounting is useful. The elimination of this information from financial statements as a result of SFAS #89 places the burden on the analyst to request the information directly from the client. If depreciation methods and FIFO accounting are critical to the net income figure, then this information should be requested. In too many cases, FIFO and depreciation are at issue; therefore, the *determination of debt repayment capacity must be based not only on the profit margins but also on the other derivative indicators of funds flow.*

Consider the changes inflationary accounting would have on some of the ratios we have considered.

- LIFO inventory turnover would decrease because inventory would be reported at the higher current cost.
- The current ratio would most likely improve because of higher LIFO inventory values.
- The profit margin would decline because current cost depreciation would be higher.

- Return on assets would fall because net income would be smaller and current cost assets would be much larger.

How is the analyst to balance the spreadsheet after making changes to the financial statements to reflect inflation-adjusted accounting? For the sake of simplicity, reflect determined differences in the net worth section without having changes flow through net income. In this way, the issue of whether holding gains on inventory should be considered a part of recurring earnings is

Exhibit 9-2.

BREAK EVEN ANALYSIS

Example of HIGH FIXED costs and LOW VARIABLE costs

Year	1985	1986	1987	1988	1989	1990
Sales in units	150.00	200.00	225.00	250.00	300.00	325.00
Sales	187.50	250.00	281.25	312.50	375.00	406.25
Variable Costs	56.25	75.00	84.38	93.75	112.50	121.88
Fixed Costs	180.00	180.00	180.00	180.00	180.00	180.00
Total Costs	236.25	255.00	264.38	273.75	292.50	301.88
Net Income	-48.75	-5.00	16.88	38.75	82.50	104.38

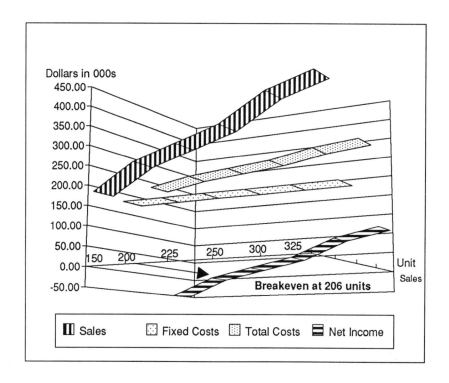

BREAK EVEN ANALYSIS, part 2

Example of LOW FIXED costs and HIGH VARIABLE costs

Year	1985	1986	1987	1988	1989	1990
Sales in units	150.00	200.00	225.00	250.00	300.00	325.00
Sales	187.50	250.00	281.25	312.50	375.00	406.25
Variable Costs	131.25	175.00	196.88	218.75	262.50	284.38
Fixed Costs	75.00	75.00	75.00	75.00	75.00	75.00
Total Costs	206.25	250.00	271.88	293.75	337.50	359.38
Net Income	-18.75	0.00	9.38	18.75	37.50	46.88

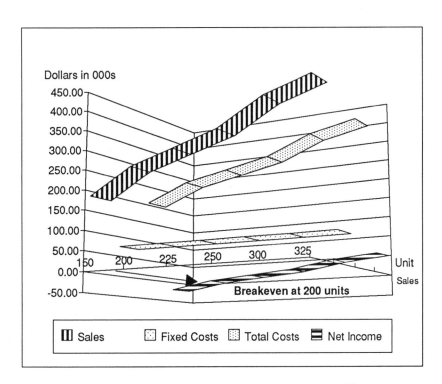

eliminated because the increased value of the inventory will show up in the revised balance sheet. Running these adjustments through the income statements is not really helpful because it creates sporadic (non-recurring) earnings that are not necessarily in line with the inflation rate. Furthermore, in evidence of the propriety of the approach consider the accounting for overseas subsidiaries (currency translation), and recently for pensions (unfunded pension liability), in which both of these FASB statements permit posting to segregated reserve accounts within the net worth section of the balance sheet *without* accounting for the change within the income statement.

Break-Even Calculations

Now let's look at operating leverage, a factor in earnings variability and, thus, earnings quality. Refer to the tables and graphs in Exhibit 9-2 exemplifying, first, high fixed costs (low variable costs) and, second, low fixed costs (high variable costs) for the discussion.

The theory of operating leverage is similar to that of financial leverage: There are fixed costs that must be met on a regular basis. These are shown as the flat line on each of the graphs. In contrast, variable costs are incurred only if products are moving through the plant. The variable expenses are shown on a line with an upward slope less than the sales line slope. It is labeled "Total Costs" on the graph because it is being added on top of the fixed costs.

Understanding its fixed and variable costs, a firm should be able to forecast its costs relative to sales volume. The sales line runs from the intersection of the horizontal axis and the vertical axis toward the upper right, at approximately a 45-degree angle. (This analysis assumes that as much can be sold as can be made and offered at the market price, similar to the farm industry. Unfortunately for the model, many product manufacturers and service providers supply markets in which they cannot endlessly expand production and sales.)

By reviewing the sales and costs figures, a firm can calculate two important derivatives of break-even analysis: the break-even point and the contribution margin. This analysis can be used by management in making decisions about whether to emphasize one product at the expense of other products since it can show which product contributes more to overhead. By examining closely the contribution margin, the firm can anticipate the results of different sales and production strategies.

The first graph shown in Exhibit 9-2 has high fixed costs relative to variable ones. This would be the profile of a heavy manufacturing firm. On the upswing, once break-even is reached, profits expand very rapidly. On the downside, once break-even is reached, profits can drop off just as quickly. This creates earnings instability. The quality of earnings for a capital-intensive firm is thus lower than the quality of earnings for a firm with low fixed costs.

The situation for a firm with low fixed costs is illustrated in the second graph of Exhibit 9-2. The ability to reduce variable costs (and total costs) significantly as production falls permits this firm to show much less of a loss in down times; however, it is more difficult for this firm to earn large profits with a sharp increase in sales. (The firm's operations are not leveraged.) An example of a firm that has high variable costs is an accounting firm. Besides a portable computer for its employees, the firm need not even provide desk space for all associates, since auditors often must work at their client's place of business. As work expands, more associates can be hired. As work slows down, associates can be laid off.

> **Key Points:** A firm with high operating leverage will have greater variability in earnings year to year than a firm with low operating leverage, assuming the latter firm's variable costs have been correctly identified. This variability reduces the quality of earnings.

Chapter 10

Comparative Analysis: Intra-Industry and Trend

Previous chapters have explained how to calculate ratios and have defined them in the abstract. In this chapter, ratio *comparison* is the focal point. You will learn how to compare one company's ratios to its own past performance as well as to compare ratios of its competitors in the same industry.

Historically, **intra-industry analysis,** comparing the firm with its peers of the same size in the same industry, has provided an important means for assessing a firm's operations. Today, research indicates that intra-industry analysis provides the most decisive data for assessing the financial standing of a firm. While the lender still has to figure out whether to participate in a particular industry, once there, it can rank prospective clients and decide how far down in the list of potential clients to go. Intra-industry analysis will be the subject of this chapter's first section.

The second section will cover **trend analysis**—examining historical relationships among one company's ratios. Trend analysis is important since it helps lenders detect adverse changes in the company's operation or environment that might impair its chances for future success. Trend analysis is preeminently important for some lenders who are disposed to have client relationships for many years and are constantly on the alert for some adverse change in the company's operation or its environment that impairs its chances for future success. Furthermore, it is sometimes easier to ask company managers (who tend to view their firm as a special case) about variances in their own trends than it is to ask them about deviations from industry averages.

Intra-Industry Comparative Analysis

There are two approaches to intra-industry analysis. The first is to *compare directly one firm with another of the same size and in the same industry*. The second firm against which the subject firm is compared could be one with which the analyst is familiar, a well-regarded client, or it could be one about which the lender has been able to obtain an independent analysis, possibly from a brokerage firm. This last example is appropriate for lenders to extremely large firms, and the security analyst's perspective can provide useful input, although security analysts tend to focus on net income performance and growth rather than on debt repayment capacity. In any case, the analyst must have a complete set of financials for the two firms to compare. This practice avoids the problems of averages or medians and instead focuses on the reasonable differences between firms.

The second approach it to *compare the firm under study to industry averages* published by Standard & Poor's, Moody's Investors Service, Value Line, Robert Morris Associates (RMA), or Dun & Bradstreet (D&B). These firms conduct ongoing research to create average ratios by industry, and in the case of Robert Morris Associates, by asset size within the industry. This asset size variation can be very important when looking at smaller companies. It is reasonable to compare Chrysler Corporation with General Motors, even though one is several times larger than the other, because they are both billion-dollar assets firms. It is less meaningful, however, to compare ratios of firms with $10 million in assets with those of $100 million because the management infrastructure is so different at the higher level. The lack of a breakdown by asset size increases the value of the industry ratio studies; thus, this chapter discusses the averages prepared by Robert Morris Associates.

Robert Morris Associates' Statement Studies

Robert Morris Associates (RMA) is the national association for bank loan and credit officers. It has over 15,000 associate members. Exhibit 10-1 is from the RMA *Annual Statement Studies* book [1987]. Each year RMA requests that members complete a limited detail statement spreadsheet, by SIC code and asset sizes, for companies to which the banks lend. RMA then computes common sizes and ratios for each company (nearly 86,000 in 1987) and calculates the averages by asset sizes as follows:

Up to $1 million in assets—for the smallest firm
$1 to $10 million in assets—for the smaller medium-size firms
$10 million to $50 million in assets—for the larger medium-size firms
$50 million to $100 million in assets—for the largest firms, except in the
    section on contractors, which is based on revenues

Robert Morris Associates' disclaimer statement reads as follows:

RMA cautions that the *Studies* be regarded only as a general guideline and not as an absolute industry norm. This is due to limited samples within categories, the categorization of companies by their primary Standard Industrial Classification (SIC) number only, and different methods of operations by companies within the same industry. For these reasons, RMA recommends that the figures be used only as general guidelines in addition to other methods of financial analysis.

Exhibit 10-1 shows the page for manufacturers of general industrial machinery and equipment (SIC #3561, 3564, 3566, 3567, and 3569), which has been chosen for discussion here because of the large number of statements averaged and the broad industry covered. As the sample sheet shows, RMA occasionally does not get a sufficient number (more than ten) of large-size company data to produce statistically significant averages. Therefore, cells for those companies are left blank, although they are included in averages in the right-hand columns (the ones labeled "All"). For an example, see the "EBIT/Interest" ratio cell, fourth column.

RMA Common Sizes

The top half of the sheet lists the type and number of statements incorporated into each category. Next, is a straightforward common-size analysis of the balance sheet. Assets are listed as a percentage of total assets; liabilities and net worth are listed as a percentage of total liabilities and net worth. Users select the relationships they wish to scrutinize. The RMA spread is so abbreviated compared to the usual multipage spreadsheet used by lenders that the analyst will have to respread the subject firm's financials in order to make a comparison. (This should present no problem if a computerized spreadsheet is available.)

The right-hand columns present five-year historical comparisons. These columns contain unweighted averages of "All" financial statements' results rather than weighting firms by asset size. The numbers in these columns are consequently less reliable for comparison purposes. For instance, the net sales (the bottom row of the spreadsheet) in the $10 million to $50 million company range are nearly 16 times the net sales of the firms in the up to $1 million category. The difference is even greater for total assets. Since the right-hand columns average all firms together, the smaller firm contributes as much to the average as a larger firm. Each lending organization is likely to have a unique size composition in portfolio, making comparison with this version of the whole industry less useful. Therefore, the right-hand ("All") columns should be avoided for individual firm comparison. Instead, *the columns to the right of the categories should be used only to look at trends within the industry as a whole.*

If analysts take their individual companies and compare them with the specific sheet in the Robert Morris book, it should be easy to detect which balance sheet or income statement items are out of line. In many industries (but not manufacturers of general industrial machinery and equipment), the smaller firms are less profitable. This is because owners of smaller companies frequently pay themselves salaries or other fringe benefits to reduce income. Otherwise the owners would subject themselves to double taxation. (That is, the firm would have to pay taxes on income, and the owners have to pay taxes on dividend income.)

Smaller companies also typically have older, fully depreciated equipment with which they make do. This can be verified by looking at the common-size percent. Larger businesses often find they can achieve real productivity gains with newer equipment and as a consequence the common-size analysis will show a higher percentage of total assets invested in fixed assets.

Another feature more commonly related to size than to different industries is the percentage of long-term debt relative to trade debt. Inevitably small

(Text continued on page 244.)

Exhibit 10-1.

MANUFACTURERS - GENERAL INDUSTRIAL MACHINERY & EQUIPMENT   SIC# 3551 (64,66,67,69)   117

	Current Data					Comparative Historical Data				
Type of Statement	**0-1MM**	**1-10MM**	**10-50MM**	**50-100MM**	**ALL**	**6/30/82-3/31/83 ALL**	**6/30/83-3/31/84 ALL**	**6/30/84-3/31/85 ALL**	**6/30/85-3/31/86 ALL**	**6/30/86-3/31/87 ALL**
Unqualified	5	77	43	10	135			161	138	135
Qualified	5	13	6		24	DATA NOT	AVAILABLE	11	7	24
Reviewed	28	68	1		97			80	87	97
Compiled	35	28	1		64			73	63	64
Other	17	35	12	1	65			57	71	65
			180(6/30-9/30/86)	205(10/1/86-3/31/87)						
NUMBER OF STATEMENTS	**90**	**221**	**63**	**11**	**385**	**411**	**372**	**382**	**366**	**385**
ASSETS	%	%	%	%	%	%	%	%	%	%
Cash & Equivalents	10.5	5.9	8.3	7.5	7.4	8.8	7.9	7.7	7.1	7.4
Trade Receivables - (net)	32.8	28.8	23.0	22.5	28.6	25.8	27.3	29.1	28.9	28.6
Inventory	27.7	31.1	26.1	25.7	29.4	28.0	28.7	28.5	30.0	29.4
All Other Current	2.9	1.9	4.4	2.1	2.6	3.0	2.8	2.2	2.5	2.6
Total Current	73.9	67.8	61.8	57.8	68.0	65.6	66.7	67.6	68.5	68.0
Fixed Assets (net)	19.1	23.8	30.5	27.9	23.9	26.4	25.2	24.5	24.2	23.9
Intangibles (net)	1.8	1.6	2.0	2.5	1.7	1.0	1.0	.9	1.3	1.7
All Other Non-Current	5.2	6.9	5.7	11.8	6.4	7.1	7.1	7.0	6.1	6.4
Total	100.0	100.0	100.0	100.0	100.0	100.0	100.0	100.0	100.0	100.0
LIABILITIES										
Notes Payable-Short Term	11.1	10.9	6.2	3.0	10.0	8.6	9.3	10.4	10.8	10.0
Cur. Mat.-LT/D	4.5	3.6	3.8	1.2	3.8	3.6	2.9	4.0	3.8	3.8
Trade Payables	18.7	14.6	9.3	8.0	14.5	13.2	14.3	15.4	15.4	14.5
Income Taxes Payable	.9	.9	1.0	1.0	1.0	—	—	1.5	1.3	1.0
All Other Current	10.2	11.9	9.9	9.0	11.1	12.0	12.2	10.6	11.7	11.1
Total Current	45.5	42.0	30.3	22.3	40.3	37.4	38.6	41.9	42.9	40.3
Long Term Debt	12.7	14.7	20.7	14.2	15.2	16.1	16.3	16.1	15.6	15.2
Deferred Taxes	.4	1.1	2.5	1.8	1.2	—	—	1.1	1.1	1.2
All Other Non-Current	1.9	2.4	1.5	8.2	2.3	1.9	3.0	2.2	1.8	2.3
Net Worth	39.5	39.8	45.0	53.5	41.0	44.5	42.0	38.8	38.7	41.0
Total Liabilities & Net Worth	100.0	100.0	100.0	100.0	100.0	100.0	100.0	100.0	100.0	100.0
INCOME DATA										
Net Sales	100.0	100.0	100.0	100.0	100.0	100.0	100.0	100.0	100.0	100.0
Gross Profit	37.6	31.3	31.9	32.2	32.9	30.8	31.1	32.3	32.4	32.9
Operating Expenses	32.1	26.1	25.8	29.2	27.5	26.0	28.0	26.4	27.4	27.5
Operating Profit	5.5	5.2	6.1	3.0	5.4	4.9	3.1	5.9	5.0	5.4
All Other Expenses (net)	1.2	1.4	3.1	1.2	1.6	1.8	1.4	1.5	1.5	1.6
Profit Before Taxes	4.3	3.8	3.0	1.8	3.7	3.0	1.7	4.4	3.5	3.7
RATIOS										
Current	2.3	2.5	3.3	4.1	2.6	3.0	2.9	2.5	2.5	2.6
	1.6	1.5	2.2	2.9	1.7	1.9	1.8	1.7	1.6	1.7
	1.2	1.2	1.5	1.8	1.3	1.3	1.3	1.3	1.3	1.3
Quick	1.5	1.3	1.6	1.9	1.5	1.6	1.6	1.4	1.3	1.5
	1.0	.8	1.0	1.7	.9	1.0	.9	.9	.9	.9
	.7	.6	.7	1.0	.6	.6	.6	.6	.6	.6

L1	L2	L3	L4	L5		R1	R2	R3	R4	R5
30 / 43 / 61	41 / 54 / 65	48 / 59 / 79	51 / 70 / 76	40 / 53 / 68	**Sales/Receivables**	36 / 49 / 64	43 / 57 / 72	41 / 55 / 72	39 / 51 / 65	40 / 53 / 68
12.1 / 8.5 / 6.0	8.8 / 6.8 / 5.6	7.9 / 6.2 / 4.6	7.2 / 5.2 / 4.8	9.1 / 6.9 / 5.4		10.2 / 7.4 / 5.7	8.4 / 6.4 / 5.1	9.0 / 6.6 / 5.1	9.3 / 7.1 / 5.6	9.1 / 6.9 / 5.4
23 / 49 / 101	55 / 87 / 130	59 / 99 / 146	79 / 114 / 135	49 / 85 / 130	**Cost of Sales/Inventory**	45 / 83 / 130	56 / 94 / 135	49 / 83 / 130	48 / 83 / 130	49 / 85 / 130
15.8 / 7.5 / 3.6	6.6 / 4.2 / 2.8	6.2 / 3.7 / 2.5	4.6 / 3.2 / 2.7	7.5 / 4.3 / 2.8		8.1 / 4.4 / 2.8	6.5 / 3.9 / 2.7	7.4 / 4.4 / 2.8	7.6 / 4.4 / 2.8	7.5 / 4.3 / 2.8
17 / 35 / 56	20 / 37 / 56	20 / 33 / 46	24 / 31 / 45	20 / 35 / 54	**Cost of Sales/Payables**	17 / 29 / 49	24 / 37 / 59	23 / 38 / 58	22 / 35 / 55	20 / 35 / 54
21.8 / 10.4 / 6.5	18.2 / 10.0 / 6.5	18.0 / 11.1 / 7.9	15.1 / 11.7 / 8.1	18.1 / 10.3 / 6.7		21.3 / 12.5 / 7.4	15.3 / 9.8 / 6.2	15.9 / 9.7 / 6.3	16.7 / 10.3 / 6.6	18.1 / 10.3 / 6.7
6.4 / 10.2 / 22.3	4.6 / 8.1 / 15.4	2.6 / 4.8 / 7.2	2.6 / 3.8 / 3.9	4.1 / 7.1 / 14.0	**Sales/Working Capital**	3.7 / 6.4 / 15.9	3.4 / 5.8 / 11.6	4.3 / 7.2 / 16.6	4.3 / 7.8 / 16.1	4.1 / 7.1 / 14.0
(80) 11.1 / 4.1 / 1.2	(196) 6.6 / 2.9 / 1.5	(58) 5.8 / 2.5 / 1.0		(343) 7.3 / 3.0 / 1.3	**EBIT/Interest**	(340) 6.0 / 2.2 / 1.0	(335) 6.0 / 2.5 / .4	(339) 8.2 / 3.2 / 1.4	(325) 6.4 / 3.0 / 1.4	(343) 7.3 / 3.0 / 1.3
(40) 7.5 / 2.9 / .9	(147) 5.2 / 2.5 / 1.2	(51) 5.3 / 2.7 / 1.0		(246) 5.3 / 2.5 / 1.1	**Net Profit + Depr., Dep., Amort./Cur. Mat. L/T/D**	(247) 7.8 / 3.0 / 1.0	(227) 7.1 / 2.7 / .7	(244) 6.5 / 2.8 / 1.4	(243) 6.1 / 3.1 / 1.2	(246) 5.3 / 2.5 / 1.1
.2 / .4 / .9	.3 / .6 / 1.2	.4 / .6 / 1.0	.4 / .6 / .9	.3 / .6 / 1.0	**Fixed/Worth**	.3 / .6 / 1.1	.3 / .6 / 1.0	.3 / .6 / 1.1	.3 / .6 / 1.2	.3 / .6 / 1.0
.7 / 1.6 / 3.4	.9 / 1.8 / 3.4	.8 / 1.4 / 2.2	.3 / 1.1 / 1.7	.8 / 1.5 / 3.1	**Debt/Worth**	.6 / 1.3 / 2.6	.7 / 1.4 / 2.9	.8 / 1.5 / 3.4	.8 / 1.7 / 4.0	.8 / 1.5 / 3.1
(82) 56.9 / 28.5 / 5.9	(213) 35.9 / 17.1 / 4.3	(61) 27.5 / 8.2 / 2.1	18.8 / 6.4 / -24.3	(367) 36.8 / 17.3 / 3.6	**% Profit Before Taxes/Tangible Net Worth**	(402) 29.1 / 13.9 / 1.3	(356) 27.7 / 11.8 / -3.9	(360) 39.6 / 20.9 / 8.7	(347) 41.2 / 17.9 / 5.4	(367) 36.8 / 17.3 / 3.6
21.5 / 9.1 / .8	11.8 / 5.7 / 1.7	11.4 / 4.1 / .5	15.4 / 4.5 / -7.2	12.9 / 6.1 / .9	**% Profit Before Taxes/Total Assets**	12.6 / 5.3 / .4	10.9 / 5.2 / -3.0	14.0 / 8.5 / 2.0	13.6 / 6.7 / 1.8	12.9 / 6.1 / .9
38.0 / 16.8 / 8.9	18.4 / 9.0 / 4.9	7.0 / 4.6 / 3.3	6.6 / 4.0 / 3.2	19.9 / 8.6 / 4.6	**Sales/Net Fixed Assets**	15.1 / 7.4 / 4.1	14.7 / 7.5 / 3.9	16.4 / 8.3 / 4.4	19.1 / 8.6 / 4.5	19.9 / 8.6 / 4.6
3.4 / 2.6 / 2.1	2.3 / 1.9 / 1.4	1.8 / 1.3 / 1.1	1.5 / 1.2 / 1.0	2.4 / 1.9 / 1.3	**Sales/Total Assets**	2.3 / 1.8 / 1.3	2.2 / 1.6 / 1.2	2.5 / 1.8 / 1.3	2.5 / 1.9 / 1.3	2.4 / 1.9 / 1.3
(74) 1.0 / 2.0 / 3.6	(201) 1.4 / 2.3 / 4.5	(57) 2.1 / 3.0 / 5.2	1.6 / 4.4 / 5.1	(343) 1.4 / 2.4 / 4.4	**% Depr., Dep. Amort./Sales**	(356) 1.3 / 2.3 / 3.6	(335) 1.5 / 2.3 / 3.9	(338) 1.3 / 2.3 / 3.5	(325) 1.4 / 2.4 / 4.2	(343) 1.4 / 2.4 / 4.4
(41) 4.8 / 6.7 / 10.7	(69) 2.8 / 4.2 / 6.7		(113) 3.1 / 4.8 / 8.5	(113) 3.1 / 4.8 / 8.5	**% Officers' Comp/Sales**	(140) 2.7 / 4.6 / 8.4	(113) 2.9 / 4.3 / 8.6	(121) 2.6 / 5.4 / 8.6	(113) 2.9 / 4.8 / 8.2	(113) 3.1 / 4.8 / 8.5
118066M	1343298M	1859476M	993946M	4314786M	**Net Sales ($)**	4809385M	4277387M	6237080M	4528308M	4314786M
44398M	757431M	1383473M	814063M	2999355M	**Total Assets ($)**	3365506M	3197572M	3608929M	3041581M	2999355M

© Robert Morris Associates 1987

M = $thousand   MM = $million

See Pages 1 through 13 for Explanation of Ratios and Data

businesses depend much more on trade credit and, compared to larger competitors, do not have significant long-term financing from outside lenders.

> **Key Points:** The left-hand columns are more useful for comparison purposes because their averages are segregated for firms of different asset sizes. The right-hand columns of the RMA ratio sheet contain data that are useful primarily for overall industry trends, because the data represent straight averages of ratios for companies of many different sizes.

RMA Ratios

The bottom two thirds of Exhibit 10-1 lists ratios. There are three values presented for each ratio. The middle number is the median (middle) score of all companies individually. The top number is the median for the better half of those individual companies. The lower number is the median for the worse half. These three medians give rise to four quartiles. The first quartile of firms have ratios falling entirely above the top number; firms in the second quartile have ratios that fall between the top and middle number; the ratios of firms in the third quartile fall between the middle and lower number; the fourth-quartile firms have ratios that fall below the lowest number. Thus, 50% of the companies have ratios that are between the top and bottom numbers.

Some analysts refer to the quartile position of the subject firm in the credit write-ups. RMA arranges all ratio calculations so that the quartiles accurately position the best firms in the top quartile and vice versa. For example, in the current ratio, quick ratio, accounts receivable turnover, and inventory turnover, the higher the ratio, the better the quality is. Therefore, the highest values are the top numbers. In sales as a percentage of working capital, the lower the ratio, the more select it is. Therefore, the low values are at the top.

Liquidity. Let's review the individual ratios to highlight the better ones for analysis. The current and quick ratios, misleading measures of liquidity, are followed by the quality-focused ratios of *receivables, inventory, and payable turnovers*. There are two columns of ratios for the accounts receivable and inventory turnovers. The column to the left lists the number of days per turnover and the other column lists the turnover times per year.

Solvency. The *interest coverage* ratio, so important to debt-rating agencies (and still valuable for firms with little amortizing debt), is listed after the innocuous sales to working capital ratio. Interest coverage is followed by derived *funds (from operations) divided by current maturities long-term debt*. This ratio is a useful variation of the funds flow to total term debt ratio. It has a slight defect in that it will fail to bring any bulges in the long-term debt repayment schedule to the analyst's attention. Nevertheless, it is a reasonable ratio for measuring debt repayment obligations of the coming year. Another innocuous ratio, fixed assets to net worth, is followed by debt to worth, a ratio discussed in Chapter 8.

Performance. Next is the return on net worth, which is calculated by taking profits before taxes and dividing by tangible net worth. The notion of tangible net worth needs further investigation because some firms have undervalued assets. Moreover, because tangible net worth is smaller than total assets less liabilities, the return on net worth percentage will appear to be better than if intangibles are included. It seems incongruous to artificially improve a return percentage by eliminating intangibles.

Fortunately, the analyst can reconstruct this ratio and calculate some other useful ratios by using the percentages in the common-size analysis along with the total sales and assets listed below. For example, the return on total net worth percentage for the $50 million to $100 million asset companies is calculated as follows:

Item	Percentage	Raw Numbers
Net Sales	100.0	$993,946
Profit Before Taxes	1.8	17,891
Total Assets	100.0	$814,053
Net Worth	53.5	435,518
Profit Before Taxes to Net Worth		4.1%

This answer is properly lower than the 6.4% median given on the RMA page for return on tangible net worth.

The next ratio listed is profit before taxes to total assets. Unfortunately, this is an incomplete calculation of the return on assets. As discussed in Chapter 9, this formulation of ROA sharply penalizes firms that have significant debt in their capital structures. Unfortunately, interest expense is not reported separately on RMA sheets, so in this case, you cannot adjust the ratio.

The last two ratios are sales to net fixed assets (fixed asset turnover) and sales to total assets (total asset turnover). They have earned a reputation for being good industry benchmarks since Dupont's treasury division popularized them for inter-divisional analysis. If a subject firm is significantly above or below industry averages in these ratios, it may be evidence of either strikingly superior management or serious problems ahead.

> **Key Points:** Most of the traditional financial condition ratios are found in the RMA *Studies*. In some cases, it is possible to adjust RMA ratios so that they give a more discriminating indication of intra-industry performance.

Development of Industry Databases

Since most analysts have personal computers, many lenders have developed or acquired industry databases for their unique needs and markets. A database of spreadsheets can be used for several different purposes, including reviewing decisions made by specific investment officers or establishing comprehensive policies for investment in particular industries. One of the more ingenious ideas is for qualified licensees to obtain the Robert Morris or Securities and Exchange Commission statistics by industry on computerized database and to develop a loan scoring technique from them.

From the RMA analysis, the reviewer could derive a scoring system by calculating how many subject firm ratios fell in the upper quartiles as opposed to the lower quartiles. An investment officer having many borrowers whose ratios unfortunately fall into the lower quartiles could be easily detected by the loan review department. Another option is to input the financial statement information of all the lenders' accounts into a database and calculate statistics similar to those expressed in the Robert Morris Associates' *Statement Studies* book. Many lenders feel that their particular portfolio imparts a value to the database because it is specific to their loan policies and geographic area.

A customized database can be especially useful for those investors with a narrow market reach. The smaller lender's activities are slightly curbed by the regional economics of its particular geographic area. The limited database might be tailored to include an economic analysis of the industries served by that lender. This analysis would help the investor determine whether it should expand lending activity in its traditional markets. A database cross-referenced with Standard Industrial Classification codes (SICs) might also be designed to allow analysts to compare their subject firm to other individual firms or averages of firms extracted from the database.

A database gives the smaller institution the opportunity to match the bigger institution in analytical sophistication. Better debt repayment forecasts are made with which at least two independent reviewers can agree. The analyst's comparing and contrasting different companies, possibly using reports prepared by others, will more likely result in a better forecast.

Key Points: A financial spreadsheet database can offer the small investor a level of analytical sophistication that usually is found only in larger institutions.

Financial Information Trend Analysis

Trend analysis is the second major analytical technique used with historical financial statements. A discussion of trends is especially appropriate for this chapter because the next chapter focuses on forecasting analysis. Historical trend information is needed for forecasting. Some analysts typically believe that monitoring trends in the financial statements and in commonly used ratios is the most important part of the investment analysis. Financial spreadsheets are always designed to show several consecutive years of data, or several consecutive interim periods.

Unfortunately, because inflation levels and accounting principles change more frequently than in the past, trend analysis is more difficult now than ever before. In addition, corporate treasurers' concerns with trends are second only to their concerns about the immediate statements. Their desire to look good over time thus affects their decisions about the accounting alternatives facing them.

Elevator Analysis

Since trends are so important, most credit analysis write-ups are filled with references to how a company's percentages have changed from period to period. *The analyst errs in not investigating the reason for these differences.* The monotonous repetition of how each account on the balance sheet was one percentage of total assets last year and another percentage this year, with no explanation for the change, is called **elevator analysis**.

An even greater problem than elevator analysis is restating a self-explanatory idea. Consider the following sentence:

> The current ratio was 2.05:1 in 1988, down from 2.15:1 in 1987, because current assets have declined relative to current liabilities.

This statement fails to explain the change in the current ratio. The second part of the statement merely restates the initial concept, a tautology. The analyst's job is to find out what business condition or transaction(s) changed in a company's operation to cause a decline in the current ratio. Another part of the analyst's job is to make a value judgment about that change as in the following statement:

> The current ratio declined slightly in 1988 to 2.05:1 because the firm decided to push for sales by offering extended payment terms to large customers. While accounts receivable increased more than proportionally to sales as a result, sales increased at a faster rate than some competitors'.

These comments allow the senior lending officer to make her own value judgment about the change and to understand something about the firm. Review the explanations for differences between firms of different sizes given in the RMA common-size section above for more ideas.

Changes in Accounting Principles

Trend analysis is made more difficult by the changes in accounting principles that cause restatement of a company's past financial statements. The problem is that one year's footnotes do not aggregate the changes of previous years; moreover, the restatement is usually limited to two years of details. This prevents the analyst from restating the five years customarily preferred for trend analysis. Occasionally restatement may be found in the ten years of financial highlights portion of a firm's annual report. However, financial highlights are hardly a substitute for the detailed information necessary for analysis. Moreover, smaller firms rarely include the ten-years-of-highlights page prominently displayed in public companies' financial reports.

Inflation and Indexing

Analysts once thought they could solve inflation adjustment problems by using an index system. The index system required setting each account in a base year at 100 and increasing it each succeeding year at a percent of the base year as in the consumer price index published by the Department of Labor. Analysts reasoned that if all accounts were increasing, they would be able to distinguish inflation's impact on the raw numbers in the financial statements.

Today, analysts have become more sophisticated about how inflation affects asset values. The outcome of inflation is different depending on the *specific* industry and assets. Therefore, the application of the index system is not a proper way to eliminate inflation's impact on the statement of a particular firm, and the once-common ten-year spreadsheets for company analysis are rarely in use today.

Volatility of Earnings and Cash Flow

With regard to the quality of earnings issue discussed in Chapter 9—stability and reliability of debt repayment capability—identifying the volatility of earnings and cash flow should be the major goal of trend analysis. To the extent that analysts observe volatility in a firm's earnings and cash flow, they can further examine several possibilities:

- Is the firm operating in a risky environment? If profits are high, and then low in alternate years, the analyst might investigate individual divisions or products experiencing volatile results.
- Does the firm have high operating and financial leverage? As previously discussed, high operating and financial leverage can increase the instability of the financial reports of firms that are already affected by frequent changes in their market environment, such as residential builders. High operating or financial leverage, or both, do not necessarily create volatility in earnings, but they should be closely examined if volatility exists.
- Is management too inexperienced or unskilled to consistently produce similar results? This problem can be determined by the process of elimination. If the previous two possibilities are not the source of volatility, management may be the problem.

These issues raise important questions about the firm's ability to repay debt. Lenders structuring transactions with firms with volatile earnings and cash flows should consider extending repayments, setting financial covenants, and taking collateral.

> **Key Points:** Exogenous industry variables, financial and operating leverage, and management experience all affect variability of earnings and cash flow.

Collateral and Covenants

Creditors may attempt to reduce their risks by taking liens on those assets that they believe to be of high quality, including accounts receivable and land. Taking a security interest in a fixed asset, including contract rights, can help to significantly protect the lender, especially *if the fixed assets are appraised and are periodically monitored to assure their condition.*

If sufficient equity exists in the property, or in the real estate company itself, it is preferable to obtain a lien on the assets as pledged collateral on the loan along with the owner's personal guarantee. The unsecured guarantee is not immediately enforceable and may be of less certain value. (The owner can transfer the title to his assets into the names of his children or spouse who are not involved in the business.)

Creditors, especially unsecured creditors, typically seek strong covenant protection from risky borrowers. The covenants protect the lenders' status by setting minimum requirements for liquidity and maximum allowances for leverage. Unfortunately, covenant ratio restrictions, although they may give the lender some comfort, are unlikely to help the investor save a deteriorating firm.

If the lender carefully constructs a restrictive set of covenants, it should be difficult for the borrower to leverage itself beyond what the lender feels is prudent. Covenants based on funds flow to total debt should protect the institution from the borrower's skirting long-term borrowing restrictions and from using short-term loans to invest in fixed assets. Repayments required for the short-term facilities can rapidly deplete working capital and cause a solvency crisis.

Typically, if a client's financial statement report shows that a ratio violates a covenant, the analyst must bring the borrower's problems to the attention of his supervisors, since senior approvals are generally required for waivers. Lenders often fail to take any action when covenants are broken except to attend creditor meetings and ask some penetrating questions that should have been asked earlier.

Nonetheless, in unsecured transactions covenant protection is better than nothing, because covenants alert to trouble. Covenants set forth the financial institution's expectations from the borrower. For example, a covenant forbidding shareholder dividends is the financial institution's way of indicating a need for increased equity. Since there are many ways that owners of a medium-size company can take money out if they wish, restricting dividends may not make a difference. It does indicate, however, that the lender does not want owners taking money out of the company prior to the loan repayment.

> **Key Points:** Collateral, a direct lien on assets, is preferable to personal guarantees or financial covenants.

Macroeconomic Trends

Business Cycles

Short-term business trends need to be distinguished from the longer-lasting secular trends usually affecting particular industries. For example, short-term trends include business cycle shifts as well as peaks and valleys in seasonal businesses. The analyst needs to assess the ability of the firm to weather these cycles.

New England Companies

> During the recession of 1982, the number of U.S. firms going into bankruptcy equaled those in 1932, the worst year of the Great Depression. New England

firms, however, had struggled against deep recessions and shallow growth cycles and had been experiencing firsthand the difficulties faced by declining industries for 20 years. They were survivors, and as a result, this region had the lowest bankruptcy rate of any region in the United States.

Macroeconomic Variables

Part of the analysis of a firm's earnings and cash flow variability should include correlation with the larger economic variables: gross national product, growth in the money supply, or regional economic information. Past data and forecasts on these variables can be obtained from the *Federal Reserve Bulletin* and the Bureau of Labor Statistics in Washington. The analyst can identify correlations between these data and the historical performance of a firm. Once these relationships are established, the economic forecasts of these economic variables can guide the lender's decision in extending credit to a firm.

Seasonality

Seasonality in industries involves peak sales or production periods during discrete parts of the year. At these times, the entire firm is straining to survive the oncoming slow season. Retailers and toy companies, for instance, do 35% to 45% of their annual business in the 45-day Christmas season. Food producers have harvest periods when they are in peak operation.

The analyst must be sensitive to the fact that *the financial strength of any firm will be strained during these times.* Accordingly, the year-end statement's liquidity is usually deceivingly high. The analyst must determine which times of year borrowing will be critical to business success. This is also partially accommodated by deriving a cash budget as discussed in Chapter 11.

Secular Trends

Secular trends regularly affect particular industries. One of the most disturbing elements of secular trends, as opposed to business cycle trends, is that management is often unable to see the change occurring in its own industry. Short-term trends resulting from macroeconomic changes are noticed because there is so much in the media about them. The early 1980s secular drop in oil prices and the following "oil patch" recession is a case in point.

Excess Supply

Permanent changes in supply/demand industry characteristics can affect even strong industries. For example the fallout was extensive in oil.

Oil Industry

In 1981 oil price growth slowed. High prices had stimulated oil exploration throughout the world, resulting in new sources of oil. Conservation efforts in the United States and Europe, the major energy-using areas, had stopped the growth in demand for oil products. More supply and curtailed demand inevitably led to a fall in the price of oil. Political issues also played a role as OPEC (Organization of Petroleum Exporting Countries) had greater difficulty in restricting output among members.

After ten years of uninterrupted growth, the price of oil fell. As exploration for expensive oil was halted, in Houston, in the second and third quarters of 1982, 30% of all the machine tool shops (which prepared pipe for use by drilling rigs) *went out of business.* Many financial institutions had granted credit to companies that showed ten years of uninterrupted upward growth in their financial statements. When the recession hit, the owners just gave up. They had not experienced such an austere period, and their lenders were not reviewing the financials to determine whether they would be survivors.

To fully understand the 1982 collapse of business in the Southwest, the analyst should understand that although the strain of the drop in oil prices (a secular trend affecting the energy industry) caused the 1982 business crisis, *unseasoned managers and financial fragility characterized the firms that failed. Other firms survived.*

Farm Industry

The agricultural market also suffered reversals starting in the early 1980s. The high value of the dollar forced a drop in exports, causing farm income to plummet. As a result, land prices fell along with expectations about the potential revenues that could be earned from farming.

The value of farmland from the 1981–1983 period declined by $230 billion according to the Federal Reserve Bank of St. Louis's *Review* [Carraro, 1988]. As this and other articles have noted, the drop in farm income along with high interest rates primarily hurt those farmers who had expanded rapidly during the run-up in land values and were overextended financially. *Those farmers who had maintained a better relationship between revenues and debt payments survived.*

Deregulation

A reduction of federal regulation of the transportation, communication, and financial services industries began in earnest in the late 1970s. Faced not only with high inflation but also with slow economic growth, the managers of these businesses had to contend with unbridled competition for the first time. The initial reduction in costs brought benefits to consumers, but created excesses that caused continuing hardships.

The trucking industry was particularly hard-hit by deregulation because it was dominated by small individual operators. These operators were typically more concerned with making their next installment loan payments than with industrial trends. In the late 1970s, as oil prices rose and deregulation took hold, it should have been clear that profits would be lower than they had been in 20 years.

Additionally, three important changes were missed by trucking managers: (1) the growing popularity of air freight, (2) increased customer self-trucking, and (3) excessive increases in the number of owner operators. The owner operators were caught with high finance payments and a disappearing spot market that previously paid high daily rates and competed at operating cost rates as long as the equity in their vehicles permitted it.

Ryder Truck Lines

The plight of Ryder Truck Lines exemplified that of larger companies. Ryder expanded rapidly through the 1960s and 1970s. Its last major acquisition was PIE (Pacific Intermountain Express), giving it a nationwide reach. Still, through 1984, International Utilities, the parent holding company of Ryder, which had been losing money since deregulation, believed it could turn Ryder around. Its overly optimistic view of the industry's future kept the price for disposing of Ryder so high that the eventual sale of Ryder took a long time to complete.

Fads

Fads are another example of secular trends.

Video Games

In the early 1980s, USI Credit was besieged by entrepreneurs requesting financing on commercial (coin) video game machines that cost $2,000 to $3,000. These machines could allegedly earn $200 to $300 per week, the earnings being split half and half between the location owner and the machine owner. The machines could thus pay for themselves in 20 weeks. Entrepreneurs wanted financing so that they could invest in more machines than their own capital permitted. They proposed 3-year (156-week) amortization schedules.

Some creditors found it difficult to see why a machine that could pay for itself in 20 weeks required 3-year financing. Nevertheless, the entrepreneurs were sure that they were going to find some financial institution that would agree to finance them. They brushed aside the risk of the faddish nature of the products such as "Pac Man."

Overexpansion soon required an industry restructuring that left some lenders sadder but hopefully wiser.

Bankruptcy Prediction With Trend Analysis

The last section of this chapter is devoted to using trend analysis to predict bankruptcy. The discussion on bankruptcy prediction in Chapter 8 was focused on the absolute values of ratios. A qualitative approach to this analysis is championed by John Argenti [1976], a British theoretician. His book *Corporate Collapse* surveys many theories of corporate collapse and bankruptcy around the world. Argenti is unimpressed with empirical research with ratios and has focused on managerial behavior to derive some applicable theories. He outlines three trends that can lead to financial failure.

Exhibit 10-2.

Three Failure Types
Earnings Trajectory A

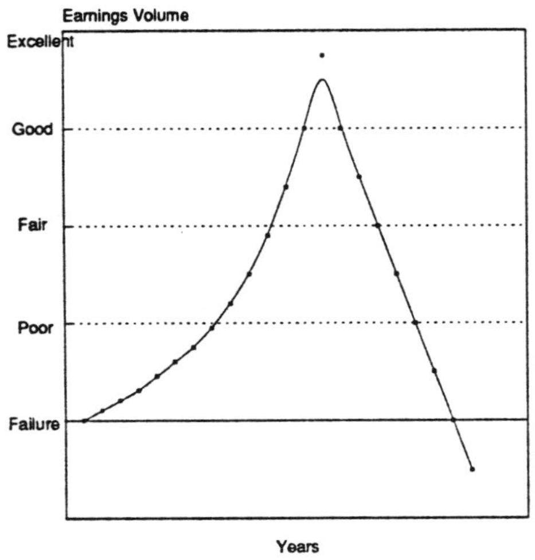

Three Failure Types
Earnings Trajectory B

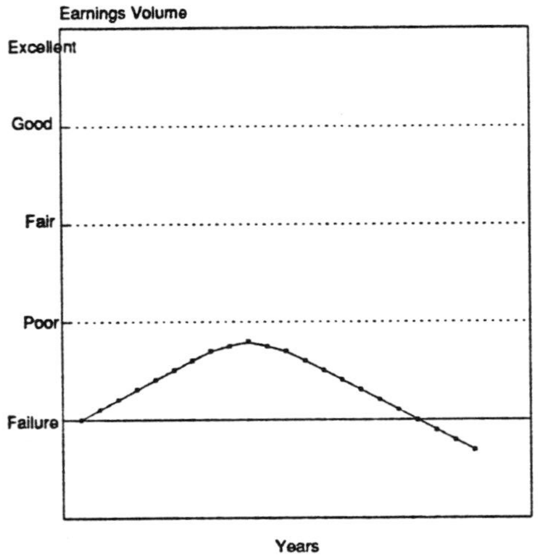

Three Failure Types
Earnings Trajectory C

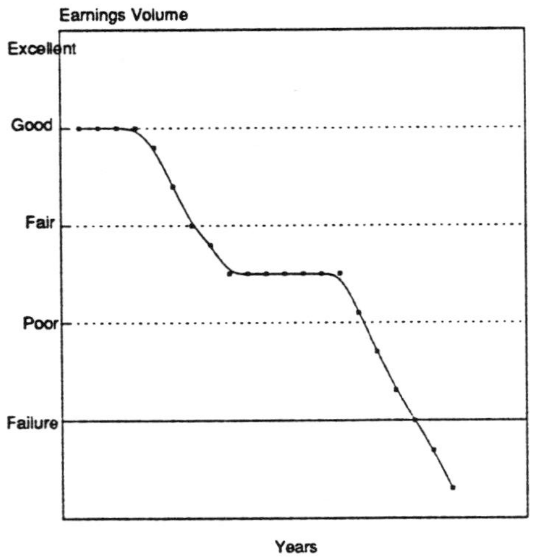

The analyst must compare recent performance of the firm to the three failure paths shown in Exhibit 10-2. If there is a match, then failure may occur. The paths are briefly described as follows:

- *Trajectory A:* The company takes off rapidly and then crashes. This type of firm may have strong one-person rule. If so, the owner may be strong in marketing or in production but rarely in both. Because of superb strength in one field, she is able to move the company off to a rapid start, but as expansion takes place, weaknesses in other areas multiply and the firm fails.
- *Trajectory B:* The company never gets off the ground. Sales build at first and then gradually start to fall off. Management is weak in all areas and is never able to get the firm to run successfully.
- *Trajectory C:* A more mature firm falls off sharply to a plateau. It is unable to regain its position from the plateau; it continues to coast until it eventually collapses.

The analyst should be exceptionally wary of any drop in a firm's net income performance. To forestall a calling of the loan, the firm's managers must be able to convince the analyst that they comprehend the causes of the decline. Management also should be able to enumerate the steps they are taking to assure a recovery.

Conclusion

Trend and intra-industry analyses are important ways of measuring a company's health and capability of repaying debt. They are more natural ways of scrutinizing company financials than looking at individual ratios and comparing them to a rule of thumb. This is not to say that trend analysis does not use ratios or measure them against standards. It does use standards, but they are derived from the former performance of the company or of its industry.

Application: United Enterprises, Inc. Ratio Analysis

By way of concluding this discussion on ratios, worksheets are presented in Exhibit 10-3 that display the ratios resulting from the spreadsheets of United Enterprises, presented as Exhibits 4-3 and 7-3. The top of each worksheet brings in information from the other worksheet to allow the calculation of ratios which require inputs from both financial statements.

Beginning with the balance sheet liquidity ratios, the breakup value column shows the traditional current ratio and working capital ratios are generally poor scores. The current ratio has dropped below the 2:1 rule of thumb and working capital also is showing substantially less, demonstrating our skill at eliminating management's efforts at window dressing. Nevertheless, the turnover ratios appear to be relatively unaffected and the trend from 1989 to 1990 appears excellent because turnover increased while sales dropped, indicating good

Exhibit 10-3.

BALANCE SHEET: RATIOS   WORKSHEET 1B

Company Name: United Enterprises, Inc. and Consolidated Subsidiaries

Balance Sheet Date:	31-Dec-89	31-Dec-90	31-Dec-90
ADDITIONAL INFORMATION			**BREAKUP VAL**
1 Estimate of Contingent Liabs.	$26.7	$26.7	$26.7
2 Sales	$1,041.3	$971.4	$971.4
3 Cost of Goods Sold	$783.4	$733.8	$746.6
4 Market Value of Equity	$211.5	$248.1	$248.1
5 Returns of Merchandise			
6 Earnings before Interest and Taxes	$94.1	$71.4	$0.0
7 LIFO Reserve			
8 Reserve for Accounts Rec. Losses	$2.8	$3.0	$3.0
BALANCE SHEET RATIOS			
LIQUIDITY			**BREAKUP VAL**
7 Current Assets/Current Liabs	2.02	2.17	1.70
8 Quick Assets/Current Liabs	0.76	0.92	0.78
9 Sales/Receivables (Turnover Times)	8.61 X	8.75 X	8.75 X
10 Receivables Turnover (Days)	41.80 Days	41.14 Days	41.14 Days
11 Reserve for Loss/Gross Accts. Rec.	2.26%	2.63%	2.63%
12 Returns of Merchandise/Sales			
13 Long Receivables / Total Receivables			23.71%
14 Net Working Capital	$183.1	$188.5	$112.9
15 Tot Inventory Turnover (Days)	86.30 Days	82.27 Days	71.12 Days
16 Inventory/Current Assets	51.85%	48.05%	53.95%
17 Raw Mat Invent Turnover (Days)	27.20 Days	25.76 Days	25.31 Days
18 Wk/I/Progress Invent Turnover (Days)	23.39 Days	19.82 Days	9.74 Days
19 Finished Gds Invent Turnover (Days)	35.71 Days	36.70 Days	36.07 Days
20 Cost of Goods Sold/Payables (Times)	25.60 Days	22.32 Days	21.94 Days
21 Payables Turnover (Days)	25.60	22.32	21.94
22			

	31-Dec-89	31-Dec-90	31-Dec-90
CAPITAL STRUCTURE			
23 Debt (Total Liabilities)/ Net Worth	0.62	0.69	0.62
24 Long Term Debt/Total Capital	0.16	0.22	0.21
25 Fixed Asset Turnover (S/FA)	3.19	2.97	2.12
26 Sales/ Current Assets	2.87	2.78	3.55
27 Total Asset Turnover (S/TA)	1.51	1.44	1.33
28			

ALTMAN MULTIPLE VARIABLE STUDY : Bankruptcy predicted if % column <=1.87, Best if > 2.68		%		%		%
37 Working Capital/Total Assets	$0.3	0.32	$0.3	0.33	$0.2	0.19
38 Retained Earnings/Total Assets	$0.4	0.56	$0.4	0.59	$0.4	0.62
39 EBIT/Total Assets	$0.1	0.45	$0.1	0.35	$0.0	0.00
40 Mkt Val Equity/Total Debt	$0.8	0.48	$0.9	0.54	$0.9	0.53
41 Sales/Total Assets	$1.5	1.51	$1.4	1.44	$1.3	1.33
42 TOTAL		3.33		3.25		2.67

INCOME STATEMENT AND CASH FLOW RATIOS   **WORKSHEET 2B**

Company Name:	United Enterprises, Inc. and Consolidated Subsidiaries		
Statement Date:	**Dec-89**	**Dec-90**	**Dec-90**
ADDITIONAL INFORMATION FOR RATIO DERIVATION			**Adjusted Values**
	$	**$**	**$**
1 Interest Expense Capitalized			
2 Eff. Tax Rate (Tax Net Deferred/PB	36.7%	12.9%	11.7%
3 Accounts Receivable, net	120.90	111.00	111.00
4 Accounts Payable	55.70	45.50	45.50
5 Inventory (including LIFO reserve)	187.80	167.70	147.50
6 Total Fixed Assets	326.60	327.50	458.34
7 Total Assets	688.80	676.50	731.74
8 Operating Lease Rentals			
9 Current Portion Long Term Debt	16.80	13.20	13.20
10 Total Term Debt (including CPLTD	88.20	102.90	117.60
11 Net Worth	426.20	400.30	452.30
LIQUIDITY RATIOS			
12 Times Interest Earned (EBIT/Int.)	6.6 X	6.0 X	4.2 X
13 SEC Earnings Coverage	5.8 X	4.4 X	3.1 X
(Income fr.Operations bfr.Tax & Intr.Exp.+ Op. Lease Rnt. / Intr.+ Op. Lease Rnt.)			
14 Receivables Turnover	41.8 Days	41.1 Days	41.1 Days
15 Tot Inventory Turnover	88.9 Days	85.3 Days	74.9 Days
16 Payables Turnover (ACP)	26.4 Days	23.2 Days	23.1 Days
DEBT REPAYMENT CAPACITY			**Adjusted Values**
17 Funds Available for Fixed Chgs	124.50 $	118.40 $	107.20 $
(Funds Flow From Operations + Taxes Paid + Interest Expense + Operating Lease Rentals)			
18 Debt Repayment Capacity Coverage	4.02 X	4.72 X	4.27 X
(Funds Available for Fixed Chrgs.) / (Intr.+ Op. Lease Rnt.+ Cur.Por.Long-Term Debt)			
19 EBIT/Earn Bef Taxes (Leverage)	1.18 X	1.20 X	1.32 X
20			
21 Funds Flow / Capital Equip Exp	1.91 X	2.37 X	2.25 X
22 Funds Flow / Dividends	3.39 X	3.38 X	3.20 X
23 Funds Flow/Cur. Portion LTD	4.34 X	5.43 X	5.14 X
24 Capital Equip Exp/Depreciation	1.64 X	1.14 X	0.81 X
25 Term Debt/ Funds Flow	1.21 X	1.44 X	1.73 X
OPERATING PERFORMANCE	(Common size analysis in Spread Sheet section)		
26 Operating Cycle (Days)	130.7 Days	126.5 Days	116.0 Days
27 Net Operating Cycle (Days)	104.4 Days	103.3 Days	92.9 Days
28 Fixed Asset Turnover (S/FA)	3.2 X	3.0 X	2.1 X
29 Return (Repeatable) on Assets	7.6%	6.1%	3.1%
30 Return (Repeatable) on Equity	12.3%	10.4%	5.1%

management control. The capital structure ratios evidence increasing use of debt capital with the repurchase of substantial common stock previously mentioned; fixed asset turnover was indicated lower in the breakup column because of the increase of fixed assets to current cost. Finally, the Zeta score dropped quite low, almost into the grey zone, as the working capital and return on assets tests fell sharply. We begin to see that return on assets may be one of UEI's major problems. Nevertheless, the traditional long-term-debt-to-total-capital ratio gives great comfort in that there is substantial cushion under the lender's position.

Let's move on to the performance ratios in the income statement and cash flow ratios page. As a result of the analyst's adjusting of values, the liquidity ratios show sharply lower coverage ratios than the more traditional columns. It is clear that severe problems have not occurred here, though, because the firm is not that highly leveraged. Nevertheless, the trend is not a healthy one, with deterioration in the term debt to funds flow (Beaver) ratio, indicating declining funds flow and increasing debt. In the debt repayment capacity section, the security of the firm is evidenced by improvement in the funds flow to current portion to LTD and in the debt repayment capacity coverage ratios over the two years in the face of higher debt. The remaining ratios in this section point to the first disturbing information about UEI: funds flow to capital equipment expense and capital equipment expense to depreciation.

We have reviewed the traditional liquidity and capital structure ratios of the balance sheet and the more current and dynamic turnover and debt repayment capacity (funds flow) ratios and found that United Enterprises would make a fine borrower. The last category of operating performance indicates the troubles that will befall the company. With the return on assets below the average borrowing rate, we see that UEI is liquidating itself. On an adjusted basis, the return on equity is only that of a savings account, not enough to keep UEI shareholders happy. It would appear that management is unable to generate a suitable return from the assets. Indeed, during 1991 UEI was the subject of a corporate stock raid and, while some assets were maintained by the purchaser, management was eliminated and many subsidiaries were sold off. The financial statement herein is the last one for UEI.

Chapter 11

Forecasting

Purpose

Predicting whether a firm can repay its loan is the ultimate mission of financial statement analysis. This chapter focuses on the technical aspects of forecasting. The first exercise in forecasting is to determine the firm's ability to meet its cash requirements during the next year, called the **cash budget.** This short-term budget focuses on a monthly inflow and outflow of funds. The short-term cash budget is especially important for the analysis of firms' seasonal borrowing needs.

The **long-term forecast** extends out five years. The purpose of the long-term forecast is to identify specific trends that may be helpful or harmful to the company's ability to repay debt. The long-term forecast can also give the analyst a reasonable idea of the firm's ability to produce cash and maintain a balanced financial position over the next five years, assuming either that present policies continue or that anticipated changes in the firm's environment occur.

This chapter's discussion of short- and long-term forecasting uses the United Enterprises financial statements from Chapter 1 to illustrate the calculations. In the discussion that follows, the rows are referred to using the "{ }" designation. The best method of tracing the steps through is probably (1) a careful reading of each section that has a bracket indication and then (2) locating it in the appropriate exhibit; this back-and-forth approach will ease perception of some of the more labyrinthine steps in preparing the forecasts.

As previously noted in Chapters 2 and 5, trying to fulfill the needs of proper analysis while also producing a finished report readable by senior management is a puzzle that may be partially solved by resorting to a personal computer. Separately available for this book are templates based on Lotus Development Corporation's LOTUS 1-2-3 spreadsheet program for use on microcomputers. With the computer, it is possible to set down the mathematical relationships used in these forecasts just one time in a formula in each cell of the spreadsheet. Then, the forecast is instantly recalculated every time the analyst wishes to explore the possibility of a "what if" change in one of the underlying variables. The exhibits referenced in this chapter are other worksheets included on the floppy disk available with this book.

Methods

Financial forecasting is somewhat analogous to weather forecasting. Both types can be wrong about the future, although they may be based on well-reasoned assumptions. A company's past financial performance will influence its future performance, especially if variability is low; however, its future performance will not duplicate the past. For example, a simple **projection** merely identifies the past trends and extends them into the future in the identical pattern. In contrast, a decent **long-term forecast** results from an analysis of the different factors that impact *sales growth, cost of funds, profit margins,* and *capital equipment expenditures.*

First the analyst must

1. Forecast the independent variables affecting a firm's operation, especially sales and including equipment expenditures and capital structure. Typically, sales and capital expenditures are used as independent variables, although capital expenditures clearly are positively correlated with sales levels. (If sales go up, capital expenditures do too.) The *sales level is the prime indicator of the forecast;* revenues supply cash and drive production needs.
2. Identify the interrelationships between these independent variables and relatively constant (dependent) variables like cost of goods sold and selling expense.
3. Test for implied trends in all of the relationships exhibited over the past three to five years.
4. Investigate in turn the trends in exogenous variables affecting these relationship trends (e.g., the competitive, technological, governmental, and economic environments).

Second, the analyst structures the format of the forecast.

1. Build the format of the forecast. A short-term forecast format is provided in Exhibit 11-1 and a long-term one in Exhibit 11-5.
2. Establish the primary methodology for tying together the dependent and independent variables. The most common forecasting method establishes a relationship between sales and each other element of the company's operations. This **percentage of sales** technique is used widely and will be used here. (A more sophisticated technique uses regression analysis to determine more precisely the relationships between sales and the other variables. In addition, regression analysis can be used to identify correlations between the sales and macroeconomic variables, and thus help to refine the forecast of sales itself.)
3. Calculate the inflows and outflows in the model and determine the cash outcome.

The Short-Term Forecast

The format to be used in the cash budget is shown in Exhibit 11-1. Notice that to complete a single year's forecast, monthly sales data from the previous year must be included to calculate cash collections in the first few months.

(Text continued on page 262.)

Exhibit 11-1.

CASH BUDGET

Dollar amounts in 000,000s	MONTHS	JAN	FEB	MAR
PART I - ASSUMPTIONS:				
1 MONTHLY SALES-as % of annual sales of: $				
2 COLLECTIONS: % of Acc.Rec.that turnover in 30 days				
3 (as a % of Sales) " in 60 days				
4 Initial Accts/Rec of $ " in 90 days				
5 CASH COST-OF-GOODS SLD-$ -shown % of Sales				
6 SALES & ADMINISTRATIVE EXP.-based on historic info.				
7 PURCHASES ON CREDIT-% inventory turn. in 30 days				
8 as % of Cost Goods Sold " in 60 days				
9 Initial Inventory of $ " in 90 days				
10 PAYABLES Accounts Payable turnover in 30 days				
11 (as % Cost-of-Goods Sld) " in 60 days				
12 Initial Accts/Pay of $ " in 90 days				
14 SHORT-TERM DEBT-based on init. prin. bal. of $		% Est. Interest Rate		
16 LONG-TERM DEBT-based on init. prin. bal. of $		% Est.Interest Rate		
17 Unamortized Portion-based upon row 18				
18 Amortization of Current Portion LTD of $				
PART II - CASH RECEIPTS CALCULATION				
19 MONTHLY SALES-based on annual Sales times row 1				
20 CASH COLLECTIONS-bsed.on Mnthly Sales & rows 2-4				
21 OTHER CASH RECEIPTS (fill in from avail. information)				
22 **TOTAL RECEIPTS**				
PART III - CASH DISBURSEMENTS				
23 PURCHASES-based on Cost-of-Goods Sld & Rows 7-9				
24 CASH PAYMENTS-based on Purchases & Rows 10-12				
25 SALES & ADMIN. EXP.-annl. est. of $ times row 6/12				
26 LONG TERM DEBT: Int. Exp.-based on rows 16 & 17				
27 Principal Repayment- based on row 18				
28 SHORT-TERM DEBT-Int. Exp.-based on rows 14 & 34				
29 INCOME TAX PAID-cash est. of $ (net def. tax)				
30 OTHER EXPENSE-based upon historic information				
31 **TOTAL DISBURSEMENTS**				
PART IV - SHORT-TERM DEBT REQUIREMENT				
32 Net Cash Generated this Month-Row 31 from row 22				
33 Last Month Short-Term Debt Balance				
34 TOTAL SHORT-TERM DEBT-maintains initial cash bal.				
PART V - BALANCES IN CURRENT ACCOUNTS				
35 ACCOUNTS RECEIVABLE				
36 INVENTORY				
37 ACCOUNTS PAYABLE				

	APR	MAY	JUN	JUL	AUG	SEP	OCT	NOV	DEC
PART I - ASSUMPTIONS:									
1									
2									
3									
4									
5									
6									
7									
8									
9									
10									
11									
12									
14									
16									
17									
18									
PART II - CASH RECEIPTS CALCULATION									
19									
20									
21									
22									
PART III - CASH DISBURSEMENTS									
23									
24									
25									
26									
27									
28									
29									
30									
31									
PART IV - SHORT-TERM DEBT REQUIREMENT									
32									
33									
34									
PART V - BALANCES IN CURRENT ACCOUNTS									
35									
36									
37									

Independent Variables

The first row of the forecast contains the percentage of annual sales that will occur each month. Completing these figures requires predicting the future course of the independent variable, sales. This can be done by extending previous average growth and seasonal trends (obtained from interim statements) that have occurred in sales over the past several years. Unfortunately, this straightforward procedure is problematical because sales are as dependent on externalities (that can change) as they are on past performance.

The best approach (if there is no in-house expert to do the forecast) is to obtain from the subject firm's management the sales forecasts that it must prepare each year to plan the company's operations. These forecasts result from a complex projection process involving management's understanding of the marketplace, plans for expansion, retrenchment, or maintenance of market share. They reflect management's own knowledge about pricing decisions and the availability of various components of supply and production.

Dependent Variables

From the common-size analysis of the income statement, individual expense items are calculated as a percentage of sales. These will be used as a guide to the interrelationships between sales and expenses in the forecast, since the theory of the percentage of sales forecasting method is that year after year cost of goods sold to sales and operating expenses to sales commonly stay within relatively narrow limits. For the balance sheet item forecast, the similar idea of turnover ratios, that balance sheet current accounts (current assets and liabilities) fluctuate with sales, will be used to relate the balance sheet entries to either sales or cost of goods sold. Thus, common-size income statement analysis and turnover ratios provide the basic elements of forecast interrelationships between independent sales variables and the dependent variables of the firm's financial operation.

Exhibit 7-3 shows a spreadsheet (a blank copy is in Exhibit 5-2) with income statement data for United Enterprises that can be used to illustrate these ideas. In this exhibit, the common-size calculations express income statement items as a percentage of sales. Notice the patterns of United Enterprises' variable relationships. For example, as sales change, the cost of goods sold, selling expenses, administrative expenses, and other expenses change proportionally—that is, they stay relatively the same compared to sales. With the balance sheet turnover ratios on the final page it can be seen that they also remain relatively stable.

This format will forecast based on the relationship between these balance sheet items and sales by using turnover ratios: inventory and payables expressed as a percentage of the cost of goods sold, which is itself based on sales.

Exhibit 11-2 shows a completed hypothetical cash budget for United Enterprises. Although it is not a seasonal company, a seasonal pattern has been devised for it to make the example more pertinent. Row 1 shows the hypothetical percentage of annual sales that occurs in each month. In this example the peak sales months are May and June. In many industries sales are even more seasonal than this example. For example, retail department stores and most retail establishments that sell consumer non-durable goods have 30% to 35% of their sales concentrated in one month (from November 25 to December 25).

Monthly Sales. The entries in row 19 are calculated by multiplying the percentages in row 1 by the total estimated annual dollar sales (obtained from the client and shown in row 1).

Collections {2}, {3} and {4}.* This next step builds a relationship between accounts receivables and sales. Exhibit 11-2 shows in row 4 the average annual accounts receivable ($111 million). To allocate the collections on a monthly basis, accounts receivable turnover in days needs to be calculated. For United Enterprises, accounts receivable turn over every 42 days (365 divided by $971.4/$111).

This task gives rise to the first technical problem in setting up a monthly cash budget. Since it is necessary to know only how much cash is collected in any 30-day block of time, the fact that receivables for United Enterprises turn over every 42 days is not very helpful. We need to determine how much of each month's sales will be collected during the first 30-day period and how much will be collected between 30 and 60 days, and so on. For the easiest example, a firm that has a turnover period of fewer than 30 days would properly estimate that 100% of receivables will be collected during the first 30 days. Because our example exceeds 30 days, we must calculate a weighted average to determine how receivables are collected as follows:

1. For firms that have turnovers between 30 and 60 days:

   The portion of receivables collected in 30 days equals:

   $$\frac{60 \text{ days} - \text{turnover period}}{30 \text{ days}}$$

   The portion collected in 30 to 60 days equals:

   $$\frac{\text{turnover period} - 30 \text{ days}}{30 \text{ days}}$$

   In the case of United Enterprises, which had a 42-day turnover, the calculations would be as follows:

   The portion collected in 30 days equals:

   $$\frac{60 - 42}{30} = .6$$

   This portion collected in 30 to 60 days equals:

   $$\frac{42 - 30}{30} = .4$$

2. For firms that have turnovers between 60 and 90 days, the formulas above must be reset as follows:

(Text continued on page 266.)

*Braces refer to row numbers in Exhibit 11-2.

Exhibit 11-2.

CASH BUDGET	United Enterprises and consolidated subsidiaries			
Dollar amounts in 000,000s	MONTHS	JAN	FEB	MAR
PART I - ASSUMPTIONS:				
1	MONTHLY SALES-as % of annual sales of: $971.0	5%	5%	5%
2	COLLECTIONS: % of Acc.Rec.that turnover in 30 days	60%	60%	60%
3	(as a % of Sales) " in 60 days	40%	40%	40%
4	Initial Accts/Rec of $111.0 " in 90 days	0%	0%	0%
5	CASH COST-OF-GOODS SLD-$707.4-shown % of Sales	73%	73%	73%
6	SALES & ADMINISTRATIVE EXP.-based on historic info.	19%	19%	19%
7	PURCHASES ON CREDIT-% inventory turn. in 30 days	0%	0%	0%
8	as % of Cost Goods Sold " in 60 days	17%	17%	17%
9	Initial Inventory of $167.7 " in 90 days	83%	83%	83%
10	PAYABLES Accounts Payable turnover in 30 days	100%	100%	100%
11	(as % Cost-of-Goods Sld) " in 60 days	0%	0%	0%
12	Initial Accts/Pay of $45.5 " in 90 days	0%	0%	0%
14	SHORT-TERM DEBT-based on init. prin. bal. of $18.2	12% Est. Interest Rate		
16	LONG-TERM DEBT-based on init. prin. bal. of $89.7	14% Est.Interest Rate		
17	Unamortized Portion-based upon row 18	89.7	88.6	87.5
18	Amortization of Current Portion LTD of $13.2	1.1	1.1	1.1
PART II - CASH RECEIPTS CALCULATION				
19	MONTHLY SALES-based on annual Sales times Row 1	48.6	48.6	48.6
20	CASH COLLECTIONS-bsed.on Mnthly Sales & Rows 2-4	48.6	48.6	48.6
21	OTHER CASH RECEIPTS (fill in from avail. information)			
22	**TOTAL RECEIPTS**	48.6	48.6	48.6
PART III - CASH DISBURSEMENTS				
23	PURCHASES-based on Cost-of-Goods Sld & Rows 7-9	64.8	100.2	106.1
24	CASH PAYMENTS-based on Purchases & Rows 10-12	35.4	64.8	100.2
25	SALES & ADMIN. EXP.-ann. est. of $186.7 times Row 6/12	15.5	15.5	15.5
26	LONG TERM DEBT: Int. Exp.-based on Rows 16 & 17	1.0	1.0	1.0
27	Principal Repayment- based on Row 18	1.1	1.1	1.1
28	SHORT-TERM DEBT-Int. Exp.-based on Rows 14 & 34	0.2	0.2	0.6
29	INCOME TAX PAID-cash est. of $16.3 (net def. tax)			
30	OTHER EXPENSE-based upon historic information			
31	**TOTAL DISBURSEMENTS**	53.2	82.7	118.4
PART IV - SHORT-TERM DEBT REQUIREMENT				
32	Net Cash Generated this Month-Row 31 from Row 22	(4.6)	(34.1)	(69.8)
33	Last Month Short-Term Debt Balance	18.2	22.8	57.0
34	TOTAL SHORT-TERM DEBT-maintains initial cash bal.	**22.8**	**57.0**	**126.8**
PART V - BALANCES IN CURRENT ACCOUNTS				
35	ACCOUNTS RECEIVABLE	111.0	111.0	111.0
36	INVENTORY	197.2	262.0	332.8
37	ACCOUNTS PAYABLE	75.0	110.3	116.2

	APR	MAY	JUN	JUL	AUG	SEP	OCT	NOV	DEC
	PART I - ASSUMPTIONS:								
1	10%	15%	15%	10%	10%	10%	5%	5%	5%
2	60%	60%	60%	60%	60%	60%	60%	60%	60%
3	40%	40%	40%	40%	40%	40%	40%	40%	40%
4	0%	0%	0%	0%	0%	0%	0%	0%	0%
5	73%	73%	73%	73%	73%	73%	73%	73%	73%
6	19%	19%	19%	19%	19%	19%	19%	19%	19%
7	0%	0%	0%	0%	0%	0%	0%	0%	0%
8	17%	17%	17%	17%	17%	17%	17%	17%	17%
9	83%	83%	83%	83%	83%	83%	83%	83%	83%
10	100%	100%	100%	100%	100%	100%	100%	100%	100%
11	0%	0%	0%	0%	0%	0%	0%	0%	0%
12	0%	0%	0%	0%	0%	0%	0%	0%	0%
14									
16									
17	86.4	85.3	84.2	83.1	82.0	80.9	79.8	78.7	77.6
18	1.1	1.1	1.1	1.1	1.1	1.1	1.1	1.1	1.1
	PART II - CASH RECEIPTS CALCULATION								
19	97.1	145.7	145.7	97.1	97.1	97.1	48.6	48.6	48.6
20	48.6	77.7	126.2	145.7	116.5	97.1	97.1	68.0	48.6
21									
22	**48.6**	**48.6**	**77.7**	**126.2**	**145.7**	**116.5**	**97.1**	**97.1**	**68.0**
	PART III - CASH DISBURSEMENTS								
23	76.6	70.7	70.7	41.3	35.4	35.4	35.4	35.4	35.4
24	106.1	76.6	70.7	70.7	41.3	35.4	35.4	35.4	35.4
25	15.5	15.5	15.5	15.5	15.5	15.5	15.5	15.5	15.5
26	1.0	1.0	1.0	1.0	1.0	0.9	0.9	0.9	0.9
27	1.1	1.1	1.1	1.1	1.1	1.1	1.1	1.1	1.1
28	1.3	2.1	2.3	1.9	1.4	0.8	0.4	(0.0)	(0.2)
29	4.1		4.1			4.1			4.1
30									
31	**129.0**	**96.3**	**94.6**	**90.2**	**60.2**	**57.8**	**53.3**	**52.9**	**56.8**
	PART IV - SHORT-TERM DEBT REQUIREMENT								
32	(80.5)	(18.6)	31.6	55.4	56.4	39.3	43.8	15.1	(8.2)
33	126.8	207.3	225.9	194.3	138.9	82.5	43.2	(0.6)	(15.7)
34	**207.3**	**225.9**	**194.3**	**138.9**	**82.5**	**43.2**	**(0.6)**	**(15.7)**	**(7.5)**
	PART V - BALANCES IN CURRENT ACCOUNTS								
35	159.6	227.5	247.0	198.4	179.0	179.0	130.4	111.0	111.0
36	374.0	374.0	338.7	273.8	238.4	203.1	167.7	167.7	167.7
37	86.8	80.9	80.9	51.4	45.5	45.5	45.5	45.5	45.5

The portion collected between 60 and 90 days equals:

$$\frac{90 \text{ days} - \text{turnover period}}{30 \text{ days}}$$

The portion collected between 90 and 120 days equals:

$$\frac{\text{turnover period} - 60 \text{ days}}{30 \text{ days}}$$

3. Finally, if the firm's collection period falls between 90 and 120 days the formulas are:

The portion collected in a 90- to 120-day block equals:

$$\frac{120 \text{ days} - \text{turnover period}}{30 \text{ days}}$$

The portion collected in a 120- to 150-day block equals:

$$\frac{\text{turnover period} - 90 \text{ days}}{30 \text{ days}}$$

Trial and error can also be used to produce the correct percentage for each 30-day block. This requires working backward from an approximation of the turnover days on a trial-and-error basis. For instance, if the firm collects half of its receivables in 30 days and half in 60 days, then the 50% collected in 30 days would represent an average collection period of 15 days and the 50% collected in 60 days would represent an average collection period of 30 days. Added together, this totals 45 days.

To have this trial-and-error result more closely match United Enterprises' 42-day turnover period, the tested amount of receivables collected in 30 days can be increased to, say, 60%. Collecting 60% in 30 days yields 18 days (.60 times 30 days) and collecting 40% in 60 days yields 24 days. Adding them both together gives the company's collection period of 42 days. Therefore, the correct solution has been found with some rounding involved. In forecasting, however, the precision of any one number is less important than detecting the general trends.

Now, the information is available to complete collection rows 2, 3, and 4 in Part I of the budget. If the average collection period had been 75 days, the percentages would have been entered in the 60- and 90-day rows. In point of fact, even if a firm has an average collection period of 25 days, some receivables may not be collected until possibly 90 days after the sale and some sales may be in cash. However, over time this budget averages those differences together, and it is not necessary to break down the allocation of collections into more than two periods.

Another factor that should be accounted for is the slowdown in collections at certain times of the year. For instance, consumers are always slow to pay in January and February, because they have all overspent in December. The cash forecast permits you to reflect slow collections. If monthly aging reports are obtained from the company, and it is evident that collections do change on a monthly or quarterly basis, revised percentages should be entered into the correct months.

Cash collections {20}. The next step is to derive cash collections in Part II. Each month, cash collections will equal 60% of the prior month's sales plus 40% of the monthly sales from two months earlier. As you look at the sums in the row, it should not come as a surprise that peak collections occur later than peak sales. Moreover, there is a more exaggerated peak in the collections with the major funds being collected in July versus the peak sales months of May and June.

Other cash receipts {21}. The next row in Part II is for other cash income. The firm may rent out some of its space or have short-term securities on which it collects income. In the case of United Enterprises, much of this other income was from litigation settlements. Since this is considered extraordinary income it was not included in this budget.

Total receipts {22}. Merely tally total receipts for each month.

Disbursements

Cash cost of goods sold {5}. The next step is calculating *cash* cost of goods sold as a percent of sales. The cash expense can be determined by subtracting depreciation, a non-cash expense, from the cost of goods sold. In the case of United Enterprises this remainder is 73%. It is rare for cost of goods sold to change during the year. Some firms, however, must go into a second, and even a third, work shift during their peak season. When this occurs, the cost of goods sold may rise. This increase in cost of goods sold as a percent of sales during peak months places an even heavier burden on the cash flow of the firm.

The cost of goods sold percentage and inventory turnover can be used to calculate the materials purchases each month. In the case of United Enterprises, inventory turnover is 85 days. The same weighted average calculation to determine the allocation to 30-days blocks that was done for collections can be done for purchases. However, *purchases will be in advance of when sales occur*.

Thus, the portion ordered in the 60-day block equals:

$$\frac{90 - 85}{30} \text{ or } .17$$

The portion ordered in the 90-day block equals:

$$\frac{85 - 60}{30} \text{ or } .83.$$

The weighted average in the example indicates that 83% of purchases occur on average in the 90-day block before sale and the balance of 17% occurs in the 60-day block before sale. To generate the purchases in dollars for each month, first calculate the inventories required in advance of each month's sales. For January they need to purchase 17% of anticipated March's sales plus 83% of April's sales.

For the first component, the inventory portion required 60 days in advance (17%) is multiplied by the cash cost of goods sold less depreciation and other non-cash charges (73%). This yields .12, the portion of monthly sales—two months from now—that United Enterprises needs to purchase in inventories in January, substantially ahead of sales. Thus, multiply .12 by the dollar sales occurring two months in the future; for United Enterprises, this is .12 times March's sales of $48 million, which equals $5.7 million.

For the second component (inventory required now for sales three months in the future) multiply 83% of purchases required 90 days in advance by the 73% cash cost of goods sold to yield .61. Next, multiply .61 by the dollar sales of $97 million that occur three months ahead (in April) to equal $59.1 million. Then $5.7 million and $59.1 million are added and entered as a whole number into the proper cell in the January column of row 23 in Part III ($64.8 million).

For the United Enterprises example, purchases peak during March, caused by peak sales in May and June. The seasons build wide fluctuations into the cash flow.

Cash payments {24}. Most customers do not pay for goods as soon as they receive them. Trade suppliers provide some credit. Surprisingly, United Enterprises' accounts payable turnover is 23 days; it pays its bills promptly, which means that for United Enterprises all the payments will occur in the month following the purchase of supplies. Therefore, 100% of each month's purchases appear in next month's accounts payable (disbursements) row.

Sales and administrative expense {25}. The next row is sales and administrative expense. Generally such expenses are not seasonal. For example, most sales and administrative personnel are salaried and work steadily throughout the year rather than fluctuate with sales, even if sales are concentrated in one season. Ostensibly this builds loyalty in a subjective or qualitative area where loyalty is vital to the firm. Therefore, for United Enterprises sales and administrative expenses were simply divided by 12 to arrive at even monthly disbursements.

Other disbursements {30}. In addition to the sales forecast, the analyst should also ask management about plans for capital equipment expenditures (and possibly company acquisitions) and fund sources to acquire plant and equipment. Although it is possible to estimate these values from past data or to derive them from sales levels, these are two areas where management can make changes unrelated to either sales levels or past practice. For example, if a plant is operating below capacity, then plant expenditures might not be immediately necessary even with rising sales. On the other hand, management may be planning new facilities that will take years to complete. Such plans would result in disbursements that would be unrelated to the independent sales variable.

Interest expense and principal repayment on LTD {26} & {27}. Next are interest expense {26} and principal repayment {27}. To calculate interest expense refer to long-term debt (carried in the long-term section) {17} and the current portion of long-term debt {18}. In these last two rows of the assumptions in Part I of the forecast, the beginning—January—principal balance of United Enterprises' long-term debt is $89.7 million. This balance declines each month by the amount of the current portion long-term debt (shown on the company's balance sheet) divided by 12; this assumes level amortization.

For Exhibit 11-2, level amortization was assumed without input from United Enterprises' management. It is unlikely, however, that the company would pay down long-term debt without taking out any new long-term debt. If the previous pattern of the corporation has been to finance a portion of capital equipment expenditures, the increase in long-term debt could be estimated by adding the additional cash inflows to the cash receipts row—other cash receipts {21}—and increasing the principal balance of long-term debt as necessary.

Another option to determine the repayment schedule is to review the long-term debt footnote in the financial statement. Especially with debt owned by the public, the repayment schedule is given for each separate piece indicated in the footnote. Any bulge in debt repayment should be noted by the analyst.

The principal balance of long-term debt plus the current portion equals the total long-term debt against which the firm must pay interest. The long-term debt interest expense line has been calculated using the 14% rate forecast in Part I, in row {16}. Row {27} adds in these principal payments—just a duplicate of the current portion long-term debt payments from {18}.

We have now completed the full row-by-row calculations. From now on, each month-column must be calculated separately, because the interest on short-term debt expense {28} is dependent on the previous month's outstanding short-term debt. Moreover, the income taxes {29} are partially determined, in turn, by the amount by which interest expense reduces net income.

Interest on short-term debt {28}. Interest expense for short-term debt, although insignificant in the early part of United Enterprises' year, will rise in May and June due to short-term borrowings. Only the January cell in row 28 can be filled in at the beginning of the calculation because the later interest expenses are based on the indicated short-term debt to be derived at the bottom of the cash budget.

To fill in the short-term interest expense for the month of January, multiply the principal outstanding amount for the month of December by the short-term interest rate indicated in row 14, 12%. This allows $.2 million short-term interest expense to be put into the January month cell.

Income taxes {29}. In the income tax row, the effective tax rate is filled in using a rough estimate of taxes by multiplying the effective rate percentage, calculated in Chapters 4 and 5, by the income before income tax as a percentage of the previous year's sales times the total sales. In United Enterprises' case, multiply .27 by .061 (59.5/994.1) by 971.4 for $16 million in cash taxes to be paid. Divide this total by 4 for each of the four payment months. (The exhibit shows $4.1 million per month, slightly higher, because of rounding.)

Total disbursements {31}. Now, add up the total disbursements for January. In United Enterprises' case, it comes to $53.2 million.

Short-Term Cash Requirements

Now, we identify the goal of what the short-term credit line needs to be.

Net cash generated this month {32}. Since the total receipts were only $48.6 million, United Enterprises has a deficit cash flow for January of $4.6 million.

Last month short-term debt balance {33}. The next row shows last month's short-term debt balance, here, $18.2 million.

New short-term debt {34}. Add the $18.2 million to the $4.6 million deficit and derive the new short-term debt balance of $22.8 million. The most important function of the cash budget is to determine whether there will be sufficient cash at the end of the peak season to repay loans.

Now, the interest on short-term debt expense {28} for February can be calculated as it was for January and the remainder of Part IV can be calculated in its entirety on a month-by-month order.

Conclusion

The cash budget enables the analyst to know exactly how much the company will need to borrow at any particular time. Its primary function is to help the lender avoid advancing money to a company that cannot repay its loan at the end of the seasonal period.

In the example of United Enterprises, the peaks of the current account balances will be in the months of May and June, concurrent with sales, although the inventory will peak before May. Going all the way across the year, United Enterprises' short-term debt builds to $226 million from $18 million at the beginning of the year. By the year's end, United Enterprises shows a decrease in short-term debt, although sales have not increased. This decrease results from an absence of capital expenditures, only partially offset by a decline in long-term debt. If necessary capital equipment expenditures are made or if stock repurchases continue, and these are added in (and increased long-term debt does not fully offset these), United Enterprises might not show a cash surplus.

Another reason for constructing the cash budget is that it provides a basis for systematically assessing a firm's performance. Each month or quarter the bank can check to see whether the firm's forecast was accurate. Unless the lender has a written plan at the beginning of the year, it will be unable to accomplish this assessment of the firm's performance.

Exhibit 11-2 convinces us why it is inadvisable to use year-end financial statements to derive average inventory and accounts receivable balances for turnover ratios. A company that has this much seasonal fluctuation would *not* be a candidate for the simple averaging of successive year-end balances of inventory and accounts receivable as suggested by some accounting texts. Monthly accounts receivable balances enable better reckoning of average collection assumptions for Part I. The same holds true for inventory and accounts payable balances. The only way to calculate an accurate turnover ratio is to obtain these balances at predetermined times coinciding with the firm's peak periods throughout the year.

Key Points: The cash budget is a useful tool for assessing the short-term performance of a firm. Its basic function is to help the lender avoid making short-term loans that the firm will not be able to repay by the end of the peak season.

Equipment Investment Analysis

Loan officers sometimes have the opportunity to review the analysis that a borrower has conducted to make a go-ahead decision about an investment project. While investment analyses that a borrower shows to a banker invariably reflect a good return on investment and favorable cash flows, the lender should examine the analysis and question management about it. Reviewing this sort of analysis is a way of learning about management's assumptions about their business. This section provides a brief introduction to the corporate finance issues involved in constructing an investment analysis.

Basic Principles

Investment forecasts do not rely on historical trends and macroeconomic variables as do financial statement forecasts. Investment studies start with engineering estimates, based on performance of similar equipment under similar circumstances. The analysis is not accounting-oriented. Concepts of income accrual are totally ignored. Instead, investment analysis attempts to show the economic gains that the equipment provides. All figures used in an investment analysis are based on cash flows. Economics dictates that when and until cash changes hands, nothing measurable has happened.

The most rudimentary analytical methods (like payback time) ignore the timing of cash flows. These practices of disregarding cash flow timing originated when the cost of debt capital in the United States was in the 2% range and even equity cost only 3.5% with reference to the 30 times price/earnings ratios common in the stock market. With investment yields this low, it practically does not matter when cash expended for equipment investment will return as long as it is within the foreseeable future.

Today, capital is scarce in the United States with interest rates in the 10% area and price/earnings multiples in the 10- to 15-times range, indicating a 7% to 10% after-tax equity cost. Thus, techniques that focus on present value analysis have become increasingly important. Present value penalizes funds that come back to the investor in the future based on an assumed interest rate. If the interest rate is 10%, then present value analysis would calculate that $110 to be received in one year is worth $100 today.

Basic Steps

Exhibit 11-3 shows an abbreviated example of the numerical analysis used to make a *capital budgeting decision*. The first step {I-A} identifies the cash investment outflows and some basic parameters of the operating cash flows. Outflows include the cost of the machines as well as permanent outlays for additional supplies, increased accounts receivable, installation, and possibly training. Operating cash {I-B} inflow parameters include sales units and prices, fixed and variable costs, depreciation, tax rates, and inflation rates.

The second step {II, A and B} develops an income statement to *solely determine the tax consequences* of the investment. This involves using the estimated sales, fixed and variable costs, and IRS depreciation expenses to calculate taxable income. (*Note:* Where GAAP accrual methods differ, IRS rules prevail.) Once operating income is calculated the income tax can be derived.

The next step {III} is to develop a cash flow statement, similar to the income statement but eliminating such charges as depreciation, which is not a

Exhibit 11-3.

INVESTMENT ANALYSIS

I. INPUT DATA

Dollars in 000s

A. Investment Outlay:			B. Operating Cash Flows		
Cost of new machine	$1,800.0		Unit sales	1,000	
Installation costs	$200.0		Unit price	$1.00	
Total Cost Basis	$2,000.0		Inflation rate	5%	
Increase in Working Capital	$20.0		Fixed Costs	$100	
Opportunity Cost of plant	$80.0		Variable Cost	40%	of Sales
Salvage value	$650.0		MACRS Class Life	5	Years
Cost of capital	10%		Tax rate	34%	
Year of Investment	1990				

II ANALYSIS SCHEDULES

A. Tax Depreciation Schedule	Year	5 Year MACRS Rate	Depreciation Allowance	Ending Book Value
	0			$2,000.0
	1	20.00%	$400.0	1,600.0
	2	26.74%	534.8	1,065.2
	3	17.80%	356.0	709.2
	4	14.18%	283.6	425.6
	5	14.18%	283.6	142.0

B. Income Tax Derivation	1990	1991	1992	1993	1994	1995
Number of Units Sold		1,000	1,000	1,000	1,000	1,000
Unit Price		$1.00	$1.05	$1.10	$1.16	$1.22
Total Revenues		$1,000.0	$1,050.0	$1,102.5	$1,157.6	$1,215.5
Variable Costs		400.0	420.0	441.0	463.1	486.2
Fixed Costs		100.0	105.0	110.3	115.8	121.6
Depreciation		400.0	534.8	356.0	283.6	283.6
Total Tax Deductibles		$900.0	$1,059.8	$907.3	$862.4	$891.4
Net Taxable Income		$100.0	($9.8)	$195.3	$295.2	$324.2
Taxes		34.0	(3.3)	66.4	100.4	110.2

III. Cash Flow Statement for Investment Analysis

		1990	1991	1992	1993	1994	1995
Outflows	Cost of new machine	($1,800)					
	Installation costs	(200)					
	Increase in Work. Cap.	(20)					
	Opportunity cost	(80)					
Inflows	Cash Revenues		$1,000.0	$1,050.0	$1,102.5	$1,157.6	$1,215.5
	Variable Costs		(400.0)	(420.0)	(441.0)	(463.1)	(486.2)
	Fixed Costs		(100.0)	(105.0)	(110.3)	(115.8)	(121.6)
	Taxes		(34.0)	3.3	(66.4)	(100.4)	(110.2)
	Recovery of Working Capital						20.0
	Salvage Value-net of associated taxes						477.3
Net Cash Flow		($2,100)	$466.0	$528.3	$484.9	$478.4	$994.8

IV. Valuation Methods

Payback method -Cumulative remaining balance of investment in specific yearly column					
	$2,100.0	$1,634.0	$1,105.7	$620.8	$142.4	($852.5)
	Payback=		4 years		1.72 months	

Net Present Value	$69.0	See Exhibit II-4 for an explanation of these two
Internal Rate of Return	11.15%	methods.

cash item. The taxes previously calculated are included because they are a cash outflow. Revenue collections minus the various cash expenses equals a cash inflow.

Finally, net cash flows (return) on the investment are forecasted.

Evaluation Methods {IV}

Payback Period

Of the several methods used to rank investments, the most rudimentary one is the payback period method. The payback period is the amount of time it takes for an investment to fully pay for itself. The bottom of Exhibit 11-3 shows an example of the payback evaluation: The cumulative outflows and inflows are taken until the inflows exceed the original outflow. Under this method, the project that is chosen for investment is the one that pays for itself in the least amount of time.

Net Present Value

Another, more sophisticated ranking method is net present value. Under this method, a project is charged an interest rate equal to the firm's cost of capital (cited in Chapter 8) for use of the invested funds. After all the returns are discounted by the cost of capital, if there is still some positive return remaining from the inflows, that investment is profitable.

Exhibit 11-4 {I} shows the cash inflows from the investment project in Exhibit 11-3 assuming that the firm has a cost of capital of 12% after tax. The cash flows are discounted to present value using the cost of capital as the discount rate. Thus, the inflows are reduced by a rate that reflects the return required by the long-term investors in the firm. Since, in this case, the sum of discounted cash flows (both outflows and inflows) is less than zero, the transaction will return less than the firm's cost of funds (the returns expected by both lenders and shareholders) and not be chosen. In the case of a result greater than zero, the opposite conclusions can be drawn and the excess amount can be viewed as a cushion against unexpected, unfavorable events. It can also be viewed as a way of giving higher returns to shareholders and boosting the stock price.

Internal Rate of Return

Exhibit 11-4 {II} shows a simple example of the present value analysis used to determine the internal rate of return of a particular investment proposal. The point is to find a rate of return that when applied to the incoming cash flows, using present value discounting, will cause those flows to be equal to the initial investment; in other words, the discount rate that equates the cash inflows with the beginning investment. Another method is ranking experiments by discounting the cash flows with different rates until a rate is found that produces a string of discounted cash inflows adding up to the original investment amount. This rate is called the **internal rate of return.** The "Fourth Trial," third column, {II,

Exhibit 11-4.

PRESENT VALUE METHODS OF EVALUATING INVESTMENT PROPOSALS

Values from Exhibit 11-3

I. NET PRESENT VALUE EVALUATION

YEARS	CASH FLOWS	@	PRESENT VALUE FACTORS 12.00%		NET PRESENT VALUE 12.00%
1987	($2,100,000)	X	100.00%	=	($2,100,000)
1988	466,000	X	89.29%	=	416,071
1989	528,332	X	79.72%	=	421,183
1990	484,865	X	71.18%	=	345,117
1991	478,440	X	63.55%	=	304,057
1992	994,821	X	56.74%	=	564,488
				TOTAL	($49,083)

NOTE: In this case the net present value of the cash flows is negative
and the net present value technique would advise against investing in this
project.

II. INTERNAL RATE OF RETURN EVALUATION

This is an iterative process requiring several trials using the net present
value analysis method to achieve the solution, a discount rate which
produces a zero net present value.

A. THE FIRST TRIAL at 10%

YEARS	CASH FLOWS	@	PRESENT VALUE FACTORS 10.00%		NET PRESENT VALUE 10.00%
1987	($2,100,000)	X	100.00%	=	($2,100,000)
1988	466,000	X	90.91%	=	423,636
1989	528,332	X	82.64%	=	436,638
1990	484,865	X	75.13%	=	364,286
1991	478,440	X	68.30%	=	326,781
1992	994,821	X	62.09%	=	617,706
				TOTAL	$69,047

NOTE: In this case the net present value of the cash flows is greater than
zero; therefore, it would appear that the IRR discount rate must be higher.

B. SECOND TRIAL at 11.5%

YEARS	CASH FLOWS	@	PRESENT VALUE FACTORS 11.50%		NET PRESENT VALUE 11.50%
1987	($2,100,000)	X	100.00%	=	($2,100,000)
1988	466,000	X	89.69%	=	417,937
1989	528,332	X	80.44%	=	424,969
1990	484,865	X	72.14%	=	349,781
1991	478,440	X	64.70%	=	309,548
1992	994,821	X	58.03%	=	577,259
				TOTAL	($20,506)

NOTE: In this case the net present value of the cash flows is less than
zero; therefore, it would appear that the IRR discount rate must be higher
than 10% and lower than 11.5%.

C. THIRD TRIAL at 10.5%			PRESENT		NET PRESENT
YEARS	CASH FLOWS	@	VALUE FACTORS		VALUE
			10.50%		10.50%
1987	($2,100,000)	X	100.00%	=	($2,100,000)
1988	$466,000	X	90.50%	=	$421,719
1989	$528,332	X	81.90%	=	$432,695
1990	$484,865	X	74.12%	=	$359,364
1991	$478,440	X	67.07%	=	$320,906
1992	$994,821	X	60.70%	=	$603,856
				TOTAL	$38,541

NOTE: In this case the net present value of the cash flows is still greater than zero; therefore, it would appear that the IRR discount rate must be higher than 10.5% and lower than 11.5%.

D. FOURTH TRIAL at 11.15%			PRESENT		NET PRESENT
YEARS	CASH FLOWS	@	VALUE FACTORS		VALUE
			11.15%		11.15%
1987	($2,100,000)	X	100.00%	=	($2,100,000)
1988	466,000	X	89.97%	=	419,263
1989	528,332	X	80.95%	=	427,669
1990	484,865	X	72.83%	=	353,120
1991	478,440	X	65.52%	=	313,494
1992	994,821	X	58.95%	=	586,471
				TOTAL	$15

NOTE: This trial was successful because the net present value has been reduced to zero; another way of looking at this is to say that we have found a discount rate which makes the future inflows equal to the original outflows.

D}, shows the discounted cash flows at 11.15%. By trial and error, the firm's analyst has identified that at that rate the discounted inflows from the investment are just $15 more than the cost (outflows) of the investment. Thus, the internal rate of return of the project is 11.15%.

Conclusion

All cash flows in investment analysis are calculated on an after-tax basis. To compare these rates on a pre-tax basis, the after-tax rate must be divided by 1 minus the tax bracket of the firm.

By examining the cost of capital percentage and the net present value of the investment, the analyst will be better able to assess the firm's opportunities for investment. A number of profitable investment alternatives bodes well for a company. Few investment alternatives may be symptomatic of a secular decline in the firm's future sales.

Another reason to review a firm's investment analysis is that it will reveal the firm's investment forecast. If the analysis is based on an uninterrupted upward stream of increasing sales, the source of this unbridled enthusiasm may be worth investigating. For example, if the firm does poorly in recessions, then recession forecasts should be examined before embarking on a major project. Reviewing a firm's investment analysis will enable the analyst to better understand the firm's culture and attitudes. This understanding will result in a better long-term forecast of the firm's operations.

> **Key Points:** Companies typically base investment decisions on either payback period, net present value, or internal rate of return analysis. Reviewing a firm's investment analyses can offer valuable insights on management culture and attitude. In addition, it can provide you with the firm's management sales forecast.

Long-Range Planning for Term Lending

Purpose

Long-range forecasts are used primarily to determine a firm's needs for increased cash on an annual basis. While dodging the nuances of daily or monthly cash peaks and valleys, a long-range forecast creates the option of closely examining major managerial decision making on:

1. Sales growth trends
2. Capital expenditures
3. Impact of interest rate fluctuations
4. Structuring debt layers
5. Validity of revenue/expense relationships

Furthermore, the plan focuses on *net cash changes* that, in view of the inadequacies of using net income as a debt capacity barometer, more definitely specifies debt needs. The long-range plan identifies the *ability to repay long-term obligations* apart from the seasonal borrowing examined in the cash budget section.

Additionally, a long-term forecast is indispensable when the investor makes a longer-term commitment to the firm in the form of a revolving credit term loan, an installment collateralized loan, or any other credit facility that will be categorized on the balance sheet as a long-term loan and part of the firm's capital. Unlike shareholders who are looking for the firm to produce profits, lenders receive a predetermined interest rate and have limited upside potential. (Concerning the subject of risk, of all the investors in business, shareholders shoulder the most risk; next, the managers of a firm take risk because of profit sharing or threat of firing; and so on.) Lenders prefer *not* to take risk. Therefore, any forecast should use conservative assumptions in attempting to determine what the various debt levels of the company will be over time. The lender should ensure that a company:

1. Maintains a balanced financial condition
2. Borrows on a long-term basis to support the acquisition of fixed assets
3. Keeps short-term debt in line with actual short-term needs

4. Generates increasing amounts of profit and cash flow
5. Is restrained by its fiduciary obligations

Basic Steps

As in most complex calculations, the usefulness of the result is entirely dependent on the assumptions made in developing the forecast. If the firm supplies the analyst with its own forecast, the first job is to assess it. This evaluation of the firm's forecast should center on the set of assumptions made to produce the result. Typically, self-prepared financial forecasts are extremely optimistic and never show a company failing. It is thus important to examine the assumptions behind a forecast and decide whether they are realistic.

Whether the borrower firm has prepared its own forecast or not, the analyst must prepare an independent one. This preparation step will produce analytical insights into the operations of the firm as noted above. The term of the loan should influence the length of the forecast; if the loan's amortization period is five years, then a five-year forecast should be prepared. Although a five-year forecast—especially the fifth year's results—may appear to be of debatable value, in fact, a lender makes such a forecast in agreeing to a five-year repayment schedule. The mechanical steps in developing a long-term forecast are similar to those for preparing a short-term budget.

1. The *independent variables will again be based on sales* projections obtained from management and, possibly, verified by correlation analysis. Correlation analysis is more important for the long-term forecast because management is less likely to be aware of long-term macroeconomic variables and secular changes. Sales-level projections should be justified by written assumptions about changes in the economy and in the market the firm serves.

2. The *identification of the relationships* within the financial statements must be subjected to augmented verification as well. As with the cash budget, information on capital equipment acquisition plans must be obtained from management. There are, however, possible alternatives to calculating the capital expenditure requirements. The forecast should demonstrate that the level of capital equipment is proportionately in line with any prior relationship to sales as final verification; if it is not in line, suitable justification must be made.

3. A *forecast format must be established*. The format presented in Exhibit 11-5 has several sections, similar to the cash budget. The top of the forecast lists assumptions about the income statement, the balance sheet, and cash flow adjustments. Below this section is the forecast itself in three sections: an income statement, a balance sheet, and a net cash flow statement.

Exhibit 11-5 shows that data should be presented in chronological order, starting with results from the year prior to the base year and going forward. The format is designed for a five-year forecast. The forecast could be longer; however, many bankers feel that five years is the longest period for which any detailed quantitative forecast can be useful.

Not all income statement and balance sheet accounts are separated out in the forecast. Consolidating accounts makes the forecast easier to complete and

(*Text continued on page 281.*)

Exhibit 11-5.

FINANCIAL STATEMENT PROJECTION

United Enterprises, Inc.

Dollars in 000,000s

PERIODS:	Last Year	This Year	Next Year	2nd Year	3rd Year	4th Year	5th Year
	=====ACTUALS=====		=====FORECASTS=====				
ASSUMPTIONS:	**FILL IN THE BLANKS IN THE FOLLOWING ASSUMPTIONS AREAS–Primarily in Base and Prior Years**						
Income Statement Assumptions:	*Sum all Operating Expenses into Either Cost of Goods Sold or Operating Expense*						
Actual Sales (Forecast Future Years)	NA						
Indicated Sales Growth (Rate)							
Cost of Goods Sold							
Operating Expenses							
Ave Interest Rate (Forecast Future Yr)							
Cash IncomeTax (Net Deferred)							
Balance Sheet Assumptions:	*Consolidate where necessary the firm's balance sheet items into these below.*						
Cash Balances & Marketable Securities							
Accounts Receivable							
Inventory & all remaining Current.Assets							
Accounts Payable							
Net Plant & Equipment			Ave. of actuals as % of Sales ->			Reality check w/forecast below	
Notes Payable Banks			Ave. of actuals as % of Sales ->			Reality check w/forecast below	
Taxes Payable & Accrued Expense							
Long-Term Debt			Ave. of actuals as % of Sales ->			Reality check w/forecast below	
Stock & Surplus-Est. New Issues or (Pur.)							
Retained Earnings			NA	NA	NA	NA	NA
Cash Flow Assumptions:	*Consolidate where necessary the firm's cash flow items into these below.*						
Depreciation							
Cap. Eq. Expend & Other Inv. (Est. Fut.Yr.)							
Cash Dividends-Estimate Future Years							
Additional LTD as % Capital Expenditure	NA						
Current Portion Long Term Debt							

FORECAST	Last Year	This Year	Next Year	2nd Year	3rd Year	4th Year	5th Year
	=======ACTUALS=======|		|========================FORECASTS========================|				
INCOME STATEMENT FORECAST							
Net Sales & Other Income							
Cost of Goods Sold							
Gross Profit							
Operating Expenses							
Operating Profit							
Interest Expense							
Income Tax							
NET OPERATING PROFIT							
BALANCE SHEET FORECAST							
Cash							
Receivables (Net)							
Inventories							
Total Current Assets							
Plant & Equipment (Net) & Invest							
TOTAL ASSETS							
Notes Payable Banks							
Accounts Payable							
Taxes and Accrued Expenses							
Current Operating Liabs							
Current Portion Long Term							
Long Term Debt							
TOTAL LIABILITIES							
Stock and Surplus							
Retained Earnings							
NET WORTH							
TOTAL FOOTINGS							

(continued)

Exhibit 11-5. *Continued.*

FORECAST	Last Year	This Year	Next Year	2nd Year	3rd Year	4th Year	5th Year
	=======ACTUALS=======		=======================FORECASTS======================				
CASH FLOW STATEMENT (NET) FORECAST							
Net Profit After Tax							
Depreciation & Amortization							
Funds Flow from Operations							
Increase in A/P & Accrued Exp	NA						
Decrease in Cur Assets (Increase)	NA						
Cash Flow from Operations	NA						
Increase in Long Term Debt	NA						
Sale of Stock (Purchase)	NA						
(Cash Dividends)	NA						
Total Financing Sources	NA						
Capital Expenditures	NA						
Total Investment Uses	NA						
Increased Notes Payable Banks	NA						

RATIOS		
Times Interest Earned		
Term Debt to Funds Flow		

easier to read. Moreover, *a condensed format avoids the appearance of accuracy* that greater detail tends to convey.

Income Statement Assumptions

Exhibit 11-6 shows a completed five-year forecast for United Enterprises. It will be used as a case to discuss the various elements.

Sales actual and forecast. The first row contains the dollar sales forecast. The sales data for United Enterprises is slightly unusual in that sales declined 6% from the prior year to the base year. This raises a question about forecasting the succeeding years' sales. There are two rows for sales: one for the dollar numbers and one for the percentage growth. This format enables the reader of the forecast to quickly review the sales assumptions.

In the United Enterprises example, sales were estimated to increase a modest 6.7% next year and then permitted to rise approximately 10% thereafter. Many scenarios can be played out here to test the cash required for a major expansion, or even continued contraction. Look back to Exhibits 8-5 and 8-6 for examples of expansion, contraction, and their concomitant cash requirements.

Cost of goods sold. For the base year and the year prior to the base year enter the actual cost of goods sold in dollars. The forecast percentages are calculated by taking the average of the cost of goods sold as a percentage of sales for the two given years. Throughout the forecast, use this technique of averaging data from these two years. This *averaging of two years is* a statistical technique that *may improve the accuracy of the trend* extended into the future. On the other hand, more sophisticated techniques may be used to segregate the fixed costs of a firm from variable costs; for instance a regression analysis on the various observations of cost of goods sold. By identifying the intercept of the best-fit line of the cost of goods sold with the "Y" axis, this would provide a general indication of fixed cost if sales were zero. Unfortunately, attempts at determining fixed costs for anything other than marginal, or short-term, analysis are futile because in the long run everything is variable. (See Exhibit 9-2 for more discussion.)

Some analysts might prefer to expunge 1990, in the United Enterprises example, as an exceptional year and therefore not an appropriate base for forecasting. Calculation of cost of goods sold to sales for the base year, 1990, however, is 73.8%, which is slightly lower than the 74.05% in the previous year, 1989, when sales were higher. If the forecaster has four or five years of data for a forecast, it might still be better to weight more highly or use only the last two years since the recent years' results should be more indicative of the immediate future.

If the forecaster feels that management may alter the production process and acquire highly productive capital equipment, or use some other technique to reduce cost of goods sold, the forecaster should feel free to change the assumptions in the later years of the forecast. Be wary of reducing the cost of goods sold in expectation of supply price changes, however. This is because things that allow the borrower to reduce costs may also be available to other manufacturers, who would also experience cost reductions, and competition

(Text continued on page 285.)

Exhibit 11-6.

FINANCIAL STATEMENT PROJECTION

United Enterprises, Inc.

Dollars in 000,000s

PERIODS:	Last Year	This Year	Next Year	2nd Year	3rd Year	4th Year	5th Year
	=====ACTUALS=====		=====FORECASTS=====				
ASSUMPTIONS:	FILL IN THE BLANKS IN THE FOLLOWING ASSUMPTIONS AREAS-Primarily in Base and Prior Years						
Income Statement Assumptions:	Sum all Operating Expenses into Either Cost of Goods Sold or Operating Expense						
Actual Sales (Forecast Future Years)	$1,057.4	$994.1	$1,061.0	$1,170.0	$1,280.0	$1,410.0	$1,550.0
Indicated Sales Growth (Rate)	NA	-6.0%	6.7%	10.3%	9.4%	10.2%	9.9%
Cost of Goods Sold	$783.0	$734.0	73.9%	73.9%	73.9%	73.9%	73.9%
Operating Expenses	$181.0	$189.0	18.1%	18.1%	18.1%	18.1%	18.1%
Ave Interest Rate (Forecast Future Yr)	12.1%	10.3%	10.0%	10.0%	10.0%	10.0%	10.0%
Cash IncomeTax (Net Deferred)	$30.3	$16.1	32.5%	32.5%	32.5%	32.5%	32.5%
Balance Sheet Assumptions:	Consolidate where necessary the firm's balance sheet items into these below.						
Cash Balances & Marketable Securities	$14.7	$4.9	0.9%	0.9%	0.9%	0.9%	0.9%
Accounts Receivable	$120.9	$111.0	11.3%	11.3%	11.3%	11.3%	11.3%
Inventory & all remaining Current.Assets	$226.5	$202.2	28.2%	28.2%	28.2%	28.2%	28.2%
Accounts Payable	$55.7	$45.5	6.7%	6.7%	6.7%	6.7%	6.7%
Net Plant & Equipment	$326.7	$358.5	Ave. of actuals as % of Sales -		30.7%	Reality check w/forecast below	
Notes Payable Banks	$16.0	$18.3	Ave. of actuals as % of Sales -		1.5%	Reality check w/forecast below	
Taxes Payable & Accrued Expense	$90.6	$83.5	11.5%	11.5%	11.5%	11.5%	11.5%
Long-Term Debt	$88.2	$102.9	Ave. of actuals as % of Sales -		8.6%	Reality check w/forecast below	
Stock & Surplus-Est. New Issues or (Pur.)	$161.9	$141.7	($15.0)	($15.0)	($15.0)	($15.0)	($15.0)
Retained Earnings	$276.4	$284.6	NA	NA	NA	NA	NA
Cash Flow Assumptions:	Consolidate where necessary the firm's cash flow items into these below.						
Depreciation	$23.3	$26.4	8.1%	8.1%	8.1%	8.1%	8.1%
Cap. Eq. Expend & Other Inv. (Est. Fut.Yr.)	$65.2	$63.8	$60.0	$60.0	$60.0	$60.0	$60.0
Cash Dividends-Estimate Future Years	$21.5	$21.2	$21.2	$21.2	$21.2	$21.2	$21.2
Additional LTD as % Capital Expenditure	NA	23.0%	40.0%	40.0%	40.0%	40.0%	40.0%
Current Portion Long Term Debt	$12.0	$16.8	14.97%	14.97%	14.97%	14.97%	14.97%

FORECAST	Last Year	This Year	Next Year	2nd Year	3rd Year	4th Year	5th Year
	=====ACTUALS=====			=========FORECASTS=========			
INCOME STATEMENT FORECAST							
Net Sales & Other Income	$1,057.4	$994.1	$1,061.0	$1,170.0	$1,280.0	$1,410.0	$1,550.0
Cost of Goods Sold	783.0	734.0	784.5	865.1	946.5	1,042.6	1,146.1
Gross Profit	$274.4	$260.1	$276.5	$304.9	$333.5	$367.4	$403.9
Operating Expenses	181.0	189.0	191.7	211.4	231.2	254.7	280.0
Operating Profit	$93.4	$71.1	$84.8	$93.5	$102.3	$112.7	$123.9
Interest Expense	12.6	12.5	12.1	15.9	19.3	22.1	24.6
Income Tax	30.3	16.1	23.6	25.2	27.0	29.4	32.2
NET OPERATING PROFIT	$50.5	$42.5	$49.1	$52.4	$56.0	$61.1	$67.0
BALANCE SHEET FORECAST							
Cash	$14.7	$4.9	$10.0	$11.0	$12.1	$13.3	$14.6
Receivables (Net)	120.9	111.0	119.9	132.2	144.6	159.3	175.1
Inventories	226.5	202.2	221.5	244.3	267.3	294.4	323.6
Total Current Assets	$362.1	$318.1	$351.4	$387.5	$423.9	$467.0	$513.4
Plant & Equipment (Net) & Invest	326.7	358.5	389.5	418.1	444.3	468.4	490.5
TOTAL ASSETS	$688.8	$676.6	$740.9	$805.6	$868.2	$935.4	$1,003.9
Notes Payable Banks	$16.0	$18.3	$49.3	$72.1	$90.7	$107.4	$119.5
Accounts Payable	55.7	45.5	52.2	57.6	63.0	69.4	76.3
Taxes and Accrued Expenses	90.6	83.5	90.0	99.3	108.6	119.6	131.5
Current Operating Liabs	$162.3	$147.3	$191.6	$228.9	$262.3	$296.5	$327.3
Current Portion Long Term	12.0	16.8	12.9	14.5	16.0	17.2	18.2
Long Term Debt	76.2	86.1	97.2	106.7	114.7	121.5	127.3
TOTAL LIABILITIES	$250.5	$250.2	$301.7	$350.1	$392.9	$435.2	$472.9
Stock and Surplus	$161.9	$141.7	$126.7	$111.7	$96.7	$81.7	$66.7
Retained Earnings	276.4	284.6	312.5	343.6	378.5	418.4	464.2
NET WORTH	$438.3	$426.3	$439.2	$455.3	$475.2	$500.1	$530.9
TOTAL FOOTINGS	$688.8	$676.5	$740.8	$805.5	$868.1	$935.3	$1,003.8

(continued)

Exhibit 11-6. *Continued.*

FORECAST	Last Year	This Year	Next Year	2nd Year	3rd Year	4th Year	5th Year
	=======ACTUALS=======		=========================FORECASTS=========================				
CASH FLOW STATEMENT (NET) FORECAST							
Net Profit After Tax	$50.5	$42.5	$49.1	$52.4	$56.0	$61.1	$67.0
Depreciation & Amortization	23.3	26.4	29.0	31.5	33.8	35.9	37.8
Funds Flow from Operations	**$73.8**	**$68.9**	**$78.0**	**$83.9**	**$89.8**	**$97.0**	**$104.9**
Increase in A/P & Accrued Exp	NA	(17.3)	13.2	14.6	14.7	17.4	18.8
Decrease in Cur Assets (Increase)	NA	44.0	(33.3)	(36.1)	(36.4)	(43.1)	(46.4)
Cash Flow from Operations	**NA**	**$95.6**	**$58.0**	**$62.4**	**$68.1**	**$71.4**	**$77.3**
Increase in Long Term Debt	NA	$14.7	$7.2	$11.1	$9.5	$8.0	$6.8
Sale of Stock (Purchase)	NA	($20.2)	($15.0)	($15.0)	($15.0)	($15.0)	($15.0)
(Cash Dividends)	NA	($21.2)	($21.2)	($21.2)	($21.2)	($21.2)	($21.2)
Total Financing Sources	NA	($26.7)	($29.0)	($25.1)	($26.7)	($28.2)	($29.4)
Capital Expenditures	NA	$63.8	$60.0	$60.0	$60.0	$60.0	$60.0
Total Investment Uses	NA	$63.8	$60.0	$60.0	$60.0	$60.0	$60.0
Increased Notes Payable Banks	**NA**	**($5.1)**	**$31.0**	**$22.7**	**$18.6**	**$16.7**	**$12.1**

RATIOS							
Times Interest Earned	7.44	5.68	7.00	5.87	5.29	5.09	5.03
Term Debt to Funds Flow	1.19	1.49	1.41	1.45	1.45	1.43	1.39

may cause prices to fall. Usually, the relationship between the cost of goods sold and sales remains stable.

It is expected that part of the cost of goods sold is depreciation, a non-cash expense, and the forecast will add that amount back in the cash flow section to reverse the deduction.

Operating expenses and other. For this category include all the other income and expenses on the income statement except for interest expense and taxes. It is important to include all income statement accounts in one or another of the consolidated entries in this analysis, even if they are not separated out on the forecast sheet. Since the entire statement is oriented toward determining the cash flow of a company, however, items of *expense that may be capitalized* for income statement purposes—such as interest expense incurred in the development of a large project—*should be treated as cash outflows*. In the example, the average of two years of operating expenses as a percent of sales is 18%; this percentage is carried through the forecast. Again one needs to consider various pieces of information that may change that percentage in the future.

Interest rate: average and forecast. The form shown here has calculated the previous average interest rate by dividing the sum of (1) short-term debt, (2) current portion long-term debt, and (3) long-term debt into the total interest expense for the period. The average rate calculates to 12% in 1989 and 10.3% in 1990. The forecast for the succeeding years is 10% as suggested by a hypothetical economic research letter that forecasts the rate based on macroeconomic variables. For United Enterprises, the interest expense is a slight part of total expenses, so any rate differential is not a significant concern. For a firm that is highly leveraged, accurate interest rate forecasting becomes more important. It may even be wise to do more than one analysis based on several different interest rate scenarios for more highly leveraged industries.

Effective income tax rate. The cash income taxes paid in the prior year and base year are not the actual amounts listed on United Enterprises' income statement. As a matter of fact, United Enterprises paid amounts less than shown on the audited statement, because of timing differences in depreciation and other expense accounts between Internal Revenue Service reporting and generally accepted accounting principles; as mentioned previously, the difference finds its way into the deferred tax account on the balance sheet. (See Exhibit 4-2 for more discussion.)

By deducting the difference and showing a lower effective (cash-oriented) income tax rate, however, the forecasts create additional differences between the audited financial statements and the forecast numbers. This difference may disconcert executives reviewing the assumptions; thus, another option is to calculate only future years using the effective tax rate of the subject firm so that the cash will be properly deducted, yet the two actual years' statements will balance with the audited ones.

Balance Sheet Assumptions

Average cash balances. The assumptions on the balance sheet, similar to those for the income statement, start by identifying relationships between each of the various accounts and sales. For United Enterprises, cash balances are slightly less than 1% of sales. The company's cash balances and marketable securities were reduced from the audited amounts in 1990 because a substantial block of funds was committed to purchase a company effective January 1, 1991. (Listing these funds as current assets compromises the spirit of the definition of a current asset—if not the literal definition—since the firm was legally committed to the acquisition prior to December 31.)

Accounts receivable. Place the actual accounts receivable in the base and prior year columns and then calculate the average accounts receivable as a percentage of sales, in this case 11%.

Inventory and other current assets. All remaining current assets are consolidated, to reduce the number of current asset categories to three. After placing the actual numbers in the base and prior year, their forecasted value is then calculated as a percentage of cost of goods sold, in this case, 28%. Similarly, **accounts payable** is expressed as a percentage of cost of goods sold and equals 6.6%.

Net plant and equipment. Other than filling in the 1990 and 1989 actual numbers, the relationships of net plant and equipment, **notes payable, long-term debt,** and **retained earnings** to sales will either be forecasted independently or derived by the process of the forecast. The forecaster may wish to calculate these items as a percentage of sales and use them later to test validity of preliminary forecast results. If one of these accounts is out of line with historical averages, it raises questions about the other management-derived assumptions that drive the forecast: sales, capital expenditures, and new long-term debt.

If, for example, the firm's own forecast of capital equipment expenditures generates a lower net plant and equipment percentage of sales in future years, the forecaster may wish to ask how management plans to change the standing relationship of sales to fixed assets. It may be a result of new, highly productive equipment, but it also may be just a mistake in the forecast. *Testing the outcome of the forecast against the historical relationships and assumptions that produced it is an important part of the analysis.*

Taxes payable and accrued expenses. Place actual balance sheet accounts in the base and prior years; they should include all remaining current liabilities. Consolidating many of these items is not a problem, since excessive detail is not that valuable. But all of these other liabilities must be included in the taxes payable and accrued expenses consolidation and calculated as a percentage of cost of goods sold.

Stock and surplus: new issues (purchases). This requires an estimate of either new stock issues or of a buy-back of stock outstanding. For our example, United Enterprises acquired $39 million of stock in 1990, so the forecast shows some continued acquisition of treasury stock throughout the next five years. United Enterprises' mode of acquisitions occasionally involves acquiring stock and using it to pay entrepreneurs for their companies, but in 1990 the company was defending itself against a takeover attempt by purchasing such a large block of stock. (Being able to raise funds in the stock market has become unusual in the last ten years, which is a prime reason for debt to have become so pervasive.)

Cash Flow Assumptions

Depreciation. First, place the actual depreciation from the statement of cash flow in the base and prior year cells. To determine for the forecast the amount of depreciation to add back into cash flow, calculate the rate at which equipment was expensed in the past—divide depreciation by net plant and equipment for the 2 given years and take the average. Since United Enterprises' rate appears to be 8%, the average useful life of its equipment is 12 years. Since this is an average, some of that equipment is notably long-lived.

Net capital equipment and other investments. This is one of the most important rows in the spreadsheet. Any growth in sales must be reflected here; capital expenditures are necessary even if the firm is stagnating, at least equal to depreciation counting inflation. If possible, investment amounts should be based on management opinions or plans, obtained directly from them.

Notice that all fixed assets—plant and equipment, land, investments, and so on—are counted in this row, including all new joint investments and unconsolidated affiliates. In Exhibit 11-6 the information on net capital expenditures and investment acquisitions was obtained from United Enterprises' Statement of Cash Flows, Exhibit 1-1. Some forward-looking companies such as Federal Express include forecasts of their planned capital equipment expenditures in their annual report. This is feasible since Federal Express's main acquisitions are new aircraft, and purchase contracts are signed years before delivery. Since United Enterprises did not provide this information, the example uses $60 million as an approximation of previous investment expenditures shown in the two actual years.

When analyzing the forecast later, these expenditures should be linked to sales and sales growth. The relationship of capital equipment to sales (fixed asset turnover ratio) can be checked over time to see if a sufficient amount has been invested.

Cash dividends and other cash outflows. Dividends conceptually should be based on the percentage of net income. Many firms do pay a percentage of earnings, commonly called a *payout ratio,* to shareholders. However, as exemplified by United Enterprises' making level dividend payments even with a 25% drop in earnings in 1990, sometimes dividends are fixed no matter what the earnings level.

A payout ratio is calculated by dividing the dividend (as it appears in the firm's audited financials) of $21.2 million by income from continuing operations of $31.2 million to compute 68%. In the prior year we divide $21.5 million by $43.3 million to figure a payout ratio of 50%. Obviously, United Enterprises does not use a constant payout ratio. Stable dollar per share dividend payouts in spite of declining earnings are more customary among public companies.

The analysis of the phenomenon goes like this:

- The dividend expresses management's belief in the future performance of the business; this is management's firm statement about what net operating earnings may be at a minimum in the future.
- The shareholders are entitled to all retained earnings anyway.
- If earnings drop, the shareholders should not be inconvenienced by a drop in the dividends since management feels that the fall in earnings is temporary.
- If management does drop dividends, it means they are frightened, and bad results are coming for the near term.

- Dividends should move upward in a smooth stair-step pattern; if they do not, analysts will think the company's earnings are too variable, indicating high risk, and the stock price will fall.

The forecaster may want to place a percentage for a payout ratio in this row for calculation for a privately held company, especially one for which the investor can restrict dividends through the term loan agreement. In the exhibit, the amount was held constant at $21.2 million into the future periods.

Additional long-term debt as a percent of capital expenditures. The next row represents an important estimate: additional long-term debt to maintain a specified capital structure of debt and equity as percentage of total capital. In this forecast, long-term debt must be approximated based on a percentage of capital equipment expenditures. Later, this percentage may be varied to maintain a specific target capital structure.

In the case of United Enterprises, the exhibit allocates new long-term debt at a rate of 40% of capital equipment and investment expenditures. Looking at the relationship of notes payable to banks in the fifth year of the forecasting section, we see that it has risen from only 7% of total footings to 12%. Meanwhile, the current portion long-term debt and long-term debt have risen from 19.5% of capital to slightly over 21.5% of capital. The conclusion is that the long-term debt to capital relationship is largely unchanged and that the short-term side has picked up the increase in leverage that the forecast projects. It might be better to increase the percentage to 45% to reduce the short-term debt. Here is an example of the need for the analyst to exercise judgment in the preparation of the forecast.

Current portion long-term debt. Divide the average current portion long-term debt by average long-term debt itself. In the case of United Enterprises, the long-term debt is amortizing at a 15% rate. The amortization schedule runs approximately seven years, and it continues at this rate for the rest of the forecast. Planned repayments can be obtained from the footnotes. However, since long-term debt will increase, the footnotes would not provide the correct information beyond the first year of the forecast.

Now that all of the assumptions have been listed, the question is: Are they justified? After the forecast has been completed, accuracy can be tested by calculating ratios to test conformity with reasonable corporate goals and requirements of the investing financial institution.

Completing the Financial Statements for the Actual Years

For the "Actuals" first two columns of the forecast, the firm's balance sheet and income statement data can be transferred directly to the spreadsheet, making the necessary combinations to produce the fewer number of entries allowed. As you fill in the historical numbers, check to make sure that the subtotals make sense with the original financial statements of the firm. Any changes, such as the reduction in cash mentioned previously, should be picked up in another asset account such as plant and equipment, since the funds went to acquire an outside firm possessing those assets. Be sure to keep the balance sheet balanced. By running the totals and comparing them, you can verify that you have correctly combined the new account summaries in the assumption section, and that the various relationships identified are based on a correct series of subdivisions.

The net operating profit should be similar to the one on the audited statement. Changes made to reflect capitalization of certain expenses or classifications of extraordinary items should be noted separately so that the various items on the forecast are related to the actual statements.

It is not necessary to fill in the first column (prior year) at the bottom of the net cash flow statement. The second column entries can be determined from the data above. The cash flow statement (net) has been divided into funds flow from operations, cash flow from operations (adjusted for changes in current asset and liability accounts), financial sources, and investment uses.

In the United Enterprises example, net positive funds from operations are augmented by reductions in current assets greater than reductions in current liabilities. Since the company shrank during the period, these positive flows should have been expected. More typically, current assets and current liabilities will increase. This is the norm for firms that are growing. Later in the growing firm's forecast, company growth must give rise to positive cash flow.

In the United Enterprises example, repurchase of stock is a reduction in sources. These cash flow changes confirm that management decisions have a direct effect on cash flow.

- Management's close control of the operations is implied by the fact that current assets were reduced more than proportionally to the decrease in sales.
- Management's use of cash to reacquire stock and pay dividends reduced equity and is changing the firm's capital structure toward more leverage.

After deriving total uses, increased notes payable to banks can be derived. Each entry in this column must first be calculated so that the resulting number can be entered in the notes payable cell for the next year. This process is also necessary to derive interest expense.

The Forecast

Income Statement Forecast

The next step is to forecast the next year's results. The net sales and other income number is merely carried down from the top row of the assumptions. The next entry, cost of goods sold, is calculated by multiplying the cost of goods sold percentage shown in the third column by the sales in the third column. Then subtract one from the other to get gross profit.

Operating expenses are similarly calculated by taking the percentage shown in the third column and multiplying it by the sales figure. A new subtotal is taken for operating profit.

Interest expense is calculated by multiplying the forecast interest rate in the third column by the ending debt balance of the base year. This debt balance includes notes payable to banks plus the current and long-term debt portion

from the base year, the second column. For United Enterprises, this is 10%
times the sum of (1) $18.3 million plus (2) $16.8 million plus (3) $86.1 million
equals the $12.1 million.

Income tax cash outflow is calculated by multiplying the percent of effective
income tax, third column, by the net difference between the third column
operating profit and interest expense. For United Enterprises, this equals 32.5%
times $72.7 million, the difference between $84.8 million operating profit and
$12.1 million interest expense. After deducting this $23.6 million tax calculation,
the net profit of $49.1 million can be calculated.

Balance Sheet Forecast

Moving on to the balance sheet, the first item is cash, derived by multiplying
the percentage in the balance sheet assumption section by sales for the "Next
Year." Continue this same calculation for the receivables, changing at inventories to the cost of goods sold relationship before totaling the current assets.

The calculation of net plant and equipment is somewhat more complex.

1. The base year plant and equipment of $358.5 million is added to the
   capital equipment and investment expenditures figure from the cash
   flow adjustments assumptions of $60 million for a total of $418.5 million.
2. Depreciation is calculated by multiplying the percentage shown in the
   cash flow assumptions section, of 8.08%, by the base year's net plant
   and equipment, of $358.5 million, equaling $29 million.
3. Depreciation (derived in step 2) is subtracted from the total in step 1.
   Total plant and equipment should be $389.5 million.

Now, compute the total assets cell.

In the liability section, notes payable banks can be left blank since this is
derived at the bottom of the forecast and entered later to bring the section into
balance with the assets. Accounts payable are calculated by multiplying the
percentage taken from the balance sheet assumptions section by the cost of
goods sold. The same is done for taxes and accrued expenses, using the
appropriate percentage. Now, total the current operating liabilities.

The current portion long-term debt for column three is calculated by
multiplying the percentage displayed in column three of the cash flow assumptions section by the previous long-term debt in the second column. For United
Enterprises, the current portion of long-term debt equals $12.9 million. Third-
column long-term debt is calculated by multiplying additional long-term debt as
a percent of capital expenditures by net capital equipment and other investment,
both in the cash flow assumptions section.

In the case of United Enterprises, this equals $60 million times 40%, or $24
million in additional long-term debt. From this number, the newly calculated
current portion of long-term debt needs to be subtracted to derive $97.2 million
($86.1 million plus $24 million minus $12.9 million).

For the stock and surplus forecast, take the previous balance and add or
subtract the changes noted in the balance sheet assumptions section. For
retained earnings, add the previous year's retained earnings to net operating

profit and subtract any cash dividends; derive cash dividends by multiplying the payout ratio by net operating profit or just take the assumed fixed payout. In the case of United Enterprises, dividends are fixed at $21 million. Add the stock and retained earnings accounts to obtain the total of net worth.

Cash Flow Forecast

The cash flow statement should be completed as follows: Net operating profits are entered from the income statement forecast into the net profit after tax. Depreciation is calculated by multiplying the percentage in the cash flow assumptions section by the previous year's net plant and equipment. The total of net operating profit and depreciation equals funds (gross cash) flow from operations.

For net cash flow from operations, adjust the funds flow by the changes in the current asset and liability accounts. To calculate the net changes, first for accounts payable and accruals, subtract the cells from their preceding period values. Since increases for these are sources of funds, add them if they increase, and subtract them if they decrease. Calculate the same for the current asset accounts of cash, receivables, and inventories. Since increases in these are uses of funds, subtract these latter ones if they increase and add if they decrease. Now take the total for the cash flow from operations.

For flows of funds resulting from financing, calculate changes in long-term debt. (Be sure to include the current portion.) These are to be added as a source of funds in case of an increase and subtracted as a use of funds in the event of a decrease. Treat changes in the stock area the same way. Finally, subtract any cash dividends and other outflows. Now total for the total financial sources.

For the investment uses section, bring capital expenditures from the cash flow assumptions section to both capital expenditures and total investment uses.

Having calculated the operations, investment, and financing sections, you can derive the increased notes payable to banks by adding cash flow from operations to total financing sources and subtracting investment uses. In fact, financing this is nothing more than a "fudge factor." Now, the forecaster can complete the notes payable to banks and the total liabilities cell, and the balance sheet total footings can be corroborated.

Finally, ratios can be calculated and compared with the previous two years. Especially valuable for this analysis are the times interest earned and loan payments coverage ratios. According to this forecast, United Enterprises' times interest earned ratio is slipping as leverage increases in the face of sluggish earnings. Because of significant non-cash charges of depreciation and the carrying of more short-term debt, the term debt to funds flow ratio stays essentially even.

As previously, the notes payable to banks and capital structure should also be examined since they traditionally have had a proportional relationship to the total current liabilities and net worth, respectively.

Use the procedure above to forecast as far into the future as you wish. At each step of the way, the results can be tested by looking at the ratios and changing the assumptions.

Computerized Spreadsheet

A computer spreadsheet model facilitates any recalculations. The typical "what if" scenarios played fall back on changing around or experimenting with variations in the primary determining variables:

1. Sales forecast and growth trends
2. Adequacy of capital expenditures
3. Impact of interest rate fluctuations
4. Structuring debt layers between long- and short-term debt
5. Validity of revenue/expense relationships

The forecast also is a valuable tool for detecting major trends in the company and identifying sensitivity of cash flow to these variables. Calculate cash flow deviations using consecutive changes in the above five factors; then, graph these deviations and identify high dependence by the steepest slope in the resulting "best fit" or regression line.

Conclusion

The ability to align the expected cash flows of the firm with the structure of debt repayment is a plausible objective for an analyst attempting to determine debt repayment capacity of a firm. The typical scenario is that a firm with existing debt comes to a prospective investor with an expenditure plan relatively willing to allow the investor to stipulate the structure of the debt within limits. Occasionally the lender seizes on a lending approach without giving consideration to the available cash flow. The preferred way is to go through the cash flow analysis first, then structure the debt and its concomitant repayment schedule.

The remaining items of concern are the incorporation of risk and the preparation of the loan doccumentation including covenants, the latter of which is not covered here. Chapter 12 takes the results of this chapter and incorporates a hypothetical yet innovative method for determining and joining industry risk analysis with the projected cash flow analysis above.

Chapter 12

Industry Risk and the Iota Coefficient

How Industry Risk Impacts a Firm's Debt Repayment Capacity

The key to debt repayment capacity is forecasting the funds flow of an individual firm. While the previous chapters have looked closely at the performance of the firm's management and historic financial performance, the missing element is industry risk. The following examination of industry risk attempts to describe the risk of variability in funds flow from operations that is actually produced versus what was forecasted.

This is not to ignore the issue of funds variability caused by variables within the individual firm. Indeed, the preceding chapters have attempted to identify the funds that are repeatable, less subject to variability than other components of net income such as extraordinary earnings, which are not repeatable. Also included was an attempt to bring the firm into greater comparability with its competitors by focusing more on funds flow, adding back depreciation and other non-cash charges to net income, than on net income. Besides giving the analyst problems of interpreting accrual income accounting, this reduces comparability between firms that have bought their fixed assets at different times and the consequent different inflationary impact.

Identifying the specifics of individual managers and firms aside, all businesses engage in a complex but similar sequence of transactions. These include (1) building fixed assets, ordering raw materials, hiring labor; (2) manufacturing, or providing a service; (3) marketing, selling, and distributing; and (4) collecting the accounts receivable.

Each of these factors induces some risk into forecasting a prospective outcome. Some businesses by their nature have eliminated a number of the possible steps. For example, a finance company provides a factoring service to a manufacturer; in its own operation, it does not handle physical assets but instead concentrates its efforts only on collecting funds. The fact that the other transactions are avoided reduces riskiness in its funds flow performance; this permits the finance company to take on greater debt capital and assume greater fixed charges that have to be met from funds flow. This is tolerated because its funds flow is very dependable. Of course, this is not to say that a bad management could not take absurd risks that would create more variability within a finance company's funds flow than ever conceived of by a manufacturing firm. Understanding these matters has been the focus of the previous eleven chapters.

It appears intuitive that funds flow variability in various firms could be best understood by combining the review of previous historical results of the individual firm with an understanding of its industry. Chapter 10 addressed the issue of intra-industry comparisons. These comparisons give comfort when the various ratios and performance relationships within the subject firm are closely aligned with the better firms within its industry. It feels perfectly satisfactory when the debt to worth ratio of a firm under analysis is indeed leveraged similarly to its industry; to be a little bit more specific, if the firm is no worse in its leverage than the majority or RMA's upper quartile of the firms within its industry. There is a sense that the risks within the industry have somehow been addressed by other lenders, and therefore, these better firms have demonstrated their capability of operating given those levels of leverage.

Since firms in most industries operate in similar ways, we shall refer to the variability common to similar businesses as industry risk; and the quantification of this industry risk we shall call the **Iota** coefficient, to distinguish it as a quantification. The effort here resembles the discussion of systematic risks in the capital asset pricing model used in corporate finance, in turn used to develop such concepts as market returns and Beta coefficients. Where Beta is a useful measure of risk in the area of contemplating returns on equity investments, the purpose here is to develop parameters of risk with regard to repayment of debt. Finally, looking to forecasted funds flow for a solution to the debt repayment capacity puzzle, the evaluation of this flow of funds within the context of a specific industry and its identified risks should be examined.

Having said the above, it is still unfortunately necessary to hedge the success at distilling business risks because there are some risks that the borrower faces that are not accounted for. These are risks induced by the need to borrow additional funds, usually because of sales growth or collection problems. Growth in and of itself creates risks since it either requires that the firm's employees do more work than previously or that additional employees be hired to handle the growth. This introduces a new and difficult-to-quantify element into the risk calculations. With growth comes the problem of control over new and untested elements; it is unknown whether historical performance or industry risk assessment will fully encompass this risk.

Qualitative Business and Industry Risk

The Economy and Industry Risk

Fluctuations within the general economy can greatly increase the risk to any firm that it will not produce the expected funds flow or earnings stream or be able to convert its balance sheet assets to their current market value in a crisis. Historically, the U.S. economy was frequently swept by panics and other economic disruptions that cause most industries to suffer extremely difficult times. Today things are better and the depth and boom of the business cycle have been reduced because of:

1. The continuing increase in complexity and diversification of the economy
2. The various economic controls and safety nets installed by the federal and state governments
3. The increasing availability of knowledge to overcome business crises
4. The relative dominance of American industry by larger firms

At present, assessing the likelihood of the occurrence of a recession in a particular industry is an important fundamental for the lending industry. Assessment of macroeconomic variables may be helpful in reducing credit extension in a difficult period for an industry, but the certainty of pinpointing the beginning of the difficult period, as opposed to just realizing you are already in an industry recession, is low. Finding a relationship between a specific macroeconomic variable and a specific business or industry is difficult if not impossible at the present time. Some examples are known, including anticipating (1) trouble in the housing industry if interest rates go up and (2) trouble in transportation if fuel costs go up.

The matter has been further complicated by the impact of the international marketplace on the economy.

Oil Industry (cont.)

Consider the case of the impact on the oil exploration industry of the devastating fall in international oil prices starting in 1983 and continuing to 1990. At the present time, it would appear that exploration has only partially recovered, unlike a purely domestic recession whereby the recovery would be expected to have been fully completed by now.

The boom times of the late 1970s were an aberration for the oil industry caused by OPEC and the fall from grace is likewise beyond the domestic economy. It is interesting that the shock to this industry came after nearly ten years of uninterrupted growth. Even today, the inflation-adjusted cost of oil is less than it was in the early 1970s after the creation of OPEC.

Nevertheless, the avoidance of loan losses and consequent business failures due to future shocks to the various segments of the economy will necessitate an understating of causes surrounding the most recent complete business cycle within a given industry. It will no longer be sufficient to merely review the past ten years of economic activity in general in order to make a loan. The activities within a specific industry must be reviewed.

Production, Sale, and Delivery Knowledge

The review of specific industry risk by interviewing the prospective borrower's management is the best way for the analyst to achieve confidence that production, sale, and delivery knowledge is present within any particular firm. Principally under production issues are included such things as:

1. *The supplies for raw materials, including energy, and alternate suppliers*—Cases in the previous chapters have identified problems with being dependent on only one available source of supply. In service industries, clearly, raw materials risks include that of finding workers with adequate skills. Rapid expansion within a particular service industry can drive up salaries and make it difficult for a firm to recruit additional talent in case of a loss of a particular valuable employee.

2. *The pace of technological change*—Clearly the more rapid technological change is within a specific industry, the greater degree of risk is engaged in that industry. Nevertheless, a management that has shown itself adept at managing technological change within its production and design areas should be given credit for coping with these problems.

3. *The exposure to environmental problems and other contingencies that may create problems for the manufacturer* such as in the case of Johns-Manville—This becomes exceedingly complex when one attempts to anticipate the next interest of government in altering the nature of the industry under study. One of the foremost examples of the latter are the changes forced on the interstate trucking industry by the removal of federal governmental regulations.

The sale aspect involves, first off, understanding one's market. The market has certain specifications including the following issues:

1. *The needs of individuals or users for the product.*

2. *The identification of the user and further specification* as to whether the user is the same as the purchaser and whether or not there is an additional influencer of the sales.

3. *The understanding of the competitive environment for the need fulfillment and product user*—Included would be such problems as the threat of lower-priced imports and the aggressiveness of other competitors as well as the potential barriers to entry. The barriers to entry can be heightened by the requirement of substantial advertising in order to achieve sales. This is exemplified by the tremendous cost of distribution of a major film across the United States; multiple openings in different cities require that expensive prints be made in substantial numbers and the advertising budget is frequently equal to that of the cost of making the film.

4. *Specific sales methods and special service requirements for individual products,* which have, for example, led to toll-free help advice lines for computer shrink-wrap software programs, a factor that has made WORDPERFECT the leader in the IBM-compatible word processing market.

Here are two hasty examples of approaches to the sales intricacies: First is the study of product life cycle, the sensitivity of a particular product to technological change and other changes in demand related to style and need. Marketing executives have attempted to classify these elements in a chronological spectrum predicated on the age of the particular product. The categories include titles such as:

- *Babies*—products just introduced without competition and with high initial overhead costs

- *Stars*—products on a strong upward growth path with high margins because of entry barriers and high demand
- *Dogs*—products on a downward spiral in sales with falling margins because of competitive pressures and falling demand
- *Cows*—products nearing the end of their life cycle, but still producing substantial profits because of market-perceived value

Second, not to be outdone, economists have also defined many aspects of the product market including issues of demand elasticity and inelasticity and such concepts as the substitutability with other products and interdependence with other products. An example of the latter is the relationship between sales of bacon and eggs. Essentially, these issues focus around the extent to which the market is in a growth mode or a saturation mode. The latter indicates that growth should be undertaken with great care and will be a high risk.

5. *Disruptive concerns including the overdependence on government contracts, patent protection on new products, and issues of copyright for products with that aspect*—The latter would obviously include such issues that have recently been in the courts concerning Lotus Development Corporation's belief that its menu structure of its famous LOTUS 1-2-3 software program is subject to copyright protection. Clearly, Lotus Development Corporation believes that a monopoly on its menu structure is essential to its continued dominance in the software business.

6. *The ability to accommodate various public responsibility issues, such as nondiscrimination for race, sex, or religious affiliation*—Recently issues of permitting or not permitting women who are capable of becoming pregnant to work areas that could be genetically hazardous and the publicity backlash associated with the debate is an example of the lack of easy solutions.

7. *The sensitivity of government to economy-wide impact of specific industries, especially the oil industry, for example, opening disruptive elements such as specific price controls, taxes, or duties on an industry.*

The analyst's reviewing these elements of risk with management and identifying their strategies is essential, sine qua non, to any investor exercising due diligence. The presence of strategies does not validate a forecast. Instead, they lend a base of validity to the forecast that permits the use of the forecast as a logical reference point. The optimism and skills of management are still limited by the historical experience of the whole industry over a period of many years. Historically, the qualitative evaluation of strategies to meet the individual problems of production and sales limit but do not eliminate risk. This is much in the way that putting on a safety belt in an automobile will reduce the chance of serious injury, but certainly will not control it.

In his recent book, *Financial Statement Analysis: A Strategic Perspective* [1990, Harcourt Brace Jovanovich, San Diego, CA], Clyde P. Stickney expresses the belief that there are essentially only two strategies for a firm to choose: price or quality. The price approach focuses on low production costs in order to meet and effectively stalemate or defeat any competition that wishes to enter the field. This is particularly successful in the case of a mature product line because other firms may be entering the field in this phase of the product life cycle, having discovered the engineering aspects of the product or other aspects that enable them to manufacture the product and compete with the initial designer and producer.

The alternative strategy is to attempt to convert even a commodity-like product to one that is perceived of as unusual in the eyes of the purchaser. This can involve the quality of the product's raw materials, its design, or other characteristics. Of course, patent protection is an alternative approach to this strategy. In the event that a firm is unable to distinguish the product in any of its underlying specifications, it is still possible to distinguish itself by building a name reputation through extensive advertising.

Becoming a market leader, whether by price or quality focus, is probably the accomplishment most revered by all financial analysts. Reviewing Standard & Poor's *Credit Week* magazine during October and November 1990 identified the rationale of Standard & Poor's in considering changes in ratings. Looking at the 20-plus firms that experienced changes in ratings during those two months, the position of market leadership was viewed as positive in every case. The write-up in *Credit Week* almost seemed to apologize for not reducing these ratings further, but market leadership was clearly a significant issue. Further supporting this contention is that the ratios results for the AAA firms dropped below those for the AAs for the first time in recent memory. It is clear that the primary reason whereby the AAAs maintained their status is because the firms involved are market leaders in their fields, giving them a capability of funds flow stability that is not possible in a firm that literally is at the call of the marketplace.

Risk of Bankruptcy

A number of authors have expressed various opinions about the ability of the firm to repay its debt load. The views concerning bankruptcy of Altman and Beaver were discussed in Chapter 8; these focused around individual firm ratio examination and were only validated by firms that actually failed. Firms unable to repay their debts in accordance with schedules—even if not filing for legal bankruptcy protection—are a major concern for lenders. At the least, debenture defaults chew up valuable lender time and usually result in some compromise of the lender's interest rate or principal.

Referring to the material on trend analysis (Chapter 10), John Argenti [1976] championed the qualitative approach and focused on managerial behavior to derive applicable hypotheses. After reviewing other works in the field and engaging in personal qualitative research, he expressed his five essential risk areas as follows:

1. With shallow management depth, the management team has insufficient skills in a number of areas to properly cope with various crises. An example of this is the entrepreneur who is experienced in marketing or production but has limited finance skills. The generalization is that additional risk exists for a management team lacking one of the strategy knowledge components.

2. Another area of excessive riskiness is created by the lack of accounting controls, budgets, forecasts, and costing systems. Entrepreneurs are known to

have difficulties in quantitative expression of their ideas. This tends to result in substantial variability in the outcome of their projects.

3. The inability to respond properly to changes in competition, politics, economics, societal needs, and technological change induce substantial variability to the firm's fund flows. Concern that management may lack knowledge in any of these major areas has been previously discussed and is clearly identified as a problem area.

4. Rapid growth in sales became a favorite Argenti concern as he saw many businesses expand too rapidly. Because of their inability to predict financial changes, especially the demands of working capital to feed growth, these firms deteriorate. This was one of his favorite problems because, on the one hand, the firms seem to be on the road to success and, instead, fail almost in spite of themselves.

5. Finally, the development of a major project, something Argenti referred to as a "bet-your-company" investment, is a risk undertaking that caused many firms to fail. Unfortunately, this latter issue is difficult to assimilate into credit analysis because it is frequently the major project that lifts a small- or medium-size firm from a minor role to that of being a major power in the economy. Furthermore, many firms with an established track record are able to engage in a major project, utilizing leverage or debt as the primary source of funds for the project.

Argenti concluded his analysis by recommending that the analyst focus on sudden drops in net income. There is little question that Argenti saw management as capable of hiding minor perturbations in the growth of net income over long time periods, and therefore, he saw a sudden, undisguised break with the past trend as a great cause for concern. At the very minimum, this is not the time for engaging in a new financing. If the firm's strategy is well understood, and existing lenders believe that the firm's management can recover, then continued support may be called for with an old borrower. Finally, if growth resumes, the firm may well have evidenced a greater resilience than others that have not experienced similiar difficulties.

To summarize Argenti then, a firm on a sharp recovery is a much more interesting borrower than a firm that has recently taken a drop in earnings. Most failing firms plateau in their earnings at a reduced level for a substantial time before they free fall, although some firms plummet directly to their death. In general, if the firm's growth has stopped, then the firm is not in need of additional cash, so new lenders are not asked to participate in new loans.

Conclusion

While the knowledge about successful or inadequate strategies as discussed above is essential for debt repayment analysis, it does not validate a forecast. The results varied from the large gross profit percentage of Stickney's quality-focused firm and the high volume with the low profit percentage of his low-priced strategy firm to the sudden change in fortune of a firm's net income as identified by Argenti. In the case of the Stickney firms, this analysis may tell us to steer clear of extending credit to firms that do not meet one or the other of the strategic planning modes suggested by Stickney. Similarly, steer clear of any firm that has had a sudden drop in income, according to Argenti. Unfortunately, this may be a considerable number of firms, and the only injunction given is to avoid all of these firms. The real world question remains: *How much debt can a firm safely owe to others?* The answer to this may move the analyst from a duality mode (considering whether a borrower is simply good or bad) to a situational approach of seeing that any firm that has been in business for a number of years should probably be able to borrow some funds.

Qualitative risk analysis is absorbing, but the analyst still senses a need for identifying the riskiness of an industry by something other than these non-measurable evaluations of the strategies to meet individual problems of production and sales. Further, we wish to tie a possible quantitative evaluation of industry risk back into the funds flow concept developed in the prior chapters, the **Iota** coefficient.

Statistically Quantified Risk

This section examines the idea of risk as variability, exploring concepts of the capital asset pricing model and, then, the familiar probability distribution curves. While most people see risk as a qualitative expression for which precise forecasting is not possible, they are less aware of the quantitative possibilities.

Everyday Forecast Risk

Consider an example in which the weather forecaster quantifies the risk. The person on the street is given an inkling of risk being quantified upon hearing a weather forecast similar to "There is a 60% chance of rain today." Clearly the weather forecaster is attempting to describe a situation where there are many possibilities, given the prevailing winds, weather in nearby geographical areas, humidity, pressure, and other variabilities calculated into the weather-predicting equation. What the weather person is actually reviewing is a distribution of possible outcomes; by applying a statistical inference to this range, the weather forecaster is able to relay the percentage of likelihood that rain will occur. The person on the street may be irritated at such a forecast, wishing instead that the weather forecaster would merely relay the information about whether or not an umbrella is necessary.

This same individual probably does not realize that a medical doctor is making the same kind of decision during a medical diagnosis. The physician is not really sure what is causing the problem, but selects the most likely range of possibilities as to the central cause of the medical symptoms.

Risk and Reward

A major underlying concept in finance is that in investments *individuals are averse to the risk* of a wide range of outcomes, preferring predictable outcomes. The presence of risk means that the outcome can only be accurately forecast as a range of possibilities. To carry this a step further, the presence of a wide range of possible outcomes justifies the individual requiring that the average return or yield on that investment be of greater value than on an investment in which the range of possibilities is much narrower. Let's look at an everyday example:

Everyday Variability

Most people would consider saving a few minutes by running across a major highway against a traffic signal at 2:00 in the afternoon on a bright clear day a suitable return on the risk of being injured as a result of ignoring the traffic signal. Contrast this with similar savings to be achieved by running across the same highway at 7:30 on a rainy winter night. The decision that most people will work out is that the additional increase in possible outcomes on the dark rainy night include slipping on the road, not seeing an oncoming vehicle, not being seen by an oncoming vehicle, being struck by an oncoming vehicle driven by an intoxicated driver, and being struck by an oncoming vehicle that is unable to stop on the slick road.

These factors will cause the individual to reconsider the value of the one or two minutes gained by running against the red signal. (On the other hand, additional payoff items such as not having an umbrella and wishing to keep good clothing dry might increase the payoff sufficiently to make the risk worthwhile. Most individuals, however, in the latter case will look for a temporary shelter until the light changes.) The increase in the average payoff in getting across the street is insufficient to warrant the downside potential of being struck or falling down.

This comparison of rewards for undertaking specific risks is frequently described as the **risk reward calculation** and implies that there are methodologies to quantify uncertainty: If more risk should produce greater rewards, then we must be able to compare various risks.

Risk-Related Definitions

The theory of finance attempts to derive variability in the returns on investments of, say, U.S. treasury bills in comparison to common stocks through the **capital asset pricing model (CAPM).** This model hypothesizes an efficient market whereby any information about individual firms and the economy is received and processed by investors instantaneously; then, they are able to take action on this information by borrowing funds to suit their needs at comparable rates and without concerns of taxation. This considerably simplifies reality. Via this theory, the variability in yields obtainable from stock market investment, for example, creates a specific return, which is called the **market return.** This market return is greater than the pure return for use of money, sometimes called the **risk-free rate of return** obtainable from investing in U.S. treasury bills, which are free of default risk.

Continuing in this discussion of definitions, a **probability distribution** is a statement of the different potential outcomes together with the probability percentage of each potential outcome. It can be expressed graphically as a probability distribution curve. Additionally, the **expected return** from an invest-ment is the weighted average return; it is calculated as the sum of the all of these potential returns weighted by their percentage probability of happening. Essentially, this is the equivalent to the simple mean when all outcomes are equally likely. (Thus, the expected return, the average return, and the mean return are all interchangeable terms.) *The average does not fully describe the probability distribution, unfortunately.* This is true, surprisingly enough, even though the means of the different sets of observations relating to the two variables may be identical. Upon reflection, this should not come as a complete surprise; for example, a college classroom could have the same average age as the audience at a rock concert, although it is more likely that the age range actually observed at the rock concert would be much wider than the age range in the college classroom.

Naturally, there would preferably be some method to assess the degree of risk within any distribution of outcomes. Statisticians measure this degree of variability by calculating a measure of difference from the mean of the individual observations, called the **standard deviation.** The standard deviation is the square root of the variance, which in turn is the sum of the squared deviations from the mean.

One of the greatest mathematicians of all times, Karl Friedrich Gauss (1777–1855), discovered the method of least squares for relating variables when he was 18. The reason for squaring the deviations from the expected value rather than just summing them is that a distribution that has extremely wide variations may indicate a spurious relationship. (In most analyses one variable is being pre-dicted on the basis of another variable, which makes the first variable the dependent variable and the second variable the independent variable.)

Beta and Market Returns

Returning to the discussion of the CAPM and the returns on stocks previously mentioned, this would tell us that a stock that had wide swings in value should have a higher return. If indeed we look at a particular group of stocks and find ones that are very constant, non-variable, and have as high a return as those that are widely variable in their price, we might conclude that indeed in this group of stocks there is no identifiable relationship between different risks and different returns. This is an illogical conclusion, given the original underlying concept of finance that individuals prefer high returns in exchange for high risk.

Of course, empirical analysis has demonstrated that stocks that exhibit variability in yields (including changes in dividends and in the price of the stock) are required over the long term by investors to evidence higher average returns. We quantify the riskiness of these variable returns by squaring their deviation from the mean of returns expected from all market stocks, severely penalizing these non-conforming observations, and identify a degree of risk that is a bigger standard deviation.

Finally, while we may measure the standard deviation of a series of observations (for example, the various prices and returns of a group of stocks over time), we need an additional calculation in order to allow us to *readily compare* the information between groups of variables or groups of firms, similar to common-size analysis on a spreadsheet. The calculation, therefore, of the **coefficient of variation** assists in this project. It is the ratio of the standard deviation of returns to the expected value. In other words, it gives the percentage from the mean of the standard deviation.

Empirically and graphically demonstrating this discussion is Exhibit 12-1, showing the relationship between average returns on a long-term basis and the standard deviation of those returns on a long-term basis. The Financial Analysts Research Foundation showed the interrelationship between the extremely high expected returns to be achieved on small stocks and the very wide standard deviation. This contrasts with the low mean rate of returns of U.S. treasury bills and a standard deviation that is also very narrow and tight. If we were to calculate the coefficient of variation in these cases, the coefficient for the small stocks would by 37.3/12.1, or approximately 300%. On the other hand, the U.S. treasury bills would only be approximately 100%. This exemplifies why banks are willing to finance the purchase of U.S. treasury bills on a relatively high percentage of the bills' current market value. On the other hand, financing small stocks would be viewed as an extremely risky proposition.

The distributions for small stocks are flat in comparison to the peaked curve demonstrated by U.S. treasury bills. The latter observed returns are all close to the mean, showing little variation and, thus, little risk. The standard deviation is an extremely interesting and good measure of the extent of variability of returns, as herein graphically validated.

The second principle demonstrated in these drawings is that a considerable amount of time must be taken into account in order to achieve the various mean returns. Diversification of investment is another alternative to maintaining an equilibrium in any specific portfolio. While the statistical patterns may indicate

Exhibit 12-1.

Historical Relationship Between Risk and Return

Statistical distribution parameters of investment total annual returns, 1926-1981

Series	Mean Returns	Standard Deviation (%)	Distribution
Common Stocks	9.1	21.9	
Small Stocks	12.1	37.3	
Long-term Corporate Bonds	3.6	5.6	
Long-term Government Bonds	3.0	5.7	
U.S. Treasury Bills	3.0	3.1	
Inflation	3.0	5.1	

- 0 +

Source: R. Ibbotson and R.A. Sinquefield, *Stocks, Bonds, Bills and Inflation*: "The Past and the Future" (Charlottesville, Va.: Financial Analysts Research Foundation, 1982).

long-range outcomes, they do not necessarily give us a clear indication of what will be happening on any specific day. This is especially true with regard to small stock investments.

Again, returning to the capital asset pricing model and risk of the market-place, these illustrations specifically identify the quantity of market risk. Market return is yield in exchange for the risk quantified by the indicated variability of the common stock portfolio listed at the top of Exhibit 12-1. The risk-free rate of return is the lower mean yield shown at the bottom, that of U.S. treasury bills.

The difference in risk between the yield required in the market for common stocks and that required in the market for U.S. treasury bills is the **market premium.** Thus, the capital asset pricing model quantifies this variability and calls it **systematic risk.** This is the risk that cannot be diversified against (by buying lots of different stocks) because it is inherent in all market portfolios. In contrast, the remaining risk—**unsystematic** or **individual firm risk**—is related to the issues investigated in the first section of this chapter, that of industry risk, and in its even more refined state, the risk induced by individual manage-ment strategies, the investigation of the first 11 chapters. Coupled with this latter idea is that finance specifically recognizes the extent of financial leverage as one of the elements of individual firm risk, the management-determined capital structure.

Beta is the conventional name given to identify quantified market variabil-ity, the market premium. (There are several different methods of calculating Beta.) In examining the riskiness of individual stocks, the **Beta coefficient** may be employed. This is a multiple of Beta derived by correlating the variability of a particular asset or stock to the variability of the market. Higher variability than the market means higher coefficients and vice versa. It is possible to also develop industry Beta coefficients that permit calculation of the required returns, the quantification of the riskiness of these investments, above that of the market.

There are many applications of quantified risk analysis. In formal financial capital budgeting analyses, for instance, CAPM says that the individual project's Beta must be determined for evaluation of risk, distinct from the weighted average cost of capital of the whole firm. The methodology here is to (1) identify a firm that typifies a project's assets; (2) determine its equity Beta; and (3) compensate for the risk associated with financial leverage within the identified base firm or industry by dividing the equity Beta by the quantity of one plus the ratio of debt to equity times one minus the tax rate.

An example of this theory not being applied with predictably dolorous results was demonstrated by the Quaker Oats Company, a relatively conserva-tive firm engaged in business over the past 50 years. (Even its round packaging exhibits its conservative and historic throwback nature.) When it analyzed the returns possible from a fast food restaurant chain by the name of Magic Pan, a crepe chain, the calculated returns looked like a purchase would make an excellent investment. Nevertheless, the riskiness of operating a fast food restau-rant chain, especially in comparison with rolling oats flat, is great. Magic Pan should have been evaluated against other fast food restaurants. This riskiness of course was compounded by lack of knowledge, as discussed in the first part of this chapter, and understanding on the part of Quaker Oats' management for dealing with problems in Magic Pan. Eventually Magic Pan was spun off.

Maintaining Variability

While capital budgeting is somewhat removed from the study of debt repayment capacity, nevertheless it indicates the typical desire of analysts for a simple go–no go quantification method in decision making. Naturally, this is similar to the conflict of:

1. Going to the effort of projecting fund flows and then considering how they might evolve into *best and worst cases,* an attempt to identify the range of possible outcomes

   versus
2. Just calculating simple current and debt to worth ratios and *matching that to a predetermined guideline* considered to be foolproof, such as 2 to 1 and 1 to 1, respectively

While the latter alternative appears much safer and is actually similar to investing only in U.S. treasury bonds, those with more sophisticated analyses will be able to achieve higher returns by devising means of dealing with variability in these returns. Reviewing probability distributions through both means and standard deviations allows profound understanding of risk and leads to better decisions about that risk. Those preferring the former approach may be trying to hold to unrealistically high standards while losing business.

> **Key Points:** Even with its unfortunate complexity, in order to achieve a more realistic forecast of the future, the analyst must discover and present the variability that may be discovered.

Probability Distribution Curves

The above conclusion forces the examination of additional statistical concepts. Most executives pale at the thought of looking at probability distribution curves, but it is imperative to address two important issues:

1. The extremely high likelihood that any distribution that occurs in human affairs is likely to be shaped as a normal distribution
2. The development of confidence limits that allow decision makers to make yes or no decisions, still retaining greater insight into matching (a) risk-taking inclinations with (b) risks of any particular investment as well as (c) returns to the risks that are undertaken

An example of the absence of the latter in current practice is the extremely close ranges of lending rates charged by most lending institutions over the expanse of customers, from risky to stable. Rates offered to most customers fluctuate within a percentage point of prime, whereas, even looking at Exhibit 12-1, the difference in yields between common stocks and small stocks is a factor of 30%. If lenders can attach themselves to this broader understanding of risk and returns, they may be able to make wiser choices for the individual financial institutions and the individual firms.

Within any specific industry, the risks of increasing leverage substantially may create unacceptable outcomes with such a high degree of probability that the plan should be changed. In other industries, leverage should be encouraged as a way of maximizing stockholder wealth. In the broader economic context of course, it appears that lenders control more capital than equity investors; therefore, debt capital should be used to finance industries that can absorb the additional risk of debt, conserving the limited equity capital for the relatively new and riskier situations, which have the greater likelihood of raising our standard of living.

There appears to be a bell-shaped or stepped-tower pattern evident in the discrete observations of long-term corporate bonds, long-term government bonds, and U.S. treasury bills. The distributions of outcomes and their related number of occurrences with regard to common stocks and small stocks are less easily characterized. While it is extremely difficult to create a mathematical formula that presents a curve shaped similar to that exhibited by a small stock distribution of observations, it is still true that the graphic interpretation of the mathematical form will relate variability to the wider and lower curves. The higher variability exhibited by the stocks also means that the standard deviation will be larger.

In an attempt to more closely identify the ranges of various types of distributions, Karl Gauss also discovered the mathematical formula that describes the so-called **normal distribution.** It describes the range of outcomes most frequently produced by biologically based activities. It is typically shown in the shape of a bell, where most of the measured activities are close to the mean or average; in a few cases they deviate more, and in some rare cases the measured values will be very different from the mean. In fact, in the mathematical description, the tails of the curve never actually touch the horizontal plane. It is reported that empirical studies have shown that humans appear to be very good estimators of a single standard deviation from the mean of a normal distribution. They describe it as a range beyond which they would be mildly surprised if it occurred.

The normal distribution produces the following sets of probabilities:

Standard Deviation	Percentage of Events Within (Around the Mean) Confidence Limits
1	68.26%
2	95.46%
3	99.74%

The normal distributions appears to offer insights no matter how squat the curve appears. Consider even the case of extremely wide distributions, for example, in the case of the small stocks. By multiplying the 37.3% times 3 to include 3 standard deviations, the result includes the farthest observation to the right of the mean, since the total would be approximately 124 to the right of the 0 point. (This is 111.9 plus the 12.1 mean.) Comparing the common stock alternative, 3 times 22 plus the mean of 9.1 equals 75.1 to the right of the 0 point. The vast majority of observations are included within 3 standard deviations of the mean. Thus, while the observations may not conclusively indicate a precise normal curve shape, the rules of normal distributions with regard to the standard deviations and the percentages of occurrences they embrace may be extremely valuable for quantification purposes.

Combining Probabilities With Useful Risk Judgments

Besides these double-tailed calculations, analysts frequently are interested in only one of the probability distribution curve's tails. Naturally this increases the confidence in describing the single-tailed outcomes given a single standard devation from the mean.

Debt Repayment Capacity—I

Managers might be interested in determining within certain confidence limits— an interchangeable term with the percentages encompassed by the various standard deviations—the chance of the *funds flow falling below a certain level*. For example, perhaps the need to comply with debt repayment commitments would require a minimum funds flow.

With concern only for answers in one tail (the down side), the confidence limits become more encompassing per standard deviation, since the entire upper-side distribution above the mean is of no worry. Therefore, Exhibit 12-2

Exhibit 12-2.

NORMAL PROBABILITY DISTRIBUTION TABLE

Number of Standard Deviations from the Mean	Chance of a result less than those included (One Tail)	Number of Standard Deviations from the Mean	Chance of a result less than those included (One Tail)	Number of Standard Deviations from the Mean	Chance of a result less than those included (One Tail)
0.10	46.02%	1.10	13.57%	2.10	1.79%
0.20	42.07%	1.20	11.51%	2.20	1.39%
0.30	38.21%	1.30	9.68%	2.30	1.07%
0.40	34.46%	1.40	8.08%	2.40	0.82%
0.50	30.85%	1.50	6.68%	2.50	0.62%
0.60	27.43%	1.60	5.48%	2.60	0.47%
0.70	24.21%	1.70	4.46%	2.70	0.35%
0.80	21.19%	1.80	3.59%	2.80	0.26%
0.90	18.41%	1.90	2.87%	2.90	0.19%
1.00	15.77%	2.00	2.28%	3.00	0.13%

is provided for the percentages remaining in a single tail, given various numbers of standard deviations from the mean. It can be seen that for a single standard deviation all of the possible events have been incorporated shy of only 15.77% of the total possibilities. Thus, *if the analyst has determined the value of a standard deviation of a series of observations and the average of those observations, he could conclude that with confidence limits of 84.33% (1 − .1577) any new observation will be above an amount equal to the mean less the value of that single standard deviation.* For those who are extremely risk averse, two standard deviations would include 97.72% of all the possibilities, and so on.

Debt Repayment Capacity—II

Let's continue with and apply this conclusion to the above example. Assume the analyst possesses a series of observations (at least as long as a business cycle) of the firm or industry's fund flows and has determined their standard deviation. He can express within specific confidence limits (probability) that future various funds flow outcomes will exceed a hypothetical danger point: *when funds flow cannot meet debt repayments or fixed charges.*

With the danger point known, its relationship to the standard deviation value can be calculated to produce a multiple of the standard deviation value below the mean. Then the confidence interval can be determined—that is, the likelihood of the firm's fund flows being too low.

Conversely, if a certain confidence interval is desired, based on the aversion to risk of the lender or firm, an 84.33% confidence limit, for example, would include all flows above the mean less one standard deviation.

Naturally, thinking back to Exhibit 12-1 and the many hundreds of observations available to the researchers in those calculations, the analyst may be concerned about applying the observations to a specific series of data for which there may be very few discrete observations. This can be a serious problem, and in sets of observations less than 20, the so-called "population" standard deviation calculation should not be used but instead a "sample" standard deviation, which corrects for the fact that there are so few observations that they may not be sufficiently descriptive of the overall normal curve and the interrelation of the standard deviations to confidence limits. To calculate the sample standard deviation, take the standard deviation and multiply it times the square root of the quotient of the total number of entries divided by the sum of the total number of entries minus one. This enlarges the standard deviation to permit smaller samples.

Another tool is available, sometimes called Student's "t" distribution.* Exhibit 12-3 is a table somewhat comparable to Exhibit 12-2, except that it contains the additional variable of the number of observations.

Student's "t" Distribution Table

To make an example to use this table, assume that the lender wishes to achieve 90% assurance that fixed charges will be capable of being covered, but that

*William S. Gosset, the actuary who derived this distribution, worked for the Guinness Brewery in Dublin and was required to use a pseudonym ("Student") when publishing.

there are only 10 previous observations. Now, move across the column listings to 10 and down the column to the number nearest 10%. The answer is that the funds flow would remain above 1.4 standard deviations below the mean 90% of the time.

Iota Coefficient

This section develops the Iota coefficient as a methodology for increasing the analyst's understanding of the reliability of any firm's funds flow forecast. It discusses the concept of identifying the variability of specific industry funds flow from year to year. By evaluating the variations in the funds flow in particular industries, you may exploit the various industry risks identified in the first section of this chapter in a quantitative way to the forecasted funds flow of any given firm.

Need for Historical Data

Thinking back over the contents of this book, indeed, statistical data have already been identified that may be serviceable as industry data over time. Chapter 10 in reviewing intra-industry firms looked into the Robert Morris statistics. Taking the variations of funds flow items over a period long enough to include a full business cycle within that industry, it is possible to derive the standard deviation of these funds flow variables. Further, it is a simple matter to generate a coefficient of variation for each industry that, in turn, would allow, given a specified confidence interval, calculation of the possible shortfall from the expected funds flow forecast produced by the analyst using the forecasting techniques in Chapter 11.

This could reasonably describe the possible outcomes of a subject firm's funds flow, anticipating that industries that have a relatively risky reputation would, indeed, have a relatively higher coefficient of variation than industries that have a stable reputation. While examining several industries in this section, recognize that further research clearly needs to be undertaken to assess whether calculations made using older historical data are indeed capable of being verified using current outcomes.

Determining the Iota Coefficient

This section determines the Iota coefficient for two industries using Robert Morris data as industry input. There is a problem identifying the funds flow numbers within the data sheet and finding a comparable alternative in the firm under study. For example, with the individual firm, the taxes the firm pays are an expense that is deducted before the calculation of funds flow. Of course, the change in the deferred tax account is added back into the generation of the funds flow, so that only the actual taxes paid are taken into account. This level of detail is unfortunately unavailable in the Robert Morris statistics since the income statistics end before taxes are considered; therefore, in order to generate the funds flow calculations, the only option is that taxes are ignored. Whether

(Text continued on page 312.)

Exhibit 12-3.

Student's "t" Distribution

Number of Standard Deviations from the Mean	Given a small sample, the following table predicts the chance that a result less than those included may occur. (One Tail)					
	The number of observations					
	2	3	4	5	6	7
	Probability of an outcome less than those identified (One Tail)					
0.1		46.43%	46.00%	45.97%	45.94%	45.93%
0.2	43.74%	43.03%	43.30%	43.13%	43.01%	42.94%
0.3	40.75%	39.63%	40.61%	40.28%	40.08%	39.95%
0.4	37.97%	36.62%	37.91%	37.44%	37.15%	36.95%
0.5	35.00%	33.57%	35.22%	34.60%	34.22%	33.96%
0.6	32.93%	30.52%	32.52%	31.76%	31.29%	30.97%
0.7	30.62%	28.13%	29.82%	28.92%	28.36%	27.98%
0.8	28.66%	25.88%	27.13%	26.08%	25.43%	24.99%
0.9	26.83%	23.63%	24.43%	23.24%	22.50%	22.00%
1.0	25.00%	21.37%	20.89%	20.40%	19.57%	19.01%
1.1	23.67%	19.53%	18.86%	18.20%	17.53%	17.06%
1.2	22.34%	18.32%	17.31%	16.31%	15.53%	14.99%
1.3	21.01%	17.10%	15.76%	14.41%	13.52%	12.91%
1.4	19.80%	15.89%	14.20%	12.52%	11.52%	10.83%
1.5	18.94%	14.68%	12.65%	10.63%	9.52%	8.75%
1.6	18.09%	13.47%	11.48%	9.50%	8.85%	8.41%
1.7	17.24%	12.25%	10.50%	8.75%	7.92%	7.42%
1.8	16.39%	11.04%	8.77%	6.50%	5.64%	5.48%
1.9	15.54%	9.83%	7.70%	5.57%	5.34%	5.14%
2.0	14.83%	9.44%	7.39%	5.33%	5.04%	4.81%
2.1	14.39%	8.96%	7.02%	5.08%	4.75%	4.48%
2.2	13.94%	8.47%	6.65%	4.83%	4.45%	4.14%
2.3	13.49%	7.98%	6.78%	4.58%	4.16%	3.81%
2.4	13.04%	7.49%	6.30%	4.34%	3.86%	3.48%
2.5	12.59%	7.00%	5.81%	4.09%	3.56%	3.14%
2.6	12.14%	6.51%	5.33%	3.84%	3.27%	2.81%
2.7	11.70%	6.03%	4.84%	3.59%	2.97%	2.48%
2.8	11.25%	5.54%	4.36%	3.35%	2.67%	2.14%
2.9	10.80%	5.05%	3.87%	3.10%	2.38%	1.81%
3.0	10.35%	4.56%	3.38%	2.85%	2.08%	1.58%

Number of Standard Deviations from the Mean	Given a small sample, the following table predicts the chance that a result less than those included may occur. (One Tail)					
	The number of observations					
	8	9	10	11	12	13
	Probability of an outcome less than those identified (One Tail)					
0.1	45.91%	45.92%	45.90%	45.90%	45.90%	45.90%
0.2	42.88%	42.85%	42.81%	42.79%	42.78%	42.78%
0.3	39.84%	39.79%	39.72%	39.68%	39.65%	39.63%
0.4	36.81%	36.72%	36.63%	36.57%	36.52%	36.47%
0.5	33.78%	33.65%	33.54%	33.45%	33.39%	33.29%
0.6	30.74%	30.58%	30.45%	30.34%	30.27%	30.21%
0.7	27.71%	27.52%	27.36%	27.23%	27.14%	27.05%
0.8	24.68%	24.45%	24.27%	24.12%	24.01%	23.91%
0.9	21.64%	21.38%	21.18%	21.01%	20.88%	19.72%
1.0	18.61%	18.31%	18.09%	17.89%	17.75%	17.14%
1.1	16.71%	16.45%	15.69%	14.92%	14.62%	14.56%
1.2	14.58%	14.28%	14.05%	13.82%	13.74%	13.33%
1.3	12.45%	12.11%	11.81%	11.48%	11.15%	10.66%
1.4	10.32%	9.93%	9.75%	9.68%	9.58%	9.48%
1.5	8.19%	7.76%	7.46%	7.26%	2.58%	8.31%
1.6	8.07%	7.81%	7.59%	7.41%	7.26%	7.14%
1.7	7.03%	6.73%	6.48%	6.27%	6.11%	5.96%
1.8	5.34%	5.23%	5.14%	5.05%	4.95%	4.79%
1.9	4.98%	4.85%	4.74%	4.50%	4.35%	4.26%
2.0	4.62%	4.46%	4.03%	3.88%	3.74%	3.63%
2.1	4.26%	4.07%	3.88%	3.50%	3.12%	3.00%
2.2	3.89%	3.69%	2.86%	2.68%	2.51%	2.37%
2.3	3.53%	2.98%	2.28%	2.25%	2.21%	2.14%
2.4	3.17%	2.69%	2.22%	2.07%	1.92%	1.84%
2.5	2.81%	2.41%	2.02%	1.83%	1.63%	1.54%
2.6	2.44%	2.13%	1.82%	1.58%	1.34%	1.24%
2.7	2.08%	1.85%	1.61%	1.33%	1.05%	0.97%
2.8	1.72%	1.56%	1.36%	1.15%	0.89%	0.84%
2.9	1.55%	1.28%	1.13%	0.99%	0.77%	0.71%
3.0	1.39%	1.20%	1.01%	0.82%	0.64%	0.57%

this eliminates the problem of the provision for tax numbers on the income statement being unrelated to the actual taxes paid is not known.

1. Thus, to begin the compilation of the funds flow concept, choose the value under the operating profits caption on the Robert Morris sheet (Exhibit 10-2). This gives the first major component, free from non-recurring items and the tax problems just mentioned as a percentage of sales.

2. Now, add to that the value for depreciation, depletion, and amortization (as a percentage of sales) to achieve a relatively close approximation to the funds flow, keynoted above as the principal identifier of debt repayment capacity.

Exhibit 12-4 shows the funds flow variations in the women's dress industry (Standard Industrial Code (SIC) #2335) over a full business cycle, 1978 to 1987, presented as enumerated above. This particular industry is well known to be relatively high in risk. Therefore, a relatively high coefficient of variation is expected. Continue to calculate as follows:

Exhibit 12-4.

Analysis of Funds Flow Variations in the Women's Dresses
Manufacturing Industry

COLUMN:

1	2	3	4	5	6	7
	Operating Profit as a % of Sales	Depreciation & Other as a % of Sales	Funds Flow as % of Sales (1 + 2)	Calculation of Standard Deviation		
Year				Average of Column 4	Deviation (Column 4 - Column 5)	Variance (Column 6 Squared)
1978	3.6	0.6	4.2	5.18	-0.98	0.9604
1979	3.7	0.5	4.2	5.18	-0.98	0.9604
1980	4.8	0.8	5.6	5.18	0.42	0.1764
1981	3.9	0.6	4.5	5.18	-0.68	0.4624
1982	5.9	0.6	6.5	5.18	1.32	1.7424
1983	5.3	0.8	6.1	5.18	0.92	0.8464
1984	7.2	0.7	7.9	5.18	2.72	7.3984
1985	3.5	0.8	4.3	5.18	-0.88	0.7744
1986	3	0.6	3.6	5.18	-1.58	2.4964
1987	4.2	0.7	4.9	5.18	-0.28	0.0784
	TOTAL		51.8		Variance	1.5896

FORMULAS:
(1) Expected Value (Average): Total Col. 4 / Number Entries In Col. 4 | 5.1800 |
(2) Standard Deviation: Square Root Of Weighted Ave. Variance (Col. 7) | 1.2608 |
(3) Sample Standard Deviation (Corrects For Small Samples)
      Multiply the standard deviation times the square root of the quotient of the
      total number of entries divided by the sum of the total entries minus one. | 1.3290 |
(4) Coefficient of Variation: IOTA factor | 0.2566 |
      Sample Standard Deviation / Expected Value

Funds Flow to Current Portion Long-term Debt   3.6
Debt to Worth   1.3

1. Calculate the expected value or average of all of the funds flow yearly observations. This equals 5.18%, shown in column 5.
2. Subtract the expected value from each funds flow observation to find the individual differences (Subtract column 5 from column 4 and place the results in column 6).
3. Determine the variance by first squaring the differences found in column 6 and then weighting them according to their likelihood of occurrence. In this case each is assumed to be equally likely, so they are merely averaged to equal the variance at the bottom of column 7 of 1.59. As an aside, if there have been unusual years, unrelated to the business cycle, you may wish to give some of the funds flows more weight than others.
4. Calculate the standard deviation by taking the square root of the variance to equal 1.26.
5. Calculate the sample standard deviation, correcting for small samples by multiplying the standard deviation by the square root of the total number of entries divided by the sum of the total entries minus 1 for 1.329.
6. Finally, calculate the coefficient of variation of the sample standard deviation, by dividing the sample standard deviation by the mean for 25.66% Now, considering only the lower tail is a problem, divide the result by 2 for 12.83%.

Applying the very high women's dress manufacturing industry Iota coefficient of 25.66% will sharply affect the high confidence interval cash flow availability. Assume that the analyst is reviewing the funds flow forecast of a particular women's dress manufacturer, given that their forecast had already been evaluated from the point of view of reliability of their own data. Now, some confidence interval needs to be agreed upon to take into account the various aspects of the riskiness of the industry and its possible impact on the forecasted funds flows, especially on the down side. Consider, for the sake of the example, that in view of the firm's depth of management and position in the market only one standard deviation would be satisfactory in validating the funds flow forecast. This means, using Exhibit 12-3, that we could be approximately 81.91% sure of incorporating the possible variations of one tail with a sample of ten observations. Thus, only 87.17% of the analyst-forecasted funds flow might be present in any one year for debt repayment. (This is 100% less the 12.83%.) Test this result against the firm's fixed charges at the present time. If the forecasted funds flow reduced by 12.83% is still sufficient to meet fixed charge coverage, then more debt capacity is exhibited.

Assuming that the lender wishes to be more sure of anticipating all the possible events, then a higher confidence limit must be chosen. Going back to Exhibit 12-3, picking three standard deviations will make us 99% sure (with ten observations) that all possibilities have been met. Now multiply three times 12.83% to find that required debt repayment of the individual firm must be held to less than 61.51% of the analyst forecasted funds flow (100% less 38.49%) if the lender wishes to be 99% sure of repayment.

Another element is that the type of financing naturally will affect the debt repayment requirements; for example, the firm that is arranging a thirty-year mortgage that will be able to satisfy the fixed charge coverage ratio with much less funds flow. Contrast this with a firm agreeing to repay all its term debt on a two-year basis.

The above demonstration might be contrasted with the analysis of the funds flow variations in the long-distance trucking industry, as shown in Exhibit 12-5. Here we see that the result of the coefficient of variation is only 7.00%. (Recall that this time period even includes the infamous deregulation of the long-distance trucking industry.) Here, being 99% sure would only eliminate 10.50% of the previously estimated firm's funds flow from availability for debt repayment.

Exhibit 12-6 shows a worksheet for making the above calculations on other industries of the analyst's choice. A bottom section has been added to simplify the second step of calculating the funds flow given different confidence intervals.

Preliminary Validation of the Iota Coefficient

A possible area of research is the comparison of the Iota coefficient with existing popular ratios; this assumes the efficient market hypothesis that if the industry

Exhibit 12-5.

Analysis of Funds Flow Variations in the Long-distance Trucking
Industry

COLUMN:

1	2	3	4	5	6	7
	Operating Profit as a % of Sales	Depreciation & Other as a % of Sales	Funds Flow as % of Sales (1 + 2)	Calculation of Standard Deviation		
Year				Average of Column 4	Deviation (Column 4 - Column 5)	Variance (Column 6 Squared)
1978	5.5	4	9.5	9.65	-0.15	0.0225
1979	5.9	4.5	10.4	9.65	0.75	0.5625
1980	5.3	4.7	10	9.65	0.35	0.1225
1981	4.8	4.8	9.6	9.65	-0.05	0.0025
1982	5.6	4.6	10.2	9.65	0.55	0.3025
1983	3.5	4.6	8.1	9.65	-1.55	2.4025
1984	4.2	4.8	9	9.65	-0.65	0.4225
1985	5.2	4.7	9.9	9.65	0.25	0.0625
1986	4.7	5	9.7	9.65	0.05	0.0025
1987	4.9	5.2	10.1	9.65	0.45	0.2025
	TOTAL		96.5		Variance	4.105

FORMULAS:

(1) Expected Value (Average): Total Col. 4 / Number Entries In Col. 4   9.6500

(2) Standard Deviation: Square Root Of Weighted Ave. Variance (Col. 7)   0.6407

(3) Sample Standard Deviation (Corrects For Small Samples)
  Multiply the standard deviation times the square root of the quotient of the
  total number of entries divided by the sum of the total entries minus one.   0.6754

(4) Coefficient of Variation: IOTA factor   0.0700
  Sample Standard Deviation / Expected Value

Funds Flow to Current Portion Long-term Debt   **1.6**
Debt to Worth   **2.2**

Exhibit 12-6.

INDUSTRY RISK ANALYSIS AND FUNDS FLOW FORECASTING

INDUSTRY: _____   SIC #: _____

SUBJECT FIRM: _____

STEP ONE: DETERMINE THE SAMPLE COEFFICIENT OF VARIATION OF THE INDUSTRY						
COLUMN:						
1	2	3	4	5	6	7
	Operating Profit as a % of Sales	Depreciation & Other as a % of Sales	Funds Flow as % of Sales (1 + 2)	Calculation of Standard Deviation		
Year				Average of Column 4	Deviation (Column 4 - Column 5)	Variance (Column 6 Squared)
19						
19						
19						
19						
19						
19						
19						
19						
19						
19						
		TOTAL	☐		VARIANCE	☐

FORMULAS:
(1) Expected Value (Average): Total Col. 4 / Number Entries In Col. 4   ☐
(2) Standard Deviation: Square Root Of Weighted Ave. Variance (Col. 7)   ☐
(4) Sample Standard Deviation (Corrects For Small Samples)
    Multiply the standard deviation times the square root of the quotient of the
    total number of entries divided by the sum of the total entries minus one.   ☐
(3) Coefficient of Variation: Sample Standard Deviation / Expected Value   ☐
(This is the percentage variability for each standard deviation from the mean)   **IOTA factor**
    NOTE: There may have been unusual years, and you may wish
    to weigh some of the cash flows more heavily than others.

STEP TWO: CALCULATE THE FIRM'S ESTIMATED FUNDS FLOW AND REEVALUATE BASED ON INDUSTRY COEFFICIENT OF VARIATION				
Column:				
1	2	3	4	5
Subject Firm's Estimated Funds Flow	Coefficient of Variation Multiplier	Confidence Interval (Approx.)	Subject Firm's Probable Funds Flow Range	
			High Column 1 + Column 2*1	Low Column 1 - Column 2*1
	0.67	75.0%		
	0.84	80.0%		
	1.04	85.0%		
	1.14	87.5%		
	1.28	90.0%		
	1.44	92.5%		
	1.64	95.0%		
	1.92	97.5%		

has been supplied with the correct amount of credit, given its level of riskiness, we should be able to find that the debt to worth is lower in the women's dress manufacturing industry than in the long-distance trucking industry, where the variability is less. Below, this hypothesis can be seen as true along with the average of 1981–1987 ratios of earnings coverage of interest expense and funds flow to current portion of long-term debt, both significantly higher in the dress manufacturing business than in the long-distance trucking industry. Obviously the debt to worth ratio is much lower in the women's dress manufacturing industry.

SIC#	Coefficient of Variation	EBIT to Interest	Cash Flow to CPLTD	Debt to Worth
2335	25.66%	3.52	3.6	1.3
4213	7.00%	2.24	1.6	2.2

Clearly, lenders have identified the riskiness inherent in the two different industries. It is relatively easy to see that the funds flow provided principally by depreciation not only builds the total gross cash flow of the trucking industry but also helps maintain its even values, so that the variability of gross cash flow is significantly less than that of operating profit by itself.

Conclusion

Whether or not the Iota coefficient will be countenanced by additional research is still an issue. Nevertheless, it has become increasingly important that analysts be able to quantify their risks and there are few alternatives available at this time. Even if the Iota coefficient achieves a prominent place in analytical guides of the future, it should be only the first in many statistical applications to assist the financial analyst. It may stimulate others to attempt to quantify risks and show that industry statistical information can satisfy this need.

Bibliography

Altman, E. I. *Corporate Financial Distress.* New York: Wiley, 1983.

———. *Corporate Bankruptcy in America.* Lexington, Mass.: D. C. Heath, 1971.

Altman, E. I., R. G. Haldeman, and P. Narayanan. "Zeta Analysis: A New Model to Identify Bankruptcy Risk of Corporations." *Journal of Banking and Finance.* June 1977, pp. 29–54.

Argenti, J. "Company Failure." *Accountancy.* August 1977, pp. 46–52.

———. *Corporate Collapse.* Maidenhead, United Kingdom: McGraw-Hill, 1976.

Bailey, Herbert S., Jr. "Quoth the Banker, 'Watch Cash Flow.'" *Publishers Weekly.* January 13, 1975, p. 34.

Bartley, J. W., and C. M. Bordman. "The Replacement Cost Adjusted Valuation Ratio as a Discriminator Among Takeover Target and Nontarget Firms." Unpublished paper. Salt Lake City, Utah: University of Utah, 1984.

Beaver, William H. "Current Trends in Corporate Disclosure." *Journal of Accountancy.* January 1978.

———. "Financial Ratios as Predictors of Failure." *Journal of Accounting Research.* January 1967, pp. 71–111.

Belkaoui, A. *Industrial Bonds and the Rating Process.* Westport, Conn.: Quorum Books, 1983.

Belongia, Michael T., and R. Alton Gilbert. "Agricultural Banks: Causes of Failures . . ." *Federal Reserve Bank of St. Louis Review.* May 1987, pp. 30–37.

Bernstein, Leopold A. *Analysis of Financial Statements.* Homewood, Ill.: Richard D. Irwin, Inc., 1990.

Bernstein, Leopold A., and Joel G. Siegel. "The Concept of Earnings Quality." *Financial Analysts Journal.* July–August 1979.

Bibeault, D. *Corporate Turnaround.* New York: McGraw-Hill, 1981.

Carraro, Kenneth C. "The 1987 Agricultural Recovery: A District Perspective." *Federal Reserve Bank of St. Louis Review.* March/April 1988.

Chang, L. S., K. SD. Most, and C. W. Brian. "The Utility of Annual Reports." *Journal of International Business Studies.* Spring/Summer 1983, pp. 63–84.

Coggin, T. D., and J. E. Hunter. "Analysts EPS Forecasts Nearer Actual Than Statistical Models." *The Journal of Business Forecasting.* Winter 1982–1983, pp. 20–23.

Collins, W. A., and W. S. Hopwood. "A Multivariate Analysis of Annual Earnings Forecasts Generated From Quarterly Forecasts of Financial Analysts and Univariate Time-Series Models." *Journal of Accounting Research.* Autumn 1980, pp. 390–406.

Copeland, R. M., and M. L. Moore. "The Financial Bath: Is It Common?" *MSU Business Topics.* Autumn 1972, pp. 63–69.

Danker, Deborah J., and Mary M. McLaughlin. "The Profitability of U.S. Chartered Insured Commercial Banks in 1986." *Federal Reserve Bulletin.* July 1987.

Dawson, James P., Peter M. Neupert, and Clyde P. Stickney. "Restating Financial Statements for Alternative GAAPs: Is It Worth the Effort?" *Financial Analysts Journal.* November–December 1980.

Deal, T. E., and A. Kennedy. *Corporate Cultures.* Reading, Mass.: Addison-Wesley, 1975.

Dieter, Richard, and Arthur R. Wyatt. "Get It Off the Balance Sheet!" *Financial Executive.* January 1980.

Duff and Phelps. *Credit Decisions.* Chicago: Duff and Phelps, March and November 1984.

————. *An Introduction to Duff and Phelps Fixed Income Rating Service.* Chicago: Duff and Phelps, September 1980.

Easman, William S., Jr., Angela Falkenstein, and Roman L. Weil. "The Correlation Between Sustainable Income and Stock Returns." *Financial Analysts Journal.* September–October 1979.

Edminster, R. O. "An Empirical Test of Financial Ratio Analysis for Small Business Failure Prediction." *Journal of Financial and Quantitative Analysis.* 7 (1972): 1477–1493. (Commissioned by the SBA.)

Financial Accounting Standards Board. *Statement of Financial Accounting Standards* (issued periodically). Stamford, Conn.: Financial Accounting Standards Board.

Foster, George. *Financial Statement Analysis, 2nd ed.* Englewood Cliffs, N.J.: Prentice-Hall, 1986.

Gibson, Charles H., and Patricia A. Frishkoff. *Financial Statement Analysis.* Boston, Mass.: Kent Publishing Company, 1983.

Gombola, M. J., and J. E. Ketz. "A Note on the Cash Flow and Classification Patterns of Financial Ratios." *The Accounting Review.* January 1983, pp. 105–114.

Graese, Clifford E., and Joseph R. DeMario. "Revenue Recognition for Long Term Contracts." *Journal of Accountancy.* December 1976.

Graham, B., D. L. Dodd, and S. Cottle. *Security Analysis: Principles and Techniques.* New York: McGraw-Hill, 1989.

Granof, M. H., and D. G. Short. "Why Do Companies Reject LIFO?" *Journal of Accounting, Auditing, and Finance.* Summer 1984, pp. 323–333.

Grinnell, D., Jacque and Corine T. Norgaard. "Reporting Rules for Marketable Equity Securities." *Financial Analysts Journal.* January–February 1980.

Hale, Roger H. *Credit Analysis.* New York: John Wiley & Sons, Inc., 1983.

Heath, Loyd C., and Paul Rosenfield. "Solvency: The Forgotten Half of Financial Reporting." *Journal of Accountancy.* January 1979.

Houlihan, William A., and Ashwinpaul C. Sondhi. "De Facto Capitalization of Operating Leases: The Effect on Debt Capacity." *Corporate Accounting.* Summer 1984.

Ijiri, Yuji. "Recovery Rate and Cash Flow Accounting." *Financial Executive.* March 1980.

Ingberman, Monroe, Joshua Ronen, and George H. Sorter. "How Lease Capitalization Under FASB Statement No. 13 Will Affect Financial Ratios." *Financial Analysts Journal.* January–February 1979.

Ingberman, Monroe, and George H. Sorter, "The Role of Financial Statements in an Efficient Market." *Journal of Accounting, Auditing, and Finance.* Fall 1978.

Jarnagin, Bill D. *Financial Accounting Standards.* Chicago, Ill.: Commerce Clearing House, Inc. (Published annually.)

Johnson, Sylvester, and Amelia A. Murphy. "Going Off the Balance Sheet." *Federal Reserve Bank of Atlanta Economic Review.* September/October 1987.

Keeton, William R., and Charles S. Morris. "Why Do Banks' Loan Losses Differ?" *Federal Reserve Bank of Kansas City Economic Review.* May 1987, pp. 3–21.

Kharbbanda, O. P., and E. A. Stallworthy. *Corporate Failure.* Maidenhead, United Kingdom: McGraw-Hill, 1985.

Landsittel, D. L., and J. E. Stewart. "Off-Balance-Sheet Financing: Commitments and Contingencies." *Handbook of Modern Accounting, 3rd ed.* New York: McGraw-Hill, 1983. Pages 26.1–26.24.

Largay, James A. III, and Clyde P. Stickney. "Cash Flows, Ratio Analysis, and the W. T. Grant Company Bankruptcy." *Financial Analysts Journal.* July–August 1980.

Lasman, Daniel A., and Roman L. Weil. *Financial Analysts Journal.* September–October 1978.

Leeming, Andrew, Greg Whittred, and Ian Zimmer. "Simulating Loan Reviewers' Judgements." Unpublished paper. University of New South Wales, January 1985.

Mason, John M. *Financial Management of Commercial Banks.* New York: Warren, Gorham & Lamont, 1979.

Melichar, Emanuel. "Turning the Corner on Troubled Farm Debt." *Federal Reserve Bulletin.* July 1987.

Miller, D. "Common Syndromes of Business Failure." *Business Horizons.* November 1977, pp. 43–53.

Miller, Donald E. *The Meaningful Interpretation of Financial Statements.* New York: AMACOM, 1972.

Modigliani, Franco, and Merton H. Miller. "The Cost of Capital, Corporation Finance, and the Theory of Investment." *American Economic Review.* June 1958.

Nash, Nathaniel C. "Who to Thank for the Thrift Crisis." *New York Times.* June 12, 1988, section 3, p. 1.

Norby, William C. "Accounting for Financial Analysis." *Financial Analysts Journal.* January–February 1980.

Page, John R., and Paul Hooper. "Financial Statement Analysis for Security Analysis." *Financial Analysts Journal.* September–October 1979.

Pantalone, Coleen C., and Marjorie B. Platt. "Predicting Commercial Bank Failure Since Deregulation." *New England Economic Review.* July/August 1987, pp. 37–47.

Perry, T., and J. Searfoss. "Eleven Companies' Approach to Changing Prices as of December 31, 1981." Memorandum to Financial Accounting Standards Board. Touche Ross, 1982.

Peters, T. J., and R. H. Waterman. *In Search of Excellence.* New York: Harper & Row, 1982.

Ponting, John T., and George R. Sanderson. "Profitable Loans, Risk, and the Loan Officer." *The Bankers Magazine.* Spring 1976, pp. 68–72.

Rankin, Deborah. "Cash Flow as a Guide to Growth." *New York Times.* May 23, 1978.

Reed, Edward W., Richard V. Cotter, Edward K. Gill, and Edward K. Smith. *Commercial Banking.* Englewood Cliffs, N.J.: Prentice-Hall, 1976.

Rose, Peter S., and Donald R. Fraser. *Financial Institutions, 3rd ed.* San Diego, Calif.: Business Publications, Inc., 1988.

Ross, J. E., and M. J. Kami. *Corporate Management in Crisis.* Englewood Cliffs, N.J.: Prentice-Hall, 1973.

Schiff, Allen I. "The Other Side of LIFO." *Journal of Accountancy.* May 1983.

Schwartz, J. B. "Accounting Changes by Corporations Facing Possible Insolvency." *Journal of Accounting, Auditing, and Finance.* Fall 1982, pp. 32–43.

Scott, Richard A., and Rita K. Scott. "Installment Accounting: Is It Inconsistent?" *Journal of Accountancy.* November 1979.

Slatter, S. *Corporate Recovery.* New York: Penguin Books, 1984.

Sorter, G. J., and George Benston. "Appraising the Defensive Position of a Firm: The Interval Measure." *The Accounting Review.* October 1960.

Standard and Poor's. "Corporate and International Ratings." *Credit Overview.* September 1988.

Taffler, R. J., and M. Tseung. "The Audit Going Concern Qualification in Practice." *The Accountants Magazine.* 88 (July 1984): pp. 263–269.

Taylor, William. "Staff Director of Banking Supervision and Regulation of the Board of Governors of the Federal Reserve, statement to the House Committee, March 15, 1988." *Real Estate Reform Act of 1987.* Washington, D.C.: U.S. Government Printing Office.

Urbancic, F. R. "Reporting Preferred Stock: Debt or Equity?" *Mergers and Acquisitions.* Spring 1980, pp. 15–20.

Zmijewski, M. E. "Predicting Corporate Bankruptcy: An Empirical Comparison of the Extant Financial Distress Models." Unpublished paper. Buffalo, N.Y.: State University of New York at Buffalo, 1983.

Index

(Page numbers in bold refer to either the definition, the key point, or the major discussion of that topic.)